P9-DWZ-415

Where print meets digital and engaging content meets academic rigor

THE JUSTICE SERIES

across the CJ curriculum…

Transportation first became an official aspect of England's punishment system in the seventeenth century but not a major component until the eighteenth century.

The Transportation Act of 1718 allowed transportation as a substitute to execution and also made it a punishment in its own right.

American colonies

Prisoners became indentured servants and the British gave up all responsibility for them.

Transportation sentences were typically seven years for noncapital offences or for life for those who had had their death penalties commuted.

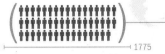
718 ———— 1775

Some **50,000 prisoners** were transported to the American colonies before 1775 when the American Revolution stopped transportation of British prisoners.

Australia

Rather than becoming indentured servants in Australia, prisoners remained the responsibility of the British government, which continued to have control over them.

1788 ———— 1868

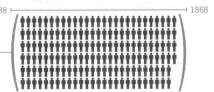

From 1788 to 1868, more than **160,000 convicts** were transported from England and Ireland to Australia. Transportation ends throughout Australia in 1868.

Norfolk Island, about 1,000 miles east of Sydney, became the most notable penal colony because of the unbearable discipline.

Norfolk Island jail

CJ2012
Fagin

Corrections
Alarid & Reichel

Policing
Worrall & Schmalleger

Criminal Investigation
Lyman

Criminal Procedure
Worrall

Juvenile Delinquency
Bartollas & Schmalleger

Coming in 2013:

CJ2013
Fagin

Criminology
Schmalleger

POLICING

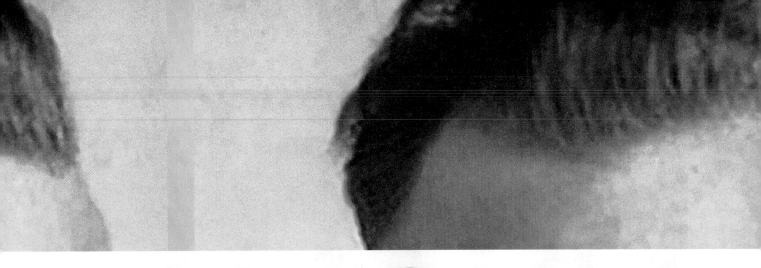

POLICING

John L. Worrall
Professor of Criminology
University of Texas at Dallas

Frank Schmalleger
Distinguished Professor Emeritus
University of North Carolina at Pembroke

PEARSON

Boston Columbus Indianapolis New York San Francisco Upper Saddle River
Amsterdam Cape Town Dubai London Madrid Milan Munich Paris Montréal Toronto
Delhi Mexico City São Paulo Sydney Hong Kong Seoul Singapore Taipei Tokyo

Editorial Director: Vernon R. Anthony
Senior Acquisitions Editor: Eric Krassow
Assistant Editor: Megan Moffo
Editorial Assistant: Lynda Cramer
Director of Marketing: David Gesell
Marketing Manager: Cyndi Eller
Senior Marketing Coordinator: Alicia Wozniak
Marketing Assistant: Les Roberts
Senior Managing Editor: JoEllen Gohr
Senior Project Manager: Steve Robb
Senior Operations Supervisor: Pat Tonneman
Creative Director: Design Development Services,
    John Christiana
Text and Cover Designer: Mary Siener
Media Project Manager: Karen Bretz
Full-Service Project Management:
    GEX Publishing Services
Composition: GEX Publishing Services
Printer/Binder: R. R. Donnelley & Sons, Inc.
Cover Printer: Lehigh/Phoenix Color Hagerstown
Text Font: MinionPro-Regular 10/12

John Dillinger From September 1933 until July 1934, John Dillinger and his violent gang terrorized the Midwest, killing 10 men, wounding 7 others, robbing banks and police arsenals, and staging 3 jail breaks—killing a sheriff during one and wounding 2 guards in another. On July 22, 1934, Dillinger was shot and killed while trying to run from FBI agents who approached him outside a Chicago theater.

Cover Image: © Everett Collection Inc/Alamy

Credits and acknowledgments borrowed from other sources and reproduced, with permission, in this textbook appear on the appropriate page within the text.

Library of Congress Cataloging-in-Publication Data
Worrall, John L.
  Policing / John L. Worrall, Frank Schmalleger.
    p. cm.
  Includes bibliographical references and index.
  ISBN-13: 978-0-13-261019-3 (pbk.)
  ISBN-10: 0-13-261019-1
  1. Police--United States. 2. Law enforcement--United States. 3. Criminal justice,
Administration of--United States. I. Schmalleger, Frank. II. Title.
  HV8139.W67 2013
  363.2'30973--dc23
                    2011045696

10 9 8 7 6 5 4 3 2 1

ISBN-10: 0-13-261019-1
ISBN-13: 978-0-13-261019-3

Brief Contents

Contents

Each chapter opener includes a quote and lists the chapter objectives to pique interest and focus students' attention on the topics to be discussed.

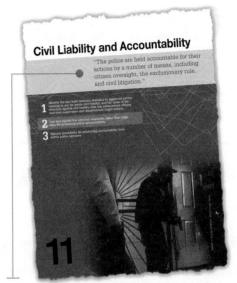

The book exhibits a balance between text, photos, and figures to present the information in both a text format and a visual format.

Each chapter introduction presents a current event or story related to chapter content followed by a discussion question. This sparks interest and promotes critical thinking about chapter concepts.

PART 2   A Career in Policing   57

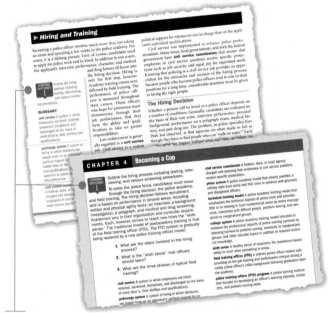

Each objective has an associated icon that also appears in the related chapter section and in the end-of-chapter material. The icon is a navigational tool, making it easy to locate explanations of or find review material for a particular topic, and is also a visual key to aid memory and retention of information related to the topic.

Key statistics are set in large blue font for easy identification.

PART 3 **On The Job** **101**

Think About It features pose questions related to chapter content, promoting critical thinking, discussion, and application.

Important quotes pulled from the text reflect the central ideas in the chapter.

A box at the end of each chapter directs students to chapter-specific resources and additional links to extend learning and investigation.

At the end of each chapter, a real-life example poses analytical discussion questions related to chapter content, promoting critical thinking and application of chapter concepts.

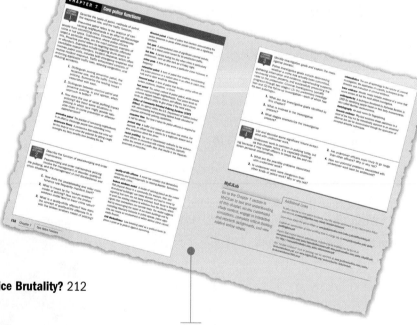

The chapter summary displays the chapter's key information as a chart with images and critical-thinking review questions embedded throughout. This visual format is designed to be a helpful study and review tool.

Preface

Introducing the Justice Series

When best-selling authors and instructional designers come together, focused on one goal—improving student performance across the CJ curriculum—you come away with a groundbreaking new series of print and digital content: the *Justice Series.*

Several years ago we embarked on a journey to create affordable texts that engage students without sacrificing academic rigor. We tested this new format with Fagin's *CJ 2010* and Schmalleger's *Criminology* and received overwhelming support from students and instructors.

The Justice Series expands this format and philosophy to more core CJ and criminology courses, providing affordable, engaging instructor and student resources across the curriculum. As you flip through the pages, you'll notice this book doesn't rely on distracting, overly used photos to add visual appeal. Every piece of art serves a purpose—to help students learn. Our authors and instructional designers worked tirelessly to build engaging info-graphics, flow charts, pull-out statistics, and other visuals that flow with the body of the text, provide context and engagement, and promote recall and understanding.

We organized our content around key learning objectives for each chapter and tied everything together in a new objective-driven end-of-chapter layout. Not only is the content engaging to the student, it's easy to follow and focuses the student on the key learning objectives.

Although brief, affordable, and visually engaging, the Justice Series is no quick, cheap way to appeal to the lowest common denominator. It's a series of texts and support tools that are instructionally sound and student approved.

Additional Highlights to the Authors' Approach

- A solid historical foundation is laid—with attention to the origins of modern policing, the nature of American law enforcement, and organizational issues—while staying connected to current events and issues.

- An evidence-based perspective takes center stage with "Think About It" boxes that appear in each chapter and in the book's comprehensive coverage of the latest in policing research.

- Theories of policing are introduced throughout, but a practical emphasis is maintained with chapters and sections on "Becoming a Cop" and "A Career in Policing."

- The text incorporates newsworthy and hot topics in policing with informative chapter-opening vignettes and compelling end-of-chapter case studies.

- Legal issues in policing, including liability and criminal procedure, and challenges, including deviance and the use of force, receive thorough treatment in four dedicated chapters.

- A concise, conversational writing style keeps student interest and facilitates comprehension.

Groundbreaking Instructor and Student Support

Just as the format of the Justice Series breaks new ground in publishing, so does the instructor support that accompanies the series.

Interactive Lecture PowerPoint Presentations

The *Interactive Lecture PowerPoints* will enhance lectures like never before. Award-winning presentation designers worked with our authors to develop PowerPoints that truly engage the student. Much like the text, the PowerPoints are full of instructionally sound graphics, tables, charts, and photos that do what presentation software is meant to do—support and enhance your lecture. Data and difficult concepts are presented in a truly interactive way, helping students connect the dots and stay focused on the lecture. The *Interactive Lecture PowerPoints* also include in-depth lecture notes and teaching tips so you have all your lecture material in one place.

A New Standard in Testing Material

Whether you use a basic test bank document or generate questions electronically through *MyTest*, every question is linked to a learning objective, page number, and level of difficulty. This allows for quick reference in the text and offers an easy way to check the difficulty level and variety of your questions. *MyTest* can be accessed at **www. PearsonMyTest.com**.

MyCJLab

MyCJLab is a dynamic program designed to support the way students learn and instructors teach. We've integrated our groundbreaking interactive simulations and media into a new, robust course management and assessment program. With *MyCJLab*, instructors can either manage their entire course online or simply allow students to study at their own pace using personalized assessment tools.

When best-selling authors and instructional designers come together, focused on one goal—improving student performance across the CJ curriculum—you come away with a groundbreaking new series of print and digital content: the Justice Series.

From practical game-like simulations to media enhanced critical thinking exercises, instructors can tailor the course to the needs of their students. In addition, our new media search tool organizes current criminal justice–related videos, news articles, and other media from the Internet for quick and easy access in and out of the classroom.

Whether you're an expert in digital learning or new to online enhancements, *MyCJLab* provides student engagement and instructor support for all levels of learning and teaching. *Note:* An access code is needed for this supplement. Students can purchase an access code at **www.MyPearsonStore.com** or from the *MyCJLab* site at **www.MyCJLab.com**.

To access supplementary materials online, instructors need to request an instructor access code. Go to **www.pearsonhighered.com/irc**, where you can register for an instructor access code. Within 48 hours after registering, you will receive a confirming e-mail, including an instructor access code. Once you have received your code, go to the site and log on for full instructions on downloading the materials you wish to use.

▶ Acknowledgments

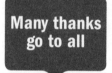
Many thanks go to all who assisted in many different ways in the development and production of this textbook. Thanks also to the hundreds of instructors whose feedback helped in the development of this series concept.

We are very grateful to the Pearson team for all their efforts in seeing this book through to production and for their many activities in getting it into the hands of students across the country. The Pearson team includes editorial director Vernon R. Anthony, acquisitions editor Eric Krassow, assistant editor Megan Moffo, interior and cover designer Mary Siener, project manager Steve Robb, audio visual project manager Janet Portisch, senior operations supervisor Pat Tonneman, director of marketing David Gesell, marketing manager Adam Kloza, senior marketing coordinator Alicia Wozniak, managing editor JoEllen Gohr, creative director John Christiana, and media project manager Karen Bretz.

The authors would like to thank their colleagues inside and outside of academia, including (but not limited to) Robert Taylor, University of North Texas; Larry Gaines, California State University–San Bernardino; Dallas police chief David Kunkle; and Michael Scott, Center for Problem-Oriented Policing. Finally, thanks go to our families whose love and continued support inspire us to write.

JOHN L. WORRALL and FRANK SCHMALLEGER

▶ About the Authors

John L. Worrall, Ph.D., is professor of criminology at the University of Texas at Dallas. A Seattle native, he received a bachelor's degree in both psychology and law and justice from Central Washington University in 1994. Both his master's degree in criminal justice and his doctorate in political science were received from Washington State University, where he completed his studies in 1999. From 1999 to 2006, he was a member of the criminal justice faculty at California State University, San Bernardino. He moved to Texas in the fall of 2006.

Dr. Worrall has published articles and book chapters on a wide range of law enforcement topics, ranging from legal issues in policing to community prosecution. He is the author of *Crime Control in America: What Works?* (Allyn and Bacon, 2008) and *Criminal Procedure: From First Contact to Appeal* (Allyn and Bacon, 2007), the coauthor of *Criminal Evidence: An Introduction* (Oxford University Press, 2005), and *Police Administration* (McGraw-Hill, 2003), and the coeditor of *The Changing Role of the American Prosecutor* (State University of New York Press, 2008).

In addition to teaching and writing, Dr. Worrall serves as a consultant, evaluator, and trainer for police departments and prosecutor's offices across the United States and Canada. In this capacity, he recently teamed up with the Center for Problem-Oriented Policing to author a guide for law enforcement officials on the use of asset forfeiture to combat illegal activity.

Dr. Worrall was recently elected to the executive board of the Academy of Criminal Justice Sciences, where he serves in the position of trustee at large (2008–2011). He is also editor of the journal *Police Quarterly*, the top-rated policing journal, and he serves as associate director for research for the W. W. Caruth, Jr., Dallas Police Institute, a collaborative research and training organization involving the Dallas Police Department, the Communities Foundation of Texas, the University of North Texas, and the University of Texas at Dallas.

Frank Schmalleger, Ph.D., holds degrees from the University of Notre Dame and Ohio State University, having earned both a master's (1970) and a doctorate (1974) in sociology with a special emphasis in criminology from Ohio State University. From 1976 to 1994, he taught criminal justice courses at the University of North Carolina at Pembroke. For the last 16 of those years, he chaired the university's Department of Sociology, Social Work, and Criminal Justice.

In 1991, he was awarded the title Distinguished Professor, and the university named him professor emeritus in 2001.

As an adjunct professor with Webster University in St. Louis, Missouri, Dr. Schmalleger helped develop the university's graduate program in security administration and loss prevention. He taught courses in that curriculum for more than a decade. Dr. Schmalleger has also taught in the online graduate program of the New School for Social Research, helping to build the world's first electronic classrooms in support of distance learning through computer telecommunications. An avid proponent of criminal justice education, he has worked with numerous schools to develop curricula at both the undergraduate and graduate levels.

Dr. Schmalleger is the author of numerous articles and many books, including the widely used *Criminal Justice Today* (Prentice Hall, 2011), *Criminology Today* (Prentice Hall, 2011), *Criminal Law Today* (Prentice Hall, 2010), and *The Definitive Guide to Criminal Justice and Criminology on the World Wide Web* (Prentice Hall, 2009).

He is also founding editor of the journal *Criminal Justice Studies*. He has served as editor for the Prentice Hall series Criminal Justice in the Twenty-First Century and as imprint adviser for Greenwood Publishing Group's criminal justice reference series.

Dr. Schmalleger's philosophy of both teaching and writing can be summed up in these words: "In order to communicate knowledge, we must first catch, then hold, a person's interest—be it student, colleague, or policymaker. Our writing, our speaking, and our teaching must be relevant to the problems facing people today, and they must in some way help solve those problems."

POLICING

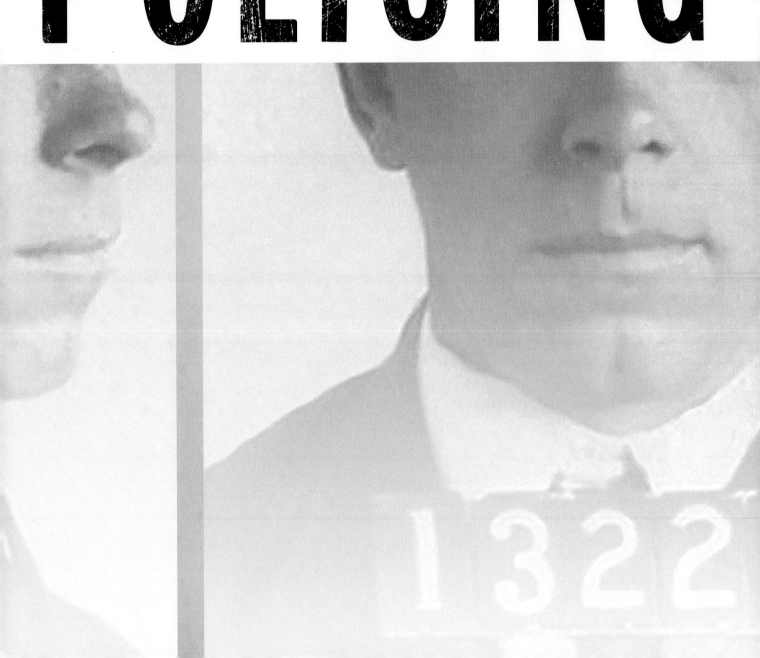

1322

Origins and Evolution of American Policing

"Police officers and police activities receive intense scrutiny by everyone."

1 Outline the origins of policing.

2 Summarize various eras of policing.

3 Outline the emergence of state and federal law enforcement agencies.

U.S. Customs and Border Protection

Source: © David R. Frazier Photolibrary, Inc./Alamy

1

In 2011, Harvard University's John F. Kennedy School of Government, in conjunction with the National Institute of Justice, released an important new publication entitled "Police Science: Toward a New Paradigm."[1] The publications' authors, George Mason University Professor David Weisburd and Peter Neyroud, Chief Executive of the National Policing Improvement Agency in the United Kingdom, called for "a radical reformation of the role of science in policing." Their purpose was to facilitate the start of a new era of evidence-based policing. As we shall see in numerous places throughout this book, evidence-based policing, which refers to the use of high-quality social science research to guide police practice, is rapidly becoming an important theme in twenty-first century law enforcement, and may be the most important innovation in policing since Sir Robert Peel formed the world's first modern-day police force.

"Advance of science in policing is essential," the Kennedy School authors wrote, "if police are to retain public support and legitimacy." Unfortunately, however, the authors point out that "evidence-based policing is [still] not the rule" today, and that "science is [still] not an essential part of [today's] police world." Worse, say Weisburd and Neyround, today's police leaders have failed to take ownership of police science, allowing outside institutions to dictate the nature of policing studies, and to produce findings that may not even be relevant to day-to-day enforcement

operations. Weisburd and Neyroud call upon police leaders to correct the situation by stepping up their use of science, and by familiarizing themselves with contemporary best practices in law enforcement agencies around the country and around the globe. It is essential, say the authors, to determine what policing programs actually work, and to use that knowledge to become wise decision-makers when asking for public moneys.

"Police Science: Toward a New Paradigm," is one of a series of articles in the Kennedy School's *New Perspectives in Policing* series, and is available on the Web at http://justicestudies.com//policing/newparadigm.pdf. It was published as part of the Kennedy School's Executive Session on Policing and Public Safety, which met from 2008 to 2010. An older series consisting of 17 articles, published between 1988 and 1993, comprise the original *Perspectives on Policing* series, and are also available on the Web. You can access them at http://tinyurl.com/6b8faze.

As you read through this text, you will learn more about evidence-based policing (see a more formal definition of the term later in this chapter) and about its relevance to policing in the twenty-first century. A good introduction to the applicability of the modern social sciences to policing and to the field of criminal justice in general can be found in National Institute of Justice Director John Laub's Web-based video presentation entitled "Embracing A Culture of Science," at http://nij.ncjrs.gov/multimedia/video-laub1.htm.

DISCUSS Why do the authors featured here say that the "advance of science in policing is essential"?

▶ *The Origins of Policing*

For students of policing, an appreciation of history is essential in order to understand the contemporary structure of law enforcement in the United States today. As a result of historical circumstances, the American system of policing is nearly unique in the world. Most countries today rely on one or only a few agencies for law enforcement. In the United States, however, there are thousands of law enforcement agencies with hundreds of thousands of employees. No other country has a policing system that looks quite like ours.

The study of policing history is important for another reason: For better or for worse, history often repeats itself. History repeats itself for worse when policy makers make decisions in a vacuum, without regard for those who have faced the same problems before. In other words, the failure to appreciate what was once tried without success leads to a costly repetition of past mistakes. Some critics of recent changes in American policing, such as the shift toward community policing, for example, argue that what we are now doing signals a return to days of old, which may not be desirable.

Alternatively, a technique or program that looks totally innovative and desirable today may have been purposefully avoided in the past. An example, which we will later cover

The American system of policing is nearly unique in the world.

more thoroughly, is federal–local law enforcement partnerships, which some see as especially important in the fight against terrorism. Critics of such efforts suggest that we are inching toward a national police force, a notion that, to the minds of many, is antithetical to our nation's system of government.

History can repeat itself for the better when we revisit the successful strategies of the past. The decentralization that served policing early on in our nation's history, for example, is now part and parcel of recent reforms in policing around the country.

From Private to Public Policing

One of the earliest known methods of policing, called *kin policing*, involved families, clans, and tribes enforcing informal rules and customs. Each member of the group was given authority to enforce the established rules, and individuals who deviated from

LEARNING OUTCOMES 1 Outline the origins of policing.

GLOSSARY

frankpledge system The ultimate outgrowth of the night watch system of social control, dating to the twelfth century, in which ten households were grouped into a tithing, and each adult male member of the tithing was held responsible for the conduct of the others.

tithing Under the frankpledge system, a group of ten households.

parish Under the frankpledge system, a group of ten tithings. Also referred to as a *hundred*.

shire Under the frankpledge system, a collection of several parishes.

sheriff The modern-day term for the Old English *shire-reeve*. In the United States today, the senior law enforcement official in a county.

shire-reeve The Old English term for *sheriff*. Literally, "the keeper of the shire."

watchman An early officer on foot patrol who, during the hours of darkness, watched for fires and criminal activities. Upon detecting such events, the watchman's role was to sound the "hue and cry" to evoke a defensive response from the citizenry. This style of policing dates back to the early to mid-eighteenth century in England.

Henry Fielding (1707–1754) An English magistrate who founded what some have called London's first police force, the Bow Street Runners.

community norms were often dealt with harshly.[4] This method of policing changed during the rise of the Greek city-states and the Roman Empire, and law enforcement evolved from what was essentially a private affair to a public one.

Greece and Rome began to use appointed magistrates to enforce the law. These unpaid individuals were largely responsible for law enforcement until about the third century BCE in Rome and the sixth century BCE in Greece. The first *paid* law enforcement official was the *praefectus urbi*, a position created in Rome about 27 BCE.[5] By 6 CE, Rome had a large force of these individuals who patrolled the streets day and night. Once the Roman Empire fell, though, law enforcement became the responsibility of the individual monarchies throughout Europe.

Kings used military forces for law enforcement, but they also relied on so-called night watches, or groups of citizens who roamed the streets looking for signs of trouble. Members of the night watch were given the authority to investigate crimes and to make arrests. The night watch system eventually evolved into the **frankpledge system**, which became more formalized around the twelfth century when kings appointed individuals known as chief-pledges to ensure that the system worked.[6] In the frankpledge system, ten households were grouped into a **tithing**, and each adult male member of the tithing was held responsible for the conduct of the others. Ten tithings were known as a hundred, or **parish**, and a group of several parishes eventually came to be called a **shire**. Shires resembled modern-day counties in terms of their size. The term **sheriff** comes from the old English word **shire-reeve**, which means "the keeper of the shire." The shire-reeve was granted authority by the Norman kings to levy fines against criminals and also to levy fines against the parishes for failing to capture criminals.

In England, the Second Statute of Westminster (1285)[7] required that each parish appoint two constables.[8] Their duties were to inspect the arms of the parish and to assist the sheriff with law enforcement. Men over the age of 15 formed the *posse comitatus*, which assisted with the pursuit and capture of dangerous criminals. Magistrates, who eventually came to be known as *justices of the peace*, began to be appointed by the king or the sheriff around the thirteenth century. They had primary responsibility for adjudicating crimes, not unlike modern-day judges. In England, from which we derive many of our traditions, this was the predominant model of law enforcement until the nineteenth century.

What set early approaches to policing apart from modern policing practices is that most of the officials charged with enforcing laws were volunteers. If paid, they were not salaried as police officers are today. Sheriffs, for example, were allowed to appropriate a portion of the money collected in the king's name.[9] Even though these developments signaled a shift from private to public policing, much of the job of enforcing the law remained largely private; there simply were not enough public officials to do the job. As the years passed, though, policing took ever greater steps in the direction of becoming a governmental function.

One of the most significant steps toward fully public policing occurred in 1735, when two London parishes were given authority to pay their **watchmen** out of tax collections.[10] Then, toward the middle of the eighteenth century, John and **Henry Fielding**, two Bow Street magistrates, started to pay men to serve as constables and patrol the streets at night.[11] These **Bow Street Runners**, or **thief takers**, patrolled the city on foot and the surrounding areas on horseback. They also performed investigations, and for that reason they have been described as the first known detective unit.[12]

In 1800, the Thames River Police were paid by public moneys.[13] Private police forces did not disappear, however. Outside London in more rural areas, much law enforcement was still the responsibility of churches, communities, parishes, magistrates, and a variety of other individuals. Moving beyond England, other countries also started to form public police agencies. France, Prussia (Germany), Russia, China, and India all made the gradual shift from private to public law enforcement.[14] As police officers came to be paid with public funds, the shift away from private policing became more apparent.

The Influence of the English Model

To a large extent, policing in London became the model for policing in America. Historians have called attention to various forces behind the emergence of American policing, several of which we will consider shortly, but what early American policing looked like stemmed a great deal from the English approach.

In 1822, British home secretary **Sir Robert Peel** criticized the state of policing in London. Some years later, he was responsible for passage of the "Act for Improving the Police in and Near the Metropolis," otherwise known as the **Metropolitan Police Act**.

Policing in London became the model for policing in America.

Bow Street Runners An early English police unit formed under the leadership of Henry Fielding, magistrate of the Bow Street region of London. Also referred to as *thief takers*.[2]

thief taker An alternative name for Henry Fielding's Bow Street Runners.

Sir Robert Peel (1788–1850) A former British home secretary whose criticisms of the state of policing in London led to the passage of the Metropolitan Police Act and the establishment of the world's first large-scale organized police force in that city in 1829.

Metropolitan Police Act The legislation adopted by the British Parliament in 1829 that established the world's first large-scale organized police force in London.

Adopted by Parliament in 1829, this legislation created the world's first large-scale organized police force in the city of London.[15] As others have noted, the Metropolitan Police Act "introduced a centralized and unified system of police in England" and constituted a revolution in traditional methods of law enforcement.[16] The legislation heralded the end of the old, fragmented, and ineffectual system of parish constables and represented the dawn of a whole new era of policing.[17]

Two men, Charles Rowan and Richard Mayne, were appointed to oversee development of the force. They adopted a military organizational model. This was resisted to a large degree by British citizens out of fear that the line between policing and the military would be too thin, and that police might behave like an occupying army. Rowan and Mayne, however, went to great lengths to ensure that their officers behaved properly, and the police force eventually gained widespread acceptance.

Sir Robert Peel's contribution lies not just in the creation of the first organized police force, however. He was among the first to envision a broader role for officers than just crime fighting. Peel emphasized the *prevention* of crime. He also felt that uniforms were necessary because they would make officers stand out in a crowd and thus discourage crime.[18] Beyond that, Peel identified a series of principles that he said ought to characterize any police force (Figure 1.1).

Policing Comes to America

The first North American colonists settled along the eastern seaboard. They hailed from a number of countries, including Spain, France, Holland, Sweden, and of course England. The first of these settlements, Jamestown, was established in 1607 in what is now Virginia. The colony at Plymouth, Massachusetts, followed, set up by the Pilgrims in 1620. Swedish and Dutch citizens settled around what is today New York City. The Spanish claimed land in what is now the southern United States and in the Caribbean. All of these people had visions of expanding their settlements, but given their distance from the European mainland, doing so was difficult. Expansion was particularly difficult for the English and French because Spain's presence was significant.

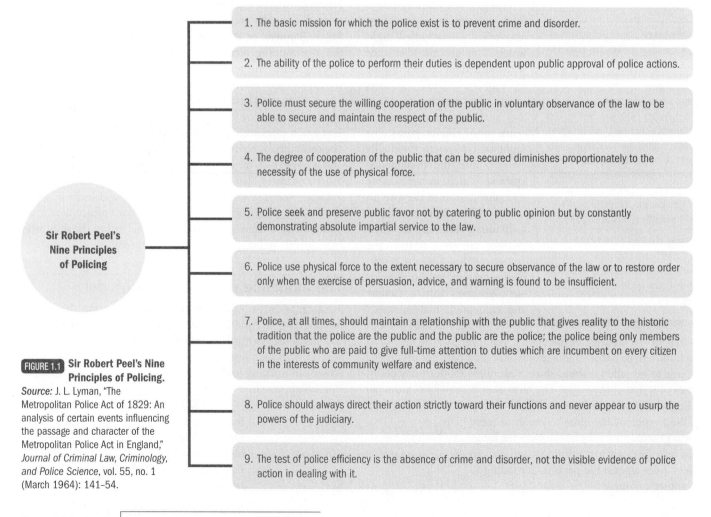

FIGURE 1.1 **Sir Robert Peel's Nine Principles of Policing.**
Source: J. L. Lyman, "The Metropolitan Police Act of 1829: An analysis of certain events influencing the passage and character of the Metropolitan Police Act in England," *Journal of Criminal Law, Criminology, and Police Science*, vol. 55, no. 1 (March 1964): 141–54.

Sir Robert Peel's Nine Principles of Policing

1. The basic mission for which the police exist is to prevent crime and disorder.

2. The ability of the police to perform their duties is dependent upon public approval of police actions.

3. Police must secure the willing cooperation of the public in voluntary observance of the law to be able to secure and maintain the respect of the public.

4. The degree of cooperation of the public that can be secured diminishes proportionately to the necessity of the use of physical force.

5. Police seek and preserve public favor not by catering to public opinion but by constantly demonstrating absolute impartial service to the law.

6. Police use physical force to the extent necessary to secure observance of the law or to restore order only when the exercise of persuasion, advice, and warning is found to be insufficient.

7. Police, at all times, should maintain a relationship with the public that gives reality to the historic tradition that the police are the public and the public are the police; the police being only members of the public who are paid to give full-time attention to duties which are incumbent on every citizen in the interests of community welfare and existence.

8. Police should always direct their action strictly toward their functions and never appear to usurp the powers of the judiciary.

9. The test of police efficiency is the absence of crime and disorder, not the visible evidence of police action in dealing with it.

Early on, churches in America were heavily involved in crime control, though without a formal criminal justice system. People who strayed from acceptable forms of conduct were often shunned by their congregations. According to one historian, church congregations functioned as the "police and courts of first resort."[19] Moreover, when corporal punishments were used, they were often carried out in public. The use of stocks, floggings in the public square, and even public hangings were common methods of dealing with wayward individuals. Public punishments, often witnessed by hundreds of people, made clear to everyone the consequences of inappropriate behavior.

As more colonists moved to the New World, however, they "brought the law in their baggage."[20] That is, they brought knowledge of English criminal codes, law enforcement agencies, and methods of punishment, and they adapted them to serve the needs of their new communities.

Chaos in the Cities

As America came of age, more immigrants arrived and settled in urban areas. Cities became increasingly crowded, dangerous, and dirty. For example, from 1850 to about 1880, New York City's population grew until almost a million people were crowded into the two-square-mile center of the city. The city's East Side housed nearly 300,000 people who lacked toilet facilities, heat, fire protection, and other essentials. Unemployment levels were high, and sickness abounded. Cholera outbreaks were common, killing thousands of people at a time.

By the mid-1800s, crime had become commonplace throughout many American cities. People stole and looted to survive. Organized gangs formed, fought for territory, and contributed to the violence and mayhem within the city. By one account, by 1850 New York City had become America's most terrifying city.[21] Other large cities like Boston, Chicago, and Philadelphia hardly fared better.

Early efforts to control crime fell on the shoulders of appointed constables and citizen volunteers. The constables patrolled during the daytime; citizens patrolled at night. But as the cities grew and became more dangerous, this system could not keep pace with crime.[22] In 1844, the first metropolitan police department was formed in the New York City area. It initially patrolled only during the daylight hours, leaving the preexisting night watch to patrol the city during darkness. The early New York City force was modeled after London's Metropolitan Police and consisted of only 16 officers appointed by the mayor.[23] The force was reorganized and expanded to 800 officers in 1845 under Mayor William Havemeyer, who divided the city into three police districts. This period also saw the elimination of the old night watch system and the construction of

station houses and local courts.[24] Twelve years later, in 1857, the police in Manhattan, Brooklyn, Staten Island, Westchester County, and the Bronx were consolidated into one department under a governor-appointed board of commissioners, becoming what we think of today as the New York City Police Department (NYPD).[25] Prior to the consolidation, 18 separate police forces patrolled within the area that comprises present-day New York City.[26] Some of them were better equipped and organized than others. Lacking, however, was a centralized police mandate, good communications, and coordinated efforts.[27]

On the one hand, the combined force of 1857, which initially consisted of 6,396 members, was welcomed by people who were distressed about problems of social disorganization and crime within the city. On the other hand, there was concern that the new police force might become a standing army (recall that our nation was founded, in part, out of frustration with overreaching, centralized government).[28] Other large cities quickly followed the New York example, establishing their own police forces. They did so in response to surges in violence, conflict, multiple riots, and citizen fears that America's experiment in self-governance might not survive.

London's police, as we have already seen, served as something of a model for policing in many American cities. Reformers in America were impressed with what London's **bobbies** did to prevent, and not just respond to, crime.[29] London's police stressed highly visible patrols intended to discourage crime. But the police forces of New York and other large cities differed from their English counterparts in at least two important ways. First, unlike police in London, America's first police officers were heavily involved in politics.[30] Most police officers at the time answered to political leaders or ward bosses in the areas they served. Officers' very jobs were dependent on remaining in the good favor of whatever political figure was in charge at the time. Second, in stark contrast to their counterparts in London, American police officers were more willing to use force.[31] These two unique features of American policing contributed in no small part to policing as it is known today.

bobby The popular British name given to a member of Sir Robert Peel's Metropolitan Police Force.[3]

Texas Rangers A militia originally formed by Stephen F. Austin in 1823 to protect the territory of Texas against Native American raids, criminals, and intruders. Today, the Rangers serve as part of the Texas Department of Public Safety.

slave patrol A crude form of private policing, often carried out by citizen volunteers. Slave patrols were created in the eighteenth century to apprehend runaway slaves and to ensure that slaves did not rise up against their owners.

due process of law A right guaranteed by the Fifth, Sixth, and Fourteenth Amendments and generally understood, in legal contexts, to mean the due course of legal proceedings according to the rules and forms established for the protection of individual rights. In criminal proceedings, due process of law is generally understood to include the following basic elements: a law creating and defining the offense, an impartial tribunal having jurisdictional authority over the case, accusation in proper form, notice and opportunity to defend, trial according to established procedure, and discharge from all restraints or obligations unless convicted.

1840s–1930

Political Era Close ties between the police and political officials

Police were organized in paramilitary style, focused on serving the politically powerful

Politicians appointed/hired the police

Came about because of a need for social order and security in a dynamic and rapidly changing society

Source: © Image Asset Management Ltd./SuperStock, Inc.

1930–1970s

Reform Era Police gained pride in their profession

Law enforcement focused on "traditional" crime-fighting and the capture of criminals

Crackdown on organized crime

Progressive policing policy led by August Vollmer and O.W. Wilson

Came about because citizens called for reform and the removal of politics from policing

Source: © SuperStock, Inc.

Source: Schmalleger, Frank J., CRIMINAL JUSTICE: A BRIEF INSTRUCTION, 9th Edition, © 2012. Reprinted by permission of Pearson Education, Inc., Upper Saddle River, NJ.

The Move West

As American pioneers moved westward, they did not leave the problems of the cities behind. In fact, the frontier mentality of fending for oneself and providing one's own self-protection fueled plenty of violence. Guns, knives, and fists were commonly used to resolve disputes in newly settled areas. Sheriffs and their marshals were appointed by town leaders to provide what little law enforcement was available on the frontier. These officials' authority, though, was not always welcomed or respected. Theirs was a lonely and dangerous job, and they repeatedly became the targets of outlaws. Making matters even more difficult, prominent outlaws of the day, including Billy the Kid and Jesse James, were apparently idolized as much, if not more, than the sheriffs and marshals themselves. Law enforcement was, at best, unreliable; at worst, it was nonexistent. Indeed, some of the new "lawmen" worked both sides of the law, depending on which side offered them the best opportunities and rewards. Consequently, frontier communities often formed their own posses and vigilante citizen groups to confront any person or group intent on disrupting social stability.[32]

Even these efforts eventually failed, despite support from the community. Not unlike what happened in the big cities, once populations in the West grew, something more was needed. It was inevitable that the kinds of agencies formed along the eastern seaboard would be replicated in cities

> *Frontier communities often formed their own posses and vigilante citizen groups.*

throughout the West. An example was Stephen Austin's corps of fighters, a group of tough men he enlisted to protect the settlers he was bringing into the Tejas, Mexico, area. This corps of rangers eventually aided in the Texas revolution against Mexico, providing scout services for the U.S. Army during the Mexican-American War. They came to be known as the **Texas Rangers**, and their efforts ushered in a period of enhanced border patrol in Arizona and New Mexico as well as the formation of state police forces throughout the Southwest.[33]

Organized police forces in early America were born of necessity. A single law enforcement official rapidly became inadequate as populations surged. Densely populated cities could not realistically be patrolled with one or even a few officers. But unlike the evolution of policing in other nations, Americans rejected centralized power and shunned any national police force. Law enforcement became a local effort that reflected local priorities and issues. That is why today we see thousands of distinct police agencies at various levels of government all across the United States. Even if there had been a desire during this period for a centralized police agency, it is doubtful it could have succeeded, given the size of the territory for which it would have been responsible. Early police agencies could not have survived without some connection to the communities they patrolled.

This decentralized policing model (which is discussed in more detail in Chapter 3) has been hailed as representing the American ideal, but there was a downside. As police agencies proliferated across America, they varied widely in terms of quality and professional commitment. Some may argue that policing today is not as highly regarded an occupation as it could be, but in the late nineteenth century, policing was generally viewed as routine, unglamorous work. Officers were held in low regard and, because the pay was poor, cities had difficulty recruiting qualified candidates. So desperate

Heavily involved in politics   More willing to use force

> *Organized police forces in early America were born of necessity.*

Community Era Police departments work to identify and serve the needs of their communities

Envisions a partnership between the police and the community

Police focus on quality-of-life offenses

Broken windows model of policing

Came about because of a realization that effective community partnerships can help prevent and solve crimes

Source: UpperCut Images/ Superstock Royalty Free

The New Era Policing to secure the homeland; emphasis on terrorism prevention and intelligence-led policing

Builds on partnership with the community to gather intelligence

Creation of counterterrorism divisions and offices within police departments and the development of actionable intelligence

Came about because of the terrorist attacks of September 11, 2001, and ongoing threats to the safety and security of Americans

---

were some cities to hire police officers that, as one historian observed, "illiteracy, poor health, chronic drunkenness, or a criminal record were no barriers to a job as a police officer."[34] Pressure for agencies to grow, combined with close relationships between the police and politicians and others in positions of influence, resulted in poor quality police work. What's worse is that a commitment to crime control and community service was secondary. Nonetheless, this period of politics and ineptitude has been described as the first significant era of policing in America.

Policing the Slaves

Unique circumstances existed in the American South during this early period. There, **slave patrols** represented a crude form of policing. Slave patrols were created in the eighteenth century to apprehend runaway slaves and to ensure that slaves did not rise up against their owners. The slave patrols were largely a private activity carried out by citizen volunteers, leading to a serious lack of control of the slave patrols' actions. When they apprehended runaway slaves, they often meted out "justice" on the spot, frequently using violence.

Due process of law was a distant concern. Slave patrols could (and did) arbitrarily enter private residences for the purpose of rounding up those who fled from bondage. The patrols were largely an outgrowth of fear on the part of wealthy white landowners that slaves were a dangerous group in need of careful scrutiny and control. With the end of the Civil War came the dissolution of the slave patrols. They did, however, provide the impetus for the Ku Klux Klan, whose mission of terrorizing

black families and black communities was not entirely different from that of the slave patrols.

▶ Policing Eras

As we have just seen, from the colonial period to the late nineteenth century, organized police forces of various kinds emerged across America. Like early policing on the other side of the Atlantic, law enforcement began as a private affair and eventually became public. Once police agencies were an established presence, they grew in number and influence. They also evolved in response to the demands and pressures of the time. Most researchers agree that these changes occurred in three distinct eras: the **political era**, the **reform era**, and the **community era**.[36]

The Political Era

In 1895, "the realities of patrol work mocked Robert Peel's dream of a continuous visible presence … police patrol barely existed at all."[37] Corruption was widespread, and some cities assigned unmanageable beats to their officers. In 1880, for example, Chicago officers patrolled more than three miles of streets—on foot. Large portions of other major metropolitan areas were not patrolled at all. Residential districts were all but ignored in most cities.[38] In addition, communication systems were inadequate, making it next to impossible for sergeants and other command officials to call officers to crime scenes.

Think About It…

An Introduction to Evidence-Based Policing Evidence-based policing is a hot topic in contemporary law enforcement. Its goal is to use research to guide practice and evaluate practitioners. There is little consensus about what is effective in policing. Many practitioners have an almost unshakable faith in the ability of police officers to prevent crime by simply driving around and keeping a watchful eye on the community. But evidence-based policing isn't about opinions; it's about the facts, about what the data and rigorous research show. How does evidence-based policing differ from the way in which policing was performed in times past? In what ways does it improve policing? Might it in some ways distract from the police mission?

Source: Rob Byron/Shutterstock.com

Regulating Criminals

Historians generally agree that police officers of the political era did more to regulate criminal activity than to control it: "Officers established relationships with professional criminals, especially pickpockets, tolerating certain kinds of crime in return for information or stolen goods."[39] They were also heavily involved in providing essential services for those in need. The recently discovered diary of a Boston police officer from 1895 reveals that one of the most common services officers provided was shelter for the homeless.[40] In Cincinnati, for instance, the police station was "a place of last resort for the desperately poor."[41] Police stations came to be dirty, disease-ridden places as a result of this practice, so the sheltering of the homeless came to a halt near the end of the nineteenth century.

Many police officers, along with the politicians and ward bosses they served, were corrupt. By one account, jobs in some early police departments were sold as investment opportunities.[42] Corruption flourished at all levels of government as a result of restrictions on various "vices." Laws limiting drinking, gambling, and sex provided ample opportunity for the criminal element to provide much-desired products and services. Such illegal activities could only thrive, of course, with support from local law enforcement. The payoffs to officers who provided protection for criminals were significant. Detective Thomas Byrnes, head of the New York City Detective Bureau from 1880 to 1895, and widely said to have been corrupt, acquired a fortune of more than $350,000 by the late 1880s (that's about $5 million today).[43] Byrnes was forced to resign by Theodore Roosevelt in 1895 when Roosevelt became head of the New York City Police Commission.

Patronage Problems

To get elected, political candidates at the turn of the twentieth century made promises to the voters, especially promises of employment. Once a candidate was elected, jobs of various sorts, including police jobs, were used to reward the politician's supporters. Newly hired police officers adopted a number of measures to ensure that their "bosses" remained in power. There are many accounts of police officers, assigned to maintain order at polling stations, who pressured voters to support particular candidates.

An example of political patronage run amok was **Tammany Hall** in New York City, the name given to the Democratic Party "machine" that played a significant role in the city's politics from the late nineteenth to the early twentieth centuries. The most notorious Tammany leader was **William M. "Boss" Tweed**. Tweed's control over the political machine was so complete

William Marcy "Boss" Tweed
Source: Library of Congress, Hoxie Collection, LC-USZ62-22467

that he was eventually elected to the New York Senate. By most accounts, he and his cronies were corrupt and heavily involved in a wide range of criminal activities. His career eventually ended in a storm of corruption controversy, and he was ultimately sent to prison. During his heyday, though, he relied heavily on police officers to keep him in office and in control of the ward.

The Reform Era

Frustrations over the likes of Boss Tweed ushered in an era of profound reform. In early 1892, Reverend Charles Parkhurst described New York City's mayor and his aides as "a lying, perjuring, rum-soaked, and libidinous lot of polluted harpies."[44] He also claimed that the police existed for no reason other than "to protect and foster crime and make capital out of it." Using his church as his forum, Parkhurst began a crusade to bring reform to the political system in New York City. He and a number of other like-minded individuals were largely responsible for the appointment of Theodore Roosevelt as commissioner of the New York City Police Department (NYPD).

Once Roosevelt took charge, he forced corrupt officers to resign and launched a series of unannounced nighttime inspections of the police department. He even took to the streets and approached officers in civilian attire. He initiated disciplinary action against officers who were asleep or away from their posts. Roosevelt resigned in 1897, claiming that the NYPD had been reformed; the reality was that little had actually changed.[45] Nonetheless, Roosevelt's efforts were quickly duplicated in a number of other cities that were experiencing similar problems. Reform efforts failed in these places, too. According to historian Sam Walker, "the reformers never came to grips with the basic problems of police administration."[46] They claimed that corrupt officers lacked moral character but ignored some of the deeper issues, such as how the department's rank structure (or absence of one) contributed to the problems reformers lamented. Reform efforts floundered for several years until police reformer August Vollmer changed their focus.

LEARNING OUTCOMES 2 Summarize various eras of policing.

GLOSSARY

political era The period of American policing during the late nineteenth and early twentieth centuries during which police forces served more to regulate crime pursuant to the wishes of corrupt politicians (who used patronage to give police jobs to handpicked loyalists) than to control crime in the interests of the public good.

reform era The period of American policing during the early to mid-twentieth century, during which efforts were made to professionalize police forces and to eliminate the influence of corrupt politicians.

community era By most accounts, the contemporary era of U.S. law enforcement, which stresses service and an almost customer-friendly approach to police work.

Tammany Hall The corrupt Democratic Party political "machine" that operated in New York City in the late nineteenth and early twentieth centuries and that used patronage to control city operations.

William M. "Boss" Tweed (1823–1878) A corrupt American politician who became notorious as the powerful leader of New York City's Tammany Hall.

August Vollmer was the leader of America's police reform movement of the early 1900s.

August Vollmer's Legacy

August Vollmer—the first police chief of Berkeley, California, and perhaps the foremost presence in America's police reform movement—argued that policing should be regarded as a public service, as a profession focused on improving society. During his address to the International Association of Chiefs of Police in 1919, Vollmer argued that the police had "far greater obligations than the mere apprehending and prosecution of lawbreakers." The police, he claimed, should go "up stream a little further" by trying to prevent crime by working with families, schools, and other influential institutions. He called for organizational reforms in police agencies, elevated standards of recruitment and retention, and the adoption of modern management techniques, such as those used in the business sector and military.[47]

There was something of a contradiction in Vollmer's message, however. On the one hand, he called for the expansion of the police role to include crime prevention. On the other, he called for increased crime-fighting efforts. It was crime fighting that won out in the end, leading to "a centralized, authoritarian bureaucracy focusing on crime control."[48]

Vollmer did more than call for reforms. As chief of the Berkeley Police Department during the early twentieth century, he transformed his department in the following ways:

- Increased the size of the force, from three officers to twenty-seven
- Put officers on bicycle and motorcycle patrol
- First to adopt fingerprinting technology to aid in criminal investigations and collaborated with University of California in making other advances
- First police leader of note to hire officers with college degrees
- Created the Berkeley Police School in 1908

In short, Vollmer's reforms were consistent with a reform mentality intended to move policing toward professional stature. He took his ideas beyond Berkeley by evaluating numerous police agencies around the country, including the scandal-ridden Los Angeles Police Department.[49] In 1921 Vollmer was elected president of the International Association of Chiefs of Police (IACP), a position he used to spread his ideas about police reform.

The Crime Commissions

As one of the authors of the 1929 **Illinois Crime Survey** (a series of influential reports on homicide, juvenile justice, and justice operations in Chicago), Vollmer criticized "the corrupt political influence exercised by administrative officials and corrupt politicians."[50] He was also the lead police consultant to the 1931 National Commission on Law Observance and Enforcement, popularly known as the **Wickersham Commission** after its head, George W. Wickersham. The commission was appointed by President Herbert Hoover in 1929 to investigate the real operations and problems of the criminal justice system. Again, Vollmer called attention to corruption, excessive political influence and meddling in criminal justice, poor leadership and management, ineffective recruitment practices, poor-quality training programs, and other issues.

The work of the Wickersham Commission and others not mentioned here, coupled with Vollmer's reformist vision, led to some consensus that a professional model of policing would greatly benefit America. It was hoped that policing would become a civil service profession divorced from politics. Reformers had faith in centralization, crime fighting, scientific investigations, and above all else police work that followed the letter of the law.

Interestingly, one of the most significant developments that fueled this change was the Great Depression. With less money to spend, many cities had to cut back on services, which included the closing of some police precincts. This brought police officers under the control of a central police station, consistent with the managerial model Vollmer had envisioned. Some have called this the *professional era*, others the *legalistic era*, and still others the *reform era*. Regardless of what it was called, what occurred was a dramatic change in the way policing was practiced in the United States. It did not happen quickly, though. The process played out over decades, leading up to the 1960s and the third of America's key policing eras: the community era.

The Community Era

The community era is, by most accounts, the era of contemporary law enforcement. It stresses service and almost a customer-friendly element to police work. Routine and traditional police functions such as patrol, investigations, and the like remain, but many police agencies have changed their mission statements to reflect a new way of thinking epitomized by O. W. Wilson.

O. W. Wilson and the Limitations of Professionalism

August Vollmer's protégé, **O. W. (Orlando Winfield) Wilson**, served as chief of the Wichita, Kansas, Police Department between 1928 and 1939. As chief, he clamped down on corruption and brutality, firing 20 percent of the officers on the force. His department's mission statement, the "Square Deal Code," eventually became the template for the code of ethics of the International Association of Chiefs of Police.[51] His reforms, many of which were quite radical, were not necessarily welcomed with open arms, even by some

---

August Vollmer (1876–1955)
An early and especially effective advocate of police reform whose collaboration with the University of California established the study of criminal justice as an academic discipline.

Illinois Crime Survey A series of influential reports, published in 1929, on homicide, juvenile justice, and justice operations in Chicago that criticized the corrupt political influence on the justice system.[35]

Wickersham Commission A commission appointed by President Herbert Hoover in 1929 to investigate the operations and problems of the criminal justice system. Formally known as the National Commission on Law Observance and Enforcement.

Orlando Winfield "O. W." Wilson (1900–1972) A progressive era reformer, professor of police administration, and protégé of August Vollmer whose writings and teachings continue to influence contemporary U.S. law enforcement.

The community era strongly influences contemporary law enforcement.

people outside the police department. For example, his efforts to aggressively enforce vice laws met with so much resistance that he resigned in 1939.

Despite Wilson's resignation, he went on to gain national prominence. His 1938 textbook, *Municipal Police Administration*, became a leading work (its eighth edition was published in 1979). A year later, he became a professor of police administration at his mentor's old stomping grounds, the University of California, Berkeley. He remained there until 1960, during which time he started the nation's first doctoral program in criminology and wrote another successful policing text, *Police Administration*.[52] He went on to write other influential works, including a manual on how to allocate police patrols according to calls for service.[53] More importantly, he called for a shift from foot patrol (the dominant mode of patrol at the time) to automobile patrol. On top of that, he called for one- rather than two-officer patrols to maximize police resources.

Although O. W. Wilson was certainly a progressive reformer, he may have done more to usher in the community era than many realize. In 1960, during the twilight of his career, Wilson was appointed by Chicago Mayor Richard Daley to reform the city's police department in the wake of a scandal. Wilson used many of the same tools as he did in Wichita, Kansas, including reorganization of the department, widespread firings, improved personnel standards, and improved communications. Despite his best efforts, however, civil rights leaders continued to criticize the department, citing police brutality and discrimination in police employment. Wilson was defensive about the discrimination allegations because he had taken significant steps to diversify the predominantly white police department.[54]

These problems led to a great deal of resentment of police in the African-American community, vestiges of which remain today in various cities. Wilson retired in 1968, marking the end of a notable career. What he did not, or could not, fix became abundantly clear in 1969, when some Chicago police officers appeared to run amok on national television, brutally beating protestors outside the Democratic Party's national convention. Wilson was clearly a progressive era reformer, but his actions (or, as some would say, failure to act) in Chicago started the push for something else.

Toward Customer Service

It is perhaps a simplification to say that the community era is characterized by customer service, but at its core, this new era of policing is about connecting the community and the police in a way that was not accomplished during the reform era. Following the public outcry in the wake of the Chicago fiasco and other publicized instances of strained police–public relations, it was no mystery why a new era emerged. Research began to reveal that the police could not reduce crime by their own efforts alone, another reason the dawn of the third era was at hand.

The sentiments of the community era were expressed in a prescient article authored by University of Alaska Professor John Angell at the beginning of the 1970s.[55] Angell argued that traditional police management practices were culture bound, that they were inconsistent with the humanistic democratic values of the United States, that they demanded that employees demonstrate "immature" personality traits, and that they couldn't cope with environmental pressures. In his view, a more community-centered model would (1) improve community relations, which suffered under the bureaucratic, military model of law enforcement; (2) improve officer morale by allowing them a measure of flexibility in the performance of their duties; and (3) improve interagency coordination.

Some aspects of the community era look remarkably similar to policing near the turn of the twentieth century, but without the corruption, patronage, and other problems that characterized the political era. Community era reformers have sought authorization from community members and extensive citizen support; a broad mandate that stresses the provision of services; a decentralized, responsive organizational structure; and close relations with citizens. A strong tie to citizens would be achieved through foot patrol, problem solving, the preservation of quality of life, and a host of other tactics—all of which were designed to ensure citizen satisfaction and all of which look remarkably similar to practices that were in place before the birth of the reform era.

Since, by most accounts, we are in the midst of the community era, much more needs to be said about it. Accordingly, we will devote a full chapter to this topic. In Chapter 8 we will look in depth at why the community era came to pass, what it looks like today, and what its prospects are for the future.

A New Era?

Few people would deny that the September 11, 2001, terrorist attacks on the United States changed the world. The attacks led

---

Think About It...

Citizen Contact Patrol One approach to improving civilian attitudes toward the police—and thereby reducing crime—consists of door-to-door visits by police officers. Consistent with the ideals of the community era, this citizen contact patrol has police officers knock on people's doors, introduce themselves, give out information, and otherwise try to make policing more personal in nature. This technique has been used by police to do everything from obtaining information about who is carrying guns on the street to providing citizens with tips about reducing burglaries.

Should police officers be encouraged to go door-to-door? Is there any possible downside to citizen contact patrol? If so, what is it?

Source: Wally Stemberger/Shutterstock.com

to one of the most dramatic reorganizations of the U.S. government, including the formation of the cabinet-level Department of Homeland Security. They also led to untold numbers of changes in America's police agencies. When, for instance, the nation's terrorist alert level is elevated, it is the local law enforcement agencies that take on most of the responsibility for increased vigilance.

Local police agencies are entering into uncharted territory with multiagency partnerships, terrorist response training, and the like. Whether the community era can survive the more militaristic style of law enforcement that followed September 11 remains to be seen. We cannot be certain a new era is upon us, but it very well could be. For the time being, however, local police agencies are struggling to fit their new antiterrorist responsibilities within their community focus and are using intelligence gathered through good community relations to further the goal of terrorism prevention.

▶ Beyond Local Law Enforcement

Most of our discussion of police history thus far has focused on local law enforcement: municipal police and sheriff's departments. There is also an interesting history behind state and federal law enforcement, but the story is much shorter. With the exception of the U.S. Marshals Service, which was founded in the late eighteenth century, the history of state and federal law enforcement goes back only to the nineteenth century.

The Emergence of State Agencies

When Texas declared its independence from Mexico in 1836, the Texas Rangers were already an established law enforcement agency. As discussed earlier, they did not begin as a state-level organization. Their initial focus was defending the community, but they adopted policing responsibilities after Texas independence was declared. The early Rangers often took the law into their own hands and were not as concerned with equal treatment and due process as police are today. In 1935, Texas created the Department of Public Safety (DPS), which remains in existence to this day. The Texas Rangers are part of the Texas DPS, as are the troopers of the Texas State Patrol. Once the Rangers came under the supervision of the DPS, conduct problems, excessive force, and the like were reined in. This hasn't stopped Hollywood from giving the impression that the Rangers are very special, as evidenced by the long-running television show *Walker, Texas Ranger*. For an overview of the Texas Rangers' *real* responsibilities, see Figure 1.2.

LEARNING OUTCOMES 3 Outline the emergence of state and federal law enforcement agencies.

The other states eventually formed their own state-level police agencies, but they often took unique forms. The Pennsylvania State Police, for example, was founded in 1905 in response to the difficulty local police were having resolving state-specific issues. For example, the western Pennsylvania mining region attracted scores of immigrant workers and experienced ethnic violence and labor disputes. A major coal strike in 1902 prompted President Theodore Roosevelt to appoint a commission to look into the problems of maintaining order in the mining region. This led to the establishment of the state

Nearly every state has at least one state-level police agency.

police. Unlike the Texas Rangers and other state agencies, the Pennsylvania State Police consisted largely of men with National Guard and army experience. The Pennsylvania State Police also had their share of problems in the beginning, just like the Rangers, but they gradually assumed greater law enforcement responsibilities and adopted professional standards.

As automobiles became more common and highways were built, state police agencies shifted much of their focus toward the enforcement of traffic laws. What we see today, then, is a mixture of state agencies, some with general law enforcement responsibilities, and others with a traffic enforcement focus. Today, nearly every state has at least one state-level police agency. We will look at them in more detail when we discuss the organization of law enforcement in America in Chapter 3.

The First Federal Agencies

U.S. Marshals

In 1789, President George Washington appointed the first 13 U.S. Marshals in accordance with the Judiciary Act. Until the Secret Service was established in 1865, the U.S. Marshals focused their efforts on apprehending counterfeiters. Between 1790 and 1870, the marshals were also required to take the national census every ten years, a responsibility that was eventually transferred to the Bureau of the Census. During the nineteenth century, the marshals did everything from arrest fugitive slaves to confiscate property used to support the Confederacy.

More than anything, though, in the latter part of the nineteenth century the marshals and their deputies were responsible for maintaining law and order in the Old West. On October 26, 1881, in Tombstone, Arizona, Marshal Virgil Earp and his deputies (brothers Wyatt and Morgan Earp and John H. "Doc" Holliday) gunned down Frank and Tom McLaury and Billy Clanton in a vacant lot just down the street from the O.K. Corral. Movies like *Tombstone* and *Wyatt Earp* have recounted this series of events. Since the nineteenth century, the U.S. Marshals Service has taken on a range of duties quite distinct from those of days past. We will look at both the history and the modern duties of the U.S. Marshals in Chapter 3.

Postal Inspectors and Secret Service

Another early federal law enforcement effort involved U.S. postal inspectors, whose job it was to target crimes committed via the mail. In 1865, the Secret Service was established with the mission to suppress counterfeiting. That responsibility remains today, along with a number of others, including the protection of the president.

The FBI

The Bureau of Investigation, now known as the *Federal Bureau of Investigation (FBI)*, was formed in 1908. The agency began with 8 Secret Service agents, 14 newly hired investigators, and 12 accountants; their task was to investigate antitrust land fraud and similar matters. The agency grew rapidly and became the primary investigative agency for federal crimes. It ascended to a position of high visibility during the 1920s, when J. Edgar Hoover was appointed to lead the agency. Under Hoover's charge from 1924 to 1972, the FBI apprehended a number of dangerous offenders and engaged in numerous high-profile investigations, perhaps most notably the kidnapping of ace flyer Charles Lindbergh's baby.

Hoover was a controversial director. He routinely fired agents who displeased him, and it is alleged that he blackmailed political leaders and illegally disrupted the activities of the Black Panther Party; Martin Luther King, Jr.'s, Southern Christian Leadership Conference; the Ku Klux Klan; and other groups. Today, FBI directors cannot serve more than a ten-year term due to concerns that they may become too powerful. To his credit, though, Hoover did a great deal to usher in the professional policing era through his insistence on a crime-fighting role for FBI agents. The FBI is discussed in greater detail in Chapter 3.

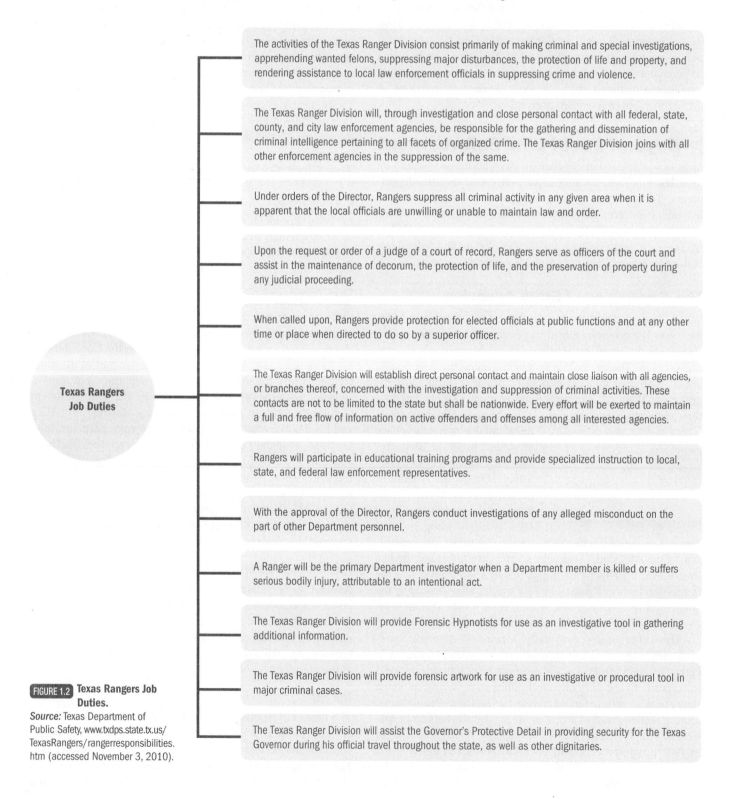

FIGURE 1.2 **Texas Rangers Job Duties.**
Source: Texas Department of Public Safety, www.txdps.state.tx.us/TexasRangers/rangerresponsibilities.htm (accessed November 3, 2010).

Texas Rangers Job Duties

The activities of the Texas Ranger Division consist primarily of making criminal and special investigations, apprehending wanted felons, suppressing major disturbances, the protection of life and property, and rendering assistance to local law enforcement officials in suppressing crime and violence.

The Texas Ranger Division will, through investigation and close personal contact with all federal, state, county, and city law enforcement agencies, be responsible for the gathering and dissemination of criminal intelligence pertaining to all facets of organized crime. The Texas Ranger Division joins with all other enforcement agencies in the suppression of the same.

Under orders of the Director, Rangers suppress all criminal activity in any given area when it is apparent that the local officials are unwilling or unable to maintain law and order.

Upon the request or order of a judge of a court of record, Rangers serve as officers of the court and assist in the maintenance of decorum, the protection of life, and the preservation of property during any judicial proceeding.

When called upon, Rangers provide protection for elected officials at public functions and at any other time or place when directed to do so by a superior officer.

The Texas Ranger Division will establish direct personal contact and maintain close liaison with all agencies, or branches thereof, concerned with the investigation and suppression of criminal activities. These contacts are not to be limited to the state but shall be nationwide. Every effort will be exerted to maintain a full and free flow of information on active offenders and offenses among all interested agencies.

Rangers will participate in educational training programs and provide specialized instruction to local, state, and federal law enforcement representatives.

With the approval of the Director, Rangers conduct investigations of any alleged misconduct on the part of other Department personnel.

A Ranger will be the primary Department investigator when a Department member is killed or suffers serious bodily injury, attributable to an intentional act.

The Texas Ranger Division will provide Forensic Hypnotists for use as an investigative tool in gathering additional information.

The Texas Ranger Division will provide forensic artwork for use as an investigative or procedural tool in major criminal cases.

The Texas Ranger Division will assist the Governor's Protective Detail in providing security for the Texas Governor during his official travel throughout the state, as well as other dignitaries.

The Minuteman Project and Border Security

The Minuteman Project raises several interesting questions:

1. Should *any* civilian volunteers get involved in actively patrolling our borders?

2. What should organizations like the Minuteman Project be allowed to do in terms of policing the borders?

3. Are the Minutemen vigilantes? If so, is there a place for vigilante groups in contemporary law enforcement?

4. Should civilian organizations be involved with general issues of crime prevention and security?

5. Where should the line be drawn between civilian and "official" law enforcement?

6. To what extent is private policing and security helpful or harmful to society's interests?

Illegal immigration is a hot-button issue today. U.S. Customs and Border Protection (CBP) agents routinely apprehend undocumented immigrants crossing the U.S.-Mexico border, but there are not enough agents to effectively stop the massive influx of illegal immigrants. In response to this concern, citizen groups are volunteering their time and energies to help with border protection. One of these groups, the Minuteman Project,[56] rose to national prominence in the early years of the twenty-first century. Its members claim to be working in collaboration with U.S. Customs and Border Protection, but that agency has not officially teamed with or endorsed the Minuteman Project's efforts.

The Minuteman Project (and its sister organization, the Minuteman Civil Defense Corps) consists mostly of civilian volunteers who literally watch portions of the U.S.-Mexico border (employing foot, car, and helicopter patrols) and alert CBP agents to possible illegal crossings. The Minuteman Project calls itself a "vigilance operation" and says that it does not advocate altercations between volunteers and those seeking to cross the border illegally; instead, it aims to provide information to officials whose legitimate responsibility is securing the border. Some volunteers, however, work together in armed patrols and sometimes detain suspected illegal immigrants until CBP agents arrive.

Whether the Minuteman volunteers are a "vigilance" group or a "vigilante" group is open to debate. There is no shortage of critics who claim that the Minutemen are concerned with anything but "vigilance." The American Civil Liberties Union (ACLU) has denounced the detentions of suspected illegal immigrants by Minuteman volunteers, and some members of the ACLU ride out into the Arizona desert to keep an eye on the Minutemen. [57]

LEARNING OUTCOMES 1

Outline the origins of policing.

Policing in the Western world began as a private affair and became a public, or governmental, responsibility. Policing in America looks as it does today largely because it was inherited from the English, beginning with the frankpledge system, the watchman system, and Henry Fielding's Bow Street Runners.

1. What were the major milestones in the historical development of policing in the Western world?

2. What is the significance of due process of law for American policing?

bobby The popular British name given to a member of Sir Robert Peel's Metropolitan Police Force.

Texas Rangers A militia originally formed by Stephen F. Austin in 1823 to protect the territory of Texas against Native American raids, criminals, and intruders. Today, the Rangers serve as part of the Texas Department of Public Safety.

slave patrol A crude form of private policing, often carried out by citizen volunteers. Slave patrols were created in the eighteenth century to apprehend runaway slaves and to ensure that slaves did not rise up against their owners.

due process of law A right guaranteed by the Fifth, Sixth, and Fourteenth Amendments and generally understood, in legal contexts, to mean the due course of legal proceedings according to the rules and forms established for the protection of individual rights. In criminal proceedings, due process of law is generally understood to include the following basic elements: a law creating and defining the offense, an impartial tribunal having jurisdictional authority over the case, accusation in proper form, notice and opportunity to defend, trial according to established procedure, and discharge from all restraints or obligations unless convicted.

frankpledge system The ultimate outgrowth of the night watch system of social control, dating to the twelfth century, in which ten households were grouped into a tithing, and each adult male member of the tithing was held responsible for the conduct of the others.

tithing Under the frankpledge system, a group of ten households.

parish Under the frankpledge system, a group of ten tithings. Also referred to as a *hundred*.

shire Under the frankpledge system, a collection of several parishes.

sheriff The modern-day term for the Old English *shire-reeve*. In the United States today, the senior law enforcement official in a county.

shire-reeve The Old English term for *sheriff*. Literally, "the keeper of the shire."

watchman An early officer on foot patrol who, during the hours of darkness, watched for fires and criminal activities. Upon detecting such events, the watchman's role was to sound the "hue and cry" to evoke a defensive response from the citizenry. This style of policing dates back to the early to mid-eighteenth century in England.

Henry Fielding (1707–1754) An English magistrate who founded what some have called London's first police force, the Bow Street Runners.

Bow Street Runners An early English police unit formed under the leadership of Henry Fielding, magistrate of the Bow Street region of London. Also referred to as *thief takers*.

thief taker An alternative name for Henry Fielding's Bow Street Runners.

Sir Robert Peel (1788–1850) A former British home secretary whose criticisms of the state of policing in London led to the passage of the Metropolitan Police Act and the establishment of the world's first large-scale organized police force in that city in 1829.

Metropolitan Police Act The legislation adopted by the British Parliament in 1829 that established the world's first large-scale organized police force in London.

LEARNING OUTCOMES 2

Summarize various eras of policing.

American policing has evolved through three distinct eras: the political, reform, and community eras. We may be on the cusp of a fourth policing era, which some are calling the homeland security era.

1. Identify and describe the major eras of policing discussed in this chapter. Are the eras distinct or overlapping? Explain.

2. What were the findings of the National Commission on Law Observance and Enforcement? What significance did those findings have for American policing?

Illinois Crime Survey A series of influential reports, published in 1929, on homicide, juvenile justice, and justice operations in Chicago that criticized the corrupt political influence on the justice system.

Wickersham Commission A commission appointed by President Herbert Hoover in 1929 to investigate the operations and problems of the criminal justice system. Formally known as the National Commission on Law Observance and Enforcement.

Orlando Winfield "O. W." Wilson (1900–1972) A progressive era reformer, professor of police administration, and protégé of August Vollmer whose writings and teachings continue to influence contemporary U.S. law enforcement.

political era The period of American policing during the late nineteenth and early twentieth centuries during which police forces served more to regulate crime pursuant to the wishes of corrupt politicians (who used patronage to give police jobs to handpicked loyalists) than to control crime in the interests of the public good.

reform era The period of American policing during the early to mid-twentieth century, during which efforts were made to professionalize police forces and to eliminate the influence of corrupt politicians.

community era By most accounts, the contemporary era of U.S. law enforcement, which stresses service and an almost customer-friendly approach to police work.

Tammany Hall The corrupt Democratic Party political "machine" that operated in New York City in the late nineteenth and early twentieth centuries and that used patronage to control city operations.

William M. "Boss" Tweed (1823–1878) A corrupt American politician who became notorious as the powerful leader of New York City's Tammany Hall.

August Vollmer (1876–1955) An early and especially effective advocate of police reform whose collaboration with the University of California established the study of criminal justice as an academic discipline.

LEARNING OUTCOMES 3

Outline the emergence of state and federal law enforcement agencies.

State and federal law enforcement agencies have their own, unique histories. With the exception of the U.S. Marshals Service, which was founded in the late eighteenth century, the history of state and federal law enforcement goes back only to the nineteenth century. Among the earliest organized state police agencies were the Texas Rangers and the Pennsylvania State Police.

1. Illustrate the development of state and federal law enforcement agencies in the United States.

2. How did the development of those agencies parallel the development of local police forces?

3. How did it differ from the pattern of development seen in local agencies?

MyCJLab

Go to the Chapter 1 section in *MyCJLab* to test your understanding of this chapter, access customized study content, engage in interactive simulations, complete critical thinking and research assignments, and view related online videos.

Additional Links

This website directs visitors to detailed information about the Wickersham Commission, including its position on the historic issue of prohibition: **www.druglibrary.org/schaffer/Library/studies/wick/index.html**. The site breaks down information through a table of contents on the home page for easy selection of material.

This link provides a PDF version of a Bureau of Justice Statistics publication covering police statistics for local departments: **http://bjs.ojp.usdoj.gov/content/pub/pdf/lpd07.pdf**. This website provides a directory of all state police agencies: **www.officer.com/links/Agency_Search/United_States/**.

This website provides a directory of federal law enforcement agencies: **www.officer.com/links/Agency_Search/Federal**.

David Weisburg and Peter Neyroud, "Police Science: Toward a New Paradigm," (Cambridge, MA: Executive Session on Policing and Public Safety at Harvard University's Kennedy School of Government, 2010). This paper provides an overview of evidence-based policing practices: **www.ncjrs.gov/pdffiles1/nij/232179.pdf**.

U.S. Government Accountability Office, *Report to Congressional Requesters: Recovery Act – Department of Justice Could Better Assess Justice Assistance Grant Program Impact* (Washington, DC: GAO, October 2010); GAO-11-87. The full report, discussed at the start of this chapter, is available here: **http://justicestudies.com//pubs/gao1187.pdf**.

Learn more about police history at **http://law.jrank.org/pages/1647/Police-History.html**. A history of British policing is available at **www.met.police.uk/history**.

The history of the New Orleans Police Department can be found here: **www.nola.gov/GOVERNMENT/NOPD/NOPD-Home/History-of-the-NOPD**.

Information about local police departments is posted here: **www.justicestudies.com/pubs/localpolice.pdf**.

Policing in American Context

"Police in the United States function within one of the most complex organizational environments imaginable."

1 Explain how the U.S. government's features of democracy and federalism impact policing.

2 Identify various elements of the policing environment in America and explain their influence on the practice of policing.

3 Summarize the police role in the criminal justice process.

2

In January, 2011, the city of Camden, New Jersey, was forced to make drastic cuts in staffing levels at the city's police department—including layoffs of more than 160 of the city's 360 sworn officers. About the same time, smaller cuts were made in other New Jersey municipalities, resulting in a loss of 167 of Camden's 1,265 officers; layoffs of 82 of Jersey City's 829 officers; and a loss of 60 officers out of Atlantic City's 365-member force.[1]

Camden, which was forced to make the staffing cuts due to significant budgetary problems, plans to rely heavily on other agencies to supplement its remaining police force. State police officers, who have been helping to patrol the city for a decade, recently started conducting "weekend surges" to put more officers on the city's streets. Similarly, county law enforcement officers will take on more duties at crime scenes, and the Camden County Prosecutor's office provides homicide investigators who also partner with the police to investigate all shootings.

Camden's poor fiscal status stems from a budget shortfall of $26.5 million in what the city had planned to spend for 2011. The shortfall developed even after a 25 percent citywide spending cut was implemented in 2010.[2]

DISCUSS How does America's current financial crisis impact policing? Might the crisis lead to improved policing?

▶ Policing in American Government

The United States is a representative democracy and the world's oldest functional federation (a union consisting of several more or less self-governing states). These unique arrangements have affected the structure and organization of government agencies at all levels, including the police.

Policing in a Democracy

Democracy is usually defined as government by the people. It vests supreme authority in the citizenry, usually through free elections and the representatives the citizens choose to elect. Other features of a democracy include equality of rights, privileges, and opportunities; open government; and due process protections against unreasonable arrest and prosecution. To many, democracy also means that people should be free from excessive government influence in their lives. See Figure 2.1 for an overview of the elements of democracy.

Nearly everyone values the full exercise of democratic principles, yet others express serious concern when those principles are threatened. Consider the recent outcries over electronic eavesdropping of domestic phone conversations by federal investigators as part of antiterrorism intelligence gathering. Some people feel that such eavesdropping is necessary to maintain security. Others, though, fear that it threatens core democratic values and is unreasonably intrusive.

In an effort to balance these opposing views, a police force in a democratic nation should be one that "is subject to the rule of law embodying values respectful of human dignity, rather than the wishes of a powerful leader or party; can intervene in the life of citizens only under limited and carefully controlled circumstances; and is publicly accountable."[3] In other words, most of us would likely agree that the police should be able to enforce the law, but they shouldn't go "too far" and run roughshod over people's rights.

Consequences of Democracy for Police

Robert Kennedy once pointed out that "every society gets the kind of criminal it deserves." Kennedy also said, "What is equally true is that every community gets the kind of law enforcement it insists on."[4]

There are many ways to interpret Kennedy's observations, but one is especially relevant here. With its concern over people's rights and privacy, democracy ensures that a certain amount of crime is inevitable. In other words, some of the crime problems our country has might be due to the very nature

The United States is a representative democracy and the world's oldest functional federation.

1. Sovereignty of the people
2. Government based upon consent of the governed
3. Majority rule
4. Minority rights
5. Guarantee of basic human rights
6. Free and fair elections
7. Equality before the law
8. Due process of law
9. Constitutional limits on government
10. Social, economic, and political pluralism
11. Values of tolerance, pragmatism, cooperation, and compromise

FIGURE 2.1 The Pillars of Democracy.
Source: U.S. Department of State, "Defining Democracy," http://usinfo.org/mirror/usinfo.state.gov/products/pubs/whatsdem/whatdm2.htm (accessed December 2, 2010).

GLOSSARY

democracy A form of government that vests supreme authority in the people, usually through their freely elected representatives.

federalism A political doctrine holding that power is divided (often constitutionally) between a central governing body (the federal government, for example) and various constituent units (the states).

dual federalism An interpretation of the U.S. Constitution that suggests a system in which the only powers vested in the federal government are those explicitly listed in the document, with the remaining powers being left to the states.

of our government. Consider those who manufacture meth-amphetamine in clandestine laboratories. If they know that the police can arbitrarily enter the facility at any time, they might choose an alternative pursuit. On the other hand, if they know that there are steps the police must take before they can enforce the law, they might be willing to take a chance. Figure 2.2 provides an overview of how democracy influences policing.

Policing and Federalism

One of democracy's most distinguishing features is policy making by majority rule, either directly by the people, as in a direct democracy, or through elected representatives, as in a representative democracy. The very term *democracy* comes from the Greek words *demos*, meaning "people," and *kratos*, meaning "rule." In other words, *democracy* means "ruled by the people." One can even go further and call ours an advanced or liberal democracy because of its concern with the rule of law, the separation of powers, and, most importantly, people's liberties. But democracy alone does not fully describe our system of government. The government structure in the United States is also characterized by **federalism**. Policing in a federalist nation is quite distinct from policing in nonfederalist nations.

Federalism, often confused with democracy, is another feature of American government that has served to shape the policing apparatus in the United States. Federalism is a political doctrine wherein power is divided (often constitutionally) between a central governing body (the federal government, for example) and various constituent units (the states).

Federalism helps facilitate democracy because it promotes participation in all levels of government. If one had ambitions to enter political office, one would likely start with the goal of becoming a county supervisor, a city council person, or an elected state official. With experience, a political veteran might then rise to ranks of U.S. senator or representative.

A perusal of the U.S. Constitution suggests a system of **dual federalism**, in which the only powers vested in the federal government are those explicitly listed in the Constitution; the rest are left to the states. This suggested arrangement is the textbook definition of federalism. In reality, though, ours is more a system of cooperative federalism, meaning that some of the lines between federal and state power are blurred or at least have fluctuated over time. For example,

American federalism effectively defines various levels of law enforcement.

Article I, Section 8 of the U.S. Constitution gives the federal government the power to regulate interstate commerce, but this authority has been interpreted so broadly that the federal government can effectively control much of what happens at the state level. To this day, we see plenty of federal influence over even local criminal justice policies.

Consequences of Federalism for Policing

Inherent in federalism is the concept of different levels of government. Consequently, American federalism effectively defines various levels of law enforcement. Our two-tiered governmental structure (states and the federal government) inherently divides law enforcement within those levels. Further, federalism can affect relationships between the agencies at the various levels of government. For example, if the federal

Features of a Democracy

- Equality of rights, privileges, and opportunities
- Open government
- Due process protections against unreasonable arrest and prosecution

Consequences of a Democracy for Police

- Concern for people's rights and privacy means that a certain amount of crime is inevitable.
- The Bill of Rights ensures that the government cannot go too far without answering to the people.
- The Fourth Amendment to the Constitution mandates that the police meet specific legal requirements before they can enter private residences, make arrests, and seize evidence.

FIGURE 2.2 Policing and Democracy.

Unified

- Central authority makes all laws and holds all power.

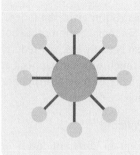

Confederation

- There is no strong central government.

- Constituent units make laws and hold power.

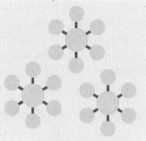

Federalist

- Laws are made by the central governing authority as well as by the constituent units. The federal government makes laws for the entire nation, but federalism also gives the states power to make their own laws.

- In the United States, we have both the federal Constitution and individual state constitutions, consistent with the idea of shared power. The federal government and each state also have their own legal codes.

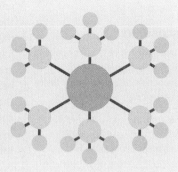

government grants money to local government, it can exercise a measure of control. Applying this to policing, the Office of Community Oriented Policing Services in the U.S. Justice Department gives various grants to local law enforcement agencies throughout the states, but typically with strings attached.

Features of a Federalist Government

- Division of power lies between a central governing body and various constituent bodies.
- Dual federalism: Any powers not explicitly vested to the federal government are left to the states.
- Cooperative federalism: Lines between federal and state power are blurred or have fluctuated over time.

Consequences of Federalism for Police

- Law enforcement is divided between federal and state levels.
- Tensions may result between federal and state agencies.
- Cooperation between various agencies is important.

FIGURE 2.3 **Policing and Federalism.**

One such string is that the money must be used to support community policing activities.

Federalism also adds to the dynamics of law enforcement because it creates relationships (and perhaps tensions) between levels of government (Figure 2.3). For example, "turf wars" sometimes occur between federal and state or local law enforcement agencies. In movies and television programs, such jurisdictional conflicts are often portrayed as some small-town police chief or sheriff laying claim to a particular criminal case before the "feds" get involved. Turf wars do indeed exist, but interagency (and interlevel) cooperation is now the word of the day, especially in the "war on terror." If it weren't for federalism, though, there would be neither tension nor cooperation across levels of government because different levels wouldn't exist in the first place.

▶ The Police Organizational Environment

Every organization operates within an environment that consists not just of the organization's physical surroundings but also has human dimensions. In a democracy where the power of the people is emphasized, this is all the more apparent. Couple this with the highly visible nature of police organizations and it becomes clear that the police in the United States function within one of the most complex organizational environments imaginable. First, they serve and interact with citizens. Second, they are government organizations and, as such, regularly interact with other government entities, such as city councils and county boards of supervisors. Third, the media in the United States keep a close eye on the police, perhaps because we as citizens are intrigued by what the police do (or don't do). Finally, police organizations interact with their peer agencies at various levels of government. See Figure 2.4 for a summary.

The Community

By far the most significant environmental factor in law enforcement is the community. In sheer magnitude, the number of citizens dwarfs all other factors that influence the police. Not every citizen carries quite the same level of influence as, say, an

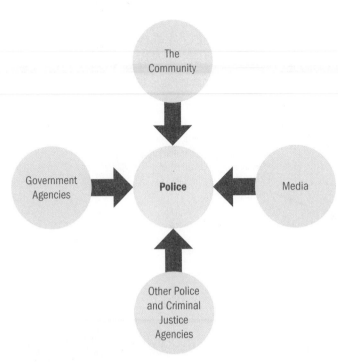

FIGURE 2.4 The Police Environment.

view police favorably.[5] One study revealed that about two-thirds of Americans felt their local police agencies and sheriff's departments were effective, friendly, and fair.[6] What about the other third? Some people regard authority figures with suspicion.[7] Moreover, a significant percentage of that one-third comprises minorities, and many minorities not only do not support police but they also view them with contempt.[8] Such perceptions are often an outgrowth of strained racial relations in some of America's high-crime, poor inner-city neighborhoods. Even that two-thirds majority is not unwavering in its support; various factors can affect whether police will be viewed favorably.

Government Officials

Law enforcement agencies are government entities, but a host of non–law enforcement government officials—at the federal, state, and local levels—exercise significant control and influence over them.

- The president appoints the heads of federal law enforcement agencies.

- Governors set state policy and prioritize spending for certain projects.

- Courts issue decisions that affect the activities of officers on the street.

- Legislatures make funding decisions.

- Mayors hire and fire police chiefs.

The list goes on, but the point is that one of the key environmental influences on law enforcement in America is government. In the sections that follow, we look at executive, legislative, and judicial influence. Although there are far more sources of influence than we can possibly cover here, there are a few standouts. For the executive, they are city councils, mayors, police commissions, and other appointing authorities. For the legislative, the roles of the U.S. Congress and the state legislatures in shaping America's law enforcement apparatus are most important. Finally, courts at all levels of government have a dramatic influence on policing (Figure 2.5).

evening newscaster, but given that there is roughly one sworn law enforcement officer for every 400 to 500 citizens in the United States, the voice of the citizenry must be reckoned with. Through the democratic process, citizens also influence the elected officials who speak for them. The president, members of Congress, county boards of supervisors, city mayors, and city councils—all of whom exert a measure of control over law enforcement activities—come to their posts with a mandate from their constituents.

Law enforcement officials have a vested interest in maintaining positive relationships with the communities they serve. The service element of the famous police mantra "protect and serve" all but requires a measure of concern for what community members think. But the protection function also requires citizen support. Much crime takes place behind closed doors, and police cannot always detect it without input from concerned citizens. A lack of citizen support can also influence law enforcement organizations through the political process. For example, public dissatisfaction with a local police department could prompt the mayor to seek a replacement for the chief.

Fortunately, the police rarely fight an uphill battle for public support. Studies reveal that the vast majority of citizens

Think About It...

Police Newsletters Some police agencies publish newsletters that are distributed throughout the community. Unfortunately, research shows that such community newsletters rarely reduce crime rates. Other forms of public education, particularly education about domestic violence, appear to be ineffective as well. However, studies show that these newsletters may have a positive effect in reinforcing citizens' participation in community safety. Should the police be responsible for disseminating newsletters to the community? Are newsletters sufficient to bolster community support?

Source: AP Photo/David Kohl

City Councils/Mayor
- Enact policies that agencies underneath them must implement
- Control purse strings: decide how much money is allocated to city agencies
- Involvement in nomination and dismissal of Police Chiefs

Police Commission
- Set policy, rules, and regulations
- Oversee department operations
- Review chief's annual proposed budget
- Investigate charges of wrongdoing brought against police department

Executive Influence

State Legislature
- It maintains office responsible for grant funding of city and county law enforcement agencies.
- Agencies must do what state wants in order to get funding.

Legislative Influence

Judicial Influence

Courts
- Court decisions on important legal issues trickle down to law enforcement.
- Police must act with regard to court decisions, or criminals may be freed due to improper procedure.

U.S. Congress
- Legislation can dispense grant money to local law enforcement.

FIGURE 2.5 The Influence of Government Officials on the Police.

Council-Manager Form

- This form is most common in cities of more than 12,000 people.

- An elected city council usually consists of 5 to 12 people.

- The city council makes all policy decisions for the city.

- The power of the mayor is significantly limited:
  - Performs ceremonial duties
  - Serves as the voice, and often the leader, of the council
  - Vote of the mayor carries no more weight than that of other council members

- A city manager presides over the city's day-to-day operations and implements policy enacted by city council.

Mayor-Council Form

- This form may be strong-mayor or weak-mayor.

- *Strong-mayor variation:* Mayor has almost limitless authority over city operations, including hiring and dismissal of key officials.

- *Weak-mayor variation:* Mayor serves largely at the behest of the city council.

- The weak-mayor variation is more common in small towns.

- In both variations, the mayor is responsible for city operations; there is no city manager.

Executive Influence

There are basically two forms of city government in the United States, the **council-manager form** and the **mayor-council form**. The difference between the mayor-council and council-manager forms is the presence or absence of a city manager. City managers are supposed to be apolitical, but mayors are not. Both systems of municipal government have interesting implications for law enforcement.

City Councils. City councils do plenty to exercise control over municipal police agencies. For example, they enact policies that agencies underneath them must implement. Likewise, they can control the purse strings, deciding how much money is allocated to city agencies. They also get involved in dismissals in the event that a police chief fails to perform important functions. In some cities, councils do this directly. Other cities give the city manager authority to make personnel decisions for all city agencies. Still other council-manager cities give the city manager authority to make decisions with the council's approval. It obviously benefits the chief to know who makes key decisions under any system of municipal government.

The council-manager form of city government gives the impression that politics are removed from the process. Presumably, with several officials instead of one partisan mayor, it would be somewhat difficult to make drastic personnel decisions concerning the police department. That does not mean, however, that city councils sit on the sidelines while problems persist in law enforcement. Just recently, the council of Troy, Texas, a city about halfway between Dallas and Austin, fired not just the police chief but the entire department.[9] The city council cited poor performance and insubordination as key reasons for its decision. While replacements were being sought, the city was forced to rely on the local sheriff's department for law enforcement services.

Mayors. As mentioned, large cities tend to favor the council-manager system of government. At the beginning of 2006, the city of San Diego changed from a city manager to a strong-mayor form of government. (See the city's organizational chart in Figure 2.6.) The change was approved by the city's voters. According to the city, "Under the new system the Mayor is the City's chief executive officer, similar to the governor or the president. The Council is the legislative body, providing checks and balances to the Mayor's new authority."[10]

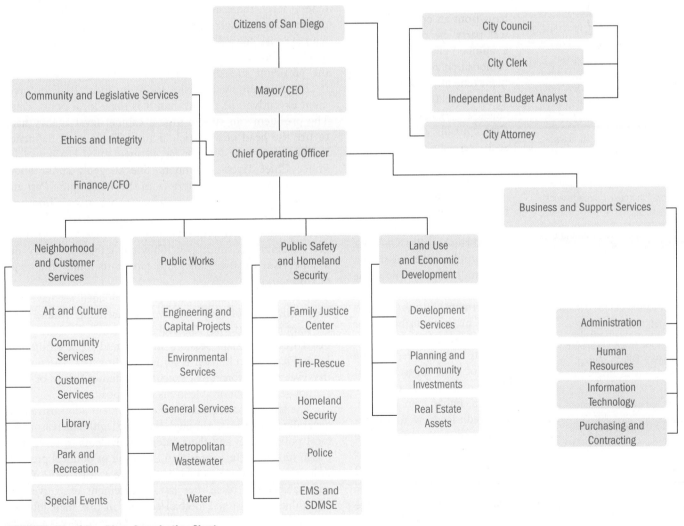

FIGURE 2.6 **City of San Diego Organization Chart.**
Source: Courtesy of the City of San Diego Police Department.

GLOSSARY

council-manager form The most common form of city government in cities of more than 12,000 people. It consists of an elected city council (usually between five and twelve people) responsible for all policy decisions for the city. Mayors under this form of municipal government generally perform ceremonial duties and serve as the voice, and often the leader, of the city council.

mayor-council form A form of municipal government that can be categorized in two ways. The strong-mayor variation gives the mayor almost limitless authority over city operations, including the hiring and dismissal of key officials. In the weak-mayor variation, which is more common in small towns, the mayor serves largely at the behest of the city council.

police commission An agency maintained in some large cities that acts like a corporate board of directors, setting policy and overseeing the police department's operations.

Violent Crime Control and Law Enforcement Act of 1994 The U.S. legislation that established the Office of Community Oriented Policing Services (the COPS Office) in the U.S. Justice Department.

impression management A media relations concept that involves controlling the presentation of information to achieve a desired public perception.

dramaturgical discipline Achieving a balance between merely reporting facts and putting a "spin" on those facts to create a desired impression.

Mayors generally wield more authority in council-mayor systems. Nowadays, though, it is fairly rare for a mayor to exercise total authority over the hiring and firing of a city's first responders. This is true for San Diego, too, despite its move to a strong-mayor system. The city's new rules allow the mayor to nominate the police chief, but the nominee must be approved by the city council. Likewise, the mayor can dismiss the police chief, but such action is subject to review by the city council.

Not every police chief can take comfort in knowing that mayors are generally prohibited from dismissing them on a whim. Oftentimes, when a new mayor is elected, perhaps from an opposing political party, he or she makes a number of changes in the composition of the city's top management. Newly elected mayors sometimes fire police chiefs to "shake things up." City councils often support such reorganizations when a new administration comes on board.

Police chiefs can sometimes make city mayors look bad. That is one of the alleged reasons why New York City's police commissioner, William J. Bratton (now the chief of the Los Angeles Police Department), was forced out of his position by Mayor Rudolph W. Giuliani in 1996. Bratton had appeared on the cover of *Time* magazine, and the accompanying article gave Bratton, rather than Giuliani, full credit for New York's precipitous drop in crime since the mid-1990s. There have also been rumors that the two men did not get along.

Police Commissions. Some large cities, regardless of their form of government, also maintain a **police commission**, which generally acts like a corporate board of directors, setting policy and overseeing the department's operations. The Los Angeles Police Commission, for example, consists of five civilian volunteers. The commissioners serving in 2008 were not just "average" citizens. Two were prominent attorneys, two were successful corporate personalities, and one was a former president of the Los Angeles Urban League. The composition of a police commission can change, however, and tends to when a new mayor is elected.

The Los Angeles Police Commission is perhaps best known for its decision in 2002 to deny embattled Police Chief Bernard Park's bid for a second five-year term. Parks asked the Los Angeles City Council to overturn the commission's decision, but it refused.[11] Hiring and firing decisions, though, are not usually the foremost responsibility of police commissions. Honolulu's police commission, while involved in such decisions, spends the bulk of its time reviewing department rules and regulations, reviewing the chief's annual proposed budget, and investigating charges of wrongdoing brought against the city's police department by members of the public and other police officers. It is critical for a police chief in a city with a police commission to understand the political process and the interplay among council, commission, and mayor.

Other Appointing Authorities. Moving from the local to the federal level, there are other appointing authorities besides mayors, city managers, city councils, and police commissions who exercise control over top law enforcement officials. The heads of federal law enforcement agencies are appointed by the president and approved by the Senate. Interestingly, it is also generally much easier for a top federal law enforcement executive to be fired than it is for a local police chief. The president can simply urge a cabinet-level agency head to fire the head of a particular unit. That's what happened in 2004, when the Interior Department fired National Park Police Chief Teresa Chambers. She allegedly spoke about "taboo" topics with reporters from the *Washington Post* and acted with a lack of discretion in various areas: "improper budget communications, making public remarks regarding security on federal property, improper disclosure of budget deliberations, improper lobbying, failure to carry out a supervisor's instructions, and failure to follow the chain of command."[12]

Justice Department law enforcement agencies have also seen their share of administrative "replacements." Some readers may recall Attorney General Janet Reno's decision to fire FBI Director William Sessions in 1993 and replace him with Louis Freeh (who himself is no longer director). The point is that every law enforcement executive, whether federal or local, cannot get too comfortable in his or her position.

The tenure of the typical law enforcement administrator is generally pretty short. Although there are legitimate reasons for local police chiefs and their federal equivalents to leave their posts, such departures are often the result of political pressure or a firing decision. Fortunately, there are at least some checks and balances in place, but law enforcement executives are not unlike professional football coaches in that their jobs are tenuous, their futures are uncertain, and job security is a far cry from that of the lower-ranking street-level police officer. The successful law enforcement administrator *must* play politics.

The Violent Crime Control and Law Enforcement Act of 1994 ushered in what is now known as the COPS Office.

Legislative Influence

Executive officials, such as mayors, are clearly important parts of the police environment. So are state legislatures and the U.S. Congress. While these bodies do not directly set local law enforcement agencies' budgets, they can exert influence in a number of key respects. Consider President Clinton's **Violent Crime Control and Law Enforcement Act of 1994**. It is the legislation that ushered in what is now known as the Office of Community Oriented Policing Services (the COPS Office) in the U.S. Justice Department. The COPS Office has dispensed billions of dollars in grant money to local law enforcement agencies to improve their community policing capabilities and hire 100,000 new officers. While the Violent Crime Control Act was one of Clinton's pet projects, it would not have succeeded were it not for Congress's decision to send the bill to the White House for that all-important signature.

Moving down from the federal level, nearly every state maintains an office that is responsible for grant funding of city and county law enforcement agencies. In California, the organization is called the Office of Emergency Services. It has no direct effect on local law enforcement, but it does have an indirect effect.

It gives out competitive grants to local agencies provided that they implement a program, or add to an existing program, that is consistent with the funding program's mission. In other words, to get the grant, the agency must do what the state desires. Some grants reflect gubernatorial priorities, others reflect the legislature's desires, and still others reflect a measure of consensus over what is important to both governors and legislatures. One point is clear, however: Governors can do next to nothing in the name of crime control and prevention without the approval of the state legislature. For this reason, local law enforcement agencies need to be in tune with what is regarded as important in the state capital, especially if they want more money.

Judicial Influence

Judicial influence over local law enforcement also cannot be ignored. So influential is the judiciary, in fact, that we devote the better part of Chapters 10 and 11 to it. The U.S. Supreme Court decides important legal issues that trickle down to law enforcement at all levels of government, and state supreme courts often resolve issues that never make it to the U.S. Supreme Court. Lower appellate courts at both the state and federal levels, coupled with state supreme courts and the U.S. Supreme Court, decide criminal appeals that often bear on whether police employed proper procedures. If police officers act without regard to what the courts decide, they will be responsible for the embarrassing release of known criminals. Considering the importance of public opinion, as we have already seen in this chapter, legal mistakes that result in criminals going free are to be avoided at all costs.

Media Portrayals of the Police

Media coverage can be inaccurate and incomplete, but can also be beneficial to police.

Inaccuracies
- Glorify the investigation aspect of policing
- Give the impression that scores of officers are routinely hurt and killed on the job[i]
- Portray an arrest rate that is far in excess of official arrest rates[ii]
- Portray the triumph of justice when, in reality, justice is not always served[iii]
- Give an impression that many criminal apprehensions are resolved with the suspect's death
- Increase people's fear of crimes
- Intensify racist sentiments

Benefits
- Help citizens understand the judicial system
- Provide positive publicity for police
- Can encourage public to provide information to police

Police Portrayals of Police Work

Police can provide information to counter inaccurate or unfavorable media portrayals.

Impression Management
- Presents information in a way that creates a favorable image of police
- Requires **dramaturgical discipline** to present an appropriate balance of facts and favorable publicity for police

The Public Information Officer
- Some police departments have a **public information officer** who provides all police information to the news media.
- A public information officer does not guarantee a good public image for the department.
- Training and encouraging all officers to provide information to the media may be a more effective strategy for improving the media image of a police department.

[i] J. Livingston, "Crime and the media: Myths and reality," *USA Today Magazine* 122 (May 1994): 40–42.
[ii] J. R. Dominick, "Crime and law enforcement on prime-time television," *Public Opinion Quarterly* 37 (1973): 241–50; and Oliver, "Portrayals of crime, race, and aggression in 'reality-based' police shows."
[iii] D. Zillman and J. Wakshlag, "Fear of victimization and the appeal of crime drama," in *Selective exposure to communication*, ed. D. Zillman and J. Bryant, pp. 141–56 (Hillsdale, NJ: Lawrence Erlbaum, 1985).

FIGURE 2.7 The Police and the Media.

The Media

The media, which include both print and television news sources, can be both the best friend and the worst enemy of every police organization. On the one hand, the media can provide favorable coverage of successful investigations, aid in the capture of fugitives, and encourage concerned citizens to call in crime tips.

Unfortunately, the media often get it wrong. This has prompted several large law enforcement agencies to hire media liaisons, some of whom are sworn officers. They assist in the preparation of press releases that present the agency's side of the story and do not give the press an opportunity to misconstrue the facts. On some occasions, though, as we saw in San Francisco, reporters take the initiative to investigate alleged wrongdoing in a police agency. Why? The answer should be pretty clear: Police agencies will not issue press releases that make themselves look incompetent or ineffective.

Media Portrayals of the Police

Most of us are familiar with how the media portray police. News reporters, who adhere to the "if it bleeds, it leads" philosophy, often make it look as though the police do nothing more than apprehend violent criminals. Television shows like *COPS* and *Dallas SWAT*, among others, highlight the most action-packed side of an occupation that is often anything but thrilling. As one researcher put it,

> these programs convey images of crime, criminals, law enforcement officials, and the criminal justice system which are incomplete, distorted, and inaccurate. . . . Viewers are led to believe policing is an action-packed profession, criminals frequently resist capture, crime is predominately violent, crime is the work of minorities, and the police regularly succeed in their endeavors to combat illicit activity.[13]

Additionally, the media have been criticized for increasing people's fear of crime, intensifying racist sentiments, and generally providing people with an incomplete picture of what police work is really like.[14]

Not all press coverage is inadequate. Freedom of the press, for better or for worse, is one of the key principles on which this country was founded. Even reality programs like *COPS* do not always get it wrong. Researchers have observed, for example, that "public display ... plays an important function for citizen understanding of the criminal justice system."[15] Moreover, "police officers received overwhelmingly positive publicity, media networks corral a healthy bottom line, and interested viewers benefit from a few minutes of action and close-to-first-hand observation of police work."[16] Generally, though, there are several limitations associated with media coverage of police work in particular and crime in general.

Freedom of the press is one of the key principles on which this country was founded.

How the media (whether via the evening news or reality police programming) portray law enforcement officials has important implications for how the police do their job. Citizen support is likely affected by media coverage. Even influential politicians can't be immune from the distorted images of police work presented on television and in newspapers. Media coverage of police work can lead to unrealistic expectations and misguided opinions about controversial incidents.

Impression Management

Smart police administrators do not let the media shape their image. Instead, they engage in what is known as **impression management**. As a police chief told the International Conference on Police-Media Relations,

> The future sees law enforcement becoming more and more transparent. We are sharing more and more information. We have to do this. We have to wake up and smell the roses. You have to really build media relations, formulate a plan, and provide other police with information on how to be prepared to deal with the media.[17]

According to one researcher, impression management best serves the public interest by reporting actual facts rather than by putting a "spin" on the information that police agencies release.[18] At the same time, though, the police are most definitely "performers" in the media relations game. They generally strive to maintain a professional image. Thus there is a balance to be achieved between putting too much spin on reporting and simply reporting the essential facts in a given case. This has been called **dramaturgical discipline**. The term *dramaturgy* refers to dramatic composition. In short, the police have to "posture and perform."[19] As one officer notes,

> We can use drama to inform the public and still be accurate. . . . And if . . . cops [don't like] this, they had better go back to a time when TV didn't exist; like it or not, we live in a media/video/showbiz world. We can either understand and work with it or live in a bubble.[20]

The police, like the media, have an interest in the portrayal of a certain form of drama. For example, while the media often report the darkest side of crime, the police routinely publicize their successful apprehensions and investigations. This is dramaturgy. Too much of it, though, is regarded unfavorably by the public—and by the press. The "discipline" side of dramaturgical discipline is about finding the appropriate mix of facts and favorable police publicity.

The Public Information Officer: An Asset?

In one of the most impressive media relations studies to date, Lovell surveyed and spent time at a number of city police departments in an effort to uncover the most successful

A public information officer is the municipal police department's equivalent of the White House's press secretary.

public information officer A police department's spokesperson. The media must go through the public information officer to gather information about the department.

International Association of Chiefs of Police (IACP) Founded in 1893, the best-known association for law enforcement professionals.

National Black Police Association The parent association, founded in 1972, for local and regional associations of African-American police professionals.

International Union of Police Associations (IUPA) An international police association, founded in 1954 and chartered by the AFL-CIO, that represents all rank-and-file officers and functions more as a lobbying group than as a professional association.

International Police Association (IPA) Founded in 1950, the largest police professional association in the world.

practices those agencies engaged in to maintain a favorable public image.[21] He did not survey citizens but rather police chiefs and those in their departments who were charged with reporting to the media. Even so, the study yielded a veritable knowledge gold mine. One important finding is that crime has little bearing on media image, that is, police departments whose jurisdictions include the most crime-prone cities are not regarded unfavorably by the press simply because crime rates are high.

Lovell also sought to determine whether having a dedicated **public information officer** was preferable over other approaches. A public information officer is the municipal police department's equivalent of the White House's press secretary. He or she is the key point of contact through which the media must go to gather information. The public information officer also crafts press releases, holds news conferences, and otherwise serves as a department liaison to the press. Relatively few agencies have public information officers, however, relying instead on either departmental policies on how officers are supposed to interact with the media or training on how to handle media inquiries. Interestingly, Lovell found that departments with comprehensive media policies or public information officers were *not* more likely to report a favorable media image than departments that allowed the press to speak with officers at all levels of the agency:

It is not so much the presence of a media police [or a public information] officer but the content of the strategy within that contributes to effective impression management. One such strategy that emerged as significantly and positively associated with a favorable police image is best summarized as department "openness." Those departments that both authorized

and encouraged its officers to communicate with news reporters were more likely to assess the quality of their department's image as favorable.[22]

Lovell also found that although media training (that is, teaching officers how to interact with the media) had a positive effect on a department's image, the effect was modest. Above all else, Lovell found that police administrators need to adopt a "media strategy" rather than a "media policy." In other words, one more entry in the typical police policy manual is not enough. Policy manuals tend to spell out what police officers *cannot* do. Lovell feels that while media policies are essential, such policies should also encourage officers to engage in proactive communications with the media when appropriate to seek out the press if the circumstances merit it.

Other Law Enforcement Agencies

Every law enforcement agency—and in fact every organization or group—communicates with others like it and with the entities that represent its employees. The chief, for example, might pick up the phone and call his or her counterpart in the next city over. Agencies also communicate with one another across radio frequencies. These varieties of communication are staples in modern law enforcement. Another key means by which police agencies communicate with one another and learn what their colleagues are up to is through participation in professional associations.

Professional Associations

Every profession has at least one association for its members. Academics join associations that are unique to their fields and participate in those associations' annual meetings. Medical doctors join huge professional groups like the American Medical Association. Lawyers, whether prosecutors, defense attorneys, or others, have their respective associations. School teachers join associations. Even occupations that are not necessarily regarded as professions have their own associations. Law enforcement personnel are no different. There are far too many police associations to list and describe here, but four are quite prominent and well known.

The **International Association of Chiefs of Police (IACP)** is the best-known law enforcement association. The organization's title suggests that membership is limited to police chiefs, but the IACP uses the term *chief* somewhat loosely. Officers with executive authority are allowed to join as so-called active members. Associate memberships are available to anyone with sufficient background in law enforcement practice or study, including academics and trainers. The association also extends honorary and distinguished

20k The IACP boasts a membership of more than 20,000 people in 89 countries across the globe.

service memberships to other people, including a number of non–law enforcement personnel. All told, the IACP boasts a membership of more than 20,000 people in 89 countries across the globe.

IACP was founded in 1893. Its constitution describes the association's mission as follows:

> As a leadership organization the Mission of the International Association of Chiefs of Police is to advance professional police services; promote enhanced administrative, technical, and operational police practices; foster cooperation and the exchange of information and experience among police leaders and police organizations of recognized professional and technical standing throughout the world; champion the recruitment and training of qualified persons in the police profession; and, encourage all police personnel worldwide to achieve and maintain the highest standards of ethics, integrity, community interaction, and professional conduct.[23]

IACP facilitates interagency communication through several means. One is an annual meeting that convenes in a different city each year. At the meeting, there are panels, presentations, and training sessions. The meetings, which are generally organized around two subjects—law enforcement technology and education—provide members ample opportunity to network with one another in both formal and informal settings. IACP also conducts various training programs throughout the year. The association's Research Center conducts a wide variety of police-related studies and disseminates the results, usually by posting them online. IACP also publishes *The Police Chief*, a print and online magazine that is widely read by law enforcement administrators throughout the United States. All in all, IACP provides a valuable interagency communication function for police administrators.

Though far from being as large as the IACP, the **National Black Police Association** was formed in 1972 as a parent association for local and regional black police associations.[24] According to the association, it "is a nationwide organization of African American Police Associations dedicated to the promotion of justice, fairness, and effectiveness in law enforcement." Basically, the National Black Police Association has succeeded in creating a network of minority police officers throughout the United States. Though the association's title suggests otherwise, membership is not restricted to African-American police officers, although they do make up the bulk of the membership. Unlike IACP, the National Black Police Association does not hold an annual meeting for all members, but its regional affiliates hold their own meetings. There are five such regions.

The **International Union of Police Associations (IUPA)** represents rank-and-file police officers and their unions from across the country. The IUPA describes itself as follows:

> The International Union of Police Associations is the only AFL-CIO union chartered exclusively for law enforcement and law enforcement support personnel. The AFL-CIO affiliation places I.U.P.A. in a position of

strength within the labor movement. While I.U.P.A.'s officers, active and retired law enforcement officers, fight to improve the lives of their brothers and sisters in law enforcement, I.U.P.A. works to improve legislation that protects and affects public safety officers, as well as representing the needs of law enforcement officers and support personnel, whether that be for better equipment, more staff or a fair wage.[25]

GLOSSARY

booking The process of fingerprinting, processing, and photographing a suspect, after which he or she is typically placed in a holding cell. The suspect may also be required to submit to testing (such as for alcohol) or be required to participate in a lineup.

The IUPA is more a lobbying organization than a professional association. It holds meetings but not on par with, for example, IACP. One of the marks of a lobbying organization is the use of us-versus-them language in its correspondence. For example, the National Rifle Association regularly battles those who would threaten Second Amendment rights, and the American Civil Liberties Union (ACLU) challenges people who threaten civil liberties. The IUPA, not surprisingly, tends to not speak highly of police administrators, who are regarded as the "bad guys" in nearly every union contract negotiation.

In addition to its lobbying efforts, the IUPA facilitates communication among police officers and among the unions that represent them. Some agencies have their own unions, and police officers in other agencies join regional and state unions. The IUPA is the body that represents *all* their interests in the nation's capital.

The largest police association in the world is the **International Police Association (IPA)**, though it is less known to most Americans than the IACP. The IPA boasts a membership of almost 376,000 people with national sections in 62 countries around the globe. The IPA's core functions are, in its words, to promote "global and cultural friendship among peace officers."[26] Beyond that, the IPA describes its other concerns:

> It is committed to the principles set out in the *Universal Declaration of Human Rights* as adopted by the United Nations in 1948 and recognizes that any form of torture is absolutely inconsistent with these principles. Its aims include the development of cultural relations amongst its members, a broadening of their general knowledge and an exchange of professional experience. In addition, it seeks to foster mutual help in the social sphere and to contribute, within the limits of its possibilities, to the peaceful co-existence of different peoples and to the preservation of world peace.[27]

The IPA's national sections (those consisting of one country's members) hold annual meetings. The main annual meeting, known as the *IPA World Congress*, provides an opportunity for law enforcement professionals from around the world to meet one another, share information, and learn of operational "best practices" that have proved successful in other agencies. The IPA's role is especially important in the wake of September 11. International cooperation is the word of the day, and the IPA serves to promote such cooperation.

▶ Police as a Piece of the Criminal Justice Puzzle

Police work does not stop with an arrest. Police officers have duties to perform throughout the criminal justice process, even well after trial. Also, police officers do not work in a criminal justice vacuum. Their relationships with prosecutors and corrections officials are important, now more than ever.

Police officers are involved in many different stages of the criminal justice process.

The Criminal Justice Process

Police officers are involved in many different stages of the criminal justice process. They are often called upon, for instance, to testify at trial. Figure 2.8 provides an overview of the criminal justice process and identifies stages where police officers may be called on to act or assist.

Police in the Pretrial Phase

Once a suspect has been arrested, he or she is searched. This is done for the protection of the officer as well as to discover any contraband in the suspect's possession. The suspect is then transported to the police station and booked. **Booking** is the process of fingerprinting, processing, and photographing the suspect, after which he or she is typically placed in a holding cell. The suspect may also be required to submit to a Breathalyzer or other test or be required to participate in a lineup.

After booking, the police present their case to the prosecutor (usually by filing a report of some sort or by contacting the prosecutor). If the prosecutor believes the evidence is persuasive enough, he or she will bring charges against the suspect, subject to certain restrictions specified in the Constitution and clarified by the Supreme Court. Once charges are brought, the suspect is then referred to as a *defendant*. If the charges are minor, the police may release the defendant rather than detaining him or her, in which case the defendant will be required to appear at court at some later date.

Through their investigations, police effectively "build" criminal cases for prosecutors. Without this assistance, prosecutors would be going into trial blind. When the process breaks down, particularly when the police forward weak cases to the prosecutor, a conviction is difficult to secure.

Some jurisdictions rely on a grand jury rather than allowing prosecutors to determine whether charges are appropriate. When a grand jury is used, it often works closely with the prosecutor, who presents the information that the grand jury needs to make its decision. Police officers often testify before grand juries in order to help make the case against a possible criminal defendant. The police role in grand jury investigations can be an important one because the suspects who are being investigated—and possibly indicted—do not enjoy the right to be present at the hearing or to offer evidence in their own defense.

Police at Trial

Once the pretrial process has concluded and the charges stand, a trial may or may not take place. If the defendant pleads guilty, then a trial is not necessary. However, if the defendant pleads *not guilty*, the case is set for trial. At trial, the prosecutor bears the burden of proving that the defendant is guilty beyond a reasonable doubt. This often entails calling on one or more investigative or arresting police officers to provide testimony. Police officers need to be prepared to be put under oath and provide testimony, usually for the prosecution, depending on the nature of the charges.

Police after Trial

Generally, police officers have little to no role during the sentencing hearing or appellate phase. They do, however, continue to work the same streets to which convicted criminals are eventually released. Clearly, many police officers thrive on putting away bad guys, but there is little excitement in arresting the same person over and over. It is therefore advantageous for police officers to work with officials whose responsibility involves the supervision of convicted criminals. Not only does such cooperation promote successful reintegration of offenders into society, but it can also assist the law enforcement function. Police officers who team with probation officers, for instance, can creatively circumvent the Fourth Amendment and search probationers with relative ease. Collaborative methods like this are taken up in the next two sections.

FIGURE 2.8 The Police in the Criminal Justice System.

Police-Corrections Partnerships A possible "dark side" to police-corrections partnerships is known as *mission distortion*. Mission distortion refers to situations where the definition of one's professional mission becomes blurred. For instance, actively working with the police makes it convenient for some community corrections officers to gravitate toward a greater emphasis on law enforcement priorities at the expense of their responsibilities to provide services to their clients. Moreover, police-probation partnerships threaten to increase the likelihood of community corrections officers serving as stalking horses for police officers. Should police officers team up with probation officers to conduct enhanced supervision of probationers? Can police-corrections partnerships lead to mission distortion?

Source: Copyright © A. Ramey/ Photo Edit

Relationships with Prosecutors

Police officers work closely with prosecutors (Figure 2.9). They may have almost no direct contact with prosecutors, save, perhaps, for testifying against a defendant in a criminal trial, but prosecutors depend on police officers to bring them cases. Were it not for police officers, few prosecutors would be employed. It is generally not their responsibility to go find suspected criminals and press charges. The police take the first step. Likewise, the police depend on prosecutors. Prosecutors present the government's case against criminal defendants. When they fail in this regard, criminals are released back into society and become police officers' problem all over again. It is in the interest of both officials to work together, whether one-on-one or otherwise.

Throughout most of this country's recent history, prosecutors have been reactive, that is, they have waited until police officers brought them cases to prosecute. To a large extent, this model persists today; many prosecutors thrive on taking serious offenders to court and sending them to prison for long periods of time. These prosecutors rely on the police for the preparation of key aspects of the cases, such as documenting a confession. This traditional prosecutorial role has been described as follows:

> The traditional . . . prosecutor likes to think of himself as the consummate carnivore: a learned lawyer, a compelling oral advocate, a relentless pursuer of the truth who fights crime by putting "bad guys" in jail. His allies in this fight are the . . . investigative agencies. Those agencies identify trends in criminal behavior and "bring" the prosecutor the significant cases.[28]

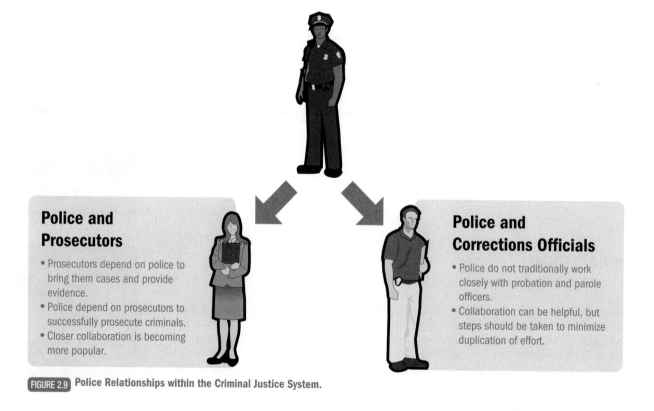

Police and Prosecutors

- Prosecutors depend on police to bring them cases and provide evidence.
- Police depend on prosecutors to successfully prosecute criminals.
- Closer collaboration is becoming more popular.

Police and Corrections Officials

- Police do not traditionally work closely with probation and parole officers.
- Collaboration can be helpful, but steps should be taken to minimize duplication of effort.

FIGURE 2.9 **Police Relationships within the Criminal Justice System.**

Some police departments are actively involving themselves in the reentry process.

It would be inaccurate to say that prosecutors are totally dependent on police officers for the preparation of their cases. Many prosecutors' offices have commissioned peace officers who serve as investigators. California is one state that follows this model. There is also much to be said about knowing the law and crafting an argument. Prosecutors cannot rely on police officers in this regard. Being lawyers, they know the law better than the typical police officer. A skilled prosecutor will take the evidence that the police present and use it creatively to mount an argument before a judge or jury.

The traditional prosecutors, then, act more or less reactively. They are not concerned with preventing crime, reaching out to other agencies, and collaborating with their law enforcement colleagues. Recently, though, prosecution has changed. Collaboration, especially with police, is gaining momentum. Prosecutors are becoming more receptive to partnering and collaboration with various entities inside and outside the criminal justice system. Police-prosecution partnerships are also becoming quite popular.

Relationships with Corrections Officials

It is perhaps easier to conceive of close working relationships between police and prosecutors than between police and corrections officials. This may be because, in terms of the criminal justice process, police and prosecutors work more closely together in time than police and corrections officials. In other words, a case moves directly from the police department to the prosecutor's office, but not from the police to, say, a parole officer. With few exceptions, corrections officials usually enter the picture after the criminal trial and sentencing stages.

When we talk about "corrections officials" in this chapter, we are not referring to jail or prison officers. Rather, our concern is with relationships between police officers and both probation officers and parole officers. Police officers have learned that such relationships can be quite helpful.

Parole officers do much of the same work as police; for efficiency's sake alone, it just makes sense to collaborate. While parole officers supervise individuals who were recently released from prison, they cannot supervise their clients perfectly, partly because of the high caseloads some parole officers oversee. Consequently, police officers often encounter parolees. When parole officers and police officers work together, however, duplication of effort should be minimized. Also, some police departments are actively involving themselves in the reentry process, especially in the days right after the parolee is released from prison.

The Fajitagate Scandal

Three off-duty San Francisco police officers became involved in a violent altercation with two men who turned out to be doing nothing more than carrying bags of fajitas. The three officers, one of whom was the son of the assistant chief and had reported using force 14 times in his first 13 months on the job, were indicted for felonies in a case that quickly captured news headlines. The case led to the resignation of two police chiefs and a short-lived grand jury indictment against other top officials for alleged obstruction of justice. The altercation and the ensuing events were quickly branded "Fajitagate," and the incident tarnished the San Francisco Police Department's image for years. The charged officers were eventually acquitted, but the incident left a sour taste in the mouths of many, including numerous local reporters.

An article in the *San Francisco Chronicle* claimed that the city's police department "failed to control officers who repeatedly resort to force, hitting, choking, clubbing and pepper-spraying citizens at rates far higher than fellow officers who patrol the same streets."[29] Staff writers at the *Chronicle* submitted a Freedom of Information Act request and obtained the department's complete use-of-force logs from 1996 to 2004. From the handwritten documents, they created a computerized database that allowed them to determine which officers reported using force and how often. According to the reporters' investigation, the "data showed the city has a core group of violence-prone officers—fewer than 100 in a force of 2,200."[30] They also made these observations:

1. Officers with questionable records were promoted to supervisory positions or were assigned to train rookies, putting them in position to carry forward a culture that tolerates and rewards the use of force.

2. Between 2001 and 2004, San Francisco officers were the subject of more allegations of improper use of force than officers in San Jose, Oakland, San Diego, and Seattle combined.

3. Taxpayers are exposed to high legal costs in defending lawsuits against officers who use force. From 1996 to 2005, the city paid more than $5 million in judgments and legal settlements related to the improper use of force. For that same amount of money it could have put 60 new officers on the street.

4. Public trust in the department has eroded, particularly among the city's African-American residents, who department records show have disproportionately experienced the use of force by police.[31]

Most of us don't have to worry about having our dirty laundry aired before scores of concerned citizens, but the police do.

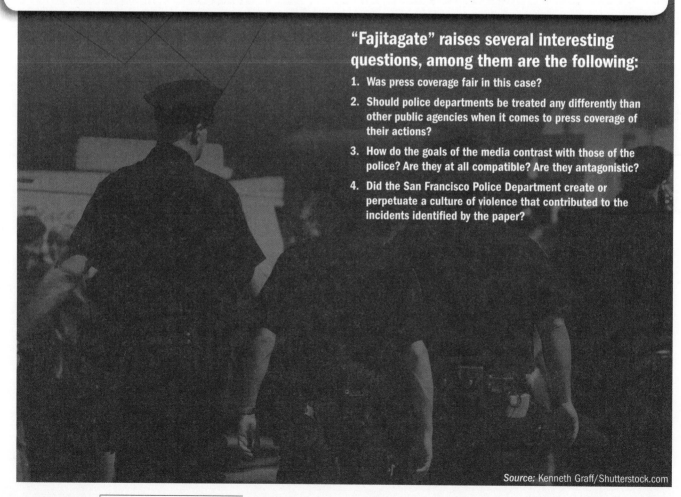

"Fajitagate" raises several interesting questions, among them are the following:

1. Was press coverage fair in this case?

2. Should police departments be treated any differently than other public agencies when it comes to press coverage of their actions?

3. How do the goals of the media contrast with those of the police? Are they at all compatible? Are they antagonistic?

4. Did the San Francisco Police Department create or perpetuate a culture of violence that contributed to the incidents identified by the paper?

LEARNING OUTCOMES 1

Explain how the U.S. government's features of democracy and federalism impact policing.

Democracy and federalism have contributed to the unique nature of policing in America. Democracy is the institutionalization of freedom. Among democracy's implications for policing is the need to balance due process against crime control. Federalism divides government power and decision-making capabilities between levels of government, and this has led to the creation of federal, state, and local law enforcement agencies in the United States.

1. What are the distinguishing features of policing in a democracy?

2. How has our system of federalism affected policing in the United States?

democracy A form of government that vests supreme authority in the people, usually through their freely elected representatives.

federalism A political doctrine holding that power is divided (often constitutionally) between a central governing body (the federal government, for example) and various constituent units (the states).

dual federalism An interpretation of the U.S. Constitution that suggests a system in which the only powers vested in the federal government are those explicitly listed in the document, with the remaining powers being left to the states.

LEARNING OUTCOMES 2

Identify various elements of the policing environment in America and explain their influence on the practice of policing.

The environment of policing includes citizens, government officials, the media, and other law enforcement agencies. Citizen support for police is affected by factors like race, age, sex, and prior contact. Government influence over policing occurs through executive, legislative, and judicial channels. The media can both help and hurt law enforcement agencies, but skilled police administrators engage in impression management to ensure a favorable public image. Two methods of promoting interagency communication are participating in professional associations and keeping abreast of research.

1. What is the policing environment?

2. Which aspect of the policing environment do you believe is most important?

council-manager form The most common form of city government in cities of more than 12,000 people. It consists of an elected city council (usually between five and twelve people) responsible for all policy decisions for the city. Mayors under this form of municipal government generally perform ceremonial duties and serve as the voice, and often the leader, of the city council.

mayor-council form A form of municipal government that can be categorized in two ways. The strong-mayor variation gives the mayor almost limitless authority over city operations, including the hiring and dismissal of key officials. In the

weak-mayor variation, which is more common in small towns, the mayor serves largely at the behest of the city council.

police commission An agency maintained in some large cities that acts like a corporate board of directors, setting policy and overseeing the police department's operations.

Violent Crime Control and Law Enforcement Act of 1994 The U.S. legislation that established the Office of Community Oriented Policing Services (the COPS Office) in the U.S. Justice Department.

impression management A media relations concept that involves controlling the presentation of information to achieve a desired public perception.

dramaturgical discipline Achieving a balance between merely reporting facts and putting a "spin" on those facts to create a desired impression.

public information officer A police department's spokesperson. The media must go through the public information officer to gather information about the department.

International Association of Chiefs of Police (IACP) Founded in 1893, the best-known association for law enforcement professionals.

National Black Police Association The parent association, founded in 1972, for local and regional associations of African-American police professionals.

International Union of Police Associations (IUPA) An international police association, founded in 1954 and chartered by the AFL-CIO, that represents all rank-and-file officers and functions more as a lobbying group than as a professional association.

International Police Association (IPA) Founded in 1950, the largest police professional association in the world.

Summarize the police role in the criminal justice process.

The police are central participants in the overall criminal justice system. They participate in the criminal justice process during the pretrial, trial, and post-trial stages, and they interact regularly with prosecutors and corrections officials.

1. What is the role of the police in the criminal justice system during trial?

2. What role do the police play in the corrections process?

booking The process of fingerprinting, processing, and photographing a suspect, after which he or she is typically placed in a holding cell. The suspect may also be required to submit to testing (such as for alcohol) or be required to participate in a lineup.

MyCJLab

Go to the Chapter 2 section in *MyCJLab* to test your understanding of this chapter, access customized study content, engage in interactive simulations, complete critical thinking and research assignments, and view related online videos.

Additional Links

This article reviews differences in perception levels about police among various demographic groups within the American population. This Department of Justice report is provided in PDF format for student viewing: **www.justicestudies.com/pubs/publicopinions.pdf**.

This National Institute of Justice article investigates the influences that cause people to favor police: **www.justicestudies.com/pubs/satisfaction.pdf**. Specifically, the authors look at how people's perceptions about the quality of their own lives affects levels of support for police.

This is a link to a first-person account of a media expert participating in an internship with police: **http://tinyurl.com/35elvy**. This first-hand account provides students with a narrative perspective on the relationship between police and the media.

This website provides an index of professional associations of law enforcement: **http://mycrimekit.pearsoncmg.com/category/professional-associations/**. Students can peruse the index and select from more than 50 websites.

An overview of public opinion as it relates to policing can be found here: **www.justicestudies.com/pubs/publicopinions.pdf**.

Information on satisfaction with the police is available at **www.justicestudies.com/pubs/satisfaction.pdf**.

The International Association of Chiefs of Police provides insight into the public image of the police on its website: **http://tinyurl.com/63ttyhh**.

An overview of police and the media can be found at **http://tinyurl.com/35elvy**.

Law Enforcement Agencies and Their Organization

"Law enforcement agencies exist at all levels of government, but the vast majority of them operate at the local level."

1 Describe the organization and roles of federal and state law enforcement agencies.

2 Summarize the differences between police departments and other types of organizations, and describe both traditional and contemporary approaches to organization.

3 Summarize the trends and issues associated with private policing.

3

INTRO THE ORGANIZED CRIME PROBLEM PERSISTS

Early on the morning of January 20, 2011, some 500 FBI agents and about 200 partner law enforcement officers from the New York Police Department and the Department of Labor Office of Inspector General began arresting nearly 130 members of organized crime in New York City and other East Coast cities.[1] The operation was the largest nationally coordinated organized crime takedown in FBI history.

Members of New York's infamous five Mafia families—the Bonanno, Colombo, Gambino, Genovese, and Luchese crime organizations—were rounded up along with members of the New Jersey–based DeCavalcante family and New England Mafia to face charges including murder, drug trafficking, arson, loan sharking, illegal gambling, witness tampering, labor racketeering, and extortion.

More than 30 of the subjects indicted were "made" members of La Cosa Nostra (LCN), including several high-ranking family members. The arrests,

predominantly in New York, were expected to seriously disrupt operations of the crime families.

"The notion that today's mob families are more genteel and less violent than in the past is put to lie by the charges contained in the indictments unsealed today," said Janice Fedarcyk, assistant director in charge of the FBI's New York Field Office. "Even more of a myth is the notion that the mob is a thing of the past; that La Cosa Nostra is a shadow of its former self." Among those arrested were Luigi Manocchio, 83, the former boss of the New England LCN; Andrew Russo, 76, street boss of the Colombo family; Benjamin Castellazzo, 73, acting underboss of the Colombo family; Richard Fusco, 74, consigliere of the Colombo family; Joseph Corozzo, 69, consigliere of the Gambino family; and Bartolomeo Vernace, 61, an important member of the Gambino family. The joint operation showcased cooperation between federal and state law enforcement agencies.

> **DISCUSS** Why is cooperation among law enforcement organizations at various levels important? How can it be achieved?

▶ Agencies of Law Enforcement

The federal government has a number of its own enforcement agencies, as does each state government. Additionally, county- and municipal-level agencies can be all across the country, including specialized agencies that don't necessarily fit neatly into any government category.

How Many Are There?

Counting the number of law enforcement agencies in America is not unlike counting the number of citizens. The decennial census of people living in the United States always falls short on some level because the number of residents does not remain constant. Some people die; others are born. Not surprisingly, police agencies follow similar patterns. New agencies are created when newly incorporated cities need their own police force. Merging municipalities and shrinking towns can lead to the combination or elimination of police departments. This makes counting cops a difficult task at best.

Some researchers have identified as few as 15,000 agencies, others as many as 40,000. What's the actual number? One of the more rigorous studies in this area relied on various sources of data and came up with a very defensible estimate of a little more than 20,000 federal, state, and local agencies.[2] The study's authors also estimated that these agencies employ some 680,000 sworn personnel.[3] That translates into roughly one sworn law enforcement officer for every 457 people.[4]

Federal Agencies

There are many federal law enforcement agencies, especially if we define them as any agency charged with the enforcement of federal laws. Most arms of the federal government have at least some enforcement component. The Internal Revenue Service, for

> **DISCUSS** Why are there so many different police agencies in the United States? Would it be better for our country to have only one centralized law enforcement agency with nationwide arrest powers than to have so many different local, state, and federal agencies?

example, has its own criminal enforcement division. Likewise, the U.S. Fish and Wildlife Service's Office of Law Enforcement ensures that relevant statutes are upheld. Even the various branches of the military have their own law enforcement arms. A comprehensive list of federal law enforcement agencies is provided in Figure 3.1. These enforcement agencies don't exactly come to mind, however, when we think about federal law enforcement. Instead, it is the familiar agencies like the FBI and the Drug Enforcement Administration that come to mind. A focus on these well-known agencies shortens the list considerably.

Before the September 11, 2001, attacks on the United States, it was somewhat difficult to succinctly describe the organization of federal law enforcement. Agencies were housed in a number of different cabinet-level departments, including Justice, Treasury, Agriculture, Energy, and Health and Human Services. After September 11, America witnessed one of the most significant efforts to restructure the federal government in generations.

The **Homeland Security Act of 2002** created what is now known as the Department

LEARNING OUTCOMES 1 Describe the organization and roles of federal and state law enforcement agencies.

GLOSSARY

Homeland Security Act of 2002 U.S. legislation enacted after the terrorist attacks of September 11, 2001, that created the cabinet-level Department of Homeland Security.

Department of Agriculture	Bureau of Prisons
U.S. Forest Service	Drug Enforcement Administration
	Federal Bureau of Investigation
Department of Commerce	U.S. Marshals Service
Bureau of Export Enforcement	
National Marine Fisheries Administration	**Department of Labor**
	Office of Labor Racketeering
Department of Defense	
Air Force Office of Special Investigations	**Department of State**
Army Criminal Investigation Division	Diplomatic Security Service
Defense Criminal Investigative Service	
Naval Investigative Service	**Department of Transportation**
	Federal Air Marshals Program
Department of Energy	
National Nuclear Safety Administration	**Department of the Treasury**
Office of Mission Operations	Internal Revenue Service–Criminal Investigation Division
Office of Secure Transportation	Treasury Inspector General for Tax Enforcement
Department of Health and Human Services	
Food and Drug Administration, Office of Criminal Investigations	**Department of Veterans Affairs**
	Office of Security and Law Enforcement
Department of Homeland Security	
Federal Law Enforcement Training Center	**U.S. Postal Service**
Federal Protective Service	Postal Inspection Service
Transportation Security Administration	**Other Offices with Enforcement Personnel**
U.S. Coast Guard	Administrative Office of the U.S. Courts
U.S. Customs and Border Protection (CBP)— includes U.S. Border Patrol	AMTRAK Police
U.S. Immigration and Customs Enforcement (ICE)	Bureau of Engraving and Printing Police
U.S. Secret Service	Environmental Protection Agency–Criminal Investigations Division
	Federal Reserve Board
Department of the Interior	Tennessee Valley Authority
Bureau of Indian Affairs	U.S. Capitol Police
Bureau of Land Management	U.S. Mint
Fish and Wildlife Service	U.S. Supreme Court Police
National Park Service	Washington, DC, Metropolitan Police Department
U.S. Park Police	
Department of Justice	
Bureau of Alcohol, Tobacco, Firearms and Explosives	

FIGURE 3.1 **Federal Law Enforcement Agencies.**
Source: © istockpoto.com/Dariusz Markowski

of Homeland Security (DHS), a cabinet-level department. Homeland Security now houses a number of law enforcement agencies that, prior to September 11, used to be found scattered throughout the federal government. The names of some of these agencies also changed. It has been a few years now since these changes were ushered in, but people are still sometimes confused about the names and parent agencies of various federal law enforcement agencies. To make sense out of the new organization, we will build our discussion of these agencies around two categories. We will begin with the

The Department of Homeland Security (DHS) houses many law enforcement agencies that, prior to September 11, 2001, used to be found scattered throughout the federal government.

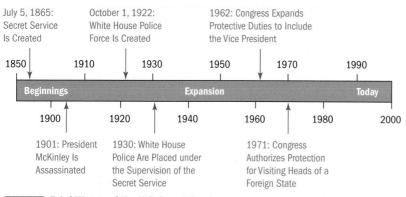

July 5, 1865: Secret Service Is Created

October 1, 1922: White House Police Force Is Created

1962: Congress Expands Protective Duties to Include the Vice President

Beginnings | Expansion | Today

1901: President McKinley Is Assassinated

1930: White House Police Are Placed under the Supervision of the Secret Service

1971: Congress Authorizes Protection for Visiting Heads of a Foreign State

FIGURE 3.2 Brief History of the U.S. Secret Service.
Source: U.S. Secret Service, "Secret Service History," www.secretservice.gov/history.shtml (accessed December 5, 2010).
p77/p77/ZUMA Press/Newscom

law enforcement agencies found within Homeland Security and then discuss those found within the U.S. Department of Justice (DOJ).

Homeland Security Agencies

The Department of Homeland Security now houses the U.S. Secret Service. The Secret Service used to be located within the Department of the Treasury. The move to DHS became effective on March 1, 2003. DHS also houses what used to be called the U.S. Customs Service. It is now called Customs and Border Protection (CBP). Finally, what used to be called the Immigration and Naturalization Service (INS) has basically been split into two separate entities, Immigration and Customs Enforcement (ICE) and Citizenship and Immigration Services (CIS). The first of these is of special interest to us here.

The Secret Service. The Secret Service is perhaps best known for its role in protecting the president and other government officials and their families. Tourists to the White House also see the Secret Service's uniformed officers protecting the president's residence. These individuals are members of the Secret Service's Uniformed Division. The agency was first created, though, to suppress counterfeit currency (Figure 3.2). From its beginnings in 1865, that has been one of the agency's primary functions. That is why, prior to

money laundering The process by which criminals or criminal organizations seek to disguise the illicit nature of their proceeds by introducing them into the stream of legitimate commerce and finance.

Customs and Border Protection (CBP) The U.S. law enforcement agency, established after the terrorist attacks on September 11, 2001, that combined the entire U.S. Border Patrol with portions of the U.S. Customs Service, U.S. Immigration, and the Animal and Plant Health Inspection Service. CBP was given the mission of controlling and protecting America's borders and ports of entry, including international airports and international shipping ports.

Immigration and Customs Enforcement (ICE) The largest investigative component of the federal Department of Homeland Security. ICE focuses specifically on illegal immigration.

Federal Bureau of Investigation (FBI) The investigative arm of the U.S. Department of Justice.

September 11, the Secret Service was housed in the Treasury Department. The Counterfeit Division, however, is only one of several nonprotection divisions within the Secret Service.

For example, the Financial Crimes Division also investigates organized crime and **money laundering**. The Secret Service's Forensic Services Division assists with these and counterfeit currency investigations. As of this writing, the Secret Service employs several thousand agents in more than 125 offices worldwide.

Customs and Border Protection. The establishment of U.S. **Customs and Border Protection (CBP)** after September 11 combined several elements of various federal agencies that had previously been separate. The entire U.S. Border Patrol was combined with portions of the U.S. Customs Service, U.S. Immigration, and the Animal and Plant Health Inspection Service. Today, the agency consists of more than 41,000 employees whose mission is, simply, to control and protect America's borders and ports of entry, including international airports and international shipping ports. Because CBP is part of the Department of Homeland Security, one of its foremost concerns is combating terrorism. The agency claims dual goals, however: fighting terrorism and "facilitating legitimate trade and travel."[5]

The most well-known component of CBP is the Border Patrol. The agents that make up this division number more than 20,000. Border Patrol agents, combined with every other official in CBP, make it one of the largest uniformed law enforcement agencies in the United States.[6]

Immigration and Customs Enforcement. Closely connected to but independent of CBP is **Immigration and Customs Enforcement (ICE)**. Whereas CBP is more concerned with border protection and customs checks, ICE focuses on investigation and is particularly concerned with illegal immigration. Indeed, it is the largest investigative component of the Department of Homeland Security. There are four main branches of ICE:

- The Office of Investigations
- The Office of Detention and Removal Operations
- The Federal Protective Service
- The Office of Intelligence

Of these, the second and third are of the most interest to us. The Office of Detention and Removal Operations enforces immigration laws by ensuring the departure from the United States of "removable aliens." The Federal Protective Service (FPS) is responsible for securing more than 8,800 federal facilities worldwide. There are nearly 2,000 FPS officers and more than 20,000 people in ICE altogether.[7]

Justice Department Agencies

With the exception of the Secret Service, the Department of Homeland Security agencies previously discussed are relatively new and unfamiliar. More accurately stated, their names are new and unfamiliar. The agents and staff who do the work have

RESPONSIBILITIES OF KEY FEDERAL LAW ENFORCEMENT AGENCIES

Department of Homeland Security		Justice Department	
The Secret Service	• Provide protection for the president and other government officials and their families • Enforce the suppression of counterfeit currency • Investigate organized crime and money laundering schemes	FBI	• Since 9/11, the FBI continues to be heavily involved in investigating terrorism; however, its primary function is enforcing federal laws
U.S. Customs and Border Protection	• Primarily responsible for controlling and protecting America's borders and ports of entry, including international airports and international shipping ports • Foremost concern is to combat terrorism	U.S. Marshals Service	• The agency's main responsibilities are judicial security and fugitive investigation
Immigration and Customs Enforcement	• Concerned primarily with illegal immigration	Bureau of Alcohol, Tobacco, Etc.	• A tax-collection, enforcement, and regulatory arm of the U.S. Department of Justice • Screens the applications and issues firearms licenses and targets illegal firearms trafficking
		Drug Enforcement Administration	• Primarily responsible for enforcing controlled substance laws and regulations

been around for some time—in one position or another. Some of the Justice Department agencies discussed in this section are, in contrast, quite familiar. Even people with no criminal justice education will recognize agencies like the Federal Bureau of Investigation or the U.S. Marshals Service (USMS). Because there is much misinformation about these agencies, we will cover them in some detail. We will also discuss the Bureau of Alcohol, Tobacco, Firearms and Explosives (ATF) and the Drug Enforcement Administration (DEA).

It should be clear why the Homeland Security agencies we have just discussed are housed where they are: Each has a unique opportunity to target terrorists and otherwise break up terrorist plots. Why are the FBI, DEA, ATF, and USMS in the Justice Department? This placement owes much to the 1870 Act to Establish the Justice Department.[8] As a result of this legislation, the Justice Department was tasked with handling the legal business (especially via prosecutions of criminal activity) of the United States and was given full control over all federal law enforcement. Of course, things have changed since 1870, and there are now law enforcement agencies, bureaus, and officials throughout the federal government. Through thick and thin, the agencies we are about to discuss have remained in the Justice Department for decades, and they will likely remain there for the foreseeable future.

Federal Bureau of Investigation. The **Federal Bureau of Investigation (FBI)** remains in the U.S. Department of Justice, but its mission has changed to some extent as a result of September 11. Its mission is now to "protect and defend the United States against terrorist and foreign intelligence threats, to uphold and enforce the criminal laws of the United States, and to

provide leadership and criminal justice services to federal, state, municipal, and international agencies and partners."[9] To be sure, the FBI had a role in terrorism investigation before September 11, but that was not one of the agency's foremost concerns. The September 11 attacks moved terrorism to the front of the line. Indeed, the FBI's "Most Wanted" list now includes known terrorists like Ayman Al-Zawahiri, bin Laden's successor.

Although the FBI is now heavily involved in investigating terrorism, its primary function is enforcing federal laws. It is to the federal government what state police agencies are to states, sheriff's departments are to counties, and municipal police agencies are to cities. It is, in short, the investigative arm of the U.S. Department of Justice. Its statutory authority can be found in Title 28, Section 533, of the U.S. Code. A number of other statutes, including the Congressional Assassination, Kidnapping, and Assault Act (Title 18, Section 351, U.S. Code), also name the FBI as the agency charged with enforcement. Moreover, the FBI has jurisdiction to enforce more than 200 categories of federal law that proscribe all sorts of criminal activity.

As of 2010, the FBI employed more than 33,000 people, including about 13,500 special agents and 18,000 support staff.[10] The agency's budget for fiscal year 2003 was approximately

Although the FBI is now heavily involved in investigating terrorism, its primary function is enforcing federal laws.

1910	1920	1920-1960
Francisco Madero revolts (on U.S. soil) against Mexican President Porfirio Diaz. U.S. Marshals protect the U.S.-Mexico border against Diaz's supporters, who were attempting to harm Madero.	Eighteenth Amendment ratified, making the manufacture, sale, and transportation of intoxicating beverages illegal. U.S. Marshals were the key enforcement agents.	U.S. Marshals started to perform bailiff functions in U.S. courts.

$8 billion. FBI officials can be found all around the globe. The headquarters is in Washington, DC, housed in the J. Edgar Hoover Building on Pennsylvania Avenue. But there are 56 field offices located in major cities, more than 400 resident agencies in smaller cities, and more than 60 international offices. The international offices are called *legal attachés* and are housed in U.S. embassies worldwide. The chain of command and various components of the FBI can be seen in the agency's organizational chart (Figure 3.3).

U.S. Marshals Service. The **U.S. Marshals Service (USMS)** is America's oldest law enforcement agency. Marshals were key law enforcement officials in the Old West, but at the turn of the twentieth century, their responsibilities started to shift.

Today, there are more than 3,300 deputy marshals throughout the United States.[12] They work for 94 presidentially appointed U.S. Marshals (one for each federal district). When staff members are added to the mix, the USMS employs nearly

3,300 Today, there are more than 3,300 deputy marshals throughout the United States.

4,500 people in more than 200 offices both in the United States and abroad. The agency's main responsibilities are judicial security and fugitive investigation. Marshals protect federal judicial officials, including judges, attorneys, and jurors. The USMS arrests more federal fugitives than all other federal agencies combined. In fiscal year 2005, for instance, marshals arrested more than 35,000 federal fugitives.

Marshals work in task forces alongside local law enforcement agencies to apprehend fugitives. Less familiar are USMS units like the Special Operations Group, which is similar to a local police agency's special weapons and tactics

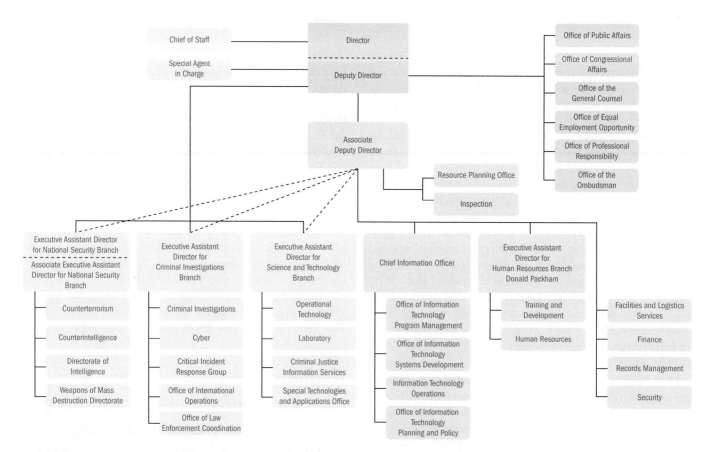

FIGURE 3.3 **Organizational Chart of the Federal Bureau of Investigation.**
Source: Federal Bureau of Investigation.

(SWAT) team. As for witness security, the agency has protected, relocated, and given new identities to nearly 8,000 individuals. The USMS has also joined up with customs enforcement and immigration officials to more efficiently deport criminal aliens. Marshals are also responsible for housing more than 50,000 federal detainees.

Bureau of Alcohol, Tobacco, Firearms and Explosives. Unlike the USMS and the FBI, the **Bureau of Alcohol, Tobacco, Firearms and Explosives (ATF)** has not been housed in the Justice Department for very long. On January 24, 2003, it was transferred from the Department of the Treasury to Justice, in accordance with the Homeland Security Act. Vestiges of ATF remain in the Treasury Department, however. Specifically, the Treasury Department is still responsible for certain tax and trade functions associated with ATF. The move from the Treasury Department to the Justice Department included a name change for the agency, from simply the Bureau of Alcohol, Tobacco, and Firearms to the Bureau of Alcohol, Tobacco, Firearms and Explosives. The *ATF* acronym remains in place, however, even though explosives are now one of the agency's key concerns.

ATF is basically a tax-collection, enforcement, and regulatory arm of the U.S. Department of Justice. The Gun Control Act of 1968 required that every manufacturer, importer, and dealer of firearms obtain a Federal Firearms License. ATF screens the applications and issues the licenses. Dealers are required to comply with applicable federal laws and to keep records of all firearms sales, and ATF conducts inspections of gun dealerships to ensure compliance. ATF also targets illegal firearms trafficking.

As for explosives, ATF investigates explosions and cases of arson. It has been particularly involved, for instance, with investigations of arson and bombings at abortion clinics throughout the United States. Finally, the agency regulates distilleries, wineries, breweries, and tobacco manufacturers and retailers. Its National Laboratory Center ensures that the labels on alcoholic beverages do not contain misleading information.

Besides staff, ATF employs both special agents and inspectors. The agents are the criminal investigators and enforcement officials. Inspectors' responsibilities do not include investigation and enforcement per se. Rather, they help people start new businesses, such as firearms dealerships, liquor stores, and

ATF is basically a tax-collection, enforcement, and regulatory arm of the U.S. Department of Justice.

the like. Inspectors also visit dealerships and retail establishments to ensure compliance with the law. ATF also employs a number of lawyers, auditors, chemists, and computer experts. The agency is headquartered in Washington, DC, where the majority of the agency's approximately 5,000 employees work. The remainder staff about 25 field offices located throughout the United States and in a handful of foreign nations.

Drug Enforcement Administration. The **Drug Enforcement Administration (DEA)** is tasked with enforcing controlled substance laws and regulations. The agency brings to justice people and organizations involved in the illegal growing, manufacture, and distribution of controlled substances. To accomplish these tasks, the DEA

- Investigates and prepares for the prosecution of major violators of controlled substance laws operating at interstate and international levels
- Investigates and prepares for the prosecution of criminals and drug gangs who perpetrate violence and terrorize citizens through fear and intimidation
- Manages a national drug-intelligence program in cooperation with federal, state, local, and foreign officials to collect, analyze, and disseminate strategic and operational drug-intelligence information
- Seizes and effects forfeiture of assets derived from, traceable to, or intended to be used for illicit drug trafficking
- Enforces the provisions of the Controlled Substances Act as they pertain to the manufacture, distribution, and dispensing of legally produced controlled substances
- Coordinates and cooperates with federal, state, and local law enforcement officials on mutual drug enforcement efforts and enhancement of such efforts through exploitation of potential interstate and international investigations beyond local or limited federal jurisdictions and resources
- Coordinates and cooperates with federal, state, and local agencies—and with foreign governments—in programs designed to reduce the availability of illicit abuse-type drugs on the U.S. market through nonenforcement methods such as crop eradication, crop substitution, and training of foreign officials[13]

The DEA is one of the larger federal law enforcement agencies. In 2010, it employed nearly 11,000 people, including more than 5,200 special agents. The agency has 227 domestic offices in 21 divisions throughout the United States and in 63 foreign countries.

TABLE 3.1

State and Local Law Enforcement Agencies and Employees in the United States.

Type of Agency	Agencies	Full-Time Employees			Part-Time Employees		
		Total	Sworn	Nonsworn	Total	Sworn	Nonsworn
Total	17,876	1,076,897	731,903	344,994	105,252	45,982	59,270
Local Police	12,766	573,152	446,974	126,178	62,693	28,712	33,981
Sheriff	3,067	326,531	175,018	151,513	27,004	11,784	15,220
Primary State	49	89,265	58,190	31,075	708	31	677
Special Jurisdiction	1,481	85,126	49,398	35,728	14,342	5,063	9,279
Constable/Marshal	513	2,823	2,323	500	505	392	113

Source: B.A. Reaves, *Census of State and Local Law Enforcement Agencies, 2004* (Washington, DC: Bureau of Justice Statistics, 2007), p. 2
http://bjs.ojp.usdoj.gov/content/pub/pdf/csllea04.pdf.

State Agencies

Most state police agencies were initially created for a specific purpose. The Texas Rangers, for example, were established in 1835, even before Texas attained statehood, and functioned largely as a military organization responsible for patrolling the republic's borders. Massachusetts was the second state to create a law enforcement agency. It was developed with the intent of targeting vice crimes. Today, numerous state policing agencies exist. Table 3.1 shows that the number of personnel employed by state law enforcement agencies is significantly less than the number employed in local police departments.

State law enforcement agencies are usually organized according to one of two models. In the first, a **centralized policing model**, the tasks of major criminal investigations are combined with the patrol of state highways. A number of states rely on these centralized agencies, the names of which often include *state police* or *state patrol*. The second model, the **decentralized policing model**, is more like a traditional municipal police agency. Figure 3.4 highlights the key points of the centralized and decentralized state policing models.

The Centralized Model

The Pennsylvania Constabulary, known today as the Pennsylvania State Police, was the first modern force to combine the duties of criminal investigations and state highway patrol. It has been described as the first modern state police agency. Michigan, New Jersey, New York, Vermont, and Delaware are a few of the states that patterned their state-level enforcement activities after the centralized Pennsylvania model. Some state agencies give greater emphasis to one or more of the responsibilities than to others. The Washington State Patrol, for example, is well known for its very active presence on state highways, but through its investigative and forensics bureaus, it assists local agencies in solving crimes throughout the state. The California Highway Patrol is also known foremost as a traffic enforcement agency because of its obvious presence on California roads and freeways. A centralized model organizational chart is shown in Figure 3.5.

The Decentralized Model

North Carolina, South Carolina, and Georgia are a few of the many states that employ both a highway patrol and a state bureau of investigation. The names of the respective agencies

State Policing Models | **Key Points**

Centralized
- Assist local law enforcement departments in criminal investigations when asked to do so
- Operate identification bureaus
- Maintain a centralized criminal records repository
- Patrol the state's highways
- Provide select training for municipal and county officers

Decentralized
- Most prevalent in the southern portion and some Midwestern portions of the United States
- Draws a clear distinction between traffic enforcement on state highways and other state-level law enforcement functions

FIGURE 3.4 Centralized versus Decentralized State Policing Models.

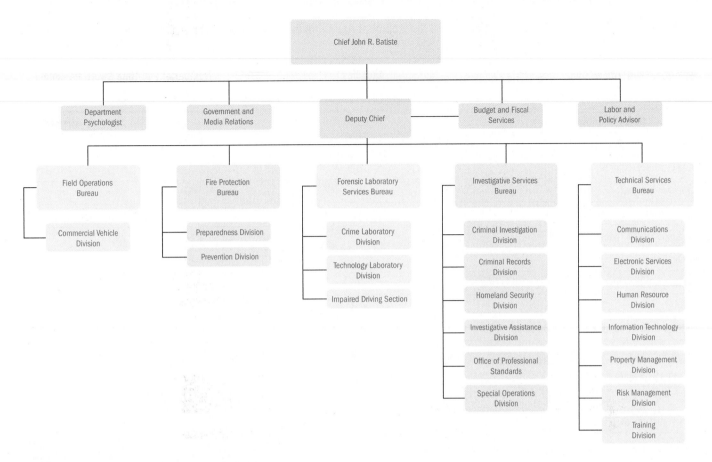

FIGURE 3.5 **Centralized Model Organizational Chart.**
Source: Washington State Patrol, "Washington State Patrol Organizational Chart, June 2009,"
www.wsp.wa.gov/about/docs/orgchart.pdf (accessed December 5, 2010).

The decentralized approach to state policing draws a clear distinction between traffic enforcement on state highways and other state-level law enforcement functions.

may vary, however, even though their functions are largely the same. In North Carolina, for example, the two major state-level law enforcement agencies are the North Carolina Highway Patrol and the State Bureau of Investigation. Georgia fields a highway patrol and the Georgia Bureau of Investigation, and South Carolina operates a highway patrol and the South Carolina Law Enforcement Division.

States that use the decentralized model usually have a number of other adjunct state-level law enforcement agencies. North Carolina, for example, has created a State Wildlife Commission with enforcement powers, a Board of Alcohol Beverage Control with additional agents, and a separate Enforcement and Theft Bureau for enforcing certain motor vehicle and theft laws. Other states have merged historically separate agencies into one parent organization. Oregon's State Police is an example. In 1993, the legislature in that state approved a law that merged the Oregon

State Fire Marshal's Office, Oregon Emergency Management, the Law Enforcement Data System, and the Oregon Boxing and Wrestling Commission into the State Police.

Local Agencies

Local police agencies, including city and county agencies, are a third level of law enforcement activity in the United States—the other two being federal and state. The term **local agencies** encompasses a wide variety of organizations. **Municipal police departments** and **sheriff's departments** are most familiar. Other lesser-known agencies, such as campus police departments and transit police, are also categorized as "local." Even some public schools have a police presence, as do airports, state capitols, medical facilities, state parks, certain prosecutor's offices, and other organizations. (See Table 3.2 for a list of some of these special jurisdiction agencies.) Viewed together, the personnel in these local

U.S. Marshals Service (USMS)
The oldest American law enforcement agency. Its mission includes judicial security and fugitive investigation and apprehension.

Bureau of Alcohol, Tobacco, Firearms and Explosives (ATF)
A tax-collection, enforcement, and regulatory arm of the U.S. Department of Justice.

Drug Enforcement Administration (DEA) The U.S. law enforcement agency tasked with enforcing controlled-substance laws and regulations.

TABLE 3.2 | Special Jurisdiction Law Enforcement Agencies by Type of Jurisdiction and Number of Full-Time Sworn Personnel.

Type of Special Jurisdiction	Agencies	Number of Full-Time Sworn Personnel
Total	1,481	49,398
Public buildings/facilities	1,011	19,247
Four-year universities/colleges	488	10,167
Public school districts	183	3,517
Two-year colleges	254	2,438
State capitol/government buildings	18	1,289
Medical schools/campuses	22	732
Public housing	12	411
Public hospitals/health facilities	30	399
Courts	4	294
Natural resources/parks and recreation	205	14,322
Fish and wildlife	50	4,937
Parks and recreational areas	95	4,212
Multifunction natural resources	25	3,550
Environmental laws	6	700
Waterways and boating	17	663
Water resources	5	129
Sanitation laws	2	97
Forest resources	5	44
Transportation systems/facilities	130	9,073
Mass transit systems/railroads	18	3,094
Airports	90	2,900
Transportation—multiple types	5	2,200
Port facilities	11	333
Commercial vehicles	2	285
Bridges, tunnels	4	261
Criminal investigations	103	4,739
County/city	62	1,756
State bureau	16	1,702
Fire marshal	17	454
Other	8	827
Special enforcement	32	2,007
Alcohol enforcement	17	1,219
Agricultural law enforcement	5	340
Gaming/racing law enforcement	6	225
Drug enforcement	4	223

Source: Brian A. Reaves, *Census of state and local law enforcement agencies, 2004* (Washington, DC: Bureau of Justice Statistics, 2007), p. 7.

agencies far outnumber all federal and state law enforcement officials combined.

Some local police departments are highly visible because of their size, huge budgets, innovative programs, and—perhaps above all else—the attention they receive from the press, television producers, and moviemakers. The nation's largest law enforcement agency, the New York City Police Department (NYPD), for example, has about 45,000 full-time employees, including about 35,000 full-time sworn officers.[14] Likewise, the police departments in Los Angeles, Chicago, Houston, and other large cities employ thousands of sworn officers. These agencies are routinely featured in television shows and "cop" movies, but far greater in number, albeit less visible, are small-town police and county sheriff's departments.

There are approximately 12,700 municipal police departments and 3,100 sheriff's departments in the United States (out of the roughly 20,000 law enforcement agencies in the country).[15] These numbers are only estimates, given the difficulty associated with counting cops, but the point is that there are many of them. Most areas are patrolled and served by officials from one or both of these types of agencies.

Municipal Police

Every incorporated municipality in the country has the authority to create its own police force. Some very small communities hire only one officer to fill the roles of chief, investigator, and night watch—as well as everything in between. The majority of local agencies employ fewer than ten full-time officers, and about three of every eight agencies (more than 7,000 in all) employ fewer than five full-time officers. These smaller agencies include 2,245 (or 12 percent) with just one full-time officer and 1,164 (or 6 percent) with only part-time officers.[16]

A few communities contract with private security firms for police services, and still others have no active police force at all, depending instead on local sheriff's departments to deal with law violators. Some cities also contract with county sheriff's

departments to provide law enforcement services. Whether a city has a police force, or any police presence at all, depends on funding, as well. Hiring a police officer, putting the person through training, paying benefits, and so on can cost hundreds of thousands of dollars.

City police chiefs are typically appointed by the mayor or selected by the city council. Their departments' jurisdictions are limited by convention to the geographic boundaries of their communities. Municipal police departments are all organized in a fairly similar fashion. Larger agencies have many more personnel and divisions, of course, but they still follow a fairly ordinary bureaucratic structure. Typically, the chief is near the top, followed by deputy chiefs, captains, lieutenants, sergeants, and so forth. The number of ranks varies from one agency to the next. To illustrate, see Figures 3.7 and 3.8. The first presents the organizational chart of the Los Angeles Police Department, while the second shows the organization of the Allen (Texas) Police Department.

Sheriff's Departments

Sheriff's departments are responsible for law enforcement throughout the counties in which they function. Sheriff's deputies mostly patrol the unincorporated areas of the county, or those that lie between municipalities. They do, however, have jurisdiction throughout the county, and in some areas they routinely work alongside municipal police to enforce laws within towns and cities. If a traffic accident occurs within city limits, for example, a sheriff's deputy may appear on the scene first and take control.

Sheriff's departments are also generally responsible for serving court papers, including civil summonses, and for maintaining security within state courtrooms. They run county jails and are responsible for more detainees awaiting trial than any other type of law enforcement department in the country.

Sheriff's departments remain strong across most of the country, although in parts of New England, deputies mostly function as court agents with limited law enforcement duties. One report reveals that most sheriff's departments are small; nearly two-thirds employ fewer than 25 sworn officers.[17] Only 12 departments employ more than 1,000 officers. Even so, sheriffs in southern and western states are still considered the chief law enforcement officers in their respective counties.

Sheriffs are usually elected officials,[18] unlike city police chiefs. This creates a somewhat different set of priorities for them. Police chiefs answer to city officials, but sheriffs answer to voters. If the voters are displeased with a sheriff's performance, come election time they can move a new sheriff into office.

In most jurisdictions, not just anyone can run for the position of sheriff. Ohio, for example, requires not only past law enforcement experience, but experience in law enforcement administration.[19] The law ensures that all unqualified candidates are screened out in advance of elections.

2/3
Nearly 2/3 of Sheriff's departments employ fewer than 25 officers.

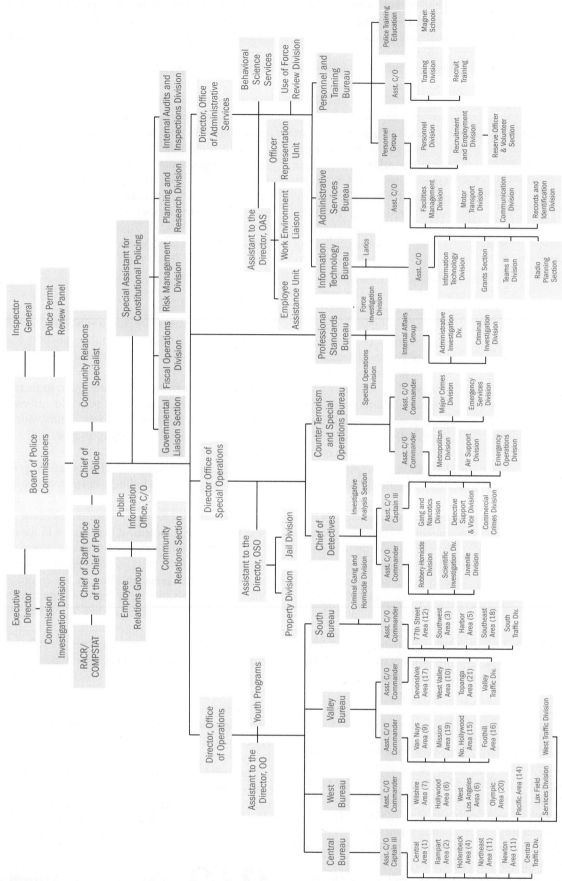

FIGURE 3.6 **Example of a Municipal Police Department Organizational Chart.**
Source: Los Angeles Police Department, "Los Angeles Police Department Organizational Chart," www.lapdonline.org/inside_the_lapd/content_basic_view/1063 (accessed December 5, 2010).

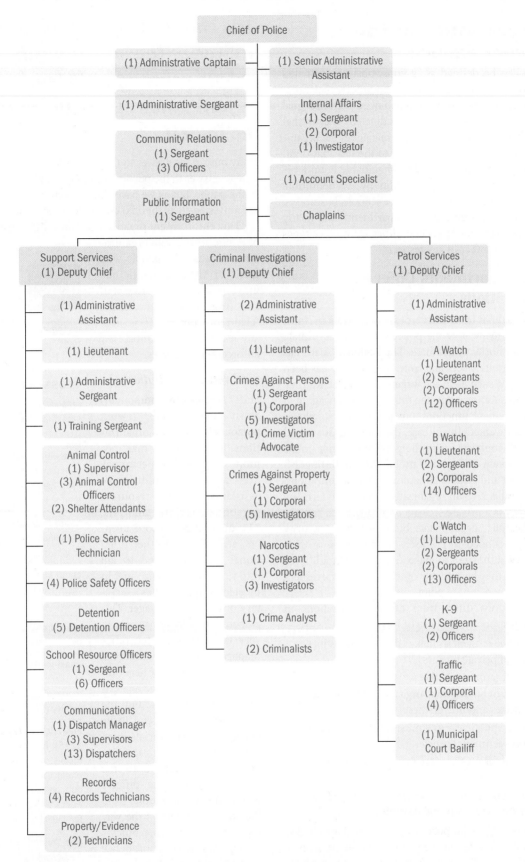

FIGURE 3.7 **Another Example of a Municipal Police Department Organizational Chart.**
Source: Allen (Texas) Police Department,
http://allen.websites.ariamedia.com/SiteContent/56/documents/Police/org%20chart.pdf (accessed December 5, 2010).

▶ The Organization of Law Enforcement Agencies

An **organization** can be defined as "a consciously coordinated social entity, with a relatively identifiable boundary, that functions on a relatively continuous basis to achieve a common goal or set of goals."[20] To be "consciously coordinated" means that someone (or perhaps a group of people) is managing the organization. The notion of "social entity" refers to the fact that organizations are groups of people. Finally, "identifiable boundary" refers to an organization's service population. By this definition, police departments are organizations, as are schools, businesses, and nonprofit groups. However, police departments, and nearly all law enforcement agencies in general, differ from other types of organizations in a number of key respects.

How Police Departments Differ from Other Organizations

Police organizations differ from other types of organizations, most obviously, because usually only the police have both legitimate arrest power and authority to use force. The National Guard has been activated in various places and from time to time has been given arrest authority, such as in the wake of Hurricane Katrina. The Posse Comitatus Act prohibits the military from engaging in domestic law enforcement functions, but if Congress so allows, the act can be circumvented. In any case, the National Guard and the military are still connected with the government, not unlike the typical police agency. Perhaps it is useful, then, to distinguish between government and civilian law enforcement organizations.

The closest parallel civilian organization to the modern law enforcement agency is a private security company. Such companies may look like police departments, but most private security officials are not sanctioned to use force in the course of their duties, nor are they authorized to make arrests in the traditional sense. In either case, they have to rely on sworn law enforcement officials to take over at a certain point.

Police organizations differ from other organizations in more than just arrest powers and use of force:

1. Their status as *public* agencies makes them quite distinct from the realm of private business.[21]
2. Unlike private organizations, they exist within a political environment, as do other public organizations, such as prosecutor's offices and universities.
3. They work in the public eye and must follow all the rules applicable to government agencies.
4. They are not run for profit, as are private security agencies and some private prisons.
5. They are often hamstrung by bureaucratic rules and regulations that can stifle creativity and flexibility.

Like most public agencies, police organizations have limited resources. They often have to pursue grants and other sources of "soft money" (that is, funding apart from their year-to-year budgets) just to make ends meet. Many private companies have no shortage of cash in the bank, and when they don't have the money they need, they can take out loans. This is not a luxury available to public-sector organizations, although parent governments can borrow typically through the issuance of bonds. Finally, whereas

The chain of command is the unbroken line of authority that extends through all levels of an organization, from the highest to the lowest.

many businesses answer to the shareholders, police organizations have to answer to the public. They may not have to answer *directly* to the public, but as we have already seen, some law enforcement executives (such as sheriffs) do answer to the voters.

Law enforcement organizations also differ from other types of public and private organizations because the people who work in them generally fall into one of two categories: staff and line officials. A distinct "chain of command" is usually established in most law enforcement agencies.

Staff versus Line Duties

Staff (**nonsworn personnel**) assist line officials (**sworn personnel**). In some organizations, there are as many or more staff than line personnel. Secretaries and administrative assistants, human resources personnel, crime analysts, 911 dispatchers, record keepers, and a host of other functional specialists tend to fall into this category. The chief in most large agencies has a secretary or an office manager. This person is usually nonsworn. In very large agencies, the office manager may have additional assistants under his or her command. Likewise, crime analysts are often nonsworn, but the units they work in tend to be headed by sworn officials, such as sergeants. By contrast, sworn personnel consist of all the commissioned peace officers within the organization, from the chief or sheriff all the way down to the frontline officers or deputies. Small rural police agencies are not always organized in this fashion, but the typical agency has at least some mix of staff and sworn personnel. This is not the case in most other public agencies.

LEARNING OUTCOMES 2 — Summarize the differences between police departments and other types of organizations, and describe both traditional and contemporary approaches to organization.

GLOSSARY

organization A group in which individuals work together to accomplish specified tasks or goals.

nonsworn personnel Support staff members of a law enforcement agency who are not empowered to make arrests.

sworn personnel Members of a law enforcement agency who are empowered to make arrests.

chain of command The supervisory channel within a law enforcement organization.

span of control The number of subordinates supervised by one person.

quasi-military An organizational structure that follows the military model to some extent, but with subtle differences.

Frederick W. Taylor (1856–1915) A classical organizational theorist who posited that worker productivity could be increased through careful attention to how work was allocated and who performed what functions.

Max Weber (1864–1920) A classical organizational theorist, widely acknowledged as the father of bureaucracy, who identified five principles that he suggested are characteristic of an effective bureaucratic organization.

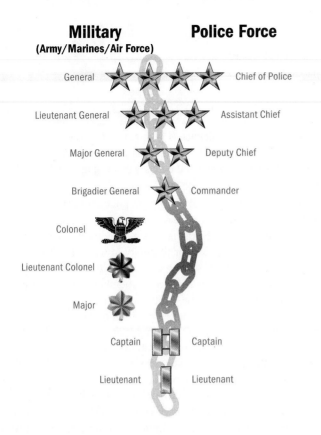

Military (Army/Marines/Air Force)		Police Force
General		Chief of Police
Lieutenant General		Assistant Chief
Major General		Deputy Chief
Brigadier General		Commander
Colonel		
Lieutenant Colonel		
Major		
Captain		Captain
Lieutenant		Lieutenant

Chain of Command

Every organization, public or private, follows a chain of command. Private companies tend to have a chief executive officer (CEO), a president, or both at the helm. Schools have principals. Most prosecutor's offices are run by an elected district attorney. In this respect, police agencies, sheriff's departments, and other law enforcement agencies are no different; someone is in charge. Where law enforcement agencies part ways with other organizations, though, is in the **chain of command**.

The functional structure of a command chain incorporates the notion of **span of control**, which refers to the number of subordinates supervised by one person. The bigger the organization and the higher up the ladder a person ascends, the greater that person's span of control.

Command structures differ from one police agency to the next, but they share much in common with the military command structure. This also makes law enforcement agencies different from most other organizations. While this command structure has its advantages, it is also significantly limited, as we will see shortly.

Traditional and Contemporary Organization

The traditional approach to police organization hails from Sir Robert Peel's recommendation that agencies follow the military model. One of the first principles Peel espoused was that "the police must be stable, efficient, and organized along military lines."[22] As we just saw, Peel's legacy lives on. But because few police organizations follow the military model in every detail, they are often said to be **quasi-military** in structure. The leaders of law enforcement agencies are not called generals, for instance. Also, there tend to be fewer distinct ranks in the typical police organization than in the military. Even so, there is much similarity to the military model in terms of how most police agencies are organized.

Classical Organizational Theory

Peel's advocacy of the military model for policing was echoed by O. W. Wilson and other influential figures in early American policing. But what is the logic for this model of organization? What makes the quasi-military model so desirable? To answer these questions, we need to look beyond policing to the realm of organizational theory—particularly to the legacy of two key individuals, **Frederick W. Taylor** and **Max Weber**.

Taylor studied organizations for the purpose of improving worker productivity. During his time, people often worked to the point of exhaustion. People were assigned tasks they were unfamiliar with or were incapable of performing adequately. In a word, they worked ineffectively. Taylor's contribution was in the area of increasing worker productivity through careful attention to how work was allocated and who performed what functions. Weber, on the other hand, studied the features of successful organizations. Together, Weber and Taylor ushered in an era of scientific management. They believed that scientific principles should be applied to workplaces so that workers could be as productive as possible with the least amount of effort. Perhaps above all else, Taylor stressed the role of managers in ensuring a smooth-running workplace.

Max Weber is widely recognized as one of the first people to study **bureaucracy**. He did not *invent* bureaucracy, nor is he responsible for all the negative connotations the term takes on today. But Weber did identify five principles that he suggested are characteristic of an effective bureaucratic organization.[23] These principles can be applied to law enforcement:

1. *Well-defined hierarchy of authority*. In every traditional police organization, superior-subordinate relationships are based on authority, from the patrol officer up to the chief. Each person at a higher position or rank has more authority than do his or her subordinates.

2. *Specialization*. Every person's job is broken into precise, routine, and well-defined tasks. By dividing tasks among several work groups, the organization becomes more efficient.

bureaucracy The administrative structure of a large or complex organization, typically employing task-specialized bureaus or departments.

participatory management A form of leadership that allows subordinates to participate in decision making and planning, especially with regard to the manner in which their own units are operated.

quality circle A group of qualified employees from all ranks who work together, often around one table, to solve organizational problems.

contingency theory A management theory that recognizes that there are often different types of tasks within a single organization, including repetitive tasks that call for standardization and control and nonrepetitive tasks that call for flexibility and participatory management.

systems perspective A view of organizational style, rooted in biology, that posits that organizations are living organisms that strive for a state of equilibrium, or balance, and that affect or are affected by their environment.

Participatory management refers to a form of leadership that allows subordinates to participate in decision making and planning.

Source: © istockpoto.com/ Dariusz Markowski

3. *Formalization.* There must be a well-established system of rules and regulations detailing workers' duties to ensure uniformity and reduce discretion.

4. *Impersonality of management.* Decisions should be made without regard to personalities or individuals. Decision making should be based on the goals and objectives of the agency.

5. *Personnel decisions based on merit.* Positions should be filled and promotions made according to merit—that is, based on the experience and qualifications of the individual. The agency must strive to put the best qualified individuals in each position.

Does this sound like the typical police agency? The answer is most certainly yes. Every agency today has clearly defined levels of authority, specialization, and formalization. Authority is accomplished via the rank structure. Specialization is evident not just in levels of supervision (the vertical dimension), but also within the agency's various divisions (the horizontal dimension). These two features can be seen in the organizational charts presented earlier in this chapter. Concerning formalization, every law enforcement agency has a policy manual that employees must follow. Also, merit-based personnel decisions are standard in modern police agencies.

Contemporary Organizational Theory

The classical model of police organization has its limitations. Critics feel that the classical approach is, in a word, "mechanistic."[24] A contrasting view of organizations is that they are "organic," like living, breathing entities made up of real human beings. The mechanistic view of organizations separates the people element from the command structure. The organic view does the opposite; it allows employees greater input and responsibility in decision making, especially at the lower levels. Applying this thinking to policing, an organic organizational structure would elevate the status of the line officers by giving them some control over the organization's mission, day-to-day operations, and key decisions. Advocates believe that this is a more flexible and adaptive method of organization.[25]

Participatory management is an important concept in police management circles today. It refers to a form of leadership that allows subordinates to participate in decision making and planning, especially with regard to the manner in which their own units are operated. Related to this is the use of **quality circles**, groups of qualified officers from all ranks who work together (often around one table) to solve organizational problems.

Contingency theory recognizes that there are often different types of tasks within a single organization: repetitive and nonrepetitive tasks. The former calls for standardization and control, while the latter calls for flexibility and participatory management.

How is this manifested in the typical police agency? On the one hand, consider the traffic enforcement division. Its tasks are repetitive, and it can easily be managed via a traditional organizational model; there is little need for flexibility in writing tickets. On the other hand, a problem-solving unit within the same agency may need to be structured to allow team members to be creative and do what it takes within the limits of the law to effectively target certain crimes. This is the very definition of contingency theory; organizational strategies are contingent on the tasks at hand.

The final approach to organizational style considered in this chapter is the **systems perspective**, which is rooted in biology. This view posits that organizations are living organisms that strive for a state of equilibrium, or balance, and that affect or are affected by their environment.[26] The last element is most telling. Nowadays, it is very clear that police organizations do not operate in a vacuum. They affect their surroundings through officers' actions and inactions. They are also affected by the environment (that is, the media, public opinion, relationships with other government officials, relationships with private business, and so on). They are, to use some organizational terminology, "open systems." Systems theory differs from the other approaches in its concern with organizational parts, and their relationships to one another, more than the whole being. The systems view of organizational design takes the same approach—making sure all the pieces of the whole work together to ensure survival.

▶ Private Policing and Security

The police are not the only ones in the business of crime control and prevention. Public police (municipal police officers, sheriff's deputies, state troopers, and so on) work alongside scores of private police and security officials.[29] People employed as private police officers or security personnel outnumber public police officers by three to one.[30] The number of companies engaged in providing private police or security services has been estimated at more than 10,000.[31] They employ more than 500,000 personnel, including more than 10,000 store detectives, nearly 100,000 managers and staff, and nearly 400,000 security officers.[32]

The contract security industry (consisting of companies that enter into contracts with businesses to provide security) estimated in 1999 that it employed 719,000 uniformed personnel.[33]

3:1 People employed as private police officers or security personnel outnumber public police officers by three to one.

Other estimates place the number of people involved in either private policing or security at more than 2 million.[34] Despite their numbers, private police and security professionals have largely escaped the notice of police scholars.[35]

Private Security versus Private Policing

Security guards are highly visible to the public. They work in retail establishments, hotels, gated communities, and sports venues, just to name a few locations. These guards come immediately to mind when we consider private policing, but they represent the proverbial tip of the iceberg. In this regard, it is useful to distinguish between **private security** and **private policing**. According to Elizabeth Joh, a law professor at the University of California–Davis, *private security* refers to the industry that provides "for-profit security products and services, which include three broad categories: the provision of guards, equipment, and investigation or consulting services."[36] Homeowners who buy a home security system do so from the private security industry. *Private policing*, on the other hand, refers to "the acquisition and use of these products and services, as well as the application of specialized knowledge in areas like crime control, investigation, and risk management."[37] In other words, private police are supplied by the private security industry.

Our concern here is not with the private security industry per se. Rather, our interest is in private policing's provision of security, crime prevention, and crime-control functions. Whether we call it *security* or *policing* is not particularly important, but for consistency's sake, we will use the term *private policing* from here on out, knowing that private policing owes its livelihood to the private security industry. Private police could be trained personnel supplied by the private security industry or ordinary people—trained in the trade or not—who are not affiliated with any known security company but are hired to provide security services.

Private Policing versus Public Policing

One of the hallmarks of public policing is that it is funded by tax dollars. One distinguishing feature of private policing, on the other hand, is its "client-driven mandate."[38] Client-driven relationships in the world of public policing are usually regarded as unethical. For example, most people regard it as inappropriate for a store owner to offer perks (such as free merchandise or discounts) to a city police officer. An officer who receives such benefits from a citizen may be more inclined to favor that person with additional security or to ignore minor criminal offenses. Stepping over into the private policing realm, though, few people would object to a store owner who hires a private police officer for additional protection.

Private Policing Methods

Private policing can also be distinguished from public policing by its methods. South African criminologist Clifford Shearing has identified four such methods.[39] First, private police personnel

One distinguishing feature of private policing is its "client-driven mandate."

focus largely on loss control and prevention. Retail security guards, for instance, are in the business of making sure their clients' products are not stolen or embezzled. The term *loss prevention* can encompass much more than lost merchandise. Some private police focus on the prevention of accidents and costly mistakes. According to Joh, "The emphasis on loss also means that private police are disengaged from the moral underpinnings of the criminal law; they focus instead on property and asset protection."[40] "Moral underpinnings" refers to the what's right/what's wrong aspect of the laws that public police are charged with enforcing. Whereas public police target situations deemed by constituents and law-making bodies to be problems, private police are not limited by these issues; they do what their clients want without regard to moral issues.

The second main private policing method is prevention: "Private police stress preventive means over detection and apprehension to control crime and disorder."[41] Their concern is not so much with the punishment of wrongdoers. Rather, it is with preventing the disruption of legitimate business activities. It is ironic, in fact, that retailers often place signs throughout their establishments warning that "shoplifters will be prosecuted to the fullest extent of the law." For one thing, retailers have limited say over whether someone will be charged with theft; prosecutors make this decision. In addition, retailers' concern with prosecution is typically incidental to their more immediate concern for making sure the business doesn't lose money.

That is why private police rely on surveillance. Casino owners, for example, go to great pains to keep an eye on things and make sure that dishonest gamblers do not line their pockets at the casino's expense.

Private policing is also distinguished from public policing by its focus on "private justice" rather than public justice. As Joh points out, private security provides a functional alternative to the public police and the criminal justice system.[42] Consider, for example, employee theft from a retail store. What would the store's owner rather do, go to the trouble of prosecuting the employee or simply fire the person? The latter choice would be the easiest. What about the gambler who counts cards in a blackjack game and gets caught? He or she would sooner be banned from the casino than charged with any criminal violation. "In a private justice system," Joh says, "the resolution of problems is left to the control and discretion of private police and their clients, who may see some incidents as unworthy of the lost time and resources necessary to assist in a public prosecution."[43] Indeed, some businesses are willing to absorb a certain amount of loss rather than incurring the costs of pursuing formal criminal charges against a wrongdoer.

GLOSSARY

private security The industry that provides for-profit security products and services, which include three broad categories: the provision of guards, equipment, and investigative or consulting services.[27]

private policing The acquisition and use of security products and services, as well as the application of specialized knowledge in areas like crime control, investigation, and risk management, by nonsworn personnel.[28]

Think About It...

Citizen Patrols Citizen crime patrols are made up of trained volunteers who drive around and "patrol" their neighborhoods looking for suspicious activity and reporting it to officers who then respond. These patrols have been touted as creating an extra barrier to criminal activity in the community.

In one survey of citizens' and police officers' attitudes about citizen patrols, people felt that patrol should be performed by armed, state-sanctioned police. Two other similar studies suggest that citizen patrols may exacerbate fear and have no discernible effect on crime. Should private citizens be permitted to assist the police with patrol? Why or why not? How effective can a citizen patrol be compared to an ordinary police patrol? Explain.

Source: p77/p77/ZUMA Press/ Newscom

The fourth distinguishing feature of private policing is a concern with private rather than public property. Generally, public police do not have the luxury of entering private places without proper cause or an invitation. At the opposite extreme, private police generally don't care what happens in public spaces. Their job is, for the most part, protecting private property. Often they work in quasi-public places, such as privately owned malls that are open to the public, but their loyalties lie with the businesses that employ them, not the general public.

Controversies in Private Policing

Private security is controversial in a number of respects. First, it is important to note that private security is but one part of a larger privatization movement in criminal justice.[44] Private prisons, for instance, have emerged to provide a presumably cost-effective alternative to state-run correctional facilities. Critics charge that privatization turns criminal justice into a for-profit venture, which could translate into detrimental cost-cutting measures. Second, some people have charged that private policing is poised to replace public policing. Nothing could be further from the truth, however. As Sklansky puts it, "Private policing poses no risk of supplanting public law enforcement entirely, at least not in our lifetime, and it is far from clear to what extent the growing numbers of private security employees are actually performing functions previously carried out by public officers."[45]

Perhaps the most significant controversy associated with private policing deals with constitutional concerns. In general, because private police are nongovernmental, they are not bound by the same legal requirements as public police. As Sklansky notes,

> Perhaps the most basic and invariable principle of criminal procedure is that constitutional restrictions on policing— the limitations imposed by the Fourth, Fifth, and Sixth Amendments, the prophylactic rules of evidentiary exclusion constructed to reinforce those limitations, and the analogous rules of state constitutional law—apply only to investigative action attributable to the government.[46]

Citizen crime patrols came into vogue in the 1980s as a way of allowing trained volunteers to serve as the eyes and ears of local police departments in neighborhoods.

The U.S. Supreme Court has yet to tackle the issue of private policing head-on. It decided one case in 1964 involving an amusement park security guard who had been "deputized" by the county sheriff,[47] ruling that the security guard was a state official and thus was bound by the same legal constraints as public police officers. Beyond that case, the Supreme Court has had little to say. State courts, however, have been much more vocal, and most of them have refused to treat private police as state actors. For example, private police have been exempted from the Fourth Amendment,[48] the *Miranda* rule,[49] and entrapment restrictions.[50] We will look at these issues from a public policing perspective in Chapter 10.

It would be a mistake to construe these decisions as granting unbridled power to private police. It is true that some private police do have more power than ordinary citizens, and deputizing private police officers gives them—briefly—the same authority as public police. Additionally, many private police officers are off-duty public police officers. Yet most private police do not enjoy the same legal powers as public police: "Many private security guards . . . possess no greater legal capabilities than do ordinary citizens to forcibly detain persons who are suspected of or have in fact committed a crime."[51] In many states, ordinary citizens can arrest people for misdemeanors committed in their presence and for felonies that they have probable cause to believe were committed.[52]

DISCUSS
1. Is the criminal justice system becoming a for-profit venture?
2. Is private policing replacing public?
3. What happens to constitutional concerns?

PRIVATE VERSUS PUBLIC POLICING

Private	Public
Focus on loss prevention	Focus on right vs. wrong and enforcing public policy
Focus on prevention, not punishment	Focus on detection, apprehension, and punishment
Private justice—punishment up to discretion of business	Public justice—punishment depends on the law
Concerned with protection of private property and clients	Concerned with protection of public property and the general public

Joe Arpaio, "America's Toughest Sheriff"

Joe Arpaio, the controversial sheriff of Maricopa County, Arizona, is well known for his desert jail's "tent city," where inmates sometimes live outside in 110-degree heat. Arpaio is also famous for the pink underwear that he requires male inmates to wear (and that is sold to them to raise revenue for the county) and for the chain gangs that he reinstituted. On one occasion, Arpaio even had his inmates march down public streets wearing only their pink underwear.

Although the sheriff has some supporters, he has also attracted criticism, both internationally and locally. In 2005, a Scottish judge decided not to extradite a Catholic priest back to Arizona to face molestation charges because Arpaio, he said, takes "a chillingly sadistic pleasure in his role as incarcerator. It [is] the duty of any Irish court to see that no citizen [is] handed over to such a regime."[53]

Some residents of Maricopa County became so critical of Arpaio's policies that a recall petition got under way in 2007. The petition was set into motion, in part, due to the suspicious death of inmate Scott Norberg in 1996. Arpaio was cleared of any personal wrongdoing, but Norberg's family filed a civil lawsuit, which the county settled for $8.25 million. In 2008, recall efforts targeting Arpaio fell by the wayside as supporters failed to get enough signatures to have it placed on the county's ballot.

Sheriff Arpaio represents an "extreme case" in the world of law enforcement executives—a phrase that he applied to himself in a book he coauthored with Len Sherman, *America's Toughest Sheriff: How We Can Win the War against Crime*. Arpaio has been reelected three times since he first took office in 1992.

The case of Joe Arpaio raises a number of important questions:

1. If voters are dissatisfied with the performance of an elected sheriff, should they recall the sheriff or simply allow him or her to serve out the term?

2. Are Sheriff Arpaio's policies outrageous?

3. Would an appointed city police chief be allowed to adopt policies similar to Arpaio's?

Source: Chris Curtis/Shutterstock.com

LEARNING OUTCOMES 1

Describe the organization and roles of federal and state law enforcement agencies.

The roughly 20,000 law enforcement agencies in the United States are found at the federal, state, and local levels. Most federal law enforcement agencies are located in the Department of Homeland Security and the Department of Justice. Most state police agencies follow either a centralized or decentralized model. Local law enforcement agencies consist mostly of municipal police departments and county sheriff's offices. Other agencies operate at the local level, but they are the exception.

1. Identify and describe a number of key federal law enforcement agencies, and explain their roles.

2. What two models of state law enforcement can be identified? What are the differences between them?

Homeland Security Act of 2002 U.S. legislation enacted after the terrorist attacks of September 11, 2001, that created the cabinet-level Department of Homeland Security.

money laundering The process by which criminals or criminal organizations seek to disguise the illicit nature of their proceeds by introducing them into the stream of legitimate commerce and finance.

Customs and Border Protection (CBP) The U.S. law enforcement agency, established after the terrorist attacks on September 11, 2001, that combined the entire U.S. Border Patrol with portions of the U.S. Customs Service, U.S. Immigration, and the Animal and Plant Health Inspection Service. CBP was given the mission of controlling and protecting America's borders and ports of entry, including international airports and international shipping ports.

Immigration and Customs Enforcement (ICE) The largest investigative component of the federal Department of Homeland Security. ICE focuses specifically on illegal immigration.

Federal Bureau of Investigation (FBI) The investigative arm of the U.S. Department of Justice.

U.S. Marshals Service (USMS) The oldest American law enforcement agency. Its mission includes judicial security and fugitive investigation and apprehension.

Bureau of Alcohol, Tobacco, Firearms and Explosives (ATF) A tax-collection, enforcement, and regulatory arm of the U.S. Department of Justice.

Drug Enforcement Administration (DEA) The U.S. law enforcement agency tasked with enforcing controlled-substance laws and regulations.

centralized policing model The less prevalent model of state police organization, in which the tasks of major criminal investigations are combined with the patrol of state highways.

decentralized policing model A model of policing in which central governments exercise relatively few police powers and in which the majority of police services are provided by separate local and regional agencies.

local agency One of the three levels of law enforcement activity in the United States—the other two being state and federal—that encompasses organizations like municipal police departments, sheriff's departments, and other lesser-known agencies (including campus police, transit police, and specialized agencies at public schools, airports, state capitols, medical facilities, state parks, certain prosecutors' offices, and others). Together, the personnel in these local agencies far outnumber all state and federal law enforcement officials combined.

municipal police department One of the types of local law enforcement agencies in the United States. Specifically, the law enforcement agency that serves a municipality.

sheriff's department One of the types of local law enforcement agencies in the United States. Specifically, the law enforcement agency that serves a county or parish.

LEARNING OUTCOMES 2

Summarize the differences between police departments and other types of organizations, and describe both traditional and contemporary approaches to organization.

Law enforcement organizations differ from other organizations in several respects, but there are two *key* differences: Law enforcement organizations have line and staff personnel, and most follow a quasi-military command structure. The quasi-military organizational model is not without its faults, which led to the emergence in police agencies of modern organizational theories and designs (for example, contingency theories).

1. How do police organizations differ from other types of organizations?

2. What does it mean to say that law enforcement organizations follow a quasi-military model?

3. What are the benefits as well as the disadvantages of a quasi-military model of organization for law enforcement agencies?

organization A group in which individuals work together to accomplish specified tasks or goals.

nonsworn personnel Support staff members of a law enforcement agency who are not empowered to make arrests.

sworn personnel Members of a law enforcement agency who are empowered to make arrests.

chain of command The supervisory channel within a law enforcement organization.

span of control The number of subordinates supervised by one person.

quasi-military An organizational structure that follows the military model to some extent, but with subtle differences.

Frederick W. Taylor (1856–1915) A classical organizational theorist who posited that worker productivity could be increased through careful attention to how work was allocated and who performed what functions.

Max Weber (1864–1920) A classical organizational theorist, widely acknowledged as the father of bureaucracy, who identified five principles that he suggested are characteristic of an effective bureaucratic organization.

bureaucracy The administrative structure of a large or complex organization, typically employing task-specialized bureaus or departments.

participatory management A form of leadership that allows subordinates to participate in decision making and planning, especially with regard to the manner in which their own units are operated.

quality circle A group of qualified employees from all ranks who work together, often around one table, to solve organizational problems.

contingency theory A management theory that recognizes that there are often different types of tasks within a single organization, including repetitive tasks that call for standardization and control and nonrepetitive tasks that call for flexibility and participatory management.

systems perspective A view of organizational style, rooted in biology, that posits that organizations are living organisms that strive for a state of equilibrium, or balance, and that affect or are affected by their environment.

LEARNING OUTCOMES 3

Summarize the trends and issues associated with private policing.

Private police officers outnumber sworn public police officers by roughly three to one. Private police are hired to serve a client's interests, and thus their priorities differ from those of public police. The most significant controversy in private policing is whether private police can be regarded as governmental actors for purposes of the law. The integration of private and public policing resources continues to be an ongoing challenge for public safety managers everywhere.

1. What is the relationship between public police departments and private security agencies?

2. How can public police departments and private security agencies benefit one another?

private security The industry that provides for-profit security products and services, which include three broad categories: the provision of guards, equipment, and investigative or consulting services.[54]

private policing The acquisition and use of security products and services, as well as the application of specialized knowledge in areas like crime control, investigation, and risk management, by nonsworn personnel.[55]

Additional Links

This is the home page for the Department of Homeland Security: **www.dhs.gov**. The website features links to research, prevention and protection information, travel and security procedures, and other related information. Headlines on the home page also offer the most up-to-date information available.

This is the home page for the United States Department of Justice (DOJ): **www.justice.gov**. The website features links to jobs available within the DOJ and an index list of duties performed within the DOJ. Also, headlines on the home page offer the most up-do-date information on current affairs issues.

This website features links to the FBI's "Most Wanted" list, information about crime statistics, and the types of crime that the FBI investigates: **www.fbi.gov**. There is also contact information and a "kids page" available for student use.

This is the home page for the ATF: **www.atf.gov**. It offers comprehensive information on the latest news from its field divisions, as well as a "Most Wanted" list and "kids page" similar to that of the FBI. Students can find links to in depth descriptions of the ATF duties, job opportunities, contact information, and laboratories.

This is the home page for the DEA: **www.justice.gov/dea**. There are links to information about careers within the DEA, drug type information, headlines, and to the DOJ itself.

This website is a useful tool for students looking to get into the law enforcement job market: **http://officer.com/links/Agency_Search**. Within the website, there is an index of federal, state, and local level agencies and the positions currently available. Students can search for any agency listed.

This website provides an encyclopedia of information on the management and organization of police: **http://law.jrank.org/pages/1675/Police-Organization-Management.html**. This information is indexed by topics within the subject and also provides links for various relevant keywords.

This link provides students with a PDF version of an article written for the National Institute of Justice: **http://justicestudies.com//issues.pdf**. The author examines organization and management styles and suggests helpful information for implementing new techniques within police agencies.

A law enforcement agency directory is available through Officer.com: **http://officer.com/links/Agency_Search**.

The influence of police supervisory styles on patrol officer behavior is a topic for discussion in this publication: **www.justicestudies.com/pubs/supervisorystyles.pdf**.

Becoming a Cop

"Becoming a police officer involves much more than just taking an exam and spending a few weeks in the police academy."

1 Outline the hiring process including testing, interviewing, and various screening procedures.

2 Summarize the issues faced by female and minority police officers.

3 Summarize the nature and causes of stress in policing.

4

POLICING OVER THE LIFE COURSE

In December, 2009, the National Institute of Justice released a narrated Web-based slide show presentation entitled "From the Academy to Reitrement: A Journey Through the Policing Lifecycle." The show was produced by the National Police Research Platform with funding from the National Institute of Justice's Office of Justice Programs. The presentation focused on the life course of new police officers. Begininning with slide 13, the section focusing on new recruits asks questions such as (1) "What happens in the developmental life course of a police officer?" and (2) "What determines an officer's job satisfaction and longevity?"

The presentation, which employs a number of theoretical frameworks—including life course and organizational theories—and is narrated by Kutztown University (Pennsylvania) Professor Gary Cordner, is well worth watching for students of American policing. It runs for more than 77 minutes, and can be accessed on the Web at www.nij.gov/multimedia/presenter/presenter-rosenbaum.

This chapter is about becoming a cop. We begin by taking a critical look at the hiring process. Then we move on to the academy experience and describe field training following graduation. This chapter also looks at the important issues of diversity and discrimination in law enforcement. The demographics of the typical police agency have changed in recent years, as more women and minorities are on the job than ever before. We consider the implications of this trend.

DISCUSS Why would someone want to be a police officer? Would you?

Most people are drawn to policing out of a desire to help people and catch bad guys. But policing, like any career, can have its downside. This chapter also examines issues that sometimes surprise uninformed applicants: stress, fatigue, and the prospect for sexual harassment in the workplace.

▶ Hiring and Training

Becoming a police officer involves much more than just taking an exam and spending a few weeks in the police academy. For many, it is a lifelong pursuit. First, of course, candidates need to apply for police work and be hired. In addition to test scores, the applicant's interview performance, character, and medical and drug history all factor into the hiring decision. Hiring is only the first step, however. Academy training comes next, followed by field training. The performance of police officers is measured throughout their careers. Those officers who hope for promotion must demonstrate, through their job performance, that they have the ability and qualifications to take on greater responsibilities.

Law enforcement is generally regarded as a **civil service** job. Civil service is a system in which employees are hired, retained, advanced, disciplined, and discharged on the basis of merit, or their abilities and qualifications. Civil service is in contrast to the **patronage system** of old. You may recall from Chapter 1 that during the political era, police hiring decisions were based more on an individual's political support for whomever was in charge than on the applicant's individual qualifications.

Civil service was implemented to enhance police professionalism. Many states, local governments, and even the federal government have **civil service commissions** that ensure that employees in civil service positions receive specific protections such as job security and equal pay for equivalent work. Knowing that policing is a civil service job provides an appreciation for the intricacies and nuances of the hiring process; because people who become police officers tend to stay in their positions for a long time, considerable attention must be given to hiring the right people.

The Hiring Decision

Whether a person will be hired as a police officer depends on a number of conditions. Generally, candidates are evaluated on the basis of their test score, interview performance, personal background, performance on a polygraph exam, medical history, and past drug use. The problem, as police specialist Ken Peak has observed, is that agencies are often made to feel as though they have to find people who can "walk on water."[1] Early police reformer August Vollmer once said that candidates for the position of police officer should

> have the wisdom of Solomon, the courage of David, the patience of Job and leadership of Moses, the kindness of the Good Samaritan, the diplomacy of Lincoln, the tolerance of the Carpenter of Nazareth, and, finally, an intimate knowledge of every branch of natural, biological, and social sciences.[2]

Suffice it to say, that's a tall order!

For many, policing is a lifelong pursuit.

 LEARNING OUTCOMES 1 Outline the hiring process including testing, interviewing, and various screening procedures.

GLOSSARY

civil service A system in which employees are hired, retained, advanced, disciplined, and discharged on the basis of merit (that is, their abilities and qualifications).

patronage system A system of hiring in which decisions are based more on an individual's political support for an office-holder than on his or her abilities and qualifications. Patronage was common in police agencies during the political era.

civil service commission A federal, state, or local agency charged with ensuring that employees in civil service positions receive specific protections.

Recruitment

Jobs in policing can be quite competitive, depending on the position and the timing. For positions regarded as prestigious, such as those with the federal government, getting a job can be quite difficult. Timing can be important. One applicant for the Seattle Police Department during the early 1990s took the exam with roughly a thousand other people in a lecture hall at the University of Washington, but the department had a mandate to hire only about a dozen officers.

Fortunately for those looking for police work, such stories are now the exception. In fact, police departments around the country are increasingly having to come to grips with a somewhat shallow hiring pool.[3] Recently, the National Association

50% The Los Angeles Police Department saw a 50 percent reduction in applications over the course of three years.

of Police Organizations put recruitment at the top of a list of problems facing police departments today.[4]

The hiring crisis in law enforcement is not to be taken lightly. The Los Angeles Police Department saw a 50 percent reduction in applications over the course of three years.[5] The Chicago Police Department had 25,000 applicants in 1993 and only 1,900 in 2000.[6] Why the sudden decline?

There are many reasons for today's lack of qualified applicants. One has been the war in the Middle East, which has drained young men and women from the U.S. civilian workforce. Another explanation has been the relative strength of the economy; police departments have a hard time competing with higher-paying private-sector jobs. An increasing (though relatively small) number of agencies are also requiring that their applicants have at least a few college credits, if not an actual degree. This further restricts the pool of eligible applicants. Unfavorable press coverage of scandals and corruption can further discourage people from applying.

In response, agencies are going to great pains to offer attractive schedules, benefits, and job perks and are aggressively recruiting applicants. Larger departments have officers who do nothing but travel around the country to recruit. Others have conducted studies to determine how best to attract applicants.

Testing Requirements

An applicant usually takes two tests to become an officer: a written test and a physical agility test. To ensure that their tests are valid (that is, able to measure what they intend to measure) and reliable (the results don't vary markedly from one test to the next), most agencies use exams prepared by companies that specialize in creating exams for various occupations. One of those companies.

Some departments also use the written exam as an opportunity to determine an applicant's personality type. Personality tests are also routinely used in the hiring process. They consist of numerous, sometimes odd and repetitive, questions that result in scores that agencies can then use to weed out the psychologically unfit.[7]

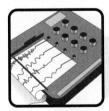

Recruitment

Position announcements placed in newspapers, career websites, college campuses, and civil service or municipal government websites

Testing Requirements

Written examination to gauge intelligence (as well as reading and writing abilities) and physical agility test to determine if the applicant is physically fit to perform the duties of a police officer

The Interview

About 90% of police departments conduct an oral interview of candidates who successfully met or exceeded the department's predetermined testing requirements.

Background Investigation

Sometimes called a *character investigation*, in which an investigator will peer into all conceivable elements of the applicant's life

Polygraph Exam

About two-thirds of America's law enforcement agencies rely on polygraph exams as part of the employment screening process to encourage honesty during questioning.

Medical and Drug Screening

Besides detecting past or current drug use, screening also assesses medical fitness to perform the job.

FIGURE 4.1 The Police Hiring Process.

As for physical testing, every applicant must meet certain criteria. Physical agility tests vary widely from agency to agency. Some focus specifically on the candidates' ability to perform the job. State trooper applicants in Washington, for example, are required to lift a tire onto the mock hub of an automobile—among other tasks. Other departments ensure that their applicants can perform a certain number of push-ups and sit-ups and run a specified distance within a limited time period. The challenge for those involved in hiring police officers is to ensure that any exam is truly job-related. In fact, tests *have* to be job-related to avoid discrimination complaints. Some agencies therefore survey their officers to determine what physical work they engage in regularly, and then they tailor the physical agility exams to meet those tasks.[8]

The Interview

The vast majority of candidates are screened out during the written and physical testing phase, leaving relatively few labor-intensive, time-consuming interviews. Oral interviews are often conducted by a board of officials, including active police officers from the jurisdiction and some civilians. Psychologists or psychiatrists might serve on such boards or might conduct separate interviews. To save time and resources, it is in the interest of hiring authorities to do as much screening as possible before the interviewing phase.

A candidate can get a stellar score on a test and yet be a lousy police officer. Consequently, oral interviews are intended to pick up where the written and agility tests leave off. They gauge factors like confidence, poise, reasoning abilities, oral skills, memory, and observational prowess. Candidates are often asked questions about what they would do in a specific situation. These questions can sometimes be difficult because candidates who have no background in law enforcement may be unsure of how to respond.

To assess observational skills, some elements of the interview may be staged (for example, there may be a phrase written on a board in the interview room). Candidates may be asked later to recall certain features of the room. Officers on patrol need to be observant; hence, this interview component might be especially useful in hiring officers seeking to work patrol.

Background Investigations

By far, the most expensive and time-consuming phase of the hiring process is the background investigation. The investigator will draw on official records and will conduct in-depth interviews with friends, family members, coworkers, acquaintances, and even former acquaintances. In short, the background investigation is intended to discover those skeletons, if any, in the applicant's closet that are not revealed during other phases of the hiring process.

Polygraph Exam

Polygraphs are used to encourage honesty during questioning. The examiner begins by asking a number of reference questions, such as, "Is your name John Smith?" Then questioning about prior criminal history, drug use, and the like begins. Polygraphs are not without their faults. Evidence from polygraph exams is not allowed in court to prove guilt, for instance. On the other hand, polygraphists feel that their devices are very difficult to fool.[9] Polygraph exams continue to be used in many police hiring decisions because many law enforcement officials believe in the polygraph's usefulness.

Medical and Drug Screening

One of the last steps in the hiring process is medical and drug screening. Although polygraphs and background checks can indicate past drug use, formal drug screening provides results that are difficult to dispute. Besides detecting past or current drug use, screening also assesses medical fitness to perform the job. A person with a serious heart condition, for instance, probably wouldn't be a good fit in any police agency, considering that officers have to physically exert themselves from time to time.

plebe system A police academy model that closely parallels a military-style boot camp and that aims to produce well-groomed and disciplined officers.

technical training model A police academy training model that emphasizes the technical aspects of police work and provides little or no training in such nontechnical areas as stress management, interaction with difficult people, problem solving, and sensitivity to marginalized groups.

college system A police academy training model intended to enhance the professional aspects of police training curricula by exposing trainees to problem solving, sensitivity to marginalized groups, and other valuable topics in addition to required technical knowledge.

sixth sense A healthy sense of suspicion; the experience-based ability to intuit when something is amiss.

field training officer (FTO) A veteran police officer tasked with providing on-the-job training and performance critique during a rookie police officer's initial assignment following graduation from the academy.

police training officer (PTO) program A police training method that focuses on developing an officer's learning capacity, leadership, and problem-solving skills.

Medical screening is also used to check applicants' vision and weight, among other factors. Most agencies will not hire candidates who fail to meet some uncorrected vision requirement. Likewise, many agencies will not hire overweight people. This may seem discriminatory on one level, but there are certain bona fide job requirements that an obese or legally blind individual cannot perform.

The Academy

Once a candidate successfully passes through all of the steps involved in the hiring process and is offered employment, he or she will go to an academy for training. The teaching methods and curricula of academies differ depending on the student's anticipated future position and the hiring agency. A common thread runs through all police academies, however: They all strive to teach candidates how to be effective officers and how to develop the all-important "sixth sense" needed for successful police work. Students must "pass" through the academy without incident, or they will be terminated.

Types of Academies

Academy training is regarded as one of the most important elements of the police hiring process. In this era of heightened civil liability, it is critical that recruits learn the limits of the law as it applies to police work. In addition, they need to learn proper procedures, including how and when to use force, how to drive a vehicle aggressively, how to make felony stops, how to deal with belligerent suspects, how to make arrests, how to document incidents, and how to investigate accidents. Needless to say, adequate coverage of these and other pertinent topics takes a great deal of time. The typical academy, in fact, trains recruits for approximately 400 hours.[10]

There are generally three types of academies: in-house, regional, and state. Candidates for the position of trooper with the Washington State Patrol, for instance, are trained at the agency's academy in Shelton, Washington. In California, the Commission on Peace Officer Standards and Training (POST) certifies city, county, and regional academies throughout the state. More than 600 agencies in California voluntarily participate in POST. There are nearly 40 different academies certified by POST, for all different types of agencies. In other states, Florida for example, police academies are often run through community colleges and other institutions of higher learning.

In a growing trend, civilians are paying their own way through police academies in the hopes of gaining employment as an officer after completing the program.[11] This saves agencies not only the expense of paying for academy training, but also the salaries that the newly hired trainees would be earning while going through their training. Some states, like New York, follow a hybrid model, allowing interested applicants to complete basic training requirements before seeking employment; once they are sworn officers, they complete additional training.[12]

Curricular Issues

Police training academies vary in terms of their curricula, but most are similar in the sense that they teach recruits the technical aspects of police work. A range of topics is usually covered,

including the criminal justice system, law, patrol, investigation procedures, job proficiency (for example, using a firearm), administration, and problems likely to be encountered on the job.[13] More recently, topics like diversity, sexual harassment, dispute resolution, victim awareness, technological applications, stress management, and courtroom demeanor have made their way into academies, as well. What we have seen is something of a move away from the traditional **plebe system**, an academy model that closely parallels a military-style boot camp and that aims to produce well-groomed and disciplined officers, to a model that stresses twenty-first-century problems.[14]

Modern police academy curricula have also moved somewhat beyond the **technical training model**[15] insofar as they expose trainees more to the less familiar dimensions of their jobs, such as managing stress, interacting with difficult people, and so on. The **college system** of training is gaining in popularity today.[16] This doesn't mean that the academy is run by a college. Rather, the academy's intent is to train budding officers to be professionals. To this end, besides gaining the needed technical knowledge, trainees learn problem solving, sensitivity to marginalized groups, and other valuable skills.

Research reveals that the college system approach to police academy training is still largely the exception rather than the rule. One study revealed that less than 3 percent of basic academy training is spent on topics other than the technical aspects of the job.[17] This concern is particularly serious in light of the recent movement toward community-oriented policing, which prides itself on relationship building, communication, and problem solving.

An overview of one of the nation's cutting-edge police academy curricula, that of the Los Angeles Police Department (LAPD), can be seen in Figure 4.2. Note that the LAPD's officers receive more than 800 hours of academy training.

Learning the Sixth Sense

Academy training also teaches recruits the so-called **sixth sense**, namely a heightened sense of suspicion. As Peak has observed, "A suspicious nature is as important to the street officer as a fine touch is to a surgeon. The officer should not only be able to visually recognize but also be able to physically sense when something is wrong or out of the ordinary."[18] Understood differently, teaching officers to be suspicious is like teaching them to be observant. They are taught how to develop knowledge of the area they work in, the people they come into contact with, and the ordinary conditions of the area. With that knowledge, they can more capably identify things that are amiss. A person who doesn't "belong" in a certain area, for instance, may be cause for suspicion.

There is a fine line between being an effective, inquisitive officer and being too suspicious. Too much suspicion can have a number of unfortunate consequences. For example, an officer who is overly suspicious of people who fit a certain profile or

A suspicious nature is as important to the street officer as a fine touch is to a surgeon.

Academics

- Arrest and booking procedures
- Preliminary investigation techniques
- Radio and communications
- Report writing
- Traffic investigation
- Traffic enforcement

Human Relations

- Cultural sensitivity training
- Sexual harassment issues
- Media relations
- Stress management
- Disability awareness
- Community relations
- Tactical communications
- Hate crimes
- Missing persons
- Domestic violence

Law

- Search and seizure
- Evidence
- Laws of arrest
- Crimes against persons and property
- Sex crimes
- Crimes against children
- Other general criminal statutes falling under the California Penal Code, Los Angeles Municipal Code, Welfare and Institutions Code, and Federal Laws

Tactics

- Patrol techniques and procedures
- Crimes in progress
- Building searches
- Vehicle stops
- Use of deadly force
- Shooting policy

Driving

Emergency Vehicle Operations Course covers
- Defensive driving
- Pursuit policy
- Safe vehicle handling

Firearms Training

- Weapon care and safety
- Marksmanship
- Tactical manipulation with the sidearm and shotgun
- Chemical agents handling
(Police candidates are strongly discouraged from seeking firearms instruction prior to entering the Police Academy. Poor marksmanship habits may be developed that are difficult or impossible to overcome.)

Physical Training

- Builds strength and endurance through physical conditioning while promoting a positive attitude toward a fitness lifestyle
- Also teaches physical arrest techniques, controls, and weaponless defense

LAPD Specific Training

- Advanced tactical training
- Mobile field force tactics
- Patrol ride-along
- Mobile digital computer (in-car computer) training
- Alcohol abuse
- Administration of discipline
- Cultural diversity
- K-9 operations
- Air support operations
- Bomb squad
- Community policing and problem solving
- Spanish language
- Civil liabilities
- Sexual harassment training

FIGURE 4.2 **The Los Angeles Police Department Academy Curriculum.**
Source: Los Angeles Police Department, "Academy training," www.joinlapd.com/academy.html (accessed December 7, 2010).

social or demographic category runs the risk of infringing on people's constitutional rights. Profiling is an important topic in modern law enforcement and, according to its critics, something to be avoided at all costs. At the same time, though, there is a clear need for healthy suspicion; even the most apparently innocuous traffic stop could turn into a violent encounter in a matter of seconds. New officers need to be prepared.

Field Training and Development

Field training is not unique to policing. It is just like the on-the-job training that comes with learning any other occupation. The first formal police field training program was implemented in San Jose, California, in the late 1960s.[19] Since then, field training programs have evolved and moved in various directions. Most, however, assign a field training officer (a veteran officer) to a recent academy graduate. But as Bob Dylan so eloquently put it, "The times, they are a-changin'." The traditional field training officer program is quickly being replaced by a new model: the police training officer model.

The Field Training Officer Approach

The traditional approach to field training typically consists of three distinct phases:[20] (1) introduction, in which the new officer learns agency policies and rules; (2) training and evaluation, in which the recruit spends the most time learning the complicated tasks police officers perform regularly; and (3) the final portion, involving first-hand observation of the new officer's actions by the **field training officer (FTO)**. The duration of FTO programs varies, but the programs typically range from 1 to 12 weeks.[21] A probationary period extending beyond that allows additional interactions between FTOs and trainees.

Toward a Police Training Officer Approach

In 1999, the Office for Community Oriented Policing Services (COPS) provided a $300,000 grant to the Reno (Nevada) Police Department to collaborate with the Police Executive Research Forum to study police training and to develop a new field training model. The collaboration produced the so-called **police training officer (PTO) program**. According to the authors of a recent report on the PTO program, "This approach is very different from traditional police training methods that emphasize mechanical repetition skills and rote memory capabilities; rather, the focus is on developing an officer's learning capacity, leadership, and problem-solving skills."[22]

The PTO model is built around John Dewey's philosophy of learning,[23] namely that there is much more to learning than can be gleaned from a lecture. The model incorporates such concepts as Malcolm Knowles's principles of self-directed learning,[24] Howard Barrows's idea of problem-based learning,[25] and Benjamin Bloom's concern with intellectual outcomes of learning.[26] The PTO model emphasizes the following:

1. Knowledge: Remembering or recalling previously learned material

2. Comprehension: Understanding meaning well enough to be able to explain and restate ideas

3. Application: Applying learned material in new and different situations

4. Analysis: Categorizing material into segments and demonstrating their relationships

5. Synthesis: Grouping or combining separate ideas to form a new whole and to establish new relationships

6. Evaluation: Assessing the material for appropriate outcomes based on established criteria[27]

This approach may not seem that dissimilar to the traditional FTO model, but its main difference lies in the manner through which material is taught and knowledge is evaluated. Problem-based learning exercises are used throughout the process. In each phase, the recruit is tasked with a structured problem. Trainees will also develop a neighborhood portfolio, which is a detailed overview of the beat in which they work. Finally, throughout the process, trainees must demonstrate competence in a number of areas, not all of which are unique to police work. Examples include problem solving, leadership, community problems, cultural diversity, ethics, safety, and report writing. The PTO model is being developed in jurisdictions across the United States and in Canada. The new model has even given rise to the Police Society for Problem Based Learning.[28]

▶ *Diversity and Discrimination*

Diversity and discrimination both have important implications for human resources. They are of great importance to administrators in terms of how they staff their agencies, and they are important to officers in lower ranks, too. New recruits, as we have just seen, are trained extensively in these areas so that they understand the importance of diversity and the avoidance of discrimination. Things were not always this way, however. It was not until the civil rights movement of the 1960s that diversity and discrimination were brought to the attention of politicians and the public.

Equal Employment Opportunity

The notion of **equal employment opportunity** has a plain meaning: Everyone should receive an equal chance at employment. The goal of equal employment opportunity did not just emerge on its own; it was legislatively mandated. Title VII of the Civil Rights Act of 1964 provides the legal basis for fair employment practices as we know them today. Section 703A of the act, for example, makes it unlawful for any employer to fail to hire, refuse to hire, discharge, or otherwise discriminate in any other manner against any individual with respect to employment compensation, terms, conditions, or privileges because of race, color, religion, sex, age, pregnancy, or national origin, among other factors.

In 1972, Title VII was revised to create the **Equal Employment Opportunity Commission (EEOC)**. The EEOC was given authority to "intervene on behalf of affected individuals" and to "file suit against businesses or governmental entities in cases of discrimination." What this means is that individuals no longer need to shoulder the burden of proving a discrimination claim; they can turn to the federal government for help.

The EEOC can also intervene in cases of alleged sexual harassment. According to Title VII, in fact, sexual harassment is a form of sex discrimination, not unlike denying employment to female candidates in favor of male candidates. Finally, the EEOC can also step in to investigate cases of employer

LEARNING OUTCOMES 2 Summarize the issues faced by female and minority police officers.

GLOSSARY

equal employment opportunity Fair employment practices mandated by Title VII of the Civil Rights Act of 1964.

Equal Employment Opportunity Commission (EEOC) The federal agency that is empowered by Title VII of the Civil Rights Act of 1964 to "intervene on behalf of affected individuals," to "file suit against businesses or governmental entities in cases of discrimination," to intervene in cases of alleged sexual harassment, and to investigate cases of employer retaliation.[29]

affirmative action The practice of taking proactive steps to boost the presence of historically marginalized groups (typically minorities and women) in the ranks of an organization by giving preference to members of those groups.

double marginality A situation in which black officers treat black suspects harshly to gain the respect of their white counterparts and to avoid giving the impression that they are biased toward members of their own race.

Americans with Disabilities Act (ADA) U.S. legislation passed in 1990 that forbids discrimination against the disabled.

racial quota A requirement for hiring and promoting a specified number of minorities.

reverse discrimination Discrimination against nonminorities that occurs when the hiring and promotion of minorities are based more on race than on any other criterion.

The EEOC	Makes it unlawful for a police department to discriminate against any individual with respect to employment because of race, color, religion, sex, age, pregnancy, or national origin
Affirmative Action	Plays a significant role in police hiring in America's 50 largest cities
Reverse Discrimination	Some police departments are now facing reverse discrimination lawsuits
Americans with Disabilities Act	Prohibits discrimination against applicants for any position if the applicant is able to perform the essential functions of the job

FIGURE 4.3 Diversity and Discrimination in Policing.

retaliation: "An employer may not fire, demote, harass or otherwise 'retaliate' against an individual for filing a charge of discrimination, participating in a discrimination proceeding, or otherwise opposing discrimination."[30]

The push for equal employment opportunity has had interesting implications for the law enforcement profession. Policing remains, by and large, a white male-dominated occupation, but women and minorities have started to make significant inroads in terms of achieving parity in the ranks with their white male counterparts. The law enforcement profession is also in the strange position of requiring a certain physical condition for job candidates while not being allowed to discriminate based on disability.

Why is diversity essential in the police ranks? In general, it is felt that a diverse organization will be more capable of effectively addressing community needs. It is also felt that a diverse police force will be regarded more favorably by citizens, especially those in minority-dominated neighborhoods. The research supports some of these claims, but only to a modest extent. For example, researchers in Detroit found that African-American citizens had more support for black than white officers.[31] Research has also revealed that New York residents had higher regard for the police department after coming into greater contact with female police officers.[32] In contrast, a study from Washington, DC, revealed little benefit resulted from assigning same-race officers to neighborhoods.[33]

Affirmative Action

Closely associated with equal employment opportunity is the practice of **affirmative action**. This is the practice of taking proactive steps to boost the presence of historically marginalized groups (typically minorities and women) in the ranks of

The notion of equal employment opportunity has a plain meaning: Everyone should receive an equal chance at employment.

an organization by giving preference to members of those groups. It is easy to see how affirmative action can further the goals of providing equal employment opportunity, but it is not part of Title VII.

There have been many court cases addressing the constitutionality of affirmative action programs. In the policing context, one researcher found that affirmative action plans played a significant role in police hiring in America's 50 largest cities.[34] It is noteworthy, however, that 23 of the affirmative action plans in these 50 cities were court mandated, not voluntary.

Minorities in Policing

It would be inaccurate to suggest that policing was exclusively a white male occupation before the 1960s. There were black police officers in Washington, DC, as early as 1861,[35] for example, but by 1940 black officers represented less than 1 percent of the nation's police forces.[36] The African-Americans who did obtain work as police officers often faced discrimination on the job. For example, a study from 1959, right before the dawn of the civil rights era, revealed that several southern cities required black officers to call on white officers when they needed to arrest a white suspect.[37] Some black officers were only allowed to drive cars marked "Colored Police" and could only arrest black suspects.[38] Additionally, job assignments for black officers were not particularly desirable, dismissals were often arbitrary, there was little integration within the ranks,[39] and promotions were few and far between. For example, a study revealed that during the 1960s, only 22 police departments had promoted black officers beyond patrol positions.[40] Times have since changed, of course. Studies now show little connection between race and promotion or disciplinary decisions.[41]

While there is little direct evidence that being a minority makes one a better cop, that claim was made during the 1960s. In the wake of various race riots during that decade, the President's Commission on Law Enforcement and Administration of Justice observed the following:

> Police officers have testified to the special competence of Negro officers in Negro neighborhoods. The reasons given include: they get along better and receive more respect from Negro residents; they receive less trouble; ... they can get more information; and they understand Negro citizens better.[42]

Similarly, some studies have revealed that black residents wanted to see more black officers patrolling the streets because they believed that understanding would improve and that abuses would decrease.[43] On the other hand, some early studies showed that black officers either felt a need to be more forceful with black suspects[44] or were actively challenged by suspects of their own race.[45] One influential author even coined the term **double marginality** to refer to a situation in which black officers treat black suspects harshly to gain the respect of their white counterparts and to avoid giving the impression that they are biased toward members of their own race.[46]

Women in Policing

Women have faced much the same fate as minorities in terms of seeking law enforcement jobs. They remain significantly underrepresented in police departments to this day. Some researchers have attributed this situation to the idea that policing requires aggression, physical exertion, and "stable" emotions—supposedly masculine traits.[47] In contrast, traits often associated with women, such as compassion, empathy, and nurturing, may not find much of a home in the law enforcement world.[48] Obviously, there are exceptions to these generalities.

Historically speaking, police departments didn't start to hire women until the early twentieth century. Lola Baldwin was the first woman to hold police powers. Hired in 1905 by Portland, Oregon, Baldwin was mostly engaged in social-work-like functions. Other police departments followed Portland's example: "Once the police began to think in terms of preventing juvenile delinquency, they responded to the traditional argument that women had a special capacity for child care."[49]

Alice Stebbins-Wells was hired by the Los Angeles Police Department in 1910. Even though her job also resembled social work, she led a movement for more female hiring, and by 1925, more than 200 cities had women working in police positions and even in jails.[50] In the ensuing years, women made some progress, but not much. By the mid-1960s, there were only around 1,700 female police officers in America's largest cities,[51] and most female officers were excluded from patrol duties.

It was not until 1968 that the first women were assigned to patrol work.[52] Indianapolis was the first city to put women on patrol, but other large cities like New York; Philadelphia; Miami; Washington, DC; and St. Louis quickly followed suit. By the end of the 1970s, nearly 90 percent of large police agencies employed female patrol officers.[53] That growth has continued at an impressive pace. Nearly all cities of more than 50,000 now have women working in the police ranks.[54] The growth is partially attributed to the fact that female and male officers perform similarly, as evidenced by some early studies on the subject.[55]

More recently, the same reasons that were once used to exclude women from the ranks of police agencies are now being used to recruit women in larger numbers. A study of patrol in New York City, for example, revealed that women are less likely than men to use firearms, to get into violent confrontations, and to become injured.[56] Some say that this means female officers are actually more emotionally stable than male officers, disavowing one of the earlier arguments that was used to keep them out of police positions.[57] A reason male and female police officers appear to perform similarly may not be so much that both sexes are equally competent, but that policing may attract a certain group of women, by either self-selection, department screening, or the recruit socialization process.[58]

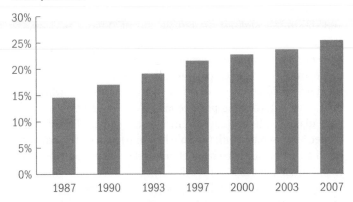

Percentage of full-time sworn personnel

Note: Includes blacks or African-Americans, Hispanics or Latinos, Asians, Native Hawaiians or other Pacific Islanders, Native Americans, Alaska Natives, and persons identifying two or more races.

FIGURE 4.4 Minority Officers in Local Police Departments.
Source: http://bjs.ojp.usdoj.gov/index.cfm?ty=pbdetail&iid=1750

Diversity in the Ranks Today

So far, we have addressed only female and African-American police officers. Other minority groups have made advances, as well. This can be seen clearly in Figure 4.4. Between 1987 and 2007 (the most recent year for which data are available), minorities increased their presence in the ranks of America's police departments. Women, as the accompanying "Think about It" box shows, have not made considerable advances in recent years. For example, in 2003, 11.3 percent of police officers were female. This number increased only to 11.9 percent by 2007.[59]

Disabled Cops

In 1990, Congress passed the **Americans with Disabilities Act (ADA)**, which forbids discrimination against the disabled. How does this apply to policing? It doesn't necessarily mean that disabled individuals can become police officers. Rather, the ADA prohibits discrimination against applicants for any position if the applicant is able to perform the essential functions of the job.

The ADA is part of the reason why medical screening occurs during the final phase of the hiring process; it prevents applicants from being rejected early on because of physical disabilities. Moreover, the ADA has required police departments (and other organizations) to develop sophisticated selection

Think About It...

Equal Employment Opportunity for Women Nearly 9 out of 10 police officers are male. Several explanations have been offered for the relatively low percentage of female police officers. One is that police departments continue to discriminate against women. Another is that not many women are drawn to a career in law enforcement because of its male-dominated culture. Yet another, perhaps more sensible explanation, is that many female candidates do not perform as well as men at certain stages of the hiring process (for example, in physical tests of upper-body strength). *Do you think women have equal employment opportunities in the police field? If not, what can be done to improve equality?*

Source: Darrin Klimek/Thinkstock

procedures that mirror the job to the fullest extent possible. Selection cannot be a haphazard process.

The term *disabled* may conjure up images of wheelchairs and significant physical limitations, but disabilities can sometimes be less visible. For example, the ADA protects people with human immunodeficiency virus (HIV); a positive test is not an outright bar to employment.[60] Indeed, a sheriff's department was ordered to pay damages to a reserve officer who was discharged after testing positive for HIV.[61] The ADA also protects diabetics. In one case, an insulin-dependent diabetic was denied employment with the Toledo (Ohio) Police Department, but the court held that a blanket policy denying employment to such individuals violates the ADA.[62]

Departments have a little more leeway, though, with serious physical disabilities. For example, a court sided with a department that put an officer on disability leave after he lost his arm in a motorcycle accident.[63] The court concluded that the department was justified in its decision because the officer could no longer perform one of the key functions of the job: making an arrest.

Reverse Discrimination: A Backlash?

The push for diversity in policing, like the push for diversity in other organizations, has sometimes gone too far. **Racial quotas**, for instance, are requirements for hiring and promoting a specified number of minorities. When minorities are hired and promoted based more on race than on any other criterion, allegations of **reverse discrimination** emerge—usually from white male officers. Reverse discrimination has also been described as entailing a "white backlash."

Reverse discrimination appears to be more than a distant concern for white officers. A study from the late 1970s revealed that white officers felt that affirmative action was a threat to their careers.[64] Twenty years later, another study found marked resentment and bitterness on the part of white officers toward several of their black supervisors.[65] Reverse discrimination appears to be a real phenomenon. During the 1970s, for example, the Detroit Police Department adopted a policy that provided for the promotion to sergeant of one black officer for every white officer. While a court struck the policy down,[66] the U.S. Supreme Court later sanctioned temporary racial quotas in police hiring.[67]

Even in the face of conflicting court decisions, claims of reverse discrimination continue. Organizations like Adversity.net have emerged to shed light on egregious abuses of racial preference and quotas. In fact, the organization recently highlighted the case of a former Dayton (Ohio) Police Department major, a white woman, who was bypassed for promotion to chief in favor of a black man. In a surprising turn of events, she was then fired so more black officers could be promoted (the department, to this day, is overwhelmingly white). The city eventually agreed to a settlement of more than $1 million.[68]

The Dayton case came on the heels of another from Milwaukee, Wisconsin, in which a jury awarded $2.2 million to 17 white police officers who, the jury felt, had been systematically bypassed for promotion in favor of minority officers.[69] Twenty of forty-one officers promoted to lieutenant were black, when the pool of applicants was more than 80 percent white.

▶ *Realities of the Job*

Once a police officer begins working, he or she is almost instantly confronted with several important "realities" of the job that may not have been made clear early on. First, police work is a stressful occupation. Stress can take its toll over the course of an officer's career. Second, fatigue is a common problem in policing, though it has historically taken a backseat to stress. Only recently have researchers started to focus their attention on the problems that can result when officers are spread too thin and forced to work long hours. Finally, as unfortunate as it sounds, sexual harassment exists in police departments just as it does in other organizations. This can be particularly difficult for female officers.

LEARNING OUTCOMES 3 Summarize the nature and causes of stress in policing.

Stress

Stress is a fact of life in many occupations, but policing has its own unique brand of stress. The nature of the job, particularly the potential for violence at any turn, takes its toll on even the most emotionally hardened officer. This toll might be manifested in the form of health-related problems,[72] family breakdown,[73] and alcoholism, to name just a few.

Nature and Symptoms of Stress

Stress has been broadly defined as anything that places an adjustive demand on the organism.[74] In other words, stressful situations require some behavioral response, and that response is usually one intended to reduce the stress being experienced. Some people thrive on what others might consider stressful situations, and stress can have both negative and positive elements. Positive stress has been called **eustress**, and negative stress has been called **distress**.[75]

Eustress is a positive form of stress that does not threaten or harm the individual but is pleasurable, challenging, or exciting. For example, the stress created by beginning a new job or a challenging assignment could qualify as eustress. The new police officer experiences eustress when going on patrol for the first time. Experienced officers

GLOSSARY

stress Anything that places a positive or negative adjustive demand on an organism.

eustress A positive form of stress that does not threaten or harm the individual but is pleasurable, challenging, or exciting.

distress A harmful form of stress that can threaten an individual's functioning or overload his or her capacity to cope with environmental stimuli.

burnout The progressive loss of idealism, energy, purpose, and concern that results from the conditions of work.

critical incident An emergency situation that evokes immediate police response and that takes priority over all other police work.

post-traumatic stress disorder (PTSD) A condition that sets in following a traumatic event with which the sufferer cannot cope. It has been described as an event outside the usual human experience—one that is experienced in a markedly distressing way, with intense fear, terror, bewilderment, and a sense of helplessness.[70]

sexual harassment Unwelcome sexual advances, requests for sexual favors, and other verbal or physical conduct of a sexual nature.

Stress is a fact of life in many occupations, but policing has its own unique brand of stress.

The Five Stages of Burnout

(1) the honeymoon/enthusiasm stage
The officer reacts enthusiastically to the challenges of the job.

(2) the fuel shortage/stagnation stage
The officer realizes that the job is not as exciting as he or she anticipated; routine sets in, and the officer may come to view the job as boring.

(3) the chronic symptoms/frustration stage
The officer has feelings of intense and seemingly irresolvable apathy and frustration.

(4) the crisis/apathy stage
Pessimism may emerge, and the officer may be plagued by feelings of self-doubt.

(5) the hitting the wall/intervention stage
The officer may reach his or her wits' end, perhaps turning to alcohol and drugs to relieve the feelings of failure and anger that have built up over time.

usually experience eustress when beginning a new assignment, such as criminal investigation. This form of stress is generally described as positive and can actually result in higher levels of motivation.

Distress is the harmful variety of stress. It threatens the individual's functioning or can overload his or her capacity to cope with environmental stimuli. Distress may result from such things as an extraordinarily high caseload, assignment to a high-crime area, inadequate equipment, or an unsupportive supervisor. All police organizations contain job assignments or situations that are perceived as threatening by most individuals, and it is these assignments or situations that create the greatest demands.

Perhaps more than anything, stress is a problem of incompatibility between a person and his or her environment. It occurs when the individual is overwhelmed by negative environmental factors or when the environment fails to provide for or meet the individual's needs. Every person has a unique set of skills, abilities, experiences, and personality traits, and every job—within the context of the environment—requires the employee to possess a certain set of skills, abilities, experiences, and personality traits. When the employee's characteristics do not match the job's requirements, a potential result is heightened stress.

Effective stress management requires that the symptoms of stress be recognized. Within a police organization, no one party should be burdened with the responsibility for recognizing these symptoms. Rather, it is vital that everyone in administrative and management positions be able to spot the signs of stress and identify possible methods for alleviating the distress. The symptoms must be acknowledged and ameliorated before they develop into excessive problems for both the stressed person and those who must associate with him or her.

Burnout

Burnout is the progressive loss of idealism, energy, purpose, and concern that results from the conditions of work. According to one team of researchers, burnout is "a debilitating psychological condition brought about by unrelieved work stress."[76] Burnout can also be understood as the final stage of mental or physical exhaustion, in which the individual is no longer able to cope with his or her job.[77]

Critical Incidents

A major source of stress in police work concerns the possibility of becoming involved in critical or traumatic incidents. A **critical incident** is an emergency situation (a crime in progress, a traffic accident with serious injuries, a natural disaster, a terrorist attack, an officer's request for assistance, and other situations in which human life may be in jeopardy) that evokes immediate police response and that takes priority over all other police work. Examples of critical-incident stressors may include apprehending a disturbed person, serving a warrant against a dangerous person, providing riot control, or dealing with a hostage taker or a barricaded suspect.

One of the most stressful events that a police officer can experience is a shooting in which the officer critically wounds or kills another person or where a fellow officer is killed or critically wounded. Most experts agree that many good officers leave policing because of postshooting trauma; such trauma can have long-lasting effects on the police officer. However, not every officer who is involved in a shooting has a traumatic reaction. The postshooting trauma reactions are almost equally divided among mild reactions, moderate reactions, and severe reactions.[78] Research reveals that officers involved in shootings experience emotional or psychological numbing.[79] Five phases have been identified for coping with critical incidents:

quid pro quo harassment A form of sexual harassment that generally involves a demand for sexual favors in exchange for some perk or benefit, such as a promotion or a favorable job assignment.

hostile work environment A form of sexual harassment involving situations in which unwelcome sexual contact and comments have the effect of "unreasonably interfering with an individual's work performance or creating an intimidating environment."[71]

1. *Denial.* The officer does not want to believe what has happened. This stage is usually very brief in officer-involved shootings.

2. *Anger and resentment.* Anger and resentment are usually nonspecific or vaguely directed at the person who was shot. This stage is usually short lived, though it may return at various times during the adaptation process.

3. *Bargaining.* This stage involves the officer wishing the shooting had never happened. It may also be due to the officer's worry about reprisals from the department.

4. *Depression.* This stage lasts the longest. The severity of the depression depends on the basic personality of the officer, the amount of trauma involved in the incident, the agency's response to the incident, the officer's social network, and other factors.

5. *Acceptance.* This stage has been reached when the officer begins to integrate the event into his or her life or makes the transition from being totally preoccupied with the event to merely acknowledging that it took place.[80]

The symptoms of postshooting trauma are usually most intense for the first 48 to 72 hours following the incident, but the various reactions to such events can come and go for some time. For example, the officer may experience a heightened sense of danger or vulnerability, fear and anxiety about future encounters, anger or rage, nightmares, sleep difficulties (insomnia, sleep disturbances, or escaping through sleep), guilt, emotional numbing, emotional withdrawal from others, sexual difficulties, physical problems (headaches, indigestion, muscle aches, diarrhea, or constipation), or anxiety reactions (difficulty concentrating, excessive worry, irritability, or nervousness).[81] The officer may continually think about the incident and may have frequent flashbacks.

Occasionally, stress arising from critical incidents can lead to a condition known as **post-traumatic stress disorder (PTSD)**. PTSD has been defined as "a condition which sets in following a traumatic event with which the sufferer cannot cope. It has been described as an event outside the usual human experience, one which is experienced in a markedly distressing way, with intense fear, terror, bewilderment and a sense of helplessness."[82] Symptoms of PTSD can include (1) persistent and recurring memories of the event, (2) loss of interest and feelings, (3) problems sleeping and concentrating, and (4) hypervigilance.[83] In the wake of particularly traumatic incidents, it is advisable to treat potential PTSD problems before they get out of control. If early treatment is offered and utilized, many of the long-term negative effects of PTSD can be prevented and eliminated.

Fatigue

Everybody gets tired on the job from time to time. Some of us can safely doze off for a few minutes without too much concern, but others work in professions in which a nap could lead to disaster. The last thing anyone would want is for an air traffic controller to snooze on the job. The same can be said of surgeons, truck drivers, and of course police officers.

Police officers, like some other workers, sometimes work lengthy shifts at odd hours. While they have more or less fixed schedules, it is sometimes impractical for police officers to just walk away at quitting time. An accident, an emergency, or a high-profile arrest could require an officer to work several extra hours, contributing to a long and unpredictable workweek. As two well-known police stress researchers point out, "It is totally reprehensible that the cops we expect to protect us, come to our aid, and respond to our needs when victimized should be allowed to have the worst fatigue and sleep conditions of any profession in our society."[84]

Tired Cops

Researchers have only recently turned their attention to police fatigue.[85] Reporters, too, have expressed concern.[86] The *Boston Globe* investigated one police agency and found that 16 officers worked more than 80 hours each week. Two averaged more than 100 hours per week over a 12-month period.[87] One even worked 130 hours in a single week, which translates into less than six hours off on any given day. Researchers identified some officers in Florida and Massachusetts who moonlighted (for example, as security guards) for 3,000 hours each year, above and beyond the hours spent performing their official duties.[88]

To further gauge the extent of police fatigue, criminologists Bryan Vila and Dennis Kenney surveyed a number of police agencies around the country and visited several more. Their survey revealed that while most officers work only a few overtime hours each month, some logged more than 100 hours of overtime.[89]

Nobody can blame police officers for wanting to increase their pay by working extra hours. Some, though, are forced to do so because of job demands. Either way, too much fatigue can lead to disaster. Vila and Kenney summarized some of the more serious incidents:

> A Michigan police officer working nearly 24 hours straight crashes his cruiser while chasing a fleeing motorist. He is critically injured. In California, a sheriff's deputy working alone drifts off a deserted highway and is killed instantly when his patrol car crashes into a tree. An officer in Florida, who has had trouble staying awake, runs a red light in her patrol car and crashes into a van driven by a deputy sheriff, injuring him severely. A police officer driving home from work in Ohio nods off at the wheel, begins swerving in and out of traffic, and runs off the road, striking and killing a man jogging down the sidewalk.[90]

Scheduling and Workload

We have looked at the most obvious cause of police fatigue: too many hours on the job. Police fatigue may also stem from shift length and shift-assignment policies. Researchers have found that police departments that use compressed work schedules (that is, fewer than five 8-hour days) see less fatigue among their officers.[91] It appears that four 10- to 12-hour shifts result in less fatigue than five 8-hour shifts.

Shift assignments, in addition to shift length, may have implications for police fatigue, as well. Vila and Kenney noted that people are less able to cope with fatigue as they grow older. They found that older officers who can select their own shifts were less fatigued than their counterparts who had no say over scheduling matters.[92] The predictability (or unpredictability) of work hours also appears to be linked to fatigue. Surprisingly, officers who work unpredictable schedules report less fatigue. According to Vila and Kenney, "One possible interpretation of this finding could be that the officers who were having problems with fatigue were actually avoiding or minimizing overtime work—perhaps by making fewer arrests or court appearances."[93] The same officers could also have had off-duty obligations (for example, caring for young children) that forced them to keep regular hours but that also contributed to fatigue.

Sexual Harassment

Sexual harassment, which consists of unwelcome sexual advances, requests for sexual favors, and other verbal or physical conduct of a sexual nature, is a sad reality in many of America's workplaces. Sexual harassment has occurred for generations, but the practice attracted national attention in 1991, when University of Oklahoma law professor Anita Hill testified at Clarence Thomas's Supreme Court confirmation hearing. Hill described Thomas's conduct as constituting sexual harassment, and it prompted many people to question the way women are treated in the workplace.

Sexual harassment is a form of discrimination under Title VII, as decided in 1977.[94] In 1986, the Supreme Court defined sexual harassment as falling into two categories: (1) **quid pro quo harassment** and (2) **hostile work environment**.[95] *Quid pro quo* harassment occurs when sexual favors are demanded in exchange for some perk or benefit, perhaps a promotion or a favorable job assignment. Viewed differently, *quid pro quo* sexual harassment occurs when there is a tangible economic detriment associated with refusing to succumb to sexual advances. A hostile work environment is said to exist when unwelcome sexual contact and comments have the effect of "unreasonably

62% 62 percent of female officers had seen or experienced sexual harassment during their careers as officers.

interfering with an individual's work performance or creating an intimidating environment."[96]

Because of the prevalence of male officers, police work has seen its share of sexual harassment. In 1993, the state of California enacted legislation requiring all peace officers to undergo sexual harassment training. The law followed several large judgments against police agencies for their officers' unscrupulous actions. In the early 1990s, the New York City Police Department went to great lengths to cover up sexual harassment allegations by a female probationary police officer. The woman alleged that she was raped and sodomized by a male officer who threatened to kill her if she reported the incident. When the facts eventually came to light, she was awarded $264,242 in damages.[97]

To this day, sexual harassment still occurs in police departments at alarming rates.[98] The author of a 1996 study interviewed 187 female police officers and found that 62 percent of them had seen or experienced sexual harassment during their careers as officers.[99] More recently, the National Center for Women and Policing concluded that "law enforcement agencies have tolerated workplace environments that are openly hostile and discriminatory toward female employees."[100]

Too Smart to be a Cop?

On March 16, 1996, Robert Jordan took a test for the position of entry-level police officer with the Law Enforcement Council of Connecticut, a consortium of 14 different cities in the eastern part of the state. The test, like many of its kind, contained questions intended to assess applicants' cognitive and scholastic abilities. Jordan was informed, along with all of the other test takers, that the test "will generate an eligibility list for distribution to the participating police departments for possible future employment."

The test, developed by Wonderlic Personnel Test, Inc. (WPT), came with an official user's manual for each exam, including a table of recommended minimum scores for a number of occupations.[101] The company recommended a score of 22 as the minimum for a police officer. Further, Wonderlic recommended hiring people who scored at most four points below and eight points above 22.

In the fall of 1996, Jordan learned that the city of New London was going to be hiring police officers, so he requested a meeting with Keith Harrigan, the assistant city manager in charge of personnel decisions. Jordan was told he was ineligible to become a police officer because he had scored too high on the written test. New London set a test score range of 20 to 27 for police officers, and Jordan had scored above 27. Jordan promptly filed a lawsuit against the city, claiming that his equal protection rights, under the Fifth Amendment to the U.S. Constitution, had been violated. The national media picked up the story, and the headline of the day declared "Too Smart to Be a Cop."

While Jordan felt that he had been discriminated against for scoring well on the exam, the city was concerned with ensuring employment longevity for its officers and minimizing turnover. City officials felt that, given Jordan's apparently extraordinary level of intelligence, he would not have been happy as a police officer and would have quickly left his post, leaving the city with little return on its investment in his selection and training. At issue in the lawsuit, then, was whether there is a justifiable relationship between high cognitive ability and job satisfaction/longevity and, if so, whether a jurisdiction can base its hiring practices on such a relationship.

Jordan's case was heard in the U.S. District Court for the District of Connecticut.[102] Interestingly, the court sided with the city of New London, finding that the city

> followed the instructions accompanying the WPT test, on which they rationally could have relied as authoritative. Additionally, a body of professional literature concludes that hiring overqualified applicants leads to subsequent job dissatisfaction and turnover. While such studies have been challenged, it cannot be said that their conclusions have been refuted.[103]

Most equal protection lawsuits have been brought by people claiming to be victims of illegitimate discrimination. If African-Americans are hired significantly less often than Caucasians, for example, then there may be a basis for a lawsuit claiming discrimination because race is not a legitimate hiring criterion. Jordan's case was different, not only because he was not a member of any historically protected group but because the city reached its hiring decision by paying attention to what the court recognized as legitimate concerns.

This raises several interesting questions:

1. Was New London's hiring decision fair in this case?

2. How many other cities throughout the United States base their hiring decisions almost exclusively on test scores?

3. Is it really possible to be too smart to be a cop?

4. How effective are written tests at screening candidates for law enforcement positions?

Source: JustASC/Shutterstock.com

Outline the hiring process including testing, interviewing, and various screening procedures.

To enter the police force, candidates must move through the hiring decision, the police academy, and field training. The hiring decision follows recruitment and is based on performance in several areas, including written and physical agility tests, an interview, a background investigation, a polygraph, and medical and drug screening. Academies vary in their organization and curricular requirements. Each, however, strives to teach new hires the "sixth sense." The traditional model of postacademy training is that of the field training officer (FTO). The FTO system is gradually being replaced by a new police training officer model.

1. What are the steps involved in the hiring process?

2. What is the "sixth sense" that officers should learn?

3. What are the three phases of typical field training?

civil service A system in which employees are hired, retained, advanced, disciplined, and discharged on the basis of merit (that is, their abilities and qualifications).

patronage system A system of hiring in which decisions are based more on an individual's political support for an officeholder than on his or her abilities and qualifications. Patronage was common in police agencies during the political era.

civil service commission A federal, state, or local agency charged with ensuring that employees in civil service positions receive specific protections.

plebe system A police academy model that closely parallels a military-style boot camp and that aims to produce well-groomed and disciplined officers.

technical training model A police academy training model that emphasizes the technical aspects of police work and provides little or no training in such nontechnical areas as stress management, interaction with difficult people, problem solving, and sensitivity to marginalized groups.

college system A police academy training model intended to enhance the professional aspects of police training curricula by exposing trainees to problem solving, sensitivity to marginalized groups, and other valuable topics in addition to required technical knowledge.

sixth sense A healthy sense of suspicion; the experience-based ability to intuit when something is amiss.

field training officer (FTO) A veteran police officer tasked with providing on-the-job training and performance critique during a rookie police officer's initial assignment following graduation from the academy.

police training officer (PTO) program A police training method that focuses on developing an officer's learning capacity, leadership, and problem-solving skills.

Summarize the issues faced by female and minority police officers.

Police departments are becoming increasingly diverse due to the Civil Rights Act of 1964, equal employment opportunity, and affirmative action—and because departments are learning the value of hiring women and minorities. However, allegations of reverse discrimination, mostly by white male police officers, have surfaced in recent years.

1. What implications has the Equal Employment Opportunity had for the law enforcement profession?

2. Why is diversity essential in the police ranks?

3. Summarize the history of minorities and women in the police field.

4. Explain the concept of reverse discrimination.

equal employment opportunity Fair employment practices mandated by Title VII of the Civil Rights Act of 1964.

Equal Employment Opportunity Commission (EEOC) The federal agency that is empowered by Title VII of the Civil Rights Act of 1964 to "intervene on behalf of affected individuals," to "file suit against businesses or governmental entities in cases of discrimination," to intervene in cases of alleged sexual harassment, and to investigate cases of employer retaliation.[104]

affirmative action The practice of taking proactive steps to boost the presence of historically marginalized groups (typically minorities and women) in the ranks of an organization by giving preference to members of those groups.

double marginality A situation in which black officers treat black suspects harshly to gain the respect of their white counterparts and to avoid giving the impression that they are biased toward members of their own race.

Americans with Disabilities Act (ADA) U.S. legislation passed in 1990 that forbids discrimination against the disabled.

racial quota A requirement for hiring and promoting a specified number of minorities.

reverse discrimination Discrimination against nonminorities that occurs when the hiring and promotion of minorities are based more on race than on any other criterion.

LEARNING OUTCOMES 3

Summarize the nature and causes of stress in policing.

Some of the realities of police work include stress, fatigue, and sexual harassment. Stress can be both positive (eustress) and negative (distress). Distress, the most destructive form of stress, can lead to numerous job-related and personal problems, including burnout. There are several sources of stress, including organizational and administrative practices, the criminal justice system, the public, stressors intrinsic to police work, and critical incidents. Fatigue is another problem for police officers. Police organizations should guard against scheduling- and workload-related fatigue. Police applicants should also be aware of occasional sexual harassment problems in police agencies, particularly for female applicants, and that some agencies have residency requirements mandating that police officers live within certain boundaries.

1. What is the difference between eustress and distress?
2. What is burnout and what are its five stages?
3. List and describe the five phases for coping with critical incidents.
4. How are scheduling and workload related to fatigue in police officers?

stress Anything that places a positive or negative adjustive demand on an organism.

eustress A positive form of stress that does not threaten or harm the individual but is pleasurable, challenging, or exciting.

distress A harmful form of stress that can threaten an individual's functioning or overload his or her capacity to cope with environmental stimuli.

burnout The progressive loss of idealism, energy, purpose, and concern that results from the conditions of work.

critical incident An emergency situation that evokes immediate police response and that takes priority over all other police work.

post-traumatic stress disorder (PTSD) A condition that sets in following a traumatic event with which the sufferer cannot cope. It has been described as an event outside the usual human experience—one that is experienced in a markedly distressing way, with intense fear, terror, bewilderment, and a sense of helplessness.[105]

sexual harassment Unwelcome sexual advances, requests for sexual favors, and other verbal or physical conduct of a sexual nature.

quid pro quo **harassment** A form of sexual harassment that generally involves a demand for sexual favors in exchange for some perk or benefit, such as a promotion or a favorable job assignment.

hostile work environment A form of sexual harassment involving situations in which unwelcome sexual contact and comments have the effect of "unreasonably interfering with an individual's work performance or creating an intimidating environment."[106]

MyCJLab

Go to the Chapter 4 section in *MyCJLab* to test your understanding of this chapter, access customized study content, engage in interactive simulations, complete critical thinking and research assignments, and view related online videos.

Additional Links

Read "A Police Officer's Mission" at **www.justicestudies.com/pubs/policemission.pdf**.

Visit the New York City Police Department's home page at **www.nyc.gov/html/nypd**.

The home page of the Los Angeles Police Department can be found here: **www.lapdonline.org**.

The article "Would You Be a Good Cop?" can be found here: **http://tinyurl.com/ywtlvp**.

Learn about an interesting new partnership between the International Association of Chiefs of Police and the Bureau of Justice Assistance for anyone interested in a career in policing here: **www.discoverpolicing.org**.

Police Subculture

"Skepticism and suspicion are essential in policing because the job can sometimes be very unpredictable."

1 Describe the elements of culture.

2 Explain the sources of police subculture.

3 Summarize the components of police subculture.

5

INTRO DANGER AND UNPREDICTABILITY: THE HALLMARKS OF POLICE WORK

On January 28, 2011, Lamar D. Moore seemed calm as he walked into the Detroit Police Department's Northwestern District station, strode past vending machines, and stepped up to the horseshoe-shaped front desk close to the station's front door. A moment later, however, he pulled out a shotgun and fired an initial blast at personnel manning the reception desk. Officers are shown hitting the floor in video taken by the station's surveillance cameras. Before the attack was over four police officers were shot, and Moore, an alleged sex crime offender also charged with kidnapping, was dead. Authorities later said that Moore had kidnapped a 13-year-old girl at knifepoint, chained her to a toilet in his basement, and sexually assaulted her for nine days. It was only after she escaped that Lamar perpetrated the station ambush. As of the printing of this book, video of the attack on the station, taken by surveillance cameras there, was available on the Web at www.youtube.com/watch?v=2qOvtDF9sCU&NR=1.

The attack in Detroit illustrates how police hang together. They run in the same circles. They work out together, vacation together, party together, go to "cop bars" together, and associate with one another when off duty. There is a tendency among most police officers to stick together. As in Detroit, they also protect one another. But cops are not the only people who work in the same field and associate with one another. Teachers often associate with other teachers, office workers relax with other office workers, and construction workers hang out with other construction workers. Yet policing is different from other occupations. Policing is, at its core, a potentially dangerous line of work, and this makes its occupational culture quite unique.

> **DISCUSS** What builds camaraderie among police officers? Is such camaraderie desirable?

► Culture: What is it?

Culture refers to a shared set of **values**, **norms**, and behaviors that form a particular way of life. Values are standards of goodness, or those things that are perceived to be important. Norms refer to rules and expectations about which forms of behavior are acceptable and which are not. Any discussion of culture should also consider social **institutions**. Institutions can be found in organizational structures—like schools, families, and churches. Social institutions communicate values and norms throughout society and over time contribute to cultural stability. In the policing context, significant research has shown that the nature of police organizations, like other social institutions, shapes police behavior. America is considered a multicultural melting pot because there are many different cultures within our borders, organized by all manner of shared sentiments.

Culture versus Subculture

The term **subculture** refers to cultural patterns that distinguish some segment of a society's population from the rest of that population. Consequently, individuals who share values and norms that differ from those of the larger culture can be said to be members of a subculture. The term **police subculture** (sometimes called *police culture*) has been used to describe the shared values and norms and the established patterns of behavior that are found among police officers. It describes the fact that police officers generally adhere to a set of values and beliefs that differ in certain crucial respects from those held by members of the wider American culture. Some of the values that characterize police subculture, like patriotism and a dedication to creating a better society, are positive values that many Americans share. Others, like suspicion and cynicism, are not always prized by others but may be necessary for effective (and safe) police work. It is important to understand that the values and norms that characterize police subculture are not unique when taken individually. It is their occurrence together that gives policing its distinctive nature. Police corruption and deviance, insofar as they stem from the subculture of policing, are taken up in Chapter 12. Our concern in this chapter is with the broader nature of police subculture in general.

The section that follows looks at the generic elements of any culture. After covering the basics, we then turn our attention to the sources of police subculture and to the specific components of police subculture.

LEARNING OUTCOMES 1 Describe the elements of culture.

GLOSSARY

culture A set of shared values, norms, and behaviors that form a way of life.

value A standard of goodness, desirability, behavior, beauty, or interaction that serves as a guideline for living within a particular culture.

norm A rule or expectation for behavior that characterizes a particular social group.

institution An organizational structure through which values and norms are transmitted over time and from one location to another within a society.

subculture Cultural patterns that distinguish some segment of a society's population.

Elements of Culture

Cultures are characterized by themes, or shared commonalities. Consider NASCAR racing. Some would say that there is not only a racing subculture in America but that there are a

The nature of police organizations shapes police behavior.

number of themes running through it, including fan loyalty to specific drivers, respect for the rules of racing, and a desire to own brand-name products associated with NASCAR winners. Themes tend to be shared by members of a particular culture. Culture also promotes the expression of norms and shared values in ways that are defined as acceptable. Let's look briefly at each of these concepts in greater detail.

Various Themes

John Crank, who has written extensively on the subject of police subculture,[1] refers to a "confluence of themes," "meaning that diverse aspects of organizational activity merge into a whole united by commonly held values and shared ways of thinking."[2]

Consider another type of culture: academia. The wider American culture often sees universities as places of learning dominated by liberal thinkers. But to characterize the culture of academia, and all academics, as "liberal" would be inaccurate. Not only do many of today's professors characterize themselves as politically conservative, but liberalism in university settings is tempered by other factors. One of those other factors is skeptical positivism (the essence of science), a theme running through academia that combines with liberal beliefs and countless other factors to create a relatively unique set of beliefs, values, and behavioral patterns. Skeptical positivism rejects beliefs based on faith or tradition alone and demands rigorous scientific proof before an idea can be accepted.

Institutional Values

Our definition of *culture* highlights the role of shared values and norms. Recall that values are what people consider important, but they can also reflect an impression of how certain things should be done. This is what is meant by **institutional values**.

There is a moral dimension to institutional values that suggests the norms we talked about earlier. Cultures contain beliefs not only about the best way to go about accomplishing tasks but also about the moral superiority of one approach over another. For example, consider how a scientific approach to a problem might differ from a faith-based approach to the same problem.

It is useful to think of organizations as promoting their particular institutional values. It is probably safe to say that most law enforcement personnel at one time felt that this was the best way to go about the business of enforcing the law.[3] An opposing view says that the traditional approach to managing police organizations is slow to adapt to new problems (such as the challenges of terrorism and homeland security) and is resistant to change.[4] Some progressive police administrators feel that decentralization, one of the hot topics in policing today, is a more effective approach. (Note that the word *progressive* is itself value-laden and that "progressive" ideas should not be accepted in place of more traditional ones unless their true "value" can be demonstrated.)

Preference for centralization or decentralization may actually represent two subcultural perspectives within the larger culture of policing. What, then, would be an example of an institutional value that is ubiquitous in policing? Returning again to Crank's observations, we note the idea of personal responsibility, one of the bedrock (though unwritten) principles on which the American system of criminal justice is built. This belief in personal responsibility is clearly manifested throughout

police subculture The shared values and norms and the established patterns of behavior that tend to characterize policing; also called *police culture.*

institutional value A sense of agreement within a particular culture about how to accomplish a valued objective.

CULTURE
A shared set of values, norms, and behaviors that form a particular way of life

SUBCULTURE
Cultural patterns that distinguish some segment of a society's population from the rest of that population

POLICE SUBCULTURE
The shared values and norms and the established patterns of behavior that are found among police officers

Some values are shared between many Americans and the police, and others are unique to the police.

(1) Shared values between many Americans and the police—patriotism, dedication to a better society

(2) Values unique to the police—suspicion, cynicism

FIGURE 5.1 The Police Subculture.

criminal justice agencies, including police departments. There is an almost unshakable faith among police administrators in preventive patrol as useful for deterring would-be criminals, even though much of the research does not necessarily support this approach. The belief seems to be that the *threat* of punishment, resulting from being caught in the act of committing a crime, serves to restrain those who would otherwise choose to break the law.

This point also illustrates the interconnectedness between cultures. Crank's observation refers to a general set of beliefs characteristic of American culture that is not limited to criminal justice. But these beliefs have clearly shaped policing—and police subculture. What make police subculture different from the broader American culture are the many additional themes that have been grafted onto it.

Emotional Expression

Businesspeople and other workers "vent" from time to time with some of their colleagues. They complain about everything from annoying or incompetent coworkers to the direction their company is headed. Likewise, college students share with their peers concerns about college life, their professors, tests they have to take, papers they are asked to write, and even their books. Indeed, everyone expresses him- or herself in one way or another.

Expression can occur through several media. Off-duty conversations between fellow officers provide a means for release. Even if an officer's feelings are not openly shared, they can still affect the officer's perception of the world and thus his or her behavior.

Police officers share many of the same sentiments in different places, and even over time.

To summarize, culture is complex, deeply entrenched, and shared. It is complex in the sense that it comprises various themes. Several sets of beliefs and values intersect to create individual cultures. Finally, culture is shared through a host of verbal and nonverbal channels: openly, subtly, and sometimes tacitly.

One does not need to venture far (geographically or professionally) in this country to discover how rapidly culture can change. This recognition enables us to present a more accurate, complete, and practical definition of *culture*. Crank's definition is useful in this regard: Culture is a body of knowledge that emerges through the shared application of practical skills to concrete problems encountered in daily routines and the normal course of activities.[5]

In closing, we should remark on the self-confirming nature of culture. This means that culture is self-reinforcing. It sustains itself and propagates itself largely intact from one generation to the next. It is no mystery why police officers share many of the same sentiments in different places, and even over time. The beliefs they carry emanate from shared training and common experiences and, as such, tend to transcend time and location. To be sure, cultures change and adapt, but this change does not occur quickly.

Various Themes — Various themes or aspects of a particular profession mix together to create a common set of beliefs, behaviors, and reactions to particular sets of circumstances.

Law enforcement officers, for example, often think in terms of "us against them."

Institutional Themes — A sense of agreement exists within a particular culture on how to accomplish valued objectives.

The traditional police department, for example, has a hierarchical, quasi-military structure, and an established formal chain of command with rigid bureaucratic structure.

Emotional Expression — Expression (as well as the mode of expression) of a culture's shared norms and values

In the police context, "war stories" told in the academy serve to build and reinforce cultural beliefs and preferences.

FIGURE 5.2 Three Elements of Culture.

▶ Sources of Police Subculture

Our discussion of culture to this point has been generic, without much reference to the unique nature of American policing. Now it is time to get more specific: What is police subculture? What does it look like? Where does it come from? This section is concerned primarily with the last question, the sources of police subculture. After we ascertain what it is that has given rise to police subculture, we will be in a better position to grasp exactly what its components are.

Organizational Factors

Although police departments are certainly not unique in this regard, police work is usually divided into at least three shifts. In larger police departments, there are often several squads of officers working each shift. In the largest agencies, these squads are organized into platoons of 25 or more officers. Platoons might be divided up based on geographic criteria.[6] Police agencies today often use terms other than *platoon* or *squad*, but the organizational makeup remains more or less the same.[7] The result, regardless of name, is a group of officers who work the same schedule.

Perhaps the most unusual shift in policing is the one stretching from midnight or so until shortly after daybreak. Officers who work this shift generally have difficulty associating with people who work normal nine-to-five jobs because they tend to sleep during daylight hours. What's more, some officers are often required to work weekends and holidays, which further interferes with their ability to socialize with and establish friendships with people outside their professional circle.

No matter what the hours, the period at the end of a shift provides ample opportunity to rehash the day's activities, further reinforcing common bonds among police officers. Two researchers who observed a Colorado police department highlighted the importance of these end-of-shift discussions, noting that the period at the end of a shift

> provided an opportunity to discuss department policies, politics, and personalities. Rumors made their rounds at this time—with a few being squelched, several being started, and many being embellished.[8]

Of course, rumors and stories do not stay confined to specific squads or platoons. With daily interaction and transfers, which are common, they spread from one group of officers to the next, as criminologist Ted Rubinstein notes:

> Occasionally a man transfers from one squad to another, bringing with him knowledge of ex-colleagues which he offers to his new colleagues, enriching their knowledge about co-workers who are frequently seen, greeted, chatted with, but rarely known in the personal way as are the [members of the] squad.[9]

This illustrates shift work's impact on the development of police subculture. Many other features of police organizations also work together to breed a relatively unique group of individuals.

We will consider the influence of administrators on subordinates, for example, but for now let's shift gears and focus on the environment as a source of police subculture.

The Street Environment

Policing is a people profession. The daily work of most police officers involves interacting with ordinary citizens and with other professionals in the criminal justice system. No other encounters have as many culture-shaping implications as those between the police and citizens.

Crank has identified two types of encounters that are especially significant in shaping police subculture. The first of these is the **street environment**. Here, an officer's personal beliefs, the circumstances of the encounter (for example, within view of others or not), and the attitudes each party brings to the encounter (hostility, cooperation, respect, and so on) can influence behavior in ways that are enduring and reinforcing.

Younger officers who have aspirations (some cynical older officers might say "delusions") of changing the world and of engaging in exciting crime-fighting activities are often soon disillusioned by the routine and even frustrating nature of many calls for service, especially those dealing with property crime. In this context, much attention usually focuses on the victim's experience. But the satisfaction that police officers get from taking property crime reports is usually quite low.[10]

Violent crimes can also prove less than exciting. Random acts of violence between total strangers are often the exception. Although the media may suggest otherwise, the typical violent encounters that officers respond to are those between friends and acquaintances,[11] and high on the list are domestic incidents. As Crank notes, "[i]nstead of providing police with a satisfactory sense of work accomplished, [these encounters] reveal the seamy, coarse, and destructive side of ordinary human relations."[12]

These observations show how the environment—especially the typical kind of contact between police and citizens—bodes ominously for police subculture. Such job frustrations, coupled with other environmental elements, lead to a unique worldview and to a characteristic set of beliefs about how to deal with most members of the public and with offenders.

The street environment is an influential shaper of police subculture, but the traffic stop is at least equally influential. Since nearly every traffic stop is involuntary (that is, drivers would rather *not* be stopped by the police), any hopes of a positive encounter between the officer and the driver are doomed from the start. As a result, traffic stop interactions negatively shape police subculture.

The street environment is an influential shaper of police subculture.

Administration

The administrative arrangements in the typical police department cannot help but inform police subculture. Interactions with superiors and the routine steps taken at the beginning and end of each shift work together with social and physical environments, organizational factors, and other factors to set policing apart from other professions.

The typical officer usually reports for duty at roll call. This may take place in a briefing room where officers are given their assignments, activities of the previous shift are recounted, new policies are discussed, and anything else of importance is brought up. Roll calls are usually presided over by sergeants or their equivalents. From a culture-forming standpoint, roll call is important for a number of reasons, not the least of which is it gives an opportunity to get together and commiserate, especially in the periods right before and after.[13]

At shift end, officers return to the briefing room or equivalent locations to finish their paperwork, change back into civilian attire, and prepare to head home. Debriefing also occurs at this time, particularly if a critical incident, such as a shooting or use of force, occurred during the shift. No matter the arrangement, this stage of the typical officer's day also shapes police subculture. Officers spend time together, relax, and share stories about their days.[14]

As for interactions with supervisors, one would suspect that sergeants (and other higher-ups) would have an influential role in the shaping of police subculture. Research reveals, interestingly, that this tends not to be the case. For example, police researchers David Allen and Michael Maxfield studied the arrest, citation, and warrant activities of police officers and found that sergeants had virtually no direct effects on their subordinates' activities—particularly the quantity of those activities:

> The influence of first-line supervisors in directing the behavior of officers is seriously limited. Even though supervisors emphasize a particular performance criterion or suggest that a certain level of performance be met, officers under their command do not seem to respond positively to these cues.[15]

Although supervisors may not directly influence the culture of line officers, there are other administrative factors that surely do. One of them, according to Crank, is the process of internal review, which encompasses everything from investigating officers whose activities are called into question to reviewing the performance of new and seasoned officers alike. Internal review activities—which are generally not openly welcomed by line officers—surely shape their worldviews, interactions with one another, and ultimately police subculture.

Finally, policies and procedures, sometimes known as *standard operating procedures*, also shape police subculture. Rules are put in place to protect citizens and to protect police organizations from undue scrutiny, complaints, criticisms, and lawsuits. Such rules are written by administrators, attorneys, or high-level officials, often with little input from the rank and file. Most people can sympathize with the resentment

Police interactions with other criminal justice agencies help shape police subculture.

that this can breed. Students often have to follow various school procedures that may seem arcane and irrelevant. This, in turn, shapes their attitudes toward administrators, possibly their instructors, and maybe their entire educational experience. The same is true in police work.

Other Criminal Justice Agencies

Police officers' interactions with other criminal justice agencies also shape police subculture. If a prosecutor rejects a case that the investigating officer perceives to be strong, for example, this can lead to disillusionment and frustration, which the officer will likely communicate to his or her peers. The more often this occurs, the more police officers may feel that they stand alone in their crime-fighting efforts and are not being supported by other criminal justice professionals.

On the other hand, if the prosecutor elects to take a case forward, this can take a significant amount of an officer's time, including his or her off-duty time. The defense will be entitled to discovery, which usually includes examination of the police report. The defense will scrutinize the report to ensure that proper procedures were followed and may even call into question the officer's integrity and worthiness—especially if the report was poorly written. All of this can be quite stressful for the officer, thus contributing to a unique set of perceptions, beliefs, and values that characterize police subculture.

The Media

The media have perhaps the most influence on police subculture. Some members of the media are supportive of the police and represent what Crank has called the "inner circle." These are often reporters who have worked with police officers for years and have come to appreciate the difficulties involved in policing.

FIGURE 5.3 Sources of Police Subculture.

Police officers can usually work constructively with these reporters to manage the release of information and to ensure that investigations proceed unfettered. But not all reporters are supportive, and at least a minority, it seems, are bent on casting law enforcement agencies in an unfavorable light.

An example can be seen in a recent incident from Houston, Texas. In 2006, the *Houston Chronicle* (a traditionally liberal newspaper) published a series of articles criticizing the Houston Police Department for its use of Tasers.[16] The department's Tasers were equipped with cameras, not unlike the cameras found in patrol cars around the country. The cameras help to ensure that officers act properly and within the law. At the same time, though, there is nothing pleasant about watching a person on the receiving end of a Taser shock. They frequently yell, howl, flail, and appear to be in great pain. The *Chronicle* posted on its website the Taser videos that it had obtained. The newspaper criticized the police department, claiming that officers were using Tasers not only to defuse hostile situations but often when use of the devices was inappropriate. The paper failed to report on any successful incidents where Taser use resulted in the apprehension of dangerous suspects without loss of life. This episode, which some saw as intentionally biased reporting, showed that the police are sometimes "damned if they do, and damned if they don't."

A police department's relationship with the media can be a double-edged sword. The media can aid in investigations, for example, by publicizing composite sketches of suspects. But they can also paint police departments in a less-than-favorable light. This is particularly true in the case of scandals. A scandal involving a small group of officers can tarnish the reputation of an entire department for years. This, in turn, takes its toll on officers who work in that department and who might come to regard members of the press skeptically.

In summary, there are five factors that have been linked to the formation of police subculture: organizational matters, the street environment, administration and administrative styles, relationships with other criminal justice agencies, and relationships with the media. This, of course, is not an exhaustive list. It would be impossible to identify all of the elements that shape police subculture in America. All of these factors interact in complex and sometimes unpredictable ways to produce a set of values and norms not found in any other occupation. What exactly are these values and norms? What is police subculture? We answer these questions in the rest of this chapter.

▶ Components of Police Subculture

In this section, we look at the values and norms that characterize police subculture in America. We examine control and territoriality; use of force; danger, unpredictability, and suspicion; solidarity; and other components of police subculture.

Control of Territory

It is the use of coercion—or at least the *authority* to use coercion—that ultimately defines police work. Sociologist Egon Bittner once described the coercive authority of policing

as the distinguishing feature that sets law enforcement apart from other professions. He called it the capacity to use force.[17] The power that officers have when it comes to the potential use of force is awesome because force can be used to deny people their freedom or even to take their lives. The ability to be coercive and to use force shapes the attitudes of police officers and sets them apart from other professionals.

Of course, force is not necessary most of the time, nor is coercion, but the maintenance of control is critical. Combined with the notion of control is territoriality, or the sense of responsibility a police officer feels for a particular area. Police officers must establish control over crime scenes and maintain social control over the neighborhoods they patrol.

Control

The term *control* sounds ominous. It suggests that police officers actively take steps to place limits on people's actions. Certainly, this does occur, especially when criminal suspects do not cooperate; however, there is more to the element of control than this. As Crank observes, "Cops may strategically use symbolic elements of their authority as coercive devices … displaying their weaponry in an intimidating way, for example."[18] Simply maintaining a police presence can do wonders in the furtherance of control.

Control is somewhat synonymous with order maintenance, one of the principal police functions we identify in Chapter 7. The issue also comes up in the next chapter, where we discuss police behavior and decision making. Viewed together, these chapters make it clear that a police officer's identity and effectiveness rest significantly on his or her ability to take control, whether that control is direct (at a crime scene, for example) or indirect (by simply maintaining a presence in the community).

LEARNING OUTCOMES 3 Summarize the components of police subculture.

GLOSSARY

dominion John Crank's substitute for the term *territoriality*, which refers to an officer's sense of personal ownership over the area for which he or she is responsible.

paradox of policing A phenomenon in which a police officer's fear of being injured or killed is stronger than is justified by actual rates of injury or death within the profession.

split-second syndrome A condition confronting police officers that involves three central features of policing—the urgency of police–citizen encounters, the involuntariness of such encounters, and a public setting—all of which combine to place officers in the position of having to make quick on-the-spot decisions.

solidarity The tendency among police officers to stick together and associate with one another.

dramaturgy In the law enforcement context, the act of putting on a display of high-mindedness.

affront According to John Van Maanen, the first of three steps police officers use in identifying an "asshole." It occurs when an officer's authority is questioned.

clarification According to John Van Maanen, the second of three steps police officers use in identifying an "asshole." It occurs when the officer attempts to ascertain what kind of person he or she is dealing with.

remedy According to John Van Maanen, the last of three steps police officers use in identifying an "asshole." It consists of the officer's response to an affront.

Territoriality

People, like animals, are all territorial to some extent. Whether we are protecting our homes, our cars, or our personal possessions, each of us takes steps to ensure "ours" does not become "theirs" without our consent. Police officers are also territorial. Instead of using the term *territoriality*, however, Crank calls this aspect of police work **dominion**, as the term "captures the divine responsibility over secular human activity that characterizes the special relationship cops have with a piece of earthly terrain."[19] John Van Maanen made this observation about territoriality:

> [Officers] come to know, in the most familiar and penetrating manner, virtually every passageway—whether alley, street, or seldom used path—located in their sector. From such knowledge of this social stage comes the corresponding evaluations of what particular conditions are to be considered good or bad, safe or unsafe, troubled or calm, usual or unusual, and so on... . These evaluations are also linked to temporal properties associated with the public use of a patrolman's area of responsibility... . The territorial perspective carried by patrolmen establishes the basic normative standard for the proper use of space.[20]

Use of Force

William Wesley was among the first police researchers to cite the importance of force as a crucial element of police culture. Others, like Bittner, also focused much of their attention on the role of force in policing. The very possibility of having to use or to face force, and the emotions that accompany the use or threat of force, is a powerful contributor to police subculture.[21]

The role force plays in shaping police culture is further magnified by the war metaphor we use to refer to crime fighting. The phrases "war on crime" and "war on drugs" are commonly used, often without much conscious thought, but the war metaphor effectively shapes police subculture. As Crank puts it, "The metaphor 'war' has had explosive mobilizing potential. It provided a way to view the police as protectors of society (read 'your wives and children'), and to view criminals as amoral enemies—less than human."[22]

It is not just force that shapes police subculture; it is specific types of force. Consider guns, perhaps the most familiar symbols of policing next to white sedans with light bars. "In the culture of policing, guns transform police work into a heroic occupation, providing both a bottom line and an unquestionable righteousness that pervades all police-citizen encounters,"[23] Crank notes. The ready availability of handguns, rifles, shotguns, and semiautomatic weapons combines with the war metaphor to create a special type of work environment, one that cannot help but mold police subculture:

> Policing in the United States is very much like going to war. Three times a day in countless locker rooms across the land, large men and a growing number of women carefully arm and armor themselves for the day's events. They begin by strapping on flak jackets... . Then they pick up a wide, heavy, black leather belt and hang around it the tools of their trade: gun, mace, handcuffs, bullets. When it is fully loaded, they swing the belt around their hips with the same practiced motion of the gun-fighter in Western movies, slugging it down and buckling it in front. Many officers slip an additional small-caliber pistol into their trouser pocket or a leg holster just above the ankle. Inspecting themselves in a full-length mirror, officers thread their night sticks into a metal ring on the side of their belt.[24]

Of all the items in a police officer's arsenal, though, it is the sidearm that is most apparent, most influential, and most significant in its contribution to occupational identity. The prospect of a deadly encounter, as Crank observes, is "etched into the personality of the police officer forever—an unrequested rite of passage that leaves a stain on the personality of the officer."[25]

There is an interesting paradox that arises with respect to guns. They shape police subculture perhaps more than any other factor, but (other than at practice ranges) police officers rarely fire their weapons.[26] To be sure, there are some police duties that require more frequent weapons usage, such as serving on a special weapons and tactics (SWAT) team. And there are some cities (and areas of those cities) that are far more dangerous than others. On the whole, though, gun use by police officers is infrequent.

Danger, Unpredictability, and Suspicion

Chapter 4 touched on academy training and recruits' learning of the so-called sixth sense (also see the accompanying "Think about It" box), the police officer's somewhat intuitive feelings of skepticism and suspicion. Skepticism and suspicion are essential in policing because the job can sometimes be very unpredictable. This section looks at how danger and unpredictability shape police subculture. Together they breed skepticism and suspicion at levels largely unmatched in other professions.

accepted lie A lie that is necessary in furthering the police mission.

tolerated lie A lie that is used to defend a questionable discretionary decision.

deviant lie A lie that expressly violates the rules and legal requirements.

Control—Synonymous with order maintenance, one of the principal police functions. Control is direct (at a crime scene, for example) or indirect (by simply maintaining a presence in the community).

Territoriality—Police officers tend to learn every aspect of the area to which they are assigned. As part of this learning, they come to appreciate what is normal or abnormal, safe or unsafe. An officer's sense of territory leads him or her to feel a sense of ownership over his or her geographical area of responsibility.

Use of Force—The very possibility of having to use or to face force, and the emotions that accompany the use or threat of force, is a powerful contributor to police subculture.

Danger—Much of police work is routine and predictable, but there is the potential, at any moment, for a violent altercation that could lead to the taking of a life, be it a suspect's life or the officer's.

Unpredictability—There are pros and cons to the unpredictability that is inherent in policing. For one thing, danger can erupt at any moment. Unpredictability, on the other hand, lends meaning and excitement to the job.

Suspicion—A simple equation characterizes much of police work: danger + unpredictability = suspicion. Cops know that given the potential for danger around any turn and the inherent uncertainty that go along with police work, a sense of suspicion is essential.

The Split-Second Syndrome—There are three features of policing—urgency of police–citizen encounters, the involuntariness of such encounters, and the public setting in which they take place—combine to put officers in the position of having to make quick on-the-spot decisions.

Moral Superiority—Moral superiority is concerned with a belief on the part of police officers that they represent a higher moral order.

Common Sense—Common sense arises from the doing of police work, what officers see and how officers act on and react to their working environment. It is the practical knowledge they use to do their work.

The Masculine Enviornment—Police officers work in a largely masculine environment. This is partly due to the fact that the profession has historically been dominated by males. Invariably, this has caused police subculture to be dominated by masculine values and orientations.

The Us-versus-Them Mentality—Police officers perception that it is "us," the police, against "them," everyone else.

Secrecy—The public does not have access to much of what happens in the world of law enforcement. Information tends to be given out on a need-to-know basis. Secrecy also insulates officers from intensive scrutiny from supervisors and the community.

Isolation—The job often requires officers to literally work in isolation. Perhaps more important, though, is the prospect of isolation from the community.

Bravery—Police officers need to possess the attribute of bravery before entering the profession. A person who does not feel comfortable in confrontational, perhaps dangerous situations (or who cannot be taught to act bravely) probably won't make a very good officer.

Art of Deception—Although somewhat controversial, some experts regard the art of deception as none other than good policing or creative detective work.

FIGURE 5.4 Components of Police Subculture.

Danger

The potential for danger sets policing apart from other occupations (also see Figure 5.5).[27] It may not be the most objectively dangerous job (timber cutters and taxi drivers, for instance, die on the job considerably more often than police officers do), but this does not discount the prominent position that perceptions of danger hold in policing. Learning about the prospect of danger begins at the academy and continues through field training, where "police vicariously experience, learn, and re-learn the potential for danger through 'war stories'" told by veteran officers.[28]

In the study of victims (known as *victimology*), there is a concept called the *victimization paradox*. It refers to the fact that some people, especially women, tend to be more fearful of crime than is justified by the likelihood of actually being victimized. A similar phenomenon has been identified in policing and has been called the **paradox of policing**. University of Cincinnati criminologist Francis Cullen and his colleagues found that while the potential for danger pervades police work, policing is not particularly hazardous compared with a number of other occupations. Officers who were interviewed felt that their personal chance of being injured or killed was slim, but they still perceived policing as a dangerous occupation.[29] In other words, policing carries a high *potential* for danger, even if the chances for *actual* danger are not all that high.

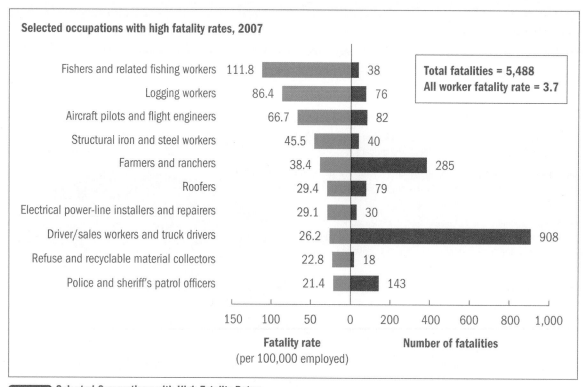

Selected occupations with high fatality rates, 2007

	Fatality rate (per 100,000 employed)	Number of fatalities
Fishers and related fishing workers	111.8	38
Logging workers	86.4	76
Aircraft pilots and flight engineers	66.7	82
Structural iron and steel workers	45.5	40
Farmers and ranchers	38.4	285
Roofers	29.4	79
Electrical power-line installers and repairers	29.1	30
Driver/sales workers and truck drivers	26.2	908
Refuse and recyclable material collectors	22.8	18
Police and sheriff's patrol officers	21.4	143

Total fatalities = 5,488
All worker fatality rate = 3.7

FIGURE 5.5 Selected Occupations with High Fatality Rates.
Source: Bureau of Labor Statistics, *National census of fatal occupational injuries in 2007* (Washington, DC: Bureau of Labor Statistics), p. 4. Available at www.bls.gov/news.release/archives/cfoi_08202008.pdf (accessed December 23, 2010).

A problem with the Cullen study and other studies of the relative dangerousness of police work is that they often focus on officer deaths. Deaths are relatively rare, especially in light of modern medical care, training, and personal protection equipment, such as bulletproof vests. So, if deaths are not a good measure of dangerousness, what is? Some researchers *have* looked at assaults against police officers. The Federal Bureau of Investigation, for example, found that 57,268 officers were assaulted throughout the United States in 2009.[30] This number vastly exceeded the number of killings of police officers; when limited to homicides; such killings tend to number below 50 in any given year. See Figure 5.6 for additional details on the events surrounding killings of, and assaults against, police officers—according to the FBI.

How does police work compare with other occupations in terms of the potential for assault? Certain elements of police work are far more dangerous than others. Researchers have not fully answered this question. Even so, it is a safe bet that few other occupations carry as much potential for employee assault as does policing.

Unpredictability

The relative dangerousness of policing can be debated. Some researchers would say perceptions of dangerousness are overplayed, and officers on the streets would likely argue the opposite. But it is difficult to dispute that levels of unpredictability are high, no matter what one's perspective.

A common saying in the police literature is some variation of this: "Police work is hours of sheer boredom punctuated by moments of sheer terror." Others have referred to the "huff and puff of the chase."[31] Indeed, a number of researchers have argued that it is those unpredictable moments of terror—the adrenaline-pumping seconds—that make policing an attractive job to many people.[32]

Unpredictability need not equate with danger, however. It can simply give rise to the bizarre. Unpredictability can also take on an air of unpleasantness, and officers need a strong stomach to deal with some of what they encounter.

Suspicion

Suspicion can creep into an officer's private life and into his or her associations with others—such as neighbors and strangers—who are not employed in the same line of work. In this vein, suspicion is more than good police work or part of the working personality. Rather, it is a key factor that defines police subculture.

By outsiders, suspicion is regarded as an unfortunate by-product of policing that slowly takes over an officer's whole personality, not just his or her working persona. Some feel that the lack of trust police officers exhibit toward others (apart from other officers) explains why they do not associate much with civilians while off the clock. Police officers regard suspicion in quite a different way. They understand that they have been *trained* to be suspicious, as failure to be "on guard" most of the time can mean the difference between life and death.[33]

Police work is hours of sheer boredom punctuated by moments of sheer terror.

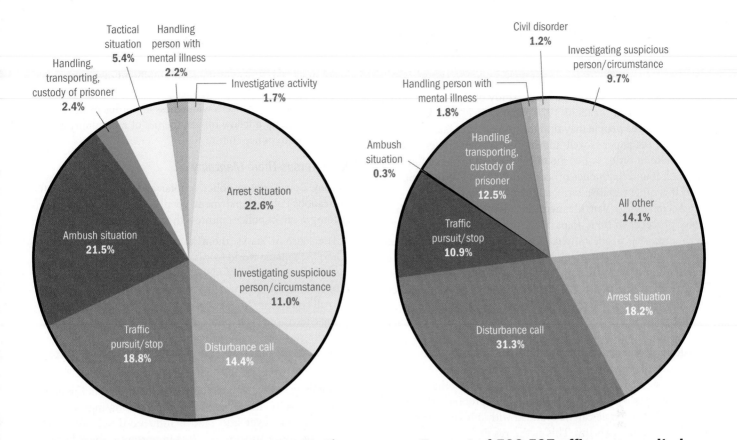

Percent of 536 officers feloniously killed[1]

Percent of 590,507 officers assaulted

FIGURE 5.6 **Law Enforcement Officers Killed and Assaulted.**
Source: Federal Bureau of Investigation, *Law enforcement officers killed and assaulted, 2009* (Washington, DC: Federal Bureau of Investigation), www2.fbi.gov/ucr/killed/2009/data/figure_04.html (accessed December 23, 2010).

The Split-Second Syndrome

If danger and unpredictability breed suspicion, then this is because of what criminologist James Fyfe has called the **split-second syndrome**.[34]

Sometimes officers' decisions are appropriate; other times they are not. If a bad decision is made, Fyfe says, it is partly due to the need to make decisions in the heat of the moment. When, for example, a police officer shoots a suspect who turns out not to be a danger, we must put ourselves in the shoes of the officer. Then it becomes a little more apparent how such decisions come to be made. Inappropriate decisions should be *expected* some of the time, given the demands placed on officers to choose a course of action in a short amount of time, and "any subsequent criticism of officers' decisions—especially by those outside the police, who can have no real appreciation of the burdens upon officers—is an unwarranted attempt to be wise after the event."[35]

Solidarity

There is a tendency among police officers to stick together and to associate with one another. In terms of police subculture, this is known as **solidarity**. Solidarity itself consists of several elements, each of which is covered in the next few subsections. We will look at moral superiority, common sense, the masculine environment, the us-versus-them mentality, and secrecy. Again, we draw on John Crank's informative examination of police subculture for guidance.

Moral Superiority

In discussing police morality, Crank points out that "police see themselves as representatives of a higher morality embodied in a blend of American traditionalism, patriotism, and religion. As moral agents, police view themselves as guardians whose responsibility is not simply to make arrests but to roust out society's trouble-makers."[36] In other words, they see themselves as morally superior in some sense. This may sound pompous, but remember that policing is about enforcing the law. Laws reflect people's perceptions of right and wrong, and those who break them are on the "wrong side," at least most of the time.

There is a darker side to the police moral sense, too. It leads to a tendency to regard ordinary citizens as different and even inferior. For example, people who get speeding tickets are often admonished by the citing officer, who might conclude by saying, "Please watch your speed now." Such statements are usually offered up out of genuine concern for the driver's safety, but they can also be said with thick sarcasm laden with an air of superiority. It is these latter tendencies that Crank points to in his discussion of the "moral mandate" inherent in police work.

Related to the moral mandate is the concept of **dramaturgy**. The simple definition of *dramaturgy* is "the art of theater, or theatrics." Applied to policing, dramaturgy refers to putting on a display of high-mindedness. This display further reinforces beliefs—on the part of police *and* citizens—that law enforcement is doing the right thing and that those who work in it are

Common sense is the lifeblood of police culture.

the "good guys." Perhaps the classic study of this higher moral sense is John Van Maanen's 1978 paper called "The Asshole."[37] Although some people may find the title of Van Maanen's paper offensive, the paper is well known in academic circles, and we use it here in order to be true to his original presentation. Van Maanen found that police officers would brand difficult people with this quite negative term, stigmatizing them.

According to Van Maanen, the identification of an "asshole" proceeds in three steps. First, the **affront** is when an officer's authority is questioned. The second stage, **clarification**, occurs when the officer attempts to ascertain what kind of person he or she is dealing with. Finally, the **remedy** consists of the officer's response. "Assholes," according to Van Maanen, are the people most likely to be on the receiving end of some "street justice."

In reflecting on Van Maanen's work, Crank observes that the term "contained a great deal of meaning for the police. The label emerged from the need to maintain control in street encounters, and from a moral imperative to assert the authority of the state when it was questioned."[38] A problem, though, is that too many people can be branded with this label or, at best, viewed as untrustworthy. This is the result of an unfortunate reality in everyday police work:

> People lie to us eight hours a day. Everybody lies to us: offenders, victims, witnesses. They all lie to the police. It gets so bad, you go to a party, somebody comes up to talk to you. You're thinking, "Why is this guy saying this to me? What's his game?" You can't turn it off.[39]

There are other terms besides "asshole" that police use to describe criminal suspects, other officers, citizens in general, superiors, and scores of other people and issues. Indeed, there is a police vocabulary that is unique and sometimes humorous.

Common Sense

According to Crank, common sense is "the lifeblood of the police culture."[40] What is common sense? The use of the term *common sense* in this context distinguishes between book learning and the ways in which actual police work is done:

> Officers take great pride in their common sense. But their common sense does not come from the world as given. To the contrary, police common sense is expressed in their ability to see the world unseen. Common sense derives from an officer's skills in recognizing the hidden danger in the seemingly safe world inhabited by ordinary citizens.[41]

The Masculine Environment

Police officers work in a largely masculine environment. This is partly due to the fact that the profession has historically been dominated by males. Invariably, this has caused police subculture to be dominated by masculine values and orientations:

> From the outset, recruits are expected to confirm their masculine images to others and to themselves by exaggerating

the characteristics associated with manhood…. Training emphasizes physical conditioning, fighting, weaponry, all skills that are associated with traditional male roles and are practiced as play in the early childhood of American males…. From crude slurs against women to the demonstration of an officer's willingness to put his or her life on the line for a fellow officer, themes of masculinity are pervasive to police culture.[42]

The Us-versus-Them Mentality

Anthony Bouza, noted police scholar and former chief of the Minneapolis Police Department, vividly captured another defining component of police culture—the us-versus-them mentality:

> The sense of "us vs. them" that develops between cops and the outside world forges a bond between cops whose strength is the stuff of fables. It is called the *brotherhood in blue*, and it inspires a fierce and unquestioning loyalty to all cops, everywhere. It is widened by the dependence cops have on each other for safety and backup. The response to a summons to help is a cop's life-line. An "assist police officer" is every cop's first priority. The ultimate betrayal is for one cop to fail to back up another.[43]

The us-versus-them mentality is also reflected in the points we have already made about officers associating with one another. It spills over into (and is influenced by) other components of police subculture. "It is important to bear in mind that being a member of the police fraternity is also a highly gratifying emotional experience in which the officer sees himself as belonging to an exclusive group of men who are braver, smarter, stronger, and more self-reliant than the civilian population they serve."[44]

Secrecy

Researchers have found that secrecy goes hand in hand with solidarity. But one doesn't need to be a researcher to get a feel for how secrecy is important in police work. The veil of secrecy that tends to pervade law enforcement has been readily revealed in high-profile investigations of police corruption. The Mollen Commission's investigation of the New York City Police Department during the 1990s reached this conclusion:

> [Secrecy and solidarity] facilitate corruption primarily in two ways. First, they encourage corruption by setting a standard that nothing is more important than the unswerving loyalty of officers to one another—not even stopping the most serious forms of corruption. Second, these attitudes thwart efforts to control corruption. They lead officers to protect or cover up for others' crimes—even crimes of which they heartily disapprove.[45]

Eastern Kentucky University police studies professor Victor Kappeler and his colleagues have identified a series of what they call "postulates shaping the ethos of secrecy." By "postulates" they mean statements that reflect the overall sentiments expressed by perhaps the majority of police officers. Here are some examples:

> * *"Don't give up another cop."* As perhaps one of the most important factors contributing to secrecy and to a sense of solidarity, this postulate admonishes officers to never,

Think About It...

One- or Two-Officer Patrols? A department's decision to adopt one- versus two-officer patrol is usually dictated by concerns like officer safety. Two-officer patrols are safer for officers, but are twice as costly and there is no conclusive research that shows two-officer patrols are any more effective in crime control. How is the topic of one- versus two-officer patrols relevant to the issue of police subculture? Which approach do you feel should be used, one- or two-officer patrol?

regardless of the seriousness or nature of a case, provide information to either superiors or nonpolice that would cause harm to a fellow police officer... .

* *"Watch out for your partner first and then the rest of the guys working that tour."* This postulate tells police officers they have an obligation to their partners first, and then to other officers working the same shift. "Watching out," in this context, means that an officer has a duty not only to protect a fellow officer from physical harm, but also to watch out for their interests in other matters.

* *"If you get caught off base, don't implicate anybody else."* Being caught off base can involve a number of activities, ranging from being out of one's assigned sector to engaging in prohibited activities. This postulate teaches officers that if they are discovered in proscribed activities, they should accept the punishment, not implicate others*.[46]

Other Components of Police Subculture

Control and territoriality, use of force, suspicion, and solidarity are key components of police culture. There are a few others, though, that do not fit neatly into any of these categories. They include isolation, bravery, and the creative use of deception.

Isolation

Police work is characterized by at least two forms of isolation. First, the job often requires officers to literally work in isolation. Consider sheriff's deputies in rural counties. They can effectively be on their own most of the time. Perhaps more important, though, is the prospect of isolation from the community. Not only are officers somewhat physically removed from the communities they serve, but they can feel isolated in terms of relationships, as well. This is especially true of relationships with nonpolice:

> Social isolation becomes both a consequence and a stimulus... . Police officers find that constraints of schedule, of secrecy, of group mystique, and of growing adaptive suspiciousness and cynicism limit their friendships and relationships in the nonpolice world.[47]

Control and territoriality, use of force, suspicion, and solidarity are key components of police culture.

Bravery

Bravery is one more key component of police subculture. New officers are taught the importance of not backing down, and veteran cops are constantly reminded not to appear "soft."

The Art of Deception

There is a clear dark side to deception. For one thing, most people do not enjoy being lied to. For another, deception can be criminal, such as in the case of providing perjured testimony. There is more to deception in the policing context, though, and it is not necessarily all bad.

Certain types of lies are necessary and desirable. Consider the usual buy-bust operation in which an undercover officer sells a willing buyer a quantity of illegal narcotics. This operation is commonplace in police agencies throughout the United States and is conducted in an effort to control a number of different types of crime. Buy-bust activities rely completely on the art of deception. For obvious reasons, buy-busts would not succeed if they were conducted by uniformed officers.

What kinds of lies are appropriate? Thomas Barker, R. N. Friery, and David L. Carter identified three types of lies and then surveyed officers concerning their perceptions of each.[48] The first were so-called **accepted lies**, those that are necessary in furthering the police mission. Second were **tolerated lies**, those that are used to defend questionable discretionary decisions. Finally, **deviant lies** expressly violate the rules and legal requirements. Interestingly, 58 percent of the officers felt deviant lies were acceptable if the end result was satisfactory. The percentages were much higher for the other types of lies.

Deception may not exactly pervade law enforcement, but it is certainly an important component of police subculture. It is but one element in a long list of values and beliefs that tend to characterize the law enforcement profession in America. Although a distinct culture characterizes many, if not all, occupations, it is safe to say that police subculture is clearly unique.

Sergeant Eileen Barry became supervisor of a New York City Police Department (NYPD) truancy unit on November 30, 1998.

After assuming her post, she learned that one of the officers under her command was falsifying truancy reports. She informed her bosses, there was an investigation, and four officers were suspended. But Barry was then demoted and assigned to undesirable shifts. She was also accused of failing to supervise the officers in her unit.

An investigative hearing revealed that the officers who were suspended had falsified their reports *before* Barry came on the job. Accordingly, Barry was exonerated, but she sued the NYPD, alleging that her First Amendment rights were compromised and that she suffered retaliation for speaking out against misconduct that was occurring in her unit. Other cops in the department allegedly called her a "rat."

Barry also claimed in her lawsuit that the actions taken against her were part of a long-standing "blue wall of silence," the unwritten practice of protecting one's fellow officers, of not cooperating with investigators, and of taking whatever steps are necessary to preserve the "secrecy" of certain aspects of police work—whether right or wrong. A judge decided her lawsuit could go forward, saying

> On balance, in light of the evidence before the court, a reasonable jury could find that a widespread custom of retaliating against officers who expose police misconduct, with officials willfully ignoring if not facilitating the practice, pervades the NYPD.[49]

Police executives, who are routinely called on by the press to comment on investigations of their officers, sometimes claim that the "blue wall of silence" is imaginary. A few years ago in Toronto, for example, a number of police officers were being investigated for theft and for offering perjured testimony. They were uncooperative and downright hostile to investigators, but the chief of the department supported his force, saying, "I don't think there is a blue wall of silence, and I can't speak to the hostility... . The way things have been portrayed—as if there is widespread corruption—that's not the case at all."[50]

Sergeant Barry's experience, along with the comments made by the Toronto police chief, raise several interesting questions:

1. Did Barry collide head-on with the "blue wall of silence"?

2. Who is right about the existence of the "blue wall"—Barry or the Toronto police chief? Can they both be right?

3. Do police officers tend to "protect their own" in cases like this?

4. Is there anything inherently wrong with looking out for one's colleagues? If not, when does it go too far?

5. Does Barry's experience reveal the negative side of police work? What other elements might be part of that "underbelly"?

Source: © Ryan McGinnis/Alamy

Describe the elements of culture.

Culture is a shared set of values, norms, and behaviors that form a way of life. Cultures are characterized by similar themes, institutional values (that is, beliefs about how things should get done), and means of expression. A segment of a larger culture that shares particular values and norms is called a *subculture*.

1. What is culture?

2. What are the differences between a culture and a subculture?

3. What is the role of institutional values in the formation of a culture?

culture A set of shared values, norms, and behaviors that form a way of life.

value A standard of goodness, desirability, behavior, beauty, or interaction that serves as a guideline for living within a particular culture.

norm A rule or expectation for behavior that characterizes a particular social group.

institution An organizational structure through which values and norms are transmitted over time and from one location to another within a society.

subculture Cultural patterns that distinguish some segment of a society's population.

police subculture The shared values and norms and the established patterns of behavior that tend to characterize policing; also called *police culture*.

institutional value A sense of agreement within a particular culture about how to accomplish a valued objective.

Explain the sources of police subculture.

The sources of police culture include organizational factors, the street environment, administration, other criminal justice agencies, and the media. Values within police subculture are not necessarily foreign to the wider culture, but their close association with one another and the exclusion of other wider norms and values are what give police subculture its characteristics.

1. From what sources does the police subculture arise?

2. How does the street environment influence police subculture?

street environment One of two settings identified by John Crank (the other is the traffic stop) in which police officers perform daily tasks that involve interaction with ordinary citizens and with other criminal justice professionals.

LEARNING OUTCOMES 3 Summarize the components of police subculture.

Police subculture is characterized by several factors, including control and territoriality; use of force; danger, unpredictability, and suspicion; and solidarity. Control refers not just to control over a particular area, but also to an officer's sense of territoriality. Police work is potentially dangerous, and work situations are commonly unpredictable. These factors lead to suspicion and force officers to make split-second decisions. Solidarity is about sticking together. It has a number of components: moral superiority, common sense, masculine values, an us-versus-them mentality, and an aura of secrecy. Policing can be isolating; officers can be physically and socially isolated from the citizens they serve. Bravery is another essential component of police subculture. Finally, police subculture is sometimes characterized by the creative use of deception.

1. What are the key components of the police subculture? Which is most important in your view?

2. What role does territoriality play in the police subculture?

3. What is meant by the term "split-second syndrome," and how does it apply to police work?

dominion John Crank's substitute for the term *territoriality*, which refers to an officer's sense of personal ownership over the area for which he or she is responsible.

paradox of policing A phenomenon in which a police officer's fear of being injured or killed is stronger than is justified by actual rates of injury or death within the profession.

split-second syndrome A condition confronting police officers that involves three central features of policing—the urgency of police–citizen encounters, the involuntariness of such encounters, and a public setting—all of which combine to place officers in the position of having to make quick on-the-spot decisions.

solidarity The tendency among police officers to stick together and associate with one another.

dramaturgy In the law enforcement context, the act of putting on a display of high-mindedness.

affront According to John Van Maanen, the first of three steps police officers use in identifying an "asshole." It occurs when an officer's authority is questioned.

clarification According to John Van Maanen, the second of three steps police officers use in identifying an "asshole." It occurs when the officer attempts to ascertain what kind of person he or she is dealing with.

remedy According to John Van Maanen, the last of three steps police officers use in identifying an "asshole." It consists of the officer's response to an affront.

accepted lie A lie that is necessary in furthering the police mission.

tolerated lie A lie that is used to defend a questionable discretionary decision.

deviant lie A lie that expressly violates the rules and legal requirements.

MyCJLab

Go to the Chapter 5 section in *MyCJLab* to test your understanding of this chapter, access customized study content, engage in interactive simulations, complete critical thinking and research assignments, and view related online videos.

Additional Links

Learn more about the nature of contacts between the police and the public at **www.justicestudies. com/pubs/contacts.pdf**.

Read about police culture and the code of silence at **http://tinyurl.com/3szx6xf**.

Police Discretion and Behavior

"Discretion allows officers to treat each situation differently, in accordance with realistic goals and humanitarian principles."

1 Describe police discretion and its advantages and disadvantages.

2 Differentiate between the universalistic and particularistic perspectives on police behavior.

3 Describe the factors that affect police decision making.

6

INTRO: THE POLICE CANNOT (AND ARE NOT REQUIRED TO) PREVENT ALL CRIMES

In 2005, the U.S. Supreme Court, in the case of *Castle Rock* v. *Gonzales*, ruled that a city police department could not be sued for failing to enforce a restraining order, even though that failure led to the brutal murder of a woman's three children by her estranged husband.[1] The facts of the case show that the husband took his daughters while they were playing outside of their home, and that the police failed to respond to the wife's repeated reports (made over a period of several hours) that her husband had taken the children in violation of the restraining order. In suing the police department, lawyers for Mrs. Gonzales cited a Colorado statute directing that law enforcement officers "shall use every reasonable means to enforce a protection order."

While the *Gonzales* case stemmed from a terrible personal tragedy, the justices' decision illustrates the protections enjoyed by police agencies whose officers exercise discretion in the performance of their duties. According to Karen J. Kruger—legal counsel for Maryland Chiefs of Police Association—writing in the journal *Police Chief*, in *Gonzales* the Court "recognized that there is a 'deep-rooted ... law enforcement discretion, even in the presence of seemingly mandatory legislative commands.'"[2] Writing for the majority in *Gonzales*, Justice Scalia noted that there is "[a] well established tradition of police discretion [that] has long

DISCUSS In what ways do police officers exercise discretion? Should police discretion be limited?

coexisted with apparently mandatory arrest statutes."[3] You can access the original article about the case in the *Police Chief* magazine's online archive at **http://tinyurl.com/3m3wyxl**.

Police officers have the authority to make decisions that can affect individuals in profound and lasting ways. One officer might decide to arrest someone for the first time, giving that person a criminal record. Another officer in the same situation might feel that arrest is unnecessary and might use an informal tactic instead. All criminal justice officials, including prosecutors, exercise discretion, but police are the gatekeepers to the criminal justice process, and without the decisions they make to begin the process, prosecutors and other criminal justice officials would never have the opportunity to decide the fate of criminal suspects.

What *explains* police action—the choices that individual officers make when faced with varying situations? Is there something about the job that causes police officers to behave in certain ways? Are there different kinds of officers, and might differing personalities shed some light on these questions? What about factors other than the officers themselves, such as the characteristics of the communities they serve? In this chapter we explore how considerations like these help explain and even predict police behavior.

► Defining Discretion

George Kelling, known for his "broken windows" perspective on crime prevention, once described the observations he made while walking with a Newark, New Jersey, police officer who was patrolling a neighborhood:

> As he saw his job, he was to keep an eye on strangers, and make certain that the disreputable regulars observed some informal but widely understood rules. Drunks and addicts could sit on the stoops, but could not lie down. People could drink on side streets, but not at the main intersection. Bottles had to be in paper bags. Talking to, bothering or begging from people waiting at the bus stop was strictly forbidden. Persons who broke the informal rules, especially [the latter], were arrested for vagrancy. Noisy teenagers were told to keep quiet.[4]

This observation captures the essence of police discretion more than any formal definition can. Although it is from a study that took place more than 25 years ago, the theme remains the same. Every community has its share of problems and priorities. Police officers must respond to those priorities and manage problems as best

Every community has its share of problems and priorities.

they can. Priorities may be assigned by residents and may have little to do with serious crime. Problems may need to be addressed in one way for some people and in another way for others. Or, in the case of Kelling's observations, *where* a problem occurs—and *how* it occurs—helps officers decide on the proper course of action.

Kelling's observations describe what discretion is, but we would be remiss to ignore more formal definitions of *police discretion*. Put simply, discretion consists of a two-part decision made by a police officer in a particular situation: (1) whether to intervene, and if the decision to intervene is made, (2) how best to intervene. But this definition is anything but simple when examined closely. Consider the typical traffic stop. Researchers have identified about ten different kinds of action that officers can take once a vehicle is stopped (for example, order the driver out of the car), seven strategies that could be used during the stop (for example, administer a field sobriety test), and 11 exit strategies that could be used (for example, arrest). These three factors alone present a total of 770 possible action

LEARNING OUTCOMES 1 Describe police discretion and its advantages and disadvantages.

Source: Orange Line Media/ Shutterstock.com

Police discretion consists of a two-part decision: (1) whether to intervene, and (2) how best to intervene.

combinations.[5] Needless to say, deciding whether and how to intervene can take an officer in *many* different directions, and he or she must be prepared for and trained to handle each one effectively.

Another way to conceive of discretion is to consider the distinction between the *letter* of the law and the *spirit* of the law. A police officer who follows the letter of the law issues a citation for every infraction, no matter how minor, and arrests every criminal suspect for all manner of criminal activity. In contrast, an officer who follows the spirit of the law looks at what the law intends and realizes that, from time to time, arrests and citations may not meet with the law's intent. The reality of policing is that officers frequently *must* make decisions, and often the law and an officer's decision correspond, but not always. Indeed, as we will see shortly, the two can be completely at odds with one another.

Note that we are not talking about police deviance, which is discussed in this book's last section. Perhaps it sounds a bit deviant that a police officer would ignore the letter of the law or let outside considerations enter into his or her decision-making process. And yes, it can be deviant—and possibly criminal— for an officer to overlook certain activities. But it can also be

necessary. There are many occasions when it is simply not practical or advisable to arrest all suspects. We see this particularly in the war on drugs. Is it advisable to arrest every person caught with a modest amount of marijuana for personal consumption? Some readers may feel the answer is yes, but the practical answer is certainly no. There is just not enough room in jail to arrest everyone who *could* be arrested. In this sense, police officers are de facto policy makers. They decide, in some respects, what is and is not right. According to one scholar,

> The police are among the most important policy makers of our entire society. And they make far more discretionary determinations in individual cases than does any other class of administrators; I know of no close second.[6]

The Pros and Cons of Police Discretion

One of the clear advantages associated with police discretion is that it gives law enforcement officers a measure of job satisfaction. Indeed, research reveals that job satisfaction improves with job conditions like autonomy.[7] Autonomy and discretionary decision making go hand in hand. Discretion is also advantageous because without it the wheels of justice would grind to a halt. The system is just not equipped to deal with the massive influx of people that would result if officers arrested every identifiable lawbreaker. On a related note, discretion allows officers to treat each situation differently, in accordance with realistic goals and humanitarian principles (Figure 6.1). Some people favor "throwing the book" at every offender, but for those who favor mercy from time to time, police discretion is the best solution.

The negative aspects of police discretion probably outweigh the positive ones, mainly because the public's attention is drawn to discretionary decisions when something goes wrong. Incidents of police abuse and corruption generally lead people to call for reforms aimed at reining in police behavior. For example, many police departments have adopted policies restricting pursuit driving. These are intended to limit officer discretion in the name of preserving public safety and minimizing injuries to

Pros	Cons
• Promotes job satisfaction	• Potential for abuse
• Promotes autonomy	• Potential for corruption
• Necessary for criminal justice system efficiency	• Potential for needless death/injury (for example, if no pursuit-driving policy)
• Promotes realistic goals	• Possible citizen complaints of unequal treatment
• Promotes humanitarian principles	• Possible litigation when things go awry

and Cons of Police Discretion.

innocent third parties. Policies restricting the use of deadly force also limit what officers can do in terms of apprehending resistant suspects. In fact, the bulk of a police department's policy manual is aimed at telling officers what they can and cannot do. When discretion runs amok, things can go wrong—resulting in needless injury or death, civil litigation, and other problems.

Discretion and Seniority

We have been discussing discretion as though it were used in the same manner by officers of all ranks. Nothing could be further from the truth. There is, as University of Nevada (Reno) professor Ken Peak has observed, an inverse relationship between discretion and seniority.[8] As an officer's rank increases, he or she is able to make fewer discretionary decisions. How is this so? The officer on the street has the greatest authority to decide who to arrest, pursue, stop, and so forth. The discretion of chiefs of police and other high-level administrators, in contrast, is limited by two factors. First, they do less ordinary police work, thus limiting the number of occasions when they may be able to employ discretion as we have defined it. Second, administrators tend to be limited by budget constraints, union pressures, governing boards, influential politicians, and others. In deciding who to hire, for instance, the chief (or whoever makes this decision) must be cognizant of diversity issues. This limits the pool of prospective officers to some extent.

This is not to say that administrators can't make decisions on their own or think outside the box. They do, but in different ways than patrol officers. For example, since money is often in short supply in some agencies, top executives have to act creatively to drum up needed revenue. The chief who sells advertising space on his department's cruisers (and some have) may be seen as a creative, forward-thinking, entrepreneurial manager. Others might regard this as unethical behavior and criticize the chief for pandering to certain interests, such as the owners of the business who buy the space. Either way, the initial decision to sell the advertising space is a discretionary one. It is safe to say, then, that while an administrative position limits one's discretionary latitude, it certainly opens the door to new types of decisions that the beat cop or frontline officer ordinarily does not get to make.

▶ Explaining Police Behavior

Police behavior can be explained from either a **universalistic perspective** or a **particularistic perspective**. The universalistic perspective is simply the view that all police officers are similar and that they exhibit some of the same characteristics and behavior patterns. The particularistic perspective, in contrast, considers how individual officers differ from one another. Similarly, we can ask whether law enforcement officers behave the way they do because of personal values and patterns of behavior they have acquired through socialization and introduction into police subculture or because of individual predispositions toward certain ways of thinking and acting.

The Universalistic Perspective

To say that all police officers are similar in some respects requires some attention to sociology, psychology, and organizational theory. Sociology, in this case, is concerned with the influence of peers and coworkers. Psychology is concerned with whether there is a distinct police personality. Organizational factors can influence police behavior as well.

Police officers are selected and trained in a very unique environment.[9] It is unlike that found in almost any other occupation. Academy training indoctrinates recruits into the world of policing and teaches trainees to view others in a particular way (that is, with a measure of suspicion). The sociological perspective is also important from a demographic standpoint. To this day, the typical police officer is a white male. Women and minorities have made great strides in terms of gaining representation in the law enforcement profession, but they are not represented in the profession in accordance with their numbers in the population as a whole. Research reveals that female officers are socialized to adapt to a largely male-dominated work environment.[10] In other words, traditional police training (in the academy and on the job) has encouraged female recruits to act in a masculine fashion.

Does policing draw a particular personality type? If so, this is an example of how psychological factors may yield common bonds among police officers. There is surprisingly little research on what types of personalities are drawn to police work. Much more accepted is the view that socialization is more influential than any degree of predisposition. Not everyone agrees, however, so we will revisit the predisposition versus socialization issue shortly. It is the law enforcement equivalent of the nature-versus-nurture argument that plays out in the criminology literature and elsewhere in human development studies.

In addition, there are organizational factors that make all officers alike. The quasi-military structure of most police agencies requires a certain pattern of behavior among all employees. Everything from chain of command to rules of dress ensures that one officer closely resembles the other officers.

Community policing may be creating suborganizations within specific police departments. Ask a special weapons and tactics (SWAT) or narcotics officer in any large urban police department what he or she thinks of the officers who work in the community policing division. Some will answer that those officers are somewhat different; some may even say that they are not doing real police work. The point is that, *traditionally*, organizational factors may have led to similarities among all officers. It is quite probable that all of this is changing in contemporary policing and that a particularistic perspective is starting to take hold.

The Particularistic Perspective

The particularistic perspective is concerned with how specific officers differ from one another. We just suggested that narcotics officers may be (and almost certainly are) different in a

Role orientation refers to an officer's individual conception of what constitutes proper and good police work.

number of respects from community police officers, although there are some officers who work both assignments at some point in their careers.

Studies of police culture and personality point to a number of characteristics that police officers share, including suspiciousness, cynicism, loyalty to colleagues, and pessimism. Particularistic perspectives, however, suggest that there is no one personality or set of traits that typifies all police officers. Robert Worden has identified five attitudinal dimensions that can be used to explain differences among individual police officers. They include role orientations, perceptions of legal restrictions, perceptions of citizen respect and cooperation, perceptions of legal institutions, and views on selective enforcement.[11]

Role orientation refers to an officer's individual conception of what constitutes proper and good police work. As might be expected, police officers differ in this regard. As Worden observes, "Some officers believe that the police role is defined wholly by the mandate to fight crime and enforce the law; they believe in the utility of an aggressive style of patrol, and they regard order maintenance and service tasks with distaste."[12] At the other extreme are officers who favor a broader police role that includes more than crime fighting. Some officers see order maintenance and service provision as higher callings than crime control and see themselves as positive rather than negative influences on people's lives.[13]

The officer who views his or her role as consisting mainly of crime control will be inclined to behave in a manner consistent with that view. This might translate into frequent stops of suspicious individuals, punitive responses to disputes (for example, arresting the parties to a domestic dispute rather than counseling them), and zealous criminal investigations. Because these officers see crime control as most important, "minor disputes fall outside of their definition of police responsibilities, and more serious disputes are police business only insofar as they constitute crimes."[14] Officers with this narrow role orientation would not have an interest in mediating disputes to settle them verbally instead of with force or by arresting someone. By contrast, officers who see themselves as having a broad role orientation will use an approach that best serves the needs of the people they serve.

All police officers are bound by various legal requirements, whether they agree with them or not. This does not mean, however, that they necessarily *like* operating under these legal limitations. In fact, there are clear differences among police officers in terms of their perceptions of legal restrictions. Some officers have total respect for the law, for department policy, and for the influence of the courts on their duties. These officers may be the exception,[15] however. According to Worden, "The stereotypical police officer chafes under due process provisions in the single-minded pursuit of criminal offenders. This officer bitterly resents legal and departmental restrictions concerning search and seizure, interrogation, and the use of force."[16]

An officer's perceptions of legal restrictions may also be indicative of his or her overall ideological stance. For example, some officers may occasionally bend the rules when it comes to accosting pedestrians or stopping motorists. If the justification for doing so is not in place in advance, these officers may fabricate a reason to justify their actions in hindsight. This resembles a conservative law-and-order mentality with a clear focus on crime control in lieu of due process. Indeed, studies of on-the-job performance have revealed numerous examples of this behavior.[17] At the other extreme, of course, are officers who both are cognizant of and strictly adhere to legal restrictions.

If a suspect physically resists police intervention, the officer will surely respond in kind—that is, uncooperative suspects will be dealt with accordingly. We will see some more evidence of this toward the end of the chapter. For now, it is also important to note that there are differences among police officers in terms of their perceptions of citizen respect and cooperation. Some officers think that the public is mostly supportive. It would be easy to get this sense if one is a recruiter, a Drug Abuse Resistance Education (DARE) program officer, or an officer who works closely with citizens in a positive sense. Other officers sometimes feel that they are held in somewhat low regard by citizens, and still others feel—rightly, much of the time—that they enjoy little respect and are viewed with nothing short of hostility and animosity.

Law enforcement is an institution, not unlike a religion. As an institution, it views itself somewhat differently, perhaps,

TABLE 6.1 | The Universalistic versus Particularistic Perspective on Police Behavior

Universalistic Perspective	Particularistic Perspective
Officers are socialized.	Officers take on different role orientations.
Officers are psychologically similar.	Officers act differently based on legal restrictions.
Police organizations force all officers to act similarly.	Officers act differently based on their perceptions of citizens.
Officers act differently based on their views of the criminal justice system.	Officers act differently based on their views of certain laws.

Source: R. Roberg, K. Novak, and G. Cordner, "The universalistic versus the particularistic," *Police and society*, 3rd ed. (New York: Oxford University Press, 2005), pp. 272–274. Reprinted by permission.

- Police officers are socialized formally and informally into their occupations.
- Formal socialization usually plays out in the academy and during the field training period.
- Informal socialization results from the new hires' interactions with seasoned officers and their colleagues.

- Recently, there has been renewed interest in whether police officers are somehow predisposed either to accept a law enforcement position or to act a certain way once employed.
- Research study findings suggest that police officers' values are somewhat entrenched before they even enter the force.

Most likely it is a mix of socialization and predisposition that determine officers' values and behaviors.

FIGURE 6.2 Socialization or Predisposition.

than other institutions. Police officers themselves have their own divergent perceptions of legal institutions. Consider the courts, for example. Some officers view the courts as supportive and helpful. Others regard them as being soft on crime or totally out of touch with the realities of police work. In a recent case, for example, the U.S. Supreme Court decided that it is not unconstitutional for a police officer to arrest someone for a traffic violation.[18] While police officers generally applauded this clarification (and seeming expansion) of their powers, the decision did not change police work very much. It does not mean that the police will begin an aggressive campaign of arresting people for not wearing their seatbelts. Police agencies have bigger fish to fry. Decisions like this, then, seem to officers to be concerned with legal minutia and do little to help the police on a practical level. Officers' perceptions of courts can be extended to include attitudes toward judges and prosecutors, as well.[19]

Some officers are more proactive in their duties than others. This may also owe to their perceptions of other criminal justice institutions—including even prisons. If an officer feels that the prosecutor will reject his or her case, that the judge will hand down a lenient decision, or that there is not enough room in the local jail or nearby prison, it may influence the arrest decision. Research on traffic enforcement makes this clearer. Forty years ago, J. A. Gardiner set out to explain why police in one city issued more traffic tickets than their counterparts in a nearby city. He traced this to the fact that the first city did not require its officers to appear in court until after a not guilty plea was entered.[20] This suggests a degree of collaboration between the police and the court that influenced police behavior. In contrast, the officers in the other city, where the court was not as supportive of their efforts, were inclined to make fewer traffic stops because it would be a burden. (See Table 6.1 for a summary of the discussion in this section.)

Research reveals—and common sense suggests—that police officers also vary in terms of their selectivity—that is, their willingness to enforce the law.[21] In the case of a murder, few would argue that any officer would not want to arrest the perpetrator. But what of less serious offenses like public intoxication, prostitution, and vagrancy? Do all officers enforce laws against these behaviors equally? Of course not. To the extent that selectivity varies among individual police officers, it is reasonable to conclude that this could affect their decisions in any number of disputes:

> Officers who believe that they should be selective in enforcing the law might be expected seldom to invoke the law in resolving disputes and instead avail themselves of informal methods; officers who are non-selective might be expected to make arrests more frequently and to adopt extra-legal strategies less frequently.[22]

Socialization or Predisposition?

We earlier raised the question of whether law enforcement officers are socialized into the perspectives they hold or whether they bring with them certain predispositions in terms of their values and behavior. Although some are more susceptible to peer influence and pressure than others, it would be impossible for any officer to completely ignore his or her colleagues, superiors, and instructors.

There has been a renewed interest in the suggestion that officers bring certain predispositions into the policing profession. Research has for decades backed up this point.[23] Research also reveals that those who enter law enforcement believe in the importance of authority and seek fulfillment in their careers. A more recent study confirms these findings, leading the authors to conclude that "individual value systems are more important than occupational socialization."[24] This means that police officers' values are somewhat entrenched before they even enter the force.[25] Chances are, though, that there is a mix of predisposition and socialization that actually takes place.

▶ *Police Decision Making*

Scores of researchers have sought to identify predictors of police decision making. We can place their findings into four general categories: organizational factors, neighborhood factors, situational factors, and individual officer characteristics. Within each of these categories are several subcategories, which we explore in this section.

Organizational Factors

The organization for which an officer works can shape his or her decision-making patterns. The bureaucratic structure of the typical police organization requires that its employees jump through certain hoops. Whether they like it or not, officers must follow the rules. This is true of any organization; people must follow the rules or risk losing their job.

Bureaucratic Structure

The typical police department adheres to a fairly rigid bureaucratic model of administration. This is done primarily to guide employee behavior and to direct and control it.[26] Part of this is accomplished through written policies. Policy manuals seek to control police decision making, such as pursuit or arrest decisions.

LEARNING OUTCOMES 3 Describe the factors that affect police decision making.

GLOSSARY

territorial imperative The sense of obligation, even protectiveness, that develops in officers who routinely patrol the same area.

Several researchers have criticized the bureaucratic control principle. Proponents of the community policing movement suggest that there may be a better way to run police departments, such as by decentralizing them and giving line officers more latitude in their decision making. More than one researcher has argued, for instance, that written policy manuals do little to affect the quality of police service.[27]

Beats and Scheduling

An officer's beat can also influence his or her behavior. In general, the larger the patrol beat, the more impersonal the relationship will be between officer and citizen.[28] In contrast, officers who patrol relatively smaller areas, such as small towns, tend to adopt more of a service orientation in their daily activities.[29] This does not mean, however, that all small areas will see a service style of policing. Some officers work dangerous beats in high-crime downtown areas on bicycle or on foot. In these places, an enforcement stance may prevail over a service orientation. Somewhat related to this is the finding that officers in larger departments are less prone to making arrests for drunk driving than their counterparts in smaller agencies.[30]

We all know that work can get boring, especially if it is routine, totally predictable, and unchanging. This extends to policing, too, but not necessarily in the way one would expect. Researchers have found that police departments that routinely rotate their officers into different beats, units, or shifts affect the relationships

The nature of the neighborhood that an officer patrols has an effect on his or her behavior.

between their officers and citizens. In particular, frequent rotation puts distance between officers and the people they serve.[31] This has been called "stranger policing,"[32] and it is not unlike what occurs when a person frequently moves from one city or state to the next; it becomes difficult to form close relationships.

When a police officer routinely works the same beat, he or she can come to form close relationships with citizens. As one researcher puts it, "An officer's continued presence in a neighborhood increases the likelihood of repeated contact with citizens and helps officers develop empathy through an understanding of problems."[33] In fact, research also reveals that officers who routinely patrol the same area develop a sense of obligation to the area and even a desire to be protective of it. This has been called the **territorial imperative**,[34] and police departments appear to be taking advantage of it.

Neighborhood Factors

Police officers who patrol America's affluent communities rarely encounter problems. They often enjoy good relationships with the vast majority of the law-abiding citizens they see daily. Then there are the officers who patrol the worst run-down neighborhoods, which are plagued by drug problems, gang violence, and serious crime. These officers are regarded with suspicion, insulted, and even shot at periodically. It is easy to understand why the nature of the neighborhood that an officer patrols has some effect on his or her behavior.

Consider, again, the broken windows theory. It argues for a certain type of law enforcement, depending on the problems a particular neighborhood faces. James Q. Wilson and George L. Kelling argue that if signs of physical and social disorder affect a neighborhood, then officers should concentrate their efforts on those problems because failure to address quality-of-life matters like these will surely invite serious crime. The broken windows theory thus provides another illustration of how neighborhood conditions can affect police strategies, decisions, and discretion.

Racial Composition and Heterogeneity

Several researchers have looked at neighborhood racial composition and its effects on police decision making. Findings reveal a greater demand for police services in minority-dominated neighborhoods.[35] This, some have argued, has been due to a

(Think About It...

Mandatory Arrests for Domestic Violence In response to the problem of domestic violence, some police agencies have implemented mandatory arrest policies. The logic behind these policies is simple: By removing one of the parties from the scene through an arrest, the problem stops—at least in the short term. The question, however, is whether mandatory arrest has long-term consequences. The issue is important because of its relevance to police discretion. Does mandatory arrest go "too far" in terms of restricting officer discretion? If so, explain. If not, in what other areas may it be beneficial to limit police discretion?

Source: Greg Lovett/Palm Beach Post/ZUMA Press/Newscom

Police Decision Making **95**

greater number of incidents as well as "a belief in the appropriateness of calling the police."[36] The relationship between neighborhood racial composition and police activity can also be understood in terms of the police being more suspicious and alert in such neighborhoods.[37]

Although it is not clear why, research also suggests that the police are more active in neighborhoods characterized by extensive racial heterogeneity.[38] Heterogeneous neighborhoods are those with ethnic or racial diversity.

Socioeconomic Status

Minority-dominated neighborhoods also tend to be comparatively less well-off. Numerous studies back this up and also show that police tend to make more arrests in poorer areas.[39] Interestingly, research also reveals that police are more likely to listen to a request for arrest in wealthier neighborhoods. For example, if one of the parties to a domestic dispute insists that an officer not make an arrest, the officer would apparently be more inclined to listen to a wealthy person's views on this subject than a poor person's. This is assuming, of course, that the officer's department does not follow a mandatory arrest policy.

Crime

Informed readers know that racial composition, socioeconomic status, and crime go hand in hand. There is more crime where there are more people. Conversely, there is much less crime in rich areas. It should be no surprise, then, to find that police make more arrests in densely populated, poor, high-crime areas. Where there is no crime, there is little need to make arrests. But there are *some* mixed findings in this area. For example, at least one author has argued that where crime is common, this may stretch police resources, forcing them to respond less vigorously than they otherwise would.[40] At the least, extensive research reveals that neighborhood crime rates can influence officer attitudes.[41]

- -

Situational Factors

Every police–citizen encounter is different. Some occur behind closed doors, such as when an arrest warrant is served in a private residence. Others occur in full view of bystanders and even cameras. Some suspects are docile and cooperative; others put up a fight. Offenses vary, too. A person facing the prospect of life in prison for his third violent felony may have little to lose if he resists arrest, but the juvenile who is arrested for the first time may not cause any trouble. Even the means by which the police arrive at the scene can have an effect on the outcome of the situation. The point is that situational factors, in addition to community-level factors, can influence an officer's decision making.

Scene and Suspects

Whether an officer arrives at the scene on his or her initiative or as a result of a call is the first important factor in determining how the officer will act. As might be expected, if someone calls the police, it generally means that the person *wants* officers there. In contrast, if officers initiate contact with people on their own, such as by engaging in preventive patrol, the contacts can be somewhat more antagonistic. Moreover, police are more likely to make arrests and treat people harshly in the second situation.[42]

Research has also cited examples of retaliation by officers who feel offended by a suspect's behavior. For example, people who are not respectful to an officer during a traffic encounter receive more traffic citations than those who show respect.[43] This also extends to other types of police–citizen encounters. In fact, the evidence is very clear that suspect demeanor is one of the most significant predictors of police behavior: Disrespectful and uncooperative people are more likely to be arrested or cited.[44] Even studies on police corruption and brutality reveal that both occur more often when a lack of respect is displayed toward the officer.[45]

One of the research problems in this area concerns the proper measurement of suspect demeanor. Many researchers have measured demeanor in terms of criminal activity (for example, assaulting the arresting officer), but one researcher found that legal forms of resistance (such as insulting the officer) did not lead to a higher probability of arrest.[46] Not everyone is in agreement with these findings, however.[47]

It is important to note that we are looking at all these predictors of police decision making in isolation. In reality, these factors occur together. Race combined with demeanor may have a stronger influence on an officer's decision. Socioeconomic status may interact with the crime rate—and even race—and also exert a substantial influence.

Suspect demographic characteristics, notably race, gender, and age, have also been shown to influence police decision making. The effects of race are consistent with the neighborhood factors we have already touched on: Minorities tend to be treated differently from whites.[48] "Some researchers contend that this situation is the result of the fact that African-Americans, and possibly other minorities, may be more likely to resist police authority or display a 'bad' attitude or outright hostility, from an officer's point of view."[49] One recent study reveals, interestingly, that race is more important in shaping an officer's level of suspicion toward someone than his or her initial decision to stop or arrest the person.[50]

Consider racial profiling. Although it is difficult to measure accurately whether profiling actually occurs, many believe it is rampant, and at least a few studies support such claims.[51] To the extent that profiling occurs, it provides perhaps the clearest evidence that race can influence officer decision making. But is that because police officers are racially biased? Is it misguided stereotyping, or is it just good policing? The answers to these questions remain somewhat elusive. Some law enforcement officials say more minorities appear to be stopped because they are where crime is; civil libertarians argue otherwise.

Gender has also been considered as a possible predictor of police decision making, although researchers have not been drawn to it as much as race. Who is more likely to be arrested, men or women? At least one study reveals, not too surprisingly, that women are less likely to be arrested than men, particularly when they display ladylike characteristics or behaviors.[52] In contrast, when women step outside the bounds of what is considered proper behavior, they are arrested more often.

Controversially, some researchers have studied police sexual violence, finding that it may be more common than once expected.[53] Others have explained this as resulting from the greater opportunities (for example, isolation from others, such as during a traffic stop) and the power and authority of police work. Indeed, some researchers have even found that attractive women are more likely to be stopped for traffic violations, mainly so the officer can make personal contact.[54]

Finally, the suspect's age may be associated with police decision making, as well. In general, young people tend to be rebellious and thus disrespectful toward police. The research bears this out,[55] particularly as it influences officer behavior. Also, younger people are more likely than older people to be arrested or dealt with harshly.[56] This may create a two-way relationship—that is, if young people are dealt with more harshly because they are disrespectful, then disrespect may be exacerbated by the fact that young people are treated harshly.[57] Of course, these are generalizations. There are different types of officers out there, as we have already made clear. Research reveals, in fact, that community police officers may be more inclined than their traditional counterparts to deal with young people informally.[58]

Relationships between Parties

The evening news makes it appear as though most crime is violent and that it occurs between strangers. Neither is correct. Most crime is nonviolent, and much of it occurs between people who know each other to some extent. When thinking about police decision making, it is also important to consider the relationship between both parties to the incident: victims and offenders. If two people know each other, does it always make sense to arrest one of the parties when, perhaps, the matter could be settled informally? The answer is often no. Several studies reveal that as relational distance between the parties increases, arrest is more likely.[59] Research also reveals that when the victim prefers that no arrest be made, officers are often influenced by such sentiments.[60]

Offense Seriousness

For obvious reasons, the seriousness of the offense will bear significantly on officer behavior. A serious crime, such as a homicide, will surely result in an arrest if a suspect is identified and located. Minor offenses and infractions are more often dealt with informally, perhaps with just a warning. An interesting question has arisen in this context, however. Do police officers make more arrests in cases of serious crime simply because the crime is serious, or is something else at work? The answer lies in what constitutes proper legal justification, or probable cause, to make an arrest. Probable cause is more likely to be present in cases of serious crime, especially violent crime, because there may be signs of physical injury, a weapon that can be located, witness accounts, and so forth. In contrast, minor offenses like shoplifting a trivial amount of merchandise may be more difficult to prove, thus making it harder for an officer to justify an arrest.[61]

Location

Consider this hypothetical scenario. An officer stops a motorist for drunk driving. He then administers a field sobriety test in broad daylight in view of several pedestrians. The driver has apparent difficulty passing the exam, but the officer lets her drive away. Would this happen? Certainly not, for two reasons. First, it would dangerous to allow an intoxicated motorist to drive off. It would also be against department rules for a police officer to allow a visibly intoxicated motorist to drive home on her own. Second, the presence of bystanders would make it even more controversial to send the motorist on her way. The location of this incident in plain view of other people would be sure to influence the officer's decision to some extent. Step outside this scenario to any other high-profile public contact between a police officer and a citizen. Officers know in these moments that they must be careful to follow proper policy to avoid complaints, litigation, and so forth. Alternatively, when police–citizen contacts take place behind closed doors, or out of public view, there is more of an opportunity to treat the matter informally.

Bystanders

Closely related to the public-private distinction is the issue of whether bystanders are present. Bystanders are, of course, more likely to be present in public places. Thus, when they are under citizen scrutiny, officers will act differently than when they are not. A different sort of situation arises when the observers are other police officers, in which case an officer's decision making will likely be influenced differently. The motivation to look good in the eyes of one's peers, for instance, may prompt an officer to act differently than he or she would otherwise behave. Researchers have found that officers who work together, as opposed to alone, are sometimes more prone to make arrests or to treat citizens harshly.[62] The combination of working in public and having bystanders present can have a profound influence on police decision making.

Individual Officer Characteristics

Thus far we have focused only on how neighborhood and situational factors affect officers' decisions. What about the officers themselves? How do differences among them affect their decision making? A number of individual officer characteristics have been linked to police decision making. These include factors such as education, age, experience, gender, ambition, and attitude toward the job.

Education, Age, and Experience

Does a well-educated officer act differently than, say, an officer with just a high school diploma? Unfortunately, researchers have yet to determine whether education affects an officer's decision to behave one way over another. The same can be said of age and experience, which tend to go hand in hand.

Younger officers are generally more aggressive and may work harder than their older counterparts, but seasoned officers may be "better" at their jobs, meaning the quality of their work could be higher.[63]

Gender

Few researchers have looked recently at gender as a possible predictor of police decision making. Some studies from the late 1980s, when women were first beginning to gain a significant presence in law enforcement, revealed that female officers tend to act less aggressively than their male counterparts.[64] On the whole, women tend to be less aggressive than men, which probably explains the differences in their decision making in the law enforcement context.

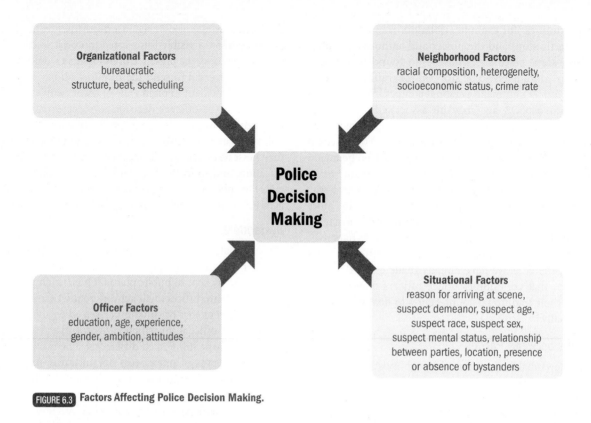

FIGURE 6.3 Factors Affecting Police Decision Making.

Ambition and Attitudes

An officer's ambition can clearly affect his or her decision making. One study revealed, for example, that officers who made the most arrests felt they needed to do so in order to gain a promotion.[65] Some of the officers who made more than their share of arrests were also motivated by the possibility of making more money from the overtime they needed to work to process all of their arrestees.

Attitudes toward the job, and particularly toward different types of police work, have also been linked to decision making. Researchers have found that an officer's perception of community

An officer's level of ambition affects his or her decision making.

policing can affect his or her arrest patterns.[66] In general, officers who view community policing favorably tend to be more selective in their arrest decisions. Circumstances, preferences, and neighborhood characteristics can call for an intervention other than arrest. Figure 6.3 summarizes the explanations of police decision making discussed in this section.

An Altercation Ends in Tragedy

In an actual case, the manager of a White Castle restaurant in Cincinnati called the fire department at about 6:00 A.M. to report that a patron was unconscious on the floor. Paramedics arrived and found Nathaniel Jones, age 41, passed out. Jones, an African-American, regained consciousness, but then he started acting strangely, so the paramedics called the police. Two white officers from the Cincinnati Police Department arrived. Their cruiser's video camera captured what happened next. One of the officers, who was out of view of the camera, was heard saying to Jones, "You gotta tell me what's going on." Jones then said, "White boy, redneck," at which point the camera caught Jones, who weighed 350 pounds, lunging at one of the officers and attempting to put him in a headlock. The two officers took Jones to the ground and tried to subdue him, but he resisted.

Soon four more officers arrived and joined the fray with their colleagues, who were using metal nightsticks to subdue a still-struggling Jones. When the video ended, Jones was on the ground and seemed to be saying, "Help!" At 6:06 A.M., an officer could be seen administering CPR to Jones. One minute later, and barely ten minutes after contact was first made, one of the officers was heard asking another if he turned his cruiser's camera off. He responded that he turned off the microphone; then seconds later the camera went blank. Jones was later pronounced dead at a local hospital. The coroner handling the case told CBS's *60 Minutes* that Jones was probably suffering from "excited delirium"—a controversial condition with a long history but no single definition—and that his heart had simply given out during the struggle.[67]

The Jones story raises several interesting questions:

1. Was Jones treated fairly by the responding officers?
2. Would the officers likely have acted differently if they had known for certain that their actions were being recorded and would be posted on the Internet and broadcast on national news programs?
3. What factors generally affect police decision making in cases like the one described here?

LEARNING OUTCOMES 1

Describe police discretion and its advantages and disadvantages.

Police discretion is the latitude an officer has in making the decision to act one way instead of another. Discretion is helpful because the police cannot be everywhere and arrest every offender. It is risky because it can lead to unequal treatment, favoritism, and even corruption.

1. What is police discretion? Is it beneficial or harmful? Explain your response.

2. What experiences in a police officer's background are likely to influence his or her discretionary decisions?

3. Should police discretion be limited? If so, how?

LEARNING OUTCOMES 2

Differentiate between the universalistic and particularistic perspectives on police behavior.

Police behavior can be perceived as being either universalistic (all officers share some of the same characteristics and attitudes) or particularistic (officers differ from one another in various respects). It is likely that officers are socialized to behave in certain ways (the socialization perspective), but there is also evidence that policing attracts a certain kind of person (the predisposition perspective).

1. What are the differences between the universalistic and particularistic perspectives on police behavior?

2. Which do you believe is more important in predicting police behavior: socialization or predisposition?

3. What kinds of personalities are most likely to be attracted to police work?

universalistic perspective The view that all police officers are similar and that they exhibit some of the same characteristics and behavior patterns.

particularistic perspective The view that individual officers differ from one another in various ways, including values, role orientation, and preferred styles of policing.

LEARNING OUTCOMES 3

Describe the factors that affect police decision making.

Police decision making can be understood in terms of (1) organizational factors, (2) neighborhood factors, (3) situational factors, and (4) individual officer characteristics. Organizational factors that can influence officer decision making include the bureaucratic structure of an agency, beats, and scheduling. Neighborhood factors include racial composition, heterogeneity, socioeconomic status, and crime. Situational factors include the reason the officer arrives at the scene (on his or her initiative or following a call for assistance), the suspect's demeanor and demographic characteristics, the relationship between the parties, the seriousness of the offense, the location of the contact, and the presence or absence of bystanders. Individual characteristics that can influence officer decision making include the officer's education, age, experience, gender, ambition, and attitudes toward the job.

1. What organizational factors have been identified as possible predictors of police decision making?

2. What neighborhood factors have been identified as possible predictors of police decision making?

3. What situational factors have been identified as possible predictors of police decision making?

4. What individual characteristics have been identified as possible predictors of police decision making?

territorial imperative The sense of obligation, even protectiveness, that develops in officers who routinely patrol the same area.

MyCJLab

Go to the Chapter 6 section in *MyCJLab* to test your understanding of this chapter, access customized study content, engage in interactive simulations, complete critical thinking and research assignments, and view related online videos

Additional Links

Learn about decision making and discretion at **www.justicestudies.com/pubs/decisionmaking.pdf**.

Additional information about police discretion can be found at **www.ncjrs.gov/pdffiles1/nij/178259.pdf** and **http://law.jrank.org/pages/1680/Police-Police-Officer-Behavior.htm**.

Information about policing a diverse community is online at **http://tinyurl.com/3x8lxr**.

Emotional intelligence in policing is the topic discussed at **http://tinyurl.com/2xaw96**.

Core Police Functions

"Research shows that only about 10 to 20 percent of all calls to the police involve situations that actually require a law enforcement response."

1 Describe types of patrol, methods of patrol, the response role, and the traffic function.

2 Describe the function of peacekeeping and order maintenance.

3 Identify investigative goals and explain the investigative process.

4 List and describe some significant issues associated with undercover work.

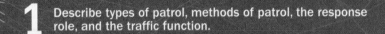

Source: Morgan Rauscher/Shutterstock.com

7

INTRO MAKING POLICING MORE COST-EFFICIENT

In late 2010, the Executive Session on Policing and Public Safety at Harvard University's John F. Kennedy School of Government released a study assessing how local governments could make policing more affordable. The paper was written partially in response to the financial crisis gripping the nation following the stock market downturn of 2008–2009 and the recession that accompanied it. "Even before the onset of the financial crisis," the authors noted, "rising expenditures on police departments stirred a debate among city managers, elected officials and police chiefs about how best to pay for policing."[1] Study authors found that increases in personnel costs, including those associated with salaries and benefits, constitute the bulk of the increases associated with the provision of police services in recent years. They also identified tactics now being used across the country to manage rising policing costs, including efforts to cut spending and raise productivity. Empirical research into the changing role of officers, the increased use of technology, and efforts to lower inefficiencies in police work were all cited as ways to help keep costs under control. The study, which also discusses creating a measure useful in estimating the social price for the effects of policing, can be accessed online at http://justicestudies.com/policing/affordablepolicing.pdf.

> **DISCUSS** How can scientific studies of policing help to lower the costs associated with effective law enforcement?

The police mission in this country is essentially fivefold: (1) to enforce and support the law; (2) to investigate crimes and apprehend offenders; (3) to prevent crime; (4) to help ensure domestic peace and tranquility; and (5) to provide local communities, states, and the nation as a whole with needed enforcement-related services.

The first police mission is the one that comes immediately to mind for most people. The police operate under an official public mandate to enforce the law. Not surprisingly, police officers see themselves as crime fighters, a view generally shared by the public and promoted by the popular media. Although it is the job of the police to enforce the law, it is not their *only* job. Most officers spend the majority of their time answering nonemergency public-service calls,[2] controlling traffic, or writing tickets. Most are not involved in intensive, ongoing crime-fighting activities. Research shows that only about 10 to 20 percent of all calls to the police involve situations that actually require a law enforcement response—that is, situations that might lead to arrest and eventual prosecution.[3]

Second, police are charged with investigating crimes and apprehending offenders. Some offenders are apprehended during the commission of a crime or immediately afterward. Fleeing Oklahoma City bomber Timothy McVeigh, for example, was stopped by an Oklahoma Highway Patrol officer on routine patrol only 90 minutes after the destruction of the Alfred P. Murrah Federal Building for driving a car with no license plate.

The third police mission, crime prevention, refers to a proactive approach to the problem of crime. Crime prevention involves "the anticipation, recognition and appraisal of a crime risk and initiation of action to remove or reduce it."[4] In preventing crime, police agencies seek to act before a crime happens, thus preventing victimization from taking place. Although the term *crime prevention* is relatively new, the idea is not. Securing valuables, limiting access to sensitive areas, and monitoring the activities of suspicious people are techniques used long before Western police forces were established in the 1800s. Modern crime-prevention efforts aim not only to reduce crime and criminal opportunities and to lower the potential rewards of criminal activity, but also to lessen the public's fear of crime.[5]

Enforcing the law, apprehending offenders, and preventing crime are all daunting tasks for police departments because there are many laws and numerous offenders. Still, crimes are clearly defined by statute and are therefore limited in number. Peacekeeping, the fourth element of the police mission, is a virtually unbounded police activity involving not only the control of activities that violate the law (and hence the community's peace) but many others as well. Law enforcement officers who supervise parades, public demonstrations, and picketing strikers, for example, attempt to ensure that the behavior of everyone involved remains "civil" and does not unduly disrupt community life. Robert H. Langworthy, who has written extensively about the police, says that keeping the peace is often left up to individual officers.[6] Basically, he says, departments depend on patrol officers "to define the peace and decide how to support it," and an officer is doing a good job when his or her "beat is quiet, meaning there are no complaints about loiterers or traffic flow, and commerce is supported."

Then there is service, perhaps the most extensive and far-reaching police mission. As writers for the National Institute of Justice note, "Any citizen from any city, suburb, or town across the United States can mobilize police resources by simply picking up the phone and placing a direct call to the police."[7] "Calling the cops" has been described as the cornerstone of policing in a democratic society.[8] About 70 percent of the half-million daily calls to 911 systems across the country are directed to the police, although callers can also request emergency medical and fire services.[9] Calls received by 911 operators are prioritized and then relayed to patrol officers, specialized field units, or other emergency personnel.

There is much more to enforcement, investigation and apprehension, crime prevention, order maintenance, and community service than we have presented thus far. Enforcement, for example, can be accomplished through several means, such as preventive patrol, broken windows law enforcement, and emergency response. Investigation can be, and often is, performed by trained detectives, but traffic cops also perform this role, such as when they investigate traffic accidents. The police service mission is extensive and includes many functions that most people are not aware of. Thus, our goal in this chapter is to present these and other police functions in more detail.

Most of us are familiar with policing because of the patrol function. Movies and television dramas seem to focus more heavily on the investigation function, but in real life most of us see patrol officers far more often than we see detectives. That is because patrol officers are the most visible aspect of the police department, engaging in preventive patrol, incident response, and traffic enforcement.

Types of Patrol

Preventive patrol refers to the practice of canvassing (that is, scrutinizing) neighborhoods in an effort to discourage people from committing crime. **Deterrence theory**, a perspective holding that crime will be less likely when the potential for getting caught outweighs any likely benefits from breaking the law, underlies this practice. Preventive patrol can occur through a number of other means, several of which we will consider here. We will also consider two interesting questions: How much patrol is really preventive, and is preventive patrol effective?

Directed patrol is, as the term suggests, patrol with direction. Unlike random patrol, directed patrol involves concentrating the police presence in areas where certain crimes are a significant problem. Two terms used in conjunction with directed patrol are **hot spots** and **hot times**. Hot spots are concentrated areas of significant criminal activity, such as a street corner well-known for its prostitution traffic. Hot times are those times of day when crime is particularly problematic, such as after dark on a Friday night.

Other terms that frequently arise with reference to directed patrol include **crime peaks**, or those times of day when certain crimes increase; **saturation patrol**, which occurs when several police officers flood a certain area in an effort to catch criminals and to deter would-be offenders; and **focused patrol**, in which police focus their efforts on certain problems, locations, or times.

Police departments today are able to identify hot spots and hot times with crime mapping. Using dispatch data, for example, police departments can plot the concentration of certain offenses on a map, including the times during which they occur. This allows officials to see firsthand where the problems are so they can allocate personnel to the areas where they are needed the most. Directed patrol is one way of making the most out of a police department's limited resources.

Patrol Methods and Techniques

Foot patrol was how policing was accomplished in America's early cities. It continues to be practiced in a number of areas, especially in strip malls, downtown shopping districts, tourist destinations, and other areas where many people are concentrated in a limited space. Being on foot, though, can clearly limit an officer's ability to give chase if the need arises. Even so, criminologist and author John Fuller has this

LEARNING OUTCOMES 1 Describe types of patrol, methods of patrol, the response role, and the traffic function.

GLOSSARY

preventive patrol The practice of canvassing neighborhoods in an effort to discourage people from committing crime.

deterrence theory A perspective that holds that crime will be less likely to occur when the potential for getting caught outweighs any likely benefits from breaking the law.

directed patrol A form of patrol that involves concentrating the police presence in areas where certain crimes are a significant problem.

hot spot A concentrated area of significant criminal activity, such as a street corner known for its prostitution traffic.

hot time A period during the day when crime is particularly problematic, such as after dark on a Friday night.

Foot patrol is the oldest method of patrol, predating the invention of the automobile.

Crime-Prevention Techniques — Access control, including barriers to entryways and exits; surveillance, including video systems; theft-deterrence devices like locks, alarms, and tethers; security lighting; visibility landscaping

Crime-Prevention Programs — Organized efforts that focus resources on reducing a specific form of criminal threat

Preventive Patrol — The practice of canvassing (that is, scrutinizing) neighborhoods in an effort to discourage people from committing crime

FIGURE 7.1 **Prevention Efforts.**

to say about foot patrol: "An aggressive, street-smart police officer, working an active post, can develop as many (or more) quality cases and arrests working foot patrol as he can working motorized patrol."[10]

Today, automobile patrol has effectively replaced foot patrol. The shift was inevitable once the automobile was invented and people began to spread out and move away from downtown areas. The act of driving itself can be a distraction, possibly diminishing even the most well-trained officer's ability to detect crimes in progress. Automobile patrol is also expensive; it requires not just an officer but a fully equipped vehicle (with all the attendant maintenance costs) for him or her to drive.

A number of other patrol methods are common and familiar. Bicycle patrol, for example, can be found in a number of relatively small towns and areas with fair weather. As police cyclist instructor Kathleen Vonk notes, "Officers on bike patrol have pursued and caught armed robbers, home invasion criminals, car thieves, criminals breaking into cars and criminals in possession of stolen property. . . . They have assisted in searches for missing children. . . . [And] housing officers have used bicycles in the areas where both stealth and speed are essential, pursuing and arresting many drug dealers, street thugs, and trespassers."[11] Additionally, "The bicycle officer is an important public relations tool and is instrumental in bringing the citizenry closer to the police. An officer on bicycle, wearing the more casual 'uniform' of a polo-type shirt and shorts, is far more approachable than an officer zipping by in an air-conditioned cruiser with the windows up."[12]

Mounted patrol is also common in some areas. As one researcher recalls, "Folklore of the frontier lawman on horseback in the American Old West evokes an image of peace and justice. . . That image of an officer on horseback remains a part

Types of Police Patrol

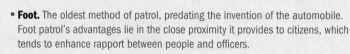

- **Foot.** The oldest method of patrol, predating the invention of the automobile. Foot patrol's advantages lie in the close proximity it provides to citizens, which tends to enhance rapport between people and officers.

- **Automobile.** Automobile patrol reverses the advantages and disadvantages of foot patrol. On the one hand, it improves officer mobility. On the other hand, it distances officers from the people they serve.

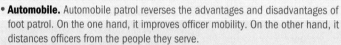

- **Bicycle.** Bicycles give officers much more mobility than foot patrol and can also be advantageous from the standpoint of community relations.

- **Mounted.** Like bicycle patrol, mounted patrol puts officers in closer contact with citizens. In addition, mounted patrol provides effective crowd control. Horses are large and heavy and put officers well above the crowd, thereby permitting them to push unruly groups back if the need arises.

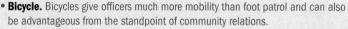

- **Air.** Air patrol is done for everything from traffic enforcement in rural areas to investigation of possible marijuana-growing operations (with thermal imagery) in inner cities.

- **Water.** Water patrol can be found on lakes and waterways throughout the United States.

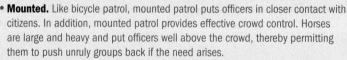

- **K9-Assisted Patrol.** Police officers who work with K9 units (police dogs) do everything from searching for elusive suspects to detecting drugs, bombs, and other threats to public safety.

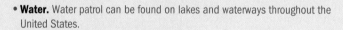

- **Special Terrain Vehicle Patrol.** Some all-terrain vehicle (ATV) parks, for instance, are patrolled by officers on off-road motorcycles. Some of the typical offenses found while patrolling are noise violations, fire hazards, illegal dumping, illegal shooting, trespassing with motor vehicles, illegal hunting, abandoning stolen vehicles, and undocumented alien trafficking.

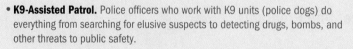
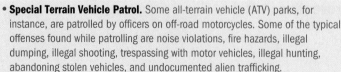

FIGURE 7.2 Types of Police Patrol.

of modern law enforcement. In the United States today, more than 600 organized mounted police patrol units form a visible pedestal and serve citizens throughout their jurisdiction. . . . An officer on horseback invites constructive community contact in its own unique way."[13] As one scholar has observed, "The horse gives the police a more visible presence in a crowd, and the horse gives the officer a better view of problems."[14] Mounted patrol is also relatively economical compared to automobile patrol.

How Much Patrol Is Really Preventive?

The public has something of a romanticized image of preventive patrol—that of police officers diligently scanning up and down every side street, alleyway, and lot as they drive through their beat. Then there is the real world, which unfortunately does not bode particularly well for the prospects of preventive patrol. Consider, for instance, the number of police officers on patrol vis-à-vis crime rates: Several large cities across the country have approximately the same number of police officers per citizen, but very different levels of crime. For example, according to the latest data, St. Louis had 39 full-time sworn police officers per 10,000 residents in 2007, while Seattle had 22.[15] At first glance, one may be inclined to conclude that St. Louis is a safer city, but such is not the case. It was the most crime-ravaged city in America during 2010.[16]

There are more reasons why preventive patrol may not do a good job of disrupting crime. First, the police presence in America is spread very thin. Even if we could double the size of our nation's police force, the number of police officers per 10,000 citizens would remain quite small. Next, according to Sam Walker, a prominent criminal justice professor, "many actual or potential offenders do not perceive police patrol as a meaningful threat."[17] Even with a substantial and visible police presence, some people cannot be deterred from committing crimes. Walker draws this conclusion: "Many crimes are inherently not 'suppressible' by patrol. . . . Because they usually occur indoors and in the heat of passion, the amount of police patrol out on the street is not going to affect them."[18]

Consider, for instance, the crime of burglary. If a burglar has at least a glimmer of intelligence, he or she will try to operate out of view of the police. Consequently, it is likely that police officers on patrol would not even notice that a burglary is taking place or has taken place. Likewise, consider both parties to an abusive relationship. How many domestic violence incidents take place in view of the police? Certainly very few. The very term *domestic* suggests that the abuse takes place in a private residence, out of view of authorities. It makes intuitive sense, therefore, that a heightened police presence cannot reduce all crime.

Office of Community Oriented Policing Services (COPS Office) An agency within the U.S. Department of Justice tasked with administering and supervising federal funds allocated to improve community policing capabilities.

response time The time it takes for police officers to respond to a call for service.

pretext stop A traffic stop based on more than one motive. For example, an officer stops a vehicle for a legitimate reason but is also suspicious about the driver.

racial profiling The use of discretionary authority by law enforcement officers in encounters with minority motorists, typically within the context of a traffic stop, that results in the disparate treatment of minorities.

COPS

Former president Bill Clinton signed the Violent Crime Control and Law Enforcement Act in September 1994. Title I of the act, known as the Public Safety Partnership and Community Policing Act of 1994, permitted the use of $8.8 billion to fund local law enforcement agencies in the fight against crime and to help improve their community policing capabilities. To spend this massive sum of money, the U.S. Department of Justice created a new agency known as the **Office of Community Oriented Policing Services** (the COPS Office). Its job was to administer and supervise the spending.

Since its creation, the COPS Office has awarded grants to law enforcement agencies throughout the United States. More than $7 billion has been spent. These grant awards have included funds for the hiring of additional police officers, for innovative community policing programs, and for improvement of law enforcement technology. COPS funds have also been used to fund regional community policing institutes, research, and training and technical assistance. All in all, the COPS Office has provided funding for the hiring of more than 100,000 new police officers throughout the United States. All of this spending has led researchers to ask whether it has reduced crime. One important study answered the question with a yes. A few others have followed suit, but at least one study, one of the more sophisticated studies to date, revealed that COPS grants have made virtually no dent in the crime problem. Thus, police officers may prevent some crimes, but certainly not all of them.

The Response Role

Perhaps one of the reasons why preventive patrol may not be the most effective approach to law enforcement is that officers are routinely responding to calls, which may limit the time they have to patrol neighborhoods and prevent crime.

Source: © Wildcat123/Dreamstime.com

Think About It. . . .

Preventive Patrol How effective is preventive patrol? This is not an easy question to answer because it is difficult to get into the heads of would-be criminals to determine whether the police presence affects their decision making. What are some possible limitations of studies that look at the aggregate relationship between the police presence and crime? What is the best way to know whether preventive patrol "works"?

Routine Incident Response

Routine incident response is the second most common activity of patrol officers.[19] As noted by the National Institute of Justice, "The specific police objective will . . . vary depending on the nature of the situation, but generally, the objective is to restore order, document information or otherwise provide some immediate service to the parties involved."[20]

One important measure of police success that is strongly linked to citizen satisfaction is **response time**: the time it takes for police officers to respond to calls for service. It is measured from the time a call for service is received by a dispatcher until an officer arrives on the scene. In 2001, for example, police response time in New York City averaged 7.2 minutes for all types of calls, 29 percent faster than the previous year and the quickest response time in a decade.[21] The average response time for critical calls in New York City decreased 20 percent, to 4.8 minutes. Response times in 2001 were cut by an average of nearly three minutes over the previous year, even in the face of an increased number of calls and budget cutbacks that resulted in fewer officers on patrol.

Emergency Response

In May 2003, Pomona, California, police officers on routine patrol responded to a dispatcher's instructions to assist in an emergency at a local coin-operated laundry.[22] On arrival, they found a two-year-old girl trapped inside an industrial-size washing machine. The officers used their batons to smash the locked glass-paned door. The girl, unconscious and nearly drowned when pulled from the machine, was taken to a local hospital, where she was expected to recover. Her mother, 35-year-old Erma Osborne, was arrested at the scene and charged with child endangerment when the on-site video surveillance cameras showed her placing her daughter in the machine and shutting the door. This is but one disturbing example of the many emergencies police officers throughout the United States respond to.

Although police respond to emergencies far less frequently than to routine incidents,[23] emergency response is a vital aspect of what police agencies do. Emergency responses take priority over all other police work, and until order is restored, the officers involved will not turn to other tasks. An important part of police training involves emergency response techniques, including first aid, hostage rescue, and the physical capture of suspects. Perhaps the ultimate critical incident these days is a terrorist attack.

Routine Responses

Police officers on patrol frequently respond to routine incidents, many of which are minor traffic accidents. Responding officers must collect information and, typically, file a written report.

Emergency Responses

Emergency Response, often called *critical incident response*, is used for crimes in progress, traffic accidents with serious injuries, natural disasters, terrorist attacks, officer requests for assistance, and other situations in which human life may be in jeopardy.

FIGURE 7.3 Routine versus Emergency Responses.

7.2 In 2001, police response time in New York City averaged 7.2 minutes for all types of calls

The Traffic Function

Most civilians are more familiar with the traffic enforcement function of police work than with any other dimension of the job—often because they've been on the receiving end of the enforcement. Traffic enforcement is generally concerned with enforcing laws pertaining to motor vehicles and their operation. It also involves the relief of congestion and the reduction of accidents. To do each of these tasks, officers may run radar surveillance, conduct checkpoints to apprehend drunk drivers, perform license and safety checks, direct traffic, enforce anti-cruising ordinances, ensure that people wear their seatbelts, target illegal street racers, nab red light runners, and keep an eye out for road rage. According to one writer, "Among the most common problems facing law enforcement today are those relating to traffic issues in their community. Citizens may call to complain about speeding cars in their neighborhood or voice concern over a nearby school crosswalk."[24]

Among the most common problems facing law enforcement officers today are those relating to traffic issues in their community.

Source: iStockphoto/Thinkstock

Think About It...

Rapid Response A common assumption is that if the police could reach crime scenes more quickly, they would have a better chance of apprehending lawbreakers. This is the essence of rapid response. One study found that probability of arrest increased when police travel time descreased, but other studies found virtually no relationship between travel time and the probability of arrest, possibly because people are slow to report crime. How do the findings from rapid response research mesh with your previous understanding of its effectiveness? If rapid response is not effective across the board, are there areas, times, and contexts in which it could be very important? Explain.

Perhaps the most controversial aspect of traffic enforcement these days involves stopping a motorist for reasons *other* than legitimate law violations, a practice known as *profiling*.

Pretext Stops and Profiling

The U.S. Supreme Court has held that police officers can stop cars based on the belief that a crime has been committed, which includes any traffic violation.[25] Once a motorist has been stopped, the officer can order him or her to stand outside of the vehicle without any justification,[26] search the vehicle with consent,[27] seize items that are in "plain view,"[28] frisk the driver and search the passenger compartment of the vehicle out of concerns for safety,[29] and search the entire car if probable cause to arrest or search is developed.[30]

Whether every motorist is stopped for a legitimate reason, though, is sometimes questionable. What's more, even if an officer has legal grounds to stop a motorist, the question of pretext presents itself: Should police with other motivations in mind (for example, to gain consent to search) be allowed to use traffic laws to stop people? In other words, should officers be able to conduct **pretext stops**, which are stops based on more than one motive? In a pretext stop, the officer stops the vehicle for a legitimate reason but is also suspicious about the driver. To the extent that pretext stops occur, too many of them can amount to **racial profiling**, which as been defined as "the use of discretionary authority by law enforcement officers in encounters with minority motorists, typically within the context of a traffic stop, that results in the disparate treatment of minorities."[31]

A driver's race obviously does not create justification to stop. Yet there are many people who have argued that the police use existing traffic laws, which are many and easy to violate, to single out certain drivers based on their race.[32] The Supreme Court has yet to decide directly on the constitutionality of this type of conduct, but at least one of its decisions has come close. In *Whren* v. *United States*,[33] Washington, DC, police made a traffic stop and observed two bags of crack cocaine in the hands of a passenger who was seated in the front of the car. The police testified that they stopped the driver because he violated traffic laws. In contrast, the defendants claimed that the stop was made based on their race and that the police used alleged traffic violations as a reason to stop them.

The Supreme Court concluded that the "constitutional reasonableness of traffic stops" does not depend "on the actual motivations of the individual officers." The Court also concluded that the only relevant inquiry is whether the officer has cause to stop the car. It rejected the argument that the Fourth Amendment requires a court to consider whether "the officer's conduct deviated materially from usual police practices, so that a reasonable officer in the same circumstances would not have made the stop for the reasons given." Simply put, the Supreme Court has stated that officers' individual motivations—whether racial or otherwise—are irrelevant. The only question worth answering, according to the Court, is whether the officer has cause to stop the vehicle. Needless to say, this decision did not satisfy critics of racial profiling.

Is racial profiling really a problem? Some studies suggest that it is. For example, in a study of drivers' characteristics during traffic stops, Robin Engel and Jennifer Calnon reached this conclusion: "The findings show that young black and Hispanic males are at increased risk for citations, searches, arrests, and use of force after other extralegal and legal characteristics are controlled."[34] Their findings are supported by other researchers.[35]

There is some concern that conclusions like these are difficult to make sense of without first considering the demographic composition of the area studied. We might expect, for example, that more blacks than whites will be stopped in an area with a large percentage of black residents. Most of us would agree that such an apparent disparity could be explained by the demographics of the area. The problem, though, is settling on the appropriate base for comparison. For example, we could look at census data to ascertain the racial composition of a particular neighborhood, but just because someone is stopped in their vehicle in that area doesn't mean they live there. The mobility of automobiles makes it difficult to find something with which to compare police traffic stop data. An alternative is driver's license databases, but even they are limited because not every driver has a license. There are ways around these types of research problems. For example, researchers can look at different officers within the same department. If one stops significantly more minorities than others, then arguably something other than legitimate enforcement is going on.

As most of us are aware, profiling has become a hot topic in the war on terror. Before September 11, 2001, critics were up in arms over the profiling of black motorists. Now the focus has shifted to people of Middle Eastern descent. But surprisingly, there is now a measure of support for profiling: "After years of enduring harsh criticism and suspicion from the public for alleged racial profiling practices, law enforcement in the aftermath of the World Trade Center disaster has suddenly found

Justification for Pretext Traffic Stops

There are numerous opportunities for the police to detect contraband during the course of a vehicle stop. And since almost every driver commits traffic law violations at some point, there is usually ample justification for stopping motorists.

Concern with Pretext Traffic Stops

There is the possibility of racial profiling: Many people have argued that the police use existing traffic laws, which are many and easy to violate, to single out certain drivers based on their race.

FIGURE 7.4 Pretext Traffic Stops.

itself on the high road, as some who once considered the practice taboo are now eager for police to bend the rules when it comes to Middle Easterners."[36] One researcher reported on a *Los Angeles Times* poll, conducted after September 11, which found that more than two-thirds of those questioned favored "randomly stopping people who may fit the profile of suspected terrorists."[37]

Accident Investigation

The traffic function involves much more than enforcement. Officers also respond to accidents. Motor vehicle crashes are all too common and exceedingly costly: "Although the traffic fatality rate has dropped dramatically since the mid-1960s, traffic crashes account for 95 percent of all transportation-related deaths and 99 percent of transportation-related injuries. Traffic crashes are the leading cause of death for people ages 4 to 34. The total economic costs of motor vehicle crashes in the United States exceeds $230 billion annually."[38] In addition, traffic crashes are the leading cause of line-of-duty deaths for police officers.[39]

After victims' needs have been met and the scene secured, officers turn to investigating the accident. The causes of some accidents are immediately apparent and require little investigation. Some even occur in plain view of an officer. The causes of many accidents, though, may not be immediately apparent. To ascertain the cause, the officer takes statements from witnesses, physically examines the vehicles involved, measures the skid marks, takes note of the final positions of vehicles on the roadway, and so on. The officer takes photographs and notes

Accident investigation begins, of course, with a response to the incident. Once an accident occurs, the officer must do the following:
- Take immediate steps to stabilize the accident scene, provide for life safety, and establish traffic control; establish a perimeter for the scene; and evacuate the injured, if required.
- Evaluate the situation and call for needed assistance.
- Triage the injured and provide appropriate field treatment and emergency care transportation.
- Extend the area of operation to ensure safe and orderly traffic flow through and around the accident scene.
- Provide for the safety, accountability, and welfare of personnel, a responsibility that continues throughout the incident.
- Restore the roadway to normal operations after the accident has been cleared.

FIGURE 7.5 Accident Investigation Steps.
Source: E. M. Sweeney, "Managing highway incidents with NIMS," *Police Chief* (July 2004): 26.

in an effort to carefully document all pertinent aspects of the accident scene. All of this helps the officer "reconstruct" the accident in order to determine who, if anyone, was at fault.

Pursuits

Every now and then suspects flee the police, and pursuits ensue. In some areas of the country, pursuits seem to be a frequent occurrence in light of all the media attention they receive. Some characteristics of police pursuits are listed in Table 7.1. The

TABLE 7.1 | Characteristics of Police Pursuits.

	Number (Percentage) of Incidents		
Reason for Pursuit	**Metro-Dade (Miami) Florida**	**Omaha, Nebraska**	**Aiken County, South Carolina**
Traffic Violation	**448 (45%)**	**112 (51%)**	**5 (36%)**
DUI/Reckless driving		8 (4%)	1 (7%)
"Suspect" vehicle		7 (3.5%)	2 (14%)
Driver known from previous incident		3 (1.5%)	
Felonies	**344 (35%)**	**89 (40%)**	**6 (43%)**
Armed robbery	117		2
Vehicular assault	67		
Aggravated assault	37		
Stolen vehicle	37	36	3
Burglary	24		
Other felonies	62	53	1
Accidents			
Personal injury	428 (41%)	31 (14%)	2 (12%)
Property damage	213 (20%)	91 (40%)	4 (24%)
Arrests	**784 (75%)**	**118 (52%)**	**14 (82%)**

Source: G. P. Alpert, *Police pursuit: Policies and training* (Washington, DC: National Institute of Justice, 1997), p. 3.

An in-depth analysis of pursuits involving the Metro-Dade Police Department revealed that four factors affect the likelihood of injury:

1. The greater the number of police cars, the greater the likelihood of injury.
2. The involvement of other police agencies also increases the likelihood of injury.
3. High-speed chases result in more injuries than low-speed pursuits.
4. Chases in residential areas result in more injuries than those conducted in nonresidential areas.

FIGURE 7.6 Injuries Resulting from Police Pursuits.
Source: G. P. Alpert and others, *Police pursuits: What we know* (Washington, DC: Police Executive Research Forum, 2000).

public seems to thrive on "the chase." There is a thrill in it for police officers, too, but there is also a dark side: Every pursuit carries with it the potential for danger to third parties. When innocent motorists or pedestrians are injured or killed in the course of a pursuit, lawsuits are often filed and sometimes the plaintiffs prevail. In Washington, DC, a jury awarded $1 million to a woman who was seriously injured when her car was struck during a high-speed police pursuit.[40] Virtually all police administrators are committed to avoiding the costs associated with such litigation.

Before initiating a high-speed pursuit, the officer must weigh two competing objectives. As Geoffrey Alpert—one of the nation's leading authorities on police pursuits—puts it, "The basic dilemma associated with high-speed pursuit of suspects is deciding whether the benefits of potential apprehension outweigh the risks of endangering police officers, the public, and suspects in the chase."[41] This dilemma becomes especially pronounced in the context of minor offenses. Research reveals that the majority of violators who flee from the police were suspected of committing offenses for which arrest would not be customary.[42]

Most police agencies have some sort of policy governing police pursuits, and these policies have a direct impact on the incidence of pursuits. A study revealed, for instance, that when the Metro-Dade (Florida) Police Department adopted a "violent felony only" pursuit policy, the number of pursuits declined markedly.[43] In contrast, Omaha adopted a more lax pursuit policy and witnessed an increase in pursuits of 600 percent in the space of one year.[44] Clearly, then, agencies can manage the incidence of police pursuits by altering their policies.

Assuming the officer decides to engage in a pursuit, what are the likely outcomes? First, research reveals that injuries are more likely to occur when people suspected of violent felonies flee the police.[45] Injuries are also likely when pursuits occur on surface streets (rather than highways) in urban and suburban (rather than rural) areas.[46]

The Washington, DC, case described at the beginning of this section might not have occurred but for apparent negligence on

Every pursuit carries with it a potential for danger to third parties.

the part of the pursuing officer. The DC police department has one of the most restrictive pursuit policies in the country, permitting officers to chase only those suspected of committing violent felonies, but the officer gave chase through a residential area after a suspect with expired license plates. Was the jury's decision a just one? Perhaps it would help to know that the woman who was injured lost three fingers and other parts of her left hand—and she was an innocent bystander to the chase.

Numerous technologies have been developed to assist police with interrupting high-speed pursuits. Most readers are probably familiar with spike strips. Recent versions of these feature hollow spikes that slowly release the air from the fleeing suspect's tires to bring the vehicle to a safe stop. The spikes can be retracted remotely so pursuing vehicles can pass over them safely. The Auto-Arrestor, another device that is currently being developed, disrupts the fleeing vehicle's electronics, kills the ignition, and brings it safely to a stop.[47]

▶ Peacekeeping and Order Maintenance

Peacekeeping and order maintenance are also critical police missions. The mere thought that police officers might be close can discourage crime and deviance, thereby fostering peace and order. On the other hand, it is sometimes necessary to take visible steps to maintain peace and order. Police officers dressed in riot gear during a high-profile public protest are an example of this. The presence of police officers at sporting events, such as on the sidelines in a football game, is another. In either case, police officers take *proactive* steps to maintain peace and order. There is also a *reactive* element to peacekeeping and order maintenance, such as when neighborhood disorder and quality-of-life problems surface in the wake of civil disobedience and during crisis situations.

Managing Disorder and Quality-of-Life Issues

Many police departments focus on quality-of-life offenses as a crime-reduction and peacekeeping strategy. **Quality-of-life offenses** are minor law violations, sometimes called *petty crimes*, that demoralize residents and businesspeople by creating disorder. Examples of petty crimes include excessive

LEARNING OUTCOMES 2
Describe the function of peacekeeping and order maintenance.

GLOSSARY

quality-of-life offense A minor law violation that demoralizes residents and businesspeople by creating disorder. Sometimes called *petty crime*.

broken windows model A model of policing based on the notion that physical decay in a community (for example, litter and abandoned buildings) can breed disorder and lead to crime by signaling that laws are not being enforced. Such decay is thought to push law-abiding citizens to withdraw from the streets, which signals that lawbreakers can operate freely. The model suggests that by encouraging the repair of run-down buildings and by controlling disorderly behavior in public spaces, police agencies can create an environment in which serious crime cannot easily flourish.

civil disobedience Law-breaking used as a political tactic to prove a point or to protest against something.

noise, graffiti, abandoned cars, and vandalism. Other quality-of-life offenses reflect social decay and include panhandling and aggressive begging, public urination, prostitution, roaming youth gangs, public consumption of alcohol, and street-level substance abuse.[48] Homelessness, while not necessarily a violation of the law unless it involves some form of trespass,[49] is also typically addressed under quality-of-life programs. Through police interviews, the homeless may be relocated to shelters or hospitals or arrested for some other offense. Some researchers claim that reducing the number of quality-of-life offenses in a community can restore a sense of order, reduce the fear of crime, and lessen the number of serious crimes that occur. However, quality-of-life programs have been criticized by those who say that the government should not be taking a law enforcement approach to social and economic problems.[50]

The Broken Windows Model

A similar approach to keeping the peace can be found in the **broken windows model** of policing.[51] This model is based on the notion that physical decay in a community, such as litter and abandoned buildings, can breed disorder and can lead to crime by signaling that laws are not being enforced (Figure 7.7).[52] Such decay, the theory postulates, pushes law-abiding citizens to withdraw from the streets, which then sends a signal that lawbreakers can operate freely.[53] The broken windows model suggests that by encouraging the repair of rundown buildings and controlling disorderly behavior in public spaces, police agencies can create an environment in which serious crime cannot easily flourish.[54] While desirable, public order has its own costs. Noted police author Charles R. Swanson says, "The degree to which any society achieves some amount of public order through police action depends in part upon the price that society is willing to pay to obtain it."[55] Swanson describes the price to be paid in terms of (1) police resources paid for by tax dollars, and (2) "a reduction in the number, kinds, and extent of liberties" that are available to members of the public.[56]

Many police departments focus on quality-of-life offenses as a crime-reduction and peacekeeping strategy.

Civil Disobedience and Crisis Situations

Civil disobedience involves law-breaking to prove a point or to protest against something. As Karen Hess and Henry Wrobleski observe, "Civil disobedience occurs daily around the world, from the fight against apartheid in South Africa, to the quest for autonomy of ethnic groups in Europe, to demonstrations in Washington, DC, against racism or for a more responsive government."[57] Police officers need to be equipped to deal with such situations.[58]

A problem with policing civil disobedience is that much of it is based on a desire to protest some perceived inequity, a right protected by the First Amendment. As the *New York Times* reported, "The death of a 21-year-old college student outside Fenway Park on October 21, [2004,] the night the Red Sox beat the Yankees for the American League pennant, is only the latest reminder that crowd control has reemerged as one of the toughest challenges for police."[59]

Crisis situations also keep the police busy. Ever wonder why the police don't just swarm a building where a person is being held hostage? The obvious answer is that doing so would be dangerous, but why? Because an assault by police threatens the lives of hostages as well as the hostage takers. Hostages could be killed by those holding them before they can be rescued, or they might be killed or injured in the battle between police and the hostage takers. An assault, of course, can also result in loss of life or injury to police personnel. Often, time is on the side of hostage negotiators.

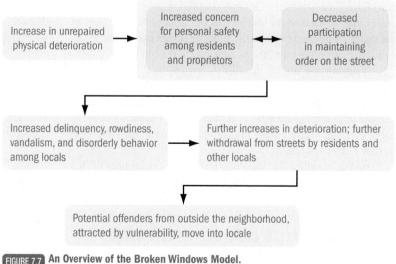

FIGURE 7.7 An Overview of the Broken Windows Model.
Source: R.B. Taylor and A.V. Harrell, *Physical environment and crime* (Washington, DC: U.S. Department of Justice, Office of Justice Programs, 1996).

Type of Situation	Example	Police Response
Civil Disobedience 	Refusing to move for police officers who are trying to establish crowd-control lines; rioting, setting fires, and looting.	Respect of constitutional rights to free expression and assembly. In celebratory gatherings, fine line between maintaining order and permitting gatherers to enjoy the moment.
Crisis Situations	Hostage taking, barricaded suspects, and suicide attempts.	The initial few hours of incident are the most dangerous. An assault by police threatens the lives of suspect and hostages. As time progresses, suspect has a chance to calm down.

FIGURE 7.8 Civil Disobedience and Crisis Situations.

▶ Investigations

Criminal investigation is one of the most important police functions—and certainly the most romanticized. Investigation is largely carried out by detectives—sworn officers who have moved up from patrol to something of a "glamour" job wherein they spend their days solving crimes. Detective work would be unnecessary if patrol officers were able to catch all crimes in progress. Of course, they hardly ever do this, in part because they are spread so thin—hence the need for a dedicated criminal investigations division.

Large police agencies often have hundreds of detectives in various divisions covering offenses that run the gamut from homicide to check fraud. Indeed, a study by the RAND Corporation revealed that police departments in every city with a population of more than 250,000 people, and 90 percent of those in smaller cities, have dedicated detectives.[60]

The Evolution of Investigations

At the heart of any investigation is the practice of **criminalistics**, which refers to the scientific study and evaluation of evidence associated with the commission of a crime. Today, this term carries connotations of recent technological advancements that detect nearly invisible **trace evidence** (for example, blood stains that someone tried to clean up) or other evidence of a crime that would escape all but the most skilled investigator. But criminalistics is about as old as policing itself. Henry Fielding's Bow Street Runners and Sir Robert Peel's bobbies experienced some early investigative success. The bobbies, for instance, were occasionally removed from their patrol duties to perform investigations.

At the heart of any investigation is the practice of criminalistics

Anthropometry and Dactylography

Some fundamentals of detective work were developed well over 100 years ago. **Anthropometry** (also known as *Bertillon measurements*), a technique for identifying people based on their body measurements, was developed in 1882. Alphonse Bertillon, who developed this technique, concluded that if just eleven measurements were taken on a person, the odds of finding someone with similar measurements were 4,191,304 to 1.[61] The problem, though, was in attempting to use these measurements to identify those who would be most likely to commit crime.

Bertillon successfully identified some criminals, but his ideas fell out of favor because they were inaccurate and a bit complicated. They were replaced with the more accurate identification practice of **dactylography**, or fingerprinting. Dactylography was proposed for criminal investigation around 1880 in England,[62] but knowledge of fingerprints far predated the routine use of such prints to identify criminals. In the first century, for example, a Roman lawyer by the name of Quintilianus used a bloody fingerprint from what was apparently a crime scene to defend a child who was accused of murdering his father.[63]

Throughout the 1880s, fingerprinting continued to gain popularity as a valid technique for identifying criminal perpetrators. Once it was accepted practice (in the mid-1890s), it was successfully used in a number of high-profile contexts. For example, in 1904, Detective Sergeant Joseph Faurot of the New York City Police Department went to England to study fingerprinting. On his return, he used his newfound knowledge to successfully identify a man accused of burglarizing a suite in the Waldorf-Astoria Hotel. The man claimed to be a respected businessman by the name of James Jones, but Faurot learned, as a result of fingerprints, that he was actually Daniel Nolan, a man with 12 prior convictions for similar crimes.[64]

LEARNING OUTCOMES 3 Identify investigative goals and explain the investigative process.

GLOSSARY

criminalistics The use of technology in the service of criminal investigation; the application of scientific techniques to the detection and evaluation of criminal evidence.

trace evidence Minute, nearly invisible evidence of a crime that would escape all but the most skilled investigators.

anthropometry A technique developed by Alphonse Bertillon in 1882 for identifying people based on their body measurements. Also called *Bertillon measurements*.

dactylography An early name for fingerprinting.

forensic evidence Physical evidence whose usefulness in a court of law may not be immediately apparent to an untrained observer but can be demonstrated through the application of accepted scientific techniques.

In another high-profile case, as Will West was being processed into the federal prison in Leavenworth, Kansas, a guard noted that there was already a photograph on file for him. West claimed to have never been in the prison before. After measurements and fingerprints were taken, it became clear that he had been mistaken for another man, William West, who had been in the same prison for some time. The concern was that Will West had tried to change his name to avoid harsh punishment for being a repeat offender, which was, of course, not the case. The two were so close in both physical appearance and Bertillon measurements—not to mention the similarity of their names—as to be virtually indistinguishable. Ultimately, it was their fingerprints that permitted authorities to distinguish one man from the other. This case earned fingerprinting a permanent place in the criminal investigator's toolkit.

Firearms Identification and Beyond

Firearms identification, or ballistics, burst onto the criminalistics scene during the mid-1800s. In 1835, Henry Goddard, who was one of the last Bow Street Runners, was the first to successfully identify a murderer from a spent bullet removed from the victim's body. He noticed that the bullet had similar characteristics as bullets fired from the suspect's gun. When confronted with the evidence, the suspect quickly confessed.[65] Near the turn of the twentieth century, Paul Jeserich, a German chemist, testified against a murder defendant on the grounds that the bullet pulled from the victim matched those fired from the defendant's gun.[65] Firearms identification gained popularity in the early 1900s. The first permanent crime laboratory was established at the Northwestern University Law School and was headed by a former army physician, Calvin Goddard, who is credited with making firearms identification a science through his development of the bullet comparison microscope.[67]

August Vollmer is credited with helping initiate the police professionalism movement, but he also made his mark in early criminal investigations. Vollmer teamed up with a chemist from the University of California, Berkeley, to help identify a poison that was allegedly used to murder someone. He also trained his officers in the identification and preservation of evidence and established a forensics lab in Los Angeles. Vollmer's partnership with the university prompted a number of scientists to become interested in criminal investigations.

Other influential figures of the early twentieth century included Albert Osborn, who wrote *Questioned Documents*,[68] an important work intended to assist in the identification of fabricated and falsified papers and records, and Leone Lattes, who pioneered a blood-typing procedure that assisted in the identification of criminals.[69]

Investigative Goals and Process

In the world of mystery novels and television shows, the goal of investigations is to discover "whodunit." In the real world, though, the goals of detective work are much more complex.

Criminal investigations typically progress through two stages: (1) the preliminary investigation and (2) the follow-up investigation. The preliminary investigation is the investigation that plays out immediately after the incident is reported.

In the vast majority of police departments, either line officers or detectives do all this work. In larger agencies, though, dedicated crime scene investigators get involved, especially in the search for

Evidence is anything useful in a court of law that tends to prove or disprove the facts at issue.

Determining whether a crime has been committed	The reporting of an alleged crime and the completion of a report by the responding officer does not necessarily mean that a crime has actually been committed. Consider, for instance, a reported sexual assault. Has it actually occurred, or is it a falsified claim made by a vindictive lover? Thorough investigations are often needed to sort out the truthfulness of such reports when the credibility of the victim is in doubt.
Obtaining information and evidence	This is perhaps the most labor-intensive and least glamorous aspect of detective work. Untold hours of interviewing and questioning can lead to a dead end.
Apprehending suspects	Detectives, as sworn police officers, may elect to arrest the individual they feel was responsible for the crime. Alternatively, they may seek a warrant that would permit any duly authorized peace officer to make the arrest.
Recovering stolen property	In cases of theft, detectives may spend a great deal of time recovering stolen property so it can be used as part of a criminal prosecution before being returned to its rightful owner.
Successfully presenting the case to the prosecutor	One of the detective's foremost responsibilities is presenting an airtight case to the prosecutor so that the correct person can be held to answer for the offense in question.

FIGURE 7.9 Investigative Goals.

forensic evidence. Generally speaking, *evidence* is anything useful in a court of law that tends to prove or disprove the facts at issue. *Physical evidence* is evidence that consists of physical material or traces of physical activity. The term *forensic* refers to that which (1) is of interest to the legal system or (2) must be adapted or suited to use through argumentation—that is, something that is not self-evident. For purposes of policing, forensic evidence, therefore, is physical evidence whose usefulness in a court of law would not be immediately apparent to an untrained observer. Argument, usually through the application of accepted scientific techniques, is necessary to demonstrate the legal value of forensic evidence. This is where crime scene investigators come on board. They often take trace evidence to a laboratory where further testing is performed with the intent of identifying the perpetrator.

The job of crime scene investigators has of course been prominently featured on television programs like *CSI*. The show and its progeny portray the crime scene investigator's life as something of an exciting frontline occupation. In reality, it is often anything but exciting. Much of the work is tedious and plays out behind the scenes. It is also performed more often by trained scientists than by police officers. These individuals, often labeled *forensic experts*, are adept at linking nearly all conceivable forms of evidence to an alleged perpetrator. Examples of such experts include forensic pathologists, toxicologists, anthropologists, odontologists, psychiatrists, and serologists, to name just a few.

The follow-up investigation proceeds through a few more steps, each with a common theme as noted below in Figure 7.10:

Preliminary Investigation Steps

Attending to emergencies, such as a fleeing suspect

Securing the scene

Measuring, photographing, and videotaping the crime scene

Searching for evidence

Identifying, collecting, and examining physical evidence (for example, suspected weapons, bloodstains, fingerprints, hair samples)

Questioning victims, witnesses, possible witnesses, and suspects

Recording all statements given for later inclusion in the written report[i]

Follow-Up Investigation Steps

Continuing the investigation. This stage, which begins when preliminary work is done, includes conducting follow-up interviews; developing a theory of the crime; analyzing the significance of information and evidence; continuing the search for witnesses; contacting crime lab technicians and assessing their analyses of the evidence; conducting surveillance, interrogations, and polygraph tests, as appropriate; and preparing the case for the prosecutor.

Reconstructing the crime. The investigator seeks a rational theory of the crime, using inductive reasoning. The collected information and evidence are carefully analyzed to develop a theory. Often, a rational theory of a crime is developed with some assistance from the careless criminal. Verbrecherpech, or "criminal's bad luck," is an unconscious act of self-betrayal. One of the major traits of criminals is vanity; their belief in their own cleverness is the key factor in their leaving a vital clue. Investigators look for mistakes.

Focusing the investigation. When this stage is reached, all investigative efforts are directed toward proving that one suspect or group of suspects is guilty of the crime. This decision is based on the investigator's analysis of the relationship among the crime, the investigation, and the habits and attitudes of the suspect or suspects.[ii]

FIGURE 7.10 **Preliminary and Follow-Up Investigation Steps.**

Undercover Work

Undercover work is closely aligned with investigations. Indeed, many detectives might as well be working undercover because they usually dress in street clothes. For the most part, though, undercover work is common in the investigation and detection of vice crimes, particularly those involving the illicit drug trade.

For obvious reasons, effective drug enforcement would be impossible if it were performed solely by uniformed officers. Police need to infiltrate the criminal underworld in order to successfully nab high-profile criminals. This is seductive work for a number of officers because of the thrill and autonomy it provides. As police scholar Ken Peak has observed, "Since only a few officers are actually selected for undercover assignments, these officers enjoy a professional latitude in their roles, minimal departmental supervision, the ability to exercise greater personal initiative, and a higher degree of professional autonomy than regular patrol officers."[70] What attracts police officers to undercover work, though, can also be their undoing. Several potential problems are associated with working undercover.

LEARNING OUTCOMES 4 List and describe some significant issues associated with undercover work.

Undercover officers enjoy a professional latitude in their roles along with minimal departmental supervision.

Problems with Undercover Work

The lack of supervision and the procedural flexibility that go with undercover work can diminish some officers' respect for procedural rules or tempt them with a number of criminal "perks." The money that changes hands in the illegal drug trade, for example, can be all too enticing to civil servants who aren't necessarily well paid.

As far as successes, the group Perverted Justice has teamed with NBC's Dateline, and various law enforcement agencies to catch sexual predators. NBC has aired a number of "To Catch a Predator" *Dateline* episodes featuring the arrests of men who troll Internet chat rooms looking for children to molest. Its volunteers continue to pose as children in Web chat rooms and then relay the information that they acquire to local police detectives. They sometimes post chat logs on the organization's website at www.perverted-justice.com.

Problems Undercover work calls for long and unpredictable hours, which can place not just a physiological strain on officers but also a strain on their personal relationships. One study revealed, for instance, that a high number of undercover assignments over the course of an officer's career was associated with problems like drug use, alcohol abuse, and disciplinary actions.[i] While many officers emerge from undercover work unscathed, not all do.

Successes One of the more celebrated examples of undercover work of late is the partnership among NBC's *Dateline*, the activist group Perverted Justice (an organization based in Portland, Oregon, that is dedicated to identifying adults who involve themselves in sexual chat room conversations with children), and various law enforcement agencies. The programs have shown the apprehension of a number of sex offenders, and Perverted Justice continues to rack up an impressive track record of apprehensions on its own. In July 2008, the organization achieved its 279th conviction and reported averaging two arrests per week.

FIGURE 7.11 Undercover Work Challenges and Successes.

High Tech Innovation Meets Law Enforcement

The human body emits a broad spectrum of electromagnetic radiation, which can be detected with the proper equipment. Inanimate objects carried on one's person do not emit such radiation and tend to stand out against the body's electromagnetic background. Using technology based on these facts, Millivision Technologies has developed a weapons-detection device that uses radiometric millimeter wave–based sensors for passive threat detection. The device, called the concealed threat detection (CTD) system, is portable, can be used from a distance, and—according to the company—does not reveal intimate anatomical information.

Millivision Technologies is but one of many companies currently developing innovative law enforcement applications. Whereas most high-tech consumer electronics tend not to be controversial, when law enforcement gets its hands on new detection and surveillance equipment, some people become alarmed. Critics of the Millivision device, for example, have charged that it reveals intimate anatomical information about people viewed with it—although the company has repeatedly denied such charges.

This raises several important questions:

1. Do threat detectors like those manufactured by Millivision unduly threaten individual privacy?

2. What other currently available law enforcement technologies might be of concern to privacy advocates?

3. Do advanced threat and surveillance technologies effectively deter criminals?

4. Can technology ever replace good old-fashioned police work?

5. Will we ever see the day when traditional preventive police patrol is completely replaced by advanced surveillance and threat-detection technologies?

Source: © Wisconsinart/Dreamstime.com

LEARNING OUTCOMES 1 Describe the types of patrol, methods of patrol, the response role, and the traffic function.

Preventive patrol refers to the practice of canvassing neighborhoods in an effort to discourage people from committing crime. Directed patrol addresses crime in hot spots. Crackdowns, where police officers target a particular area, are the most common example of this. Proactive patrol refers to targeting specific offenses or offenders. Examples include targeting drunk drivers or identifiable repeat offenders. Incident response, which often involves patrol units, includes both emergency response and routine incident response. Traffic enforcement consists of enforcing applicable traffic laws, relieving congestion, and reducing accidents.

1. Distinguish among preventive patrol, the response role, and the traffic function in policing. Summarize the leading issues associated with each.

2. Distinguish between directed patrol and proactive policing. In your opinion, which approach is better?

3. How does the use of racial profiling impact policing? Are there some situations in policing in which race might provide valuable clues in crime prevention or offender apprehension?

preventive patrol The practice of canvassing neighborhoods in an effort to discourage people from committing crime.

deterrence theory A perspective that holds that crime will be less likely to occur when the potential for getting caught outweighs any likely benefits from breaking the law.

directed patrol A form of patrol that involves concentrating the police presence in areas where certain crimes are a significant problem.

hot spot A concentrated area of significant criminal activity, such as a street corner known for its prostitution traffic.

hot time A period during the day when crime is particularly problematic, such as after dark on a Friday night.

crime peak A time of day when a particular crime increases in frequency.

saturation patrol A form of patrol that involves concentrating the police presence in a certain area in an effort to catch criminals and to deter would-be offenders.

focused patrol A form of patrol that focuses police efforts on certain problems, locations, or times.

foot patrol The oldest method of police patrol, which entails officers walking through neighborhoods. Foot patrol tends to enhance rapport between citizens and officers, but it clearly limits an officer's ability to give chase if the need arises.

Office of Community Oriented Policing Services (COPS Office) An agency within the U.S. Department of Justice tasked with administering and supervising federal funds allocated to improve community policing capabilities.

response time The time it takes for police officers to respond to a call for service.

pretext stop A traffic stop based on more than one motive. For example, an officer stops a vehicle for a legitimate reason but is also suspicious about the driver.

racial profiling The use of discretionary authority by law enforcement officers in encounters with minority motorists, typically within the context of a traffic stop, that results in the disparate treatment of minorities.

LEARNING OUTCOMES 2 Describe the function of peacekeeping and order maintenance.

Peacekeeping and order maintenance policing involve the management of disorder, quality-of-life policing, and the management of civil disobedience and crisis situations.

1. How does the peacekeeping and order maintenance role frequently manifest itself?

2. What is meant by the "broken windows" model of policing? How can the broken windows model lead to lower crime rates?

3. What is a quality-of-life offense? How does the concept of quality-of-life offenses fit in with the broken windows model of policing?

quality-of-life offense A minor law violation that demoralizes residents and businesspeople by creating disorder. Sometimes called *petty crime*.

broken windows model A model of policing based on the notion that physical decay in a community (for example, litter and abandoned buildings) can breed disorder and lead to crime by signaling that laws are not being enforced. Such decay is thought to push law-abiding citizens to withdraw from the streets, which signals that lawbreakers can operate freely. The model suggests that by encouraging the repair of run-down buildings and by controlling disorderly behavior in public spaces, police agencies can create an environment in which serious crime cannot easily flourish.

civil disobedience Law-breaking used as a political tactic to prove a point or to protest against something.

LEARNING OUTCOMES 3

Identify investigative goals and explain the investigative process.

Police investigative goals include determining whether a crime has actually been committed, gathering information and evidence, apprehending suspects, recovering stolen property, and successfully presenting the case to the prosecutor. Criminal investigations typically progress through two stages: (1) the preliminary investigation and (2) the follow-up investigation—each of which has its own substages.

1. What are the investigative goals identified by this chapter?
2. What is involved in the investigative process?
3. What stages characterize the investigative process?

criminalistics The use of technology in the service of criminal investigation; the application of scientific techniques to the detection and evaluation of criminal evidence.

trace evidence Minute, nearly invisible evidence of a crime that would escape all but the most skilled investigators.

anthropometry A technique developed by Alphonse Bertillon in 1882 for identifying people based on their body measurements. Also called *Bertillon measurements*.

dactylography An early name for fingerprinting.

forensic evidence Physical evidence whose usefulness in a court of law may not be immediately apparent to an untrained observer but can be demonstrated through the application of accepted scientific techniques.

LEARNING OUTCOMES 4

List and describe some significant issues associated with undercover work.

Undercover work is common in policing today, but as this chapter notes, it is especially challenging because it may tempt officers to break the law and can strain personal relationships.

1. What are the possible problems associated with undercover work?
2. Is undercover work more dangerous than other kinds of police work? Why or why not?

3. Are undercover officers more likely to go rouge than other officers? Why or why not?
4. How can potential problems associated with undercover work best be addressed?

MyCJLab

Go to the Chapter 7 section in *MyCJLab* to test your understanding of this chapter, access customized study content, engage in interactive simulations, complete critical thinking and research assignments, and view related online videos.

Additional Links

To get a handle on core police functions, read the mission statement of the Philadelphia Police Department at **www.phillypolice.com/about/mission-statement**.

Learn more about the patrol officer at **www.justicestudies.com/pubs/patrolofficerintel.pdf**.

Explore an examination of racial profiling data in a large city at **www.justicestudies.com/pubs/profilingdata.pdf**.

Papers that explore biased enforcement, including racial profiling can be found at **www.justicestudies.com/pubs/biasedenforcement.pdf**, **www.justicestudies.com/pubs/cdsp02.pdf**, and **http://www.justicestudies.com/pubs/citizensviews.pdf**.

The "broken windows" style of policing can be explored at **www.justicestudies.com/pubs/brokenwindows.pdf** and **www.legalaffairs.org/webexclusive/debateclub_brokenwindows1005.msp**.

Community Policing and Community Involvement

"To prevent and combat crime, the police need to work together with the communities they serve."

1 Describe community justice and problem-oriented policing.

2 Define *community policing* and list justifications for it.

3 Distinguish between citizen involvement in policing and civilianization.

4 Define *third-party policing,* and provide some examples.

8

ENCOURAGING COPS TO LIVE IN THE CITIES THEY SERVE

In 2011 Detroit mayor Dave Bing announced a plan to offer 200 of the city's police officers a chance to live near the city's center by allowing them to purchase renovated homes for as little as $1,000. The plan involved using $30 million in federal stimulus money from the Neighborhood Stabilization Fund to restore houses in run-down neighborhoods, and then sell them to police officers with no down payments required. Officials were quick to point out that more than 50 percent of Detroit's police officers live outside of the city. "We hope this can be a model for the nation," the mayor said.[1]

The last two or three decades have seen a powerful movement to bring police officers closer to the communities they serve and to get citizens more involved in policing.[2] Police officers have gone out into the community to build relationships and to establish rapport with citizens through a number of innovative programs and interventions. Citizens have

> **DISCUSS** How might police agencies enhance rapport with law-abiding citizens who live in the communities they serve?

sought out police agencies, as well, to learn what it's like to be an officer and to peek into the world of law enforcement. Some agencies have even hired civilians in place of sworn officers for certain jobs in an effort to cut costs. There are also signs of increased reliance by police departments on third parties, like landlords and apartment managers, to engage in policing-related functions.

It is important to understand why these kinds of things are happening in policing today. Accordingly, we begin this chapter with a background section that puts recent developments in context. The rest of the chapter is organized into three key sections on community policing, citizen involvement in policing, and third-party policing. Whereas Chapter 7 covered the traditional aspects of policing, this chapter shifts attention to relatively innovative, creative, and otherwise nontraditional forms of police work.

► Community Justice and Problem-Oriented Policing

It is tempting to view current trends in policing as unique to the law enforcement profession. They are not. The idea of reaching out to the community in an effort to improve relationships with citizens and to put citizens in closer touch with criminal justice professionals is part of a larger community justice movement that has been under way for some time now. Prosecutors, for example, have begun to pursue many of the same proactive, preventive, and creative crime-control strategies as those in which the police are engaged. In "community prosecution," as attorneys call it, prosecutors do much more than just charge suspected criminals and bring them to court.

Closely connected to community involvement and community policing is the idea of problem-oriented policing, which emerged at roughly the same time as the strategies we cover in this chapter. It is worth discussing separately, however, because it is the glue that holds a number of recent developments together. The idea that policing (and criminal justice in general) should be geared toward the identification and solution of root problems in the community is a relatively recent

LEARNING OUTCOMES 1 Describe community justice and problem-oriented policing.

GLOSSARY

community justice A relatively new and innovative set of ideas about how the goals of the criminal justice system can be achieved. It favors original, non-traditional approaches to crime control that draw heavily on input and cooperation from the community.

problem-oriented policing (POP) A method of policing that is geared toward identifying and solving problems within a community that are particularly troublesome and then crafting creative solutions to them. Also called *problem-solving policing*.

one. Still, it explains why police want to strengthen ties with the communities they serve and why police departments want to provide citizens with a window into the law enforcement world.

Community Justice

Community justice is a relatively new and innovative set of ideas about how the goals of the criminal justice system can be achieved. Further, community justice assumes that custom-fit crime control is better than the traditional approach, which is increasingly criticized as unimaginative. What's more, community justice emphasizes that criminal justice agencies (police, courts, corrections) cannot accomplish crime control alone; community participation is essential.

Outside of the policing context, community justice has manifested itself in our nation's courts, particularly through the creation of so-called community courts and other problem-solving courts, including drug courts, domestic violence courts, teen courts, and reentry courts. Corrections agencies are also doing community justice as we have just defined it. Approaches like restorative justice fit the community justice model, as do partnerships between probation, parole, and private companies, such as treatment facilities.

Problem-Oriented Policing

Problem-oriented policing (POP) is, as the term suggests, policing that is oriented toward problem solving. POP involves identifying areas, times of days, specific crimes, individuals, and the like that are particularly troublesome and then crafting a creative solution to these problems.[3]

Problem-oriented policing is the brainchild of law professor (emeritus) Herman Goldstein and shares much in common with some of the policing strategies discussed in the previous chapter.[4] For example, problem-oriented policing resembles directed patrol because it emphasizes direction and purpose, not just random and reactive patrol. Problem-oriented policing also resembles community policing because it usually relies on input from citizens to help identify problems. Indeed, some of the time the terms *community policing* and *problem-oriented policing* are used interchangeably. Much of the time, though, problem solving is viewed as a separate strategy unto itself.

There are at least two ways to distinguish between community policing and problem-oriented policing. First, problem-oriented policing is, as Arizona State University criminology professor, Mike Reisig has observed, "...an analytic framework used by police to identify and solve problems that result in repeated calls for service."[5] This often occurs independent of contact with citizens. In contrast, for policing to be truly community oriented, it must include some degree of citizen involvement. Another, perhaps more controversial way to distinguish between both approaches is to say that community policing focuses on citizen involvement and satisfaction as an end in itself, and problem-oriented policing is concerned with achieving a swift reduction in crime.

Despite POP's differences from community policing and community justice, it is still useful to think of it as a part of both movements because problem solving is a central feature of community policing and community justice. All three approaches necessitate an understanding of the geographic area, an in-depth understanding of the problems, and some degree of familiarity with the people in the areas where the problems occur. It is possible, of course, for POP to have no community involvement (direct or indirect), but true problem-oriented policing almost requires some outreach and relationship building with the community. See Figure 8.1 for a summary of the relationships between community justice, community policing, and problem-oriented policing.

Community Policing

Community policing emerged in the wake of the reform era discussed in Chapter 1. The reform era hasn't disappeared; there is much that occurs in the world of policing that is consistent with the ideas set forth by August Vollmer, O. W. Wilson, and others. Some not-so-desirable aspects of police professionalism, however, have been replaced with something new.

LEARNING OUTCOMES 2 — Define *community policing* and list justifications for it.

GLOSSARY

community policing A collaborative effort between the police and the community that identifies problems of crime and disorder and involves all elements of the community in the search for solutions to these problems.

What were some of the not-so-desirable aspects of reform era policing? First, police research revealed that preventive patrol wasn't particularly effective (see Chapter 7). Also, as we have already seen, the 1960s witnessed a great deal of strain in relationships between the police and the public. At the same time, the police came to realize that they couldn't reduce crime by their own efforts alone. Community-era reformers sought authorization from community members and extensive citizen support; a broad mandate that stressed the provision of services; a decentralized, responsive organizational structure; and improved relationships with citizens. These strong ties would be achieved through foot patrol, problem solving, quality-of-life preservation, and a host of other tactics—all of which were designed to ensure citizen satisfaction.

The sentiments of the community era were perhaps most clearly expressed in an important article authored by John Angell, a community policing innovator, during the early 1970s.[6] He argued that traditional police departments—and particularly their paramilitary organization and structure—are culture bound, that police bureaucracy is inconsistent with the humanistic democratic values of the United States, that it demands that employees demonstrate "immature" personality traits, and that it cannot cope with environmental pressures. The community model, he said, would (1) improve community relations, which suffered under the bureaucratic paramilitary model of law enforcement; (2) improve officers' morale by allowing them a measure of flexibility in the performance of their duties; and (3) improve interagency coordination.

There is more to the emergence of community policing than we have presented thus far. Some have argued, for instance, that it has emerged for less-than-noble purposes. It is also

Community Justice
Favors original, nontraditional approaches to crime control that draw heavily on input and cooperation from members of the community

Community Policing
Simply a part of this larger community justice movement

Problem-Oriented Policing
Geared toward identifying and solving particular and specific problems—from serious ones, such as gang shootings in one part of town, to minor ones, such as panhandlers bothering visitors at a local park

FIGURE 8.1 **Relationships between Community Justice, Community Policing, and Problem-Oriented Policing.**
Source: Worrall, John L., CRIME CONTROL IN AMERICA: WHAT WORKS?, 2nd edition, © 2008. Reprinted by permission of Pearson Education, Inc., Upper Saddle River, NJ.

important to define community policing and, from a research standpoint, to gauge its true extent. We conclude by exploring the various forms of community policing and looking at the compatibility of community policing and the "war on terror."

The Birth of Community Policing

The history of community policing is rich and nuanced. There has been a tendency to assume that community policing has emerged for simple reasons, such as poor police–citizen relations, but there is a great deal more to the origins of the new policing paradigm. Together, the explanations fall into two categories: (1) those concerned directly with crime control and (2) those involving other intentions.

Crime Control

A few writers have called attention to the many noble reasons for the present community policing era. In a discussion concerning the "drive for change," one researcher identifies three reasons for the changes that have occurred and those that are taking place now.[7] The first reason, not surprisingly, is citizen disenchantment with police services: "Minority citizens in inner cities continue to be frustrated by police who whisk in and out of their neighborhoods with little sensitivity to community norms and values."[8]

The second reason concerns social science research undertaken in the 1970s. Specifically, "research about preventive patrol, rapid response to calls for service, and investigative work—the three mainstays of police tactics—was uniformly discouraging."[9] The third reason for reform suggests that "patrol officers have been frustrated with their traditional role"[10] and that they began to demand improved methods of interacting with citizens. It is sometimes felt that such an approach improves police officer morale. Other authors have suggested that community policing can be traced to two interrelated problems: the isolation of police officers in patrol cars from citizens and the public's fear of victimization and perceptions of a rising crime rate.[11] More specifically, the authors claim that community policing "rose like a phoenix from the ashes of burned cities."[12]

Other Intentions

Is there more to the community policing movement than meets the eye? Some scholars believe there is. For example, some have argued that police organizations may have adopted community policing for selfish reasons, such as to make rank-and-file officers more content with their jobs.[13] A professional ethic, or a desire to emulate progressive police agencies, could also be responsible for the current and widespread diffusion of community policing.

Perhaps more cynically, community policing may be a means of changing the goals of police work (from crime control to service, for example), of shaping public opinion instead of responding to it,[14] or of deflecting attention away from law enforcement officials.[15] Fiscal constraints may have served as a powerful motivator. Political culture and

Some see community policing as a means of changing the goals of police work from crime control to service.

community characteristics could also explain the origins of community policing.[16]

How might community policing shape public opinion? By presenting officers in a favorable light, by making them look good in the eyes of citizens, historically strained relationships can improve. What about deflecting attention? Part of community policing puts crime control at least *partly* in the hands of citizens (as in neighborhood watch). Some have said, therefore, that community policing passes the buck. And what about fiscal constraints? Some have argued that community policing is a cheap alternative to more expensive innovations because, at its core, it is a philosophy, and a philosophical change is free. These and many other reasons to initiate community policing are summarized in Figure 8.2. Whatever the reasons for its present popularity, community policing owes its origins to multiple demands and historical contingencies.

Definitions of Community Policing

We are guilty of having talked about community policing without really defining it, but that is for good reason: It is difficult to define. Community policing is a relatively new approach to law enforcement that is premised on the assumption that the police and citizens must work together to control crime.[17] Unfortunately, this short definition fails to adequately capture all of the various aspects of community policing. A more comprehensive definition is illustrated in Figure 8.3.

1. Citizen disenfranchisement with police services
2. Research showing the ineffectiveness of random patrol and quick response times
3. Patrol officers' frustration with the traditional reactive police role
4. Isolation of officers from citizens, largely owing to increased use of patrol vehicles
5. Narrow crime-fighting police image
6. Overreliance on bureaucratic and paramilitary structure
7. Overreliance on high-tech gadgetry that diminishes personal interactions
8. Insulation of police administration from community input and accountability
9. Concern about human rights
10. Failure of police to reach out to the community
11. Desire to appear "with it" and professional
12. Desire to emulate other agencies
13. Need to change the goal of police work from crime control to service
14. Need to reduce police officers' workloads
15. Desire to deflect attention from the police department to the community
16. Need to save money
17. Needs or wants of the community
18. Political culture of the surrounding area
19. Desire to improve the police image
20. Desire to increase control over the community by adopting multiple strategies

FIGURE 8.2 **Twenty Reasons to Initiate Community Policing Services.**
Source: Worrall, John L., CRIME CONTROL IN AMERICA: WHAT WORKS?, 2nd edition, © 2008. Reprinted by permission of Pearson Education, Inc., Upper Saddle River, NJ.

Definition	Community policing is difficult to define; however, it is a reorientation of policing philosophy and strategy away from the view that police alone can reduce crime, disorder, and fear. The strategy is based on the view that police don't help their communities very much by placing primary reliance on random preventive patrolling, rapid response to calls for service irrespective of their urgency, postincident investigations to identify offenders, and other primarily reactive criminal justice system tactics.
Five Perspectives	1. *Deployment perspective*—emphasizes the fact that police officers are deployed in a way that moves them closer to citizens 2. *Community revitalization*—emphasizes the importance of the police and citizens working closely together to improve neighborhoods and make them safer places 3. *Problem-solving perspective*—an approach in which citizens and police work together to identify and respond to neighborhood problems 4. *The customer*—emphasizes the importance of the police listening to citizens and serving their needs 5. *Legitimacy*—emphasizes bolstering the credibility of the police through police–citizen partnerships
Four Dimensions	1. The *philosophical dimension* includes the ideas and beliefs surrounding a new paradigm of policing. Three ideas underlying community policing are citizen input, an enhanced and broadened police function, and personal service. 2. The *strategic dimension* consists of "the key operational concepts that translate philosophy into action." Community policing strategies include reoriented operations (for example, from cruiser patrol to foot patrol), geographic permanency (assigning patrol officers to the same areas for extended periods of time), and an emphasis on crime prevention (for example, police officers acting as mentors and role models). 3. The *tactical dimension* is best understood as the inevitable outcome of the successful implementation of the first two dimensions. "The tactical dimension of community policing ultimately translates ideas, philosophies, and strategies into concrete programs, practices, and behaviors." This dimension stresses constructive interactions between the police and citizens, improved partnerships between law enforcement officials and the public, and problem solving. 4. Finally, the organizational dimension, though not necessarily a fundamental part of community policing, is essential to its development. The structure of police agencies and their management and information services need to be adjusted to accommodate community policing through such changes as decentralization, strategic planning, and program evaluation.
Extent	The extent of community policing is widespread in that it is supported in the Violent Crime Control Act of 1994, which led to the creation of the COPS Office in the U.S. Department of Justice, and to date, billions of dollars in grants to local law enforcement agencies have been allocated to enhance their community policing capabilities.

FIGURE 8.3 Community Policing.

Sources: W. A. Geller and G. Swanger, *Managing innovation in policing: The untapped potential of the middle manager* (Washington, DC: Police Executive Research Forum, 1995).

G. W. Cordner, "Community policing: Elements an effects," in *Critical issues in policing: Contemporary readings*, 3rd ed., ed. R. G. Dunham and G. P. Alpert (Prospect Heights, IL: Waveland, 1997), p. 452.

Community Policing Perspectives and Dimensions

According to the Police Executive Research Forum (PERF), community policing consists of five different "perspectives,"[18] which are noted in Figure 8.3. Professor Gary Cordner has identified the philosophical, strategic, tactical, and organizational dimensions of community policing and has described some of the common elements within each,[19] which have also been noted in Figure 8.3.

The Extent of Community Policing

The rhetoric of community policing has become more or less institutionalized in American policing. But is there more to community policing than the term itself? Is community policing really being done, or do police departments just *say* they're doing it? Two research focuses help us answer these questions: (1) research on structural changes to police departments and (2) research on whether police officers themselves are supportive of community policing.

Structural Change

Researchers have questioned whether police departments have actually changed their structure in ways that are consistent with the spirit of community policing. A recent study on trends in police agencies' implementation of community policing from 1995 to 2000 is particularly revealing.[20] The authors of that study conclude, "Among organizational changes to support community policing activities, the most rapidly growing were those intended to signal change: revised mission statements and new performance review criteria for community police officers."[21] In other words, the study found that police departments were focusing on making mostly symbolic changes to show their acceptance of community policing.[22]

The police still cling to an institutional definition that stresses crime control and not prevention.

The author of another recent study reached the same conclusion: "The police still cling to an institutional definition that stresses crime control and not prevention."[23] He also concludes that "by all available evidence, police organizations (their structures, division of labor, and the like) have not been radically or even significantly altered in the era of community and problem-oriented policing."[24] In short, many police agencies have adopted the cosmetic tenets of community policing but without altering their basic organizational structure in a meaningful way that actually changes the substance of their performance.[25] Additional research appears to confirm the discouraging news that structural change linked to community policing is frustratingly slow and is failing to result in functional change.[26]

Attitudinal Change

If American police agencies are slow to change in response to community policing, what about police officers themselves? Here is one author's answer to this important question:

> Police have a remarkable ability to wait out efforts to reform them. Important aspects of police culture mitigate against change. Police resist the intrusion of civilians (who "can't really understand") into their business. They fear that community troublemakers will take over the program and that people will seek to use police for their private purposes or for personal revenge. When police dislike changes proposed from within, they snort that the top brass are "out of touch with the street."[27]

In short, police officers are resistant to change and, as the preceding passage suggests, will actively take steps to thwart change. In fairness to law enforcement officials, other types of agencies—especially public agencies—also respond slowly to change. Nevertheless, it seems that community policing is being resisted by police officers themselves.

Two researchers recently described the efforts to do community policing in two mid-sized U.S. cities.[28] Those cities' police departments attempted four types of community policing: participatory management, community policing training, the decentralization of certain police operations, and the creation of special community policing units. The authors then tracked the opinions of the officers in both cities over a six-year period. They found that (1) a specialized community policing unit, not full-scale implementation of community policing, is desirable because not all officers will buy in, and (2) despite the presence of different community policing approaches, much law enforcement business proceeded as it always had (for example, routine patrol remained unchanged).

In another related study, researchers sought to determine whether community policing affects police officers' decisions to use coercion during encounters with suspected criminals.[29] Studying two cities, they focused in particular on whether community policing assignments, community policing training, and community partnerships affected officers' patterns of using coercion. Their analysis showed that none of these variables had much effect on officers' decisions to use coercion, again lending support to previous studies that showed that police are resistant to change. These findings have been echoed in more recent studies.[30]

Critical Views of Community Policing

Some authors note that "community policing has become the dominant theme of contemporary police reform in America,"[31] yet problems have plagued the movement since its inception. (See Figure 8.4, "Critical Views of Community Policing.") As noted in Figure 8.4, recent findings continue to show that the attitudes of African-Americans toward the police remain poor. The wider reach of these studies, however, led evaluators to discover that this dissatisfaction may be rooted in overall quality of life and type of neighborhood.[32] Because most African-Americans continue to experience a lower quality of life than most other U.S. citizens and because they often live in neighborhoods characterized by economic problems, drug trafficking, and street crime, recent studies conclude that it is these conditions of life, rather than race, that are most predictive of citizen dissatisfaction with the police.

Those who study community policing have often been stymied by ambiguity surrounding the concept of community.[33] Sociologists, who sometimes define a community as "any

Those who study community policing have often been stymied by ambiguity surrounding the concept of community.

1.
The range, complexity, and evolving nature of community policing programs make their effectiveness difficult to measure.

2.
Citizen satisfaction with police performance can be difficult to conceptualize and quantify. Most early studies examined how citizens' attitudes developed through face-to-face interaction with individual police officers. They generally found a far higher level of dissatisfaction with the police among African-Americans than among most other groups.

3.
Sense of community is based more on interests than geography.

4.
Continuing evidence shows that not all police officers or managers are willing to accept nontraditional images of police work. Similarly, many officers are loathe to take on new responsibilities as service providers whose role is defined more by community needs and less by strict interpretation of the law.

FIGURE 8.4 Critical Views of Community Policing.

Source: © Jank1000/Dreamstime.com

area in which members of a common culture share common interests,"[34] tend to deny that a community needs to be limited geographically. Police departments, on the other hand, tend to define communities "within jurisdictional, district or precinct lines, or within the confines of public or private housing developments."[35] Robert Trojanowicz, a well-regarded community policing scholar, once cautioned police planners that "the impact of mass transit, mass communications and mass media have widened the rift between a sense of community based on geography and one [based] on interest."[36]

Researchers who follow the police definition of *community* recognize that there may be little consensus within and between members of a local community about the community's problems and about appropriate solutions. Robert Bohm and colleagues at the University of Central Florida have found, for example, that while there may be some "consensus about social problems and their solutions ... the consensus may not be community-wide." It may, in fact, exist only among "a relatively small group of 'active' stakeholders who differ significantly about the seriousness of most of the problems and the utility of some solutions."[37]

Finally, there is continuing evidence that not all police officers or managers are willing to accept nontraditional images of police work. One reason is that the goals of community policing often conflict with standard police performance criteria (such as arrests), leading to a perception among officers that community policing is inefficient at best and, at worst, a waste of time.[38] Some authors have warned that police subculture (see Chapter 5) is so committed to a traditional view of police work, which is focused almost exclusively on crime fighting, that efforts to promote community policing can demoralize an entire department, rendering it ineffective at its basic tasks.[39] As the Christopher Commission found following the Rodney King riots, "Too many ... patrol officers view citizens with resentment and hostility; too many treat the public with rudeness and disrespect."[40] Some analysts warn that only when the formal values espoused by today's innovative police administrators

begin to match those of rank-and-file officers can any police agency begin to perform well in terms of community policing.[41]

Some public officials, too, are unwilling to accept community policing. Ten years ago, for example, New York City Mayor Rudolph W. Giuliani criticized the police department's Community Police Officer Program, saying that it "has resulted in officers doing too much social work and making too few arrests."[42] Similarly, many citizens are not ready to accept a greater involvement of the police in their personal lives. Although the turbulent, protest-prone years of the 1960s and early 1970s are long gone, some groups remain suspicious of the police. No matter how inclusive community policing programs become, it is doubtful that the gap between the police and the public will ever be entirely bridged. The police role of restraining behavior that violates the law will always produce friction between police departments and some segments of the community.

Examples of Community Policing

Community policing is practiced in more forms than we can possibly list here. The majority of community policing programs, though, can be placed into one of three categories. First, some are intended to encourage citizens to take an interest in crime control. Others seek to communicate with and inform citizens. Finally, some programs expand police presence in the community, such as putting police in schools or on specialized patrols. These three categories are discussed in Figure 8.5.

An easy way for police departments to improve their communication with citizens and to foster closer relations is to develop a website.

Source: Sascha Burkard/ Shutterstock.com

Mobilizing Citizens

Formal meetings between police and community members: identify and deal with specific crime problems and locations. These meetings must be distinguished from neighborhood watch programs.

Informing Citizens

Crime-control newsletters: Often contain information on recent developments at the police department, crime statistics for the area, tips for avoiding victimization, and so on.

Websites: Allow citizens to complete hot-spot reports of criminal activity online and to submit noncriminal complaints electronically. At the same time, citizens can learn about new approaches taken by the department, see pictures of dangerous fugitives, view active warrants, and otherwise develop familiarity with their local police department.

Television: Some police departments—mostly in the largest jurisdictions—actually have their own community-access channel that broadcasts programs like "John TV," which shows the faces and names of men suspected of soliciting prostitutes. Other programming includes television shows and TV advertisements designed to improve public relations and public attitudes toward the local police force.

Engaging with Citizens

Improved police presence: For example, police officers are coming to occupy a significant position in our nation's schools. Police who work in schools are often called school resource officers.[i] They are represented by the National Association of School Resource Officers.[ii] Police are also collaborating more with schools, and some schools are opting to hire private security personnel to patrol campuses in an effort to preserve a safe learning environment and provide security in response to incidents like the infamous Columbine High School shooting.

FIGURE 8.5 Examples of Community Policing.

Community Policing and Antiterrorism

Community policing stresses improved relationships between police and citizens. The ongoing "war on terror," however, seems to place a strain on those relationships. The typical response to terrorism, particularly high terrorist alert levels, is to put more police on the streets, make more liberal use of searches, and otherwise inconvenience people in the name of national security. These tactics are somewhat at odds with building relationships and improving police-community bonds and contacts. Some have argued, though, that community policing is *not* at odds with antiterrorism efforts. According to Chuck Wexler, director of the Police Executive Research Forum,

> The events of September 11, 2001, have changed the role of local police in America—perhaps forever. Local law enforcement faces the challenges of assuming more responsibility in countering domestic terrorism threats while continuing to address crime and disorder. Success will depend on their ability to build on strong community policing networks for information exchange and to maintain a collaborative problem-solving approach to crime amid high anxiety and crisis. Now more than ever, departments need to adhere to community problem-solving principles to decrease crime and disorder in their communities, increase their departments' efficiency and strengthen their relationships with citizens.[43]

Not everyone is so convinced, however. In fact, some have argued that police departments that haven't historically favored community policing are using the "war on terror" as a reason to scrap it.[44] But they also argue that even in the face of resistance, community policing is needed to succeed against terrorism:

> Few people outside the field know about the pitched battle for the heart and soul of policing that has raged over the past decade [the traditional bureaucratic model versus community policing]. It is said that people get the police they deserve. If we are to maintain recent

Community policing stresses improved relationships between police and citizens.

reductions in violent crime and uncover the terrorists living among us, while preserving the civil rights that make our society special, we must insist on community policing now more than ever.[45]

Citizen Involvement and Civilianization

Thus far we have examined community policing strategies that are operated largely by the police. The strategies covered are best considered one-way because the police develop or coordinate them. Moreover, they are one-way in the sense that the police are the ones who go out into the community to work with citizens in numerous ways. An alternative to these approaches is to bring citizens to the police. While programs of this type are still run and coordinated by the police, they are different in that they allow citizens to view and participate in the world of law enforcement.

Citizen Patrol and Citizen Police Academies

There are hundreds, if not thousands, of **citizen patrols** around the United States.[46] An example of a volunteer citizen patrol that has received some attention is the Neighborhood Patrol Officers Program in Fort Worth, Texas.[47] Started in 1991, the program provided eight hours of training to volunteers on such topics as rules of conduct, liability issues, and legal considerations. Once training was completed, volunteers were issued an identification badge, a T-shirt, a hat, and a jacket. They also received police radios. Once trained and equipped, the volunteers used their own vehicles to patrol neighborhoods, looking for evidence of criminal activity.

Many police departments also operate so-called **citizen police academies**.[48] Although the programs differ to some extent, they all possess a common element: Citizens are given an opportunity to learn about the policing profession and even to experience some of the same sensations that uniformed officers experience.[49] Sometimes citizens even learn to use firearms and otherwise defend themselves from victimization. See Figure 8.6 for an overview of the Concord (California) Citizen Police Academy program and curriculum.

It is tempting to ask whether citizen police academies work, but in order to answer this question, we must first understand their purpose. While some critics find it difficult to fathom any crime-reduction benefits due to citizen police academies, that is not their direct goal. Rather, the academies are intended to affect citizens' perceptions of the police rather than to reduce crime, and that is what the research suggests they accomplish. The authors of

LEARNING OUTCOMES 3 Distinguish between citizen involvement in policing and civilianization.

GLOSSARY

citizen patrol A preventive patrol program staffed by citizen volunteers.

citizen police academy A training experience that offers citizens an opportunity to learn about the policing profession and even to experience some of the same situations that uniformed officers experience.

civilianization "A law enforcement agency's hiring of nonsworn personnel to replace or augment its corps of sworn officers" in an effort to reduce costs and improve service.

About the Citizen Academy

The academy provides community members with an inside look at local law enforcement. During the academy, students will be introduced to a variety of topics, as described under the curriculum outline.

The 13-week academy is designed to give citizens an overview of the police department's function and operational procedures. The curriculum and teaching methods are similar to the traditional police academy, but the weekly sessions are not designed to train the participant as a police officer.

Academy classes are taught by police executives and veteran police officers. Participants will have the opportunity to meet with the chief of police and staff members. They are encouraged to ask questions and express ideas and concerns to police employees.

Applications for the citizen academy may be submitted at any time.

For additional information about the Citizen Police Academy, please call the Community Action and Awareness Unit.

Weeks 1 & 2
- Chief of Police Introduction
- Community Policing
- Criminal Justice System
- Laws of Arrest
- Legal Issues

Weeks 3 & 4
- Traffic Investigations
- Narcotics Enforcement
- Police Facility Tour
- Criminal Investigations

Weeks 5 & 6
- Community-Oriented Government
- Community Action & Awareness
- Police Vehicle Operations
- Reserve Police Officers

Weeks 7 & 8
- Practical Pursuit Driving
- Gang Awareness
- Use of Force Issues
- Professional Standards

Weeks 9 & 10
- Crime Scene Investigations
- Communications—9-1-1
- SWAT Operations
- Hostage Negotiations

Weeks 11 & 12
- Firearms Simulation
- Use of Deadly Force
- Interview Techniques
- Practical Simulations
- K-9 Demo
- Graduation

FIGURE 8.6 A Citizen Police Academy Curriculum.
Source: Concord (California) Police Department, "Citizen Police Academy," www.ci.concord.ca.us. Reprinted by permission.

one recent study found that citizen police academy participants viewed the police more favorably after completing the program.[50] Similar findings were reported in at least two other studies.[51]

Other researchers have been critical of citizen police academies. One researcher found that academy participants tend to be mostly community "elites" and that minorities are drastically underrepresented.[52] The argument has also been raised that citizen police academies—like citizen patrol programs—perpetuate a traditional law enforcement strategy and may in fact be antithetical to the spirit of community policing.[53] This argument becomes quite convincing when police departments teach civilians many law enforcement "tricks of the trade," such as self-defense techniques.

What can be gleaned from the literature on citizen police academies? They appear to improve public perceptions of and attitudes toward the police, but people who participate in the academies may already be more prone to viewing the police favorably prior to enrolling in the curriculum. As far as the effect of citizen police academies on crime, there is no evidence that there is any. In fact, there is a total lack of research on the subject. Regardless of this, the practice of giving citizens a window into the law enforcement world is intended to do little more than improve the image of the police, and while there is nothing particularly wrong with that, an improved police image has no effect on crime.

Civilianization

Civilianization has been defined as a "law enforcement agency's hiring of nonsworn personnel to replace or augment its corps of sworn officers, typically with the aims of reducing costs and improving service."[54] (See Figure 8.7.) This definition makes it clear that civilianization is something distinct from private security, private policing, and privatization in general.

Citizen patrol and citizen police academies have largely different motivations than civilianization. They both get citizens involved in policing-related functions by having them either actively patrol neighborhoods or experience policing life through a short mock academy. Civilianization, in contrast, is largely done because it saves money. It is more expensive to have a sworn officer handle department communications when a civilian could just as easily be hired. A civilian doesn't need to go through the police academy or use the expensive specialized equipment that a sworn officer needs.

Civilianization

Civilians are hired as nonsworn personnel (communications specialists, criminalists, computer specialists, lawyers, and a host of other support positions) to replace or augment its corps of sworn officers, with the aim of reducing costs and improving service.

Citizen Patrol

Typically, citizen patrols are composed of volunteers who engage in preventive patrol. These volunteers are often provided with some type of government vehicle and patrol the streets during daylight hours. Sometimes, however, citizens volunteer to drive their own vehicles and operate independently of the police.

Citizen Police Academy

Citizens are given an opportunity to learn about the policing profession, which often consists of a watered-down version of a police academy where citizens are taught the nature, operations, and complexity of the policing profession.[i]

FIGURE 8.7 Citizen Involvement in Policing.

The hiring of civilians is the sign of a progressive, change-oriented agency.

At the same time, civilianization may not be *all* about cost savings. The hiring of civilians is, first, the sign of a progressive, change-oriented agency. As American University professor Brian Forst has observed, "While some tradition-bound police executives have been reluctant to transfer a variety of support functions to civilians, it has become increasingly clear that civilians tend to perform certain specialized roles more effectively than sworn officers."[55] Dispatch functions were largely performed by sworn officers during the 1960s; now dispatch is almost exclusively performed by nonsworn personnel. Hiring more civilians also creates an air of openness consistent with the community policing ideals of involving more and more citizens in crime-control functions.

▶ Third-Party Policing

We introduced private policing and security in Chapter 3. One could conceive of these approaches as policing by third parties—that is, by parties other than citizens or the police. When we talk about **third-party policing**, however, we are referring to something entirely different. Basically, it amounts to formal methods of policing that invoke the use of the **civil law** rather than the criminal law.

Michael Buerger and Lorraine Mazerolle, the scholars who first conceived the term *third-party policing*, distinguish it from community policing and problem-oriented policing because of its intended targets: "In community- and problem-oriented policing, the police assume an active quasi-enforcement and managerial role in addition to their more established, hortatory [encouraging] role as dispensers of expert advice."[56] They go on to argue that community policing and problem-oriented policing are simply augmented versions of traditional policing that rely heavily on citizens and guardians (those responsible for places, like landlords) for influence and control over criminals and would-be criminals. Third-party policing is different from this because "it focuses on the places that the guardians control by promoting certain collective responses as a way of controlling individual behavior."[57] In other words, third-party policing is more place oriented than person oriented.

Third-party policing should not be confused with environmental criminology, which is concerned with designing "places" to make them less vulnerable to crime (for example, access control with a tall security gate). Third-party policing is place oriented, but it is not concerned with design. Instead, it is about providing guardians with the information and tools they need to take a certain element of law enforcement into their own hands.

There is a possible "dark side" to third-party policing, however. It is not just about encouraging guardians to target

The characteristics of third-party policing
- Defined as police efforts to persuade or coerce nonoffending persons to take actions that are outside the scope of their routine activities, and that are designed to indirectly minimize disorder caused by other persons or to reduce the possibility that crime may occur.
- Pertains to formal methods of policing that invoke the use of the **civil law** rather than the criminal law.

Example of how civil law is used
- Civil law approach to policing: Not just the police but other officials relying on civil process, such as nuisance abatement and code enforcement, to reduce crime and disorder.

Third-Party Policing

Examples of third-party policing programs
- **The Beat Health Program** (Oakland, California) Police officers make the first contacts with the targeted nonoffending parties. Initial contacts are as collegial as possible. The teams attempt to build rapport with the property owners. Any owners who fail to cooperate, however, quickly encounter the more coercive arm of third-party policing.
- **Minneapolis Repeat Call Address Policing** (RECAP) Program
  - Police officers present call histories to owners and managers of problem properties.
  - They explain that improvements would be mutually beneficial
  - Benefits to businesses: Attract more customers and thereby increase profits if police are not seen arresting people on the property.
  - Benefits to owners of rental properties: Better tenants would be more likely to pay their rent and increase the profitability of the property.
- Police departments are increasingly wising up to the idea that, in some instances, civil law can work just as well for crime control as does the criminal law. Beyond the policing realm, other criminal justice officials, particularly prosecutors, are coming to the same realization. Prosecutors sometimes work closely with the police because they bring to the table the legal knowledge and ability to pursue appropriate actions in court. Although third-party policing is catching on, it hasn't been subject to extensive evaluation. Much more research remains to be done in order to identify

FIGURE 8.8 Third-Party Policing.

Third-party policing is about turning certain enforcement functions over to those who haven't traditionally done them.

problems at the places they are responsible for. It is also about coercing them to do so. Once again according to Buerger and Mazerolle, "Third-party policing constitutes a return to a compliance model of policing, although the police do not resume inspectorial functions.... Rather, these functions are performed by nominal partners of the police, or remain an implied threat behind police negotiations with guardians."[58]

In our definition of *third-party policing*, the "nonoffending" persons are the guardians. They are basically persuaded by police to do something about identified problems "or else." Simply put, "third-party policing establishes a control over nonoffending persons and persuades (or coerces) them to engage in activities thought to control crime."[59]

At its core, some would say that third-party policing is about turning certain enforcement functions over to those who haven't traditionally done them. Others, though, would argue that this is simply good law enforcement and that it is intended to bring guardians out of the shadows to take control over their properties. The police might, for instance, coerce a slumlord to fix a problem at one of his or her apartment complexes or face possible civil consequences.

Beyond the Criminal Law

Police routinely use the criminal law, local ordinances, curfew statutes, and the like to target crime. Third-party policing goes beyond the criminal law, primarily invoking civil law provisions. These, according to Buerger and Mazerolle, are "controls imported from the regulatory wing of the civil law [that] include provisions that allow the police to target deviant places, typically crackhouses, blighted homes, and false-front stores (such as 'bodegas') that sell drugs or traffic in black-market food stamps."[60] In truth, the civil law has always been available to the police, but the recent proliferation of problem-oriented and community policing has caused police officials to use more creative methods of crime control.

Civil law provisions, like those governing building codes, have been used periodically in law enforcement and, indeed, throughout the public sector to target problems. A dilapidated building that is replete with code violations can be shut down or condemned, something officials have done for years. Recently, though, scores of cities have capitalized on existing civil ordinances and created more of their own. An example is San Diego's creative ordinances aimed at the problem of illegal street racing. One of them provides that

a motor vehicle shall be declared a nuisance and forfeited subject to this division if … [i]t is used in violation of California Vehicle Code sections 23109(a) or (c); and … it is being driven by the registered owner of the vehicle, the registered owner is a passenger, the registered owner's immediate family member is driving or riding in the car, or the driver or passenger lives at the same address as the registered owner.[61]

A Digital Partnership with the Community

Some years ago, the Washington (DC) Metropolitan Police Department launched an online crime bulletin service.

The department is making use of crimereports.com, a free online service that allows police agencies to keep their communities up to date about criminal incidents in their areas. "Through this new digital partnership, we are able to provide the community with the type of information it needs to be full and active partners," said the department's chief, Charles H. Ramsey.[62]

One view of DC's crime bulletin service is that it embodies the spirit of community policing and, as the chief said, brings members of the community and the police into close contact. An opposing view is that the effort is largely symbolic—meaning that the department is giving the *appearance* of working closely with the community when in fact it is simply making use of a Web service that is readily available.

These competing views raise several interesting questions:

1. Is a Web-based approach to community policing sufficient? Is it meaningful and useful reform?

2. Is community policing an honest effort to improve police-community relations, or is it merely a symbolic gesture?

3. Where is the line between real and symbolic community policing drawn?

4. Is it realistic to expect the police and the community to work together in the name of crime prevention?

5. Is community policing effective, or is its actual intent something other than crime reduction?

Source: © Picture Contact BV/Alamy

Describe community justice and problem-oriented policing.

The contemporary notion of community justice encompasses community policing and several other recent law enforcement innovations, such as citizen patrol. Problem-oriented policing is best viewed as part of community policing. Both policing styles rely on citizen involvement.

1. What is community justice?

2. What is problem-oriented policing?

3. How are community justice and problem-oriented policing related?

community justice A relatively new and innovative set of ideas about how the goals of the criminal justice system can be achieved. It favors original, nontraditional approaches to crime control that draw heavily on input and cooperation from the community.

problem-oriented policing (POP) A method of policing that is geared toward identifying and solving problems within a community that are particularly troublesome and then crafting creative solutions to them. Also called *problem-solving policing*.

Define *community policing* and list justifications for it.

Community policing is often promoted as an effective crime-control technique, but it exists for several other reasons as well. For example, it serves to address citizen dissatisfaction, and it saves money. *Community policing* can be defined in various ways, but the essence of it is a partnership in which the police and the community work together to reduce crime.

1. What is community policing?

2. How did the concept of community policing develop?

3. What are the positive aspects of community policing, and why is it being widely promoted today?

4. What are some potentially negative aspects of community policing for law enforcement agencies?

community policing A collaborative effort between the police and the community that identifies problems of crime and disorder and involves all elements of the community in the search for solutions to these problems.

Distinguish between citizen involvement in policing and civilianization.

Citizen involvement in policing is commonplace today and occurs largely through citizen patrol and citizen police academies. Civilianization refers to the hiring of nonsworn personnel to perform certain limited functions within police departments.

1. What is the difference between citizen involvement in policing and civilianization?

2. What kinds of duties are best suited to civilians working in police departments?

3. What purposes do citizen police academies serve? Why do departments that utilize citizens for volunteer purposes find such academies important?

citizen patrol A preventive patrol program staffed by citizen volunteers.

citizen police academy A training experience that offers citizens an opportunity to learn about the policing profession and even to experience some of the same situations that uniformed officers experience.

civilianization "A law enforcement agency's hiring of nonsworn personnel to replace or augment its corps of sworn officers" in an effort to reduce costs and improve service.

LEARNING OUTCOMES 4

Define *third-party policing*, and provide some examples.

In third-party policing, the police apply pressure to nonoffending third parties (such as landlords) to improve their properties and thereby promote crime control and crime prevention.

1. What is third-party policing?

2. How can third-party policing help police departments? How might it harm them?

3. How can third-party policing help communities? How might it hurt?

4. Can you think of any potentially useful third-party policing strategies that this book doesn't discuss?

third-party policing A recently coined term that describes police efforts to persuade or coerce nonoffending persons to take actions that are outside the scope of their routine activities, and that are designed to indirectly minimize disorder caused by other persons or to reduce the possibility that crime may occur.

civil law The branch of modern law that governs relationships between parties.

MyCJLab

Go to the Chapter 8 section in *MyCJLab* to test your understanding of this chapter, access customized study content, engage in interactive simulations, complete critical thinking and research assignments, and view related online videos.

Additional Links

For insight into some of the issues involved in community policing, visit the Center for Problem-Oriented Policing at **www.popcenter.org**.

The Office of Community Oriented Policing Services is on the Web at **www.cops.usdoj.gov**.

Policing.com, which calls itself "the community policing headquarters," can be seen at **www.policing.com**.

Historical information about the evolution of community policing is posted at **law.jrank.org/pages/1653/Police-Community-Policing.html**.

The Chicago Police Department's Community Policing Page is reachable via **tinyurl.com/yroqa2**.

The role of community policing in homeland security is explored at **tinyurl.com/2bwyzr**.

Community building measures of interest to police administrators can be viewed at **www.justicestudies.com/pubs/communitybldg.pdf**.

A different aspect of community policing can be seen at the Los Angeles Police Department's E-Policing home page: **lapdonline.org/e_policing**.

An interview with Herman Goldstein, one of the founders of the community policing movement, can be seen and heard at **www.popcenter.org/learning/goldstein_interview**.

Policing in the Modern Era

"Police departments are almost wholly dependent on taxpayer funds for their continued existence, and budgets dictate their daily activities."

1 Discuss advances in information and communications technology as they apply to policing.

2 Define *intelligence-led policing* and provide examples of it.

3 Explain how terrorism has made an imprint on American policing.

9

POLICING AND THE ECONOMIC STIMULUS BILL

In recognition of the important role that police departments play in the American criminal justice system, the American Recovery and Reinvestment Act of 2009 (ARRA),[1] also known as The Recovery Act (or "the Stimulus"), provided more than $1 billion to state and local law enforcement and correctional agencies through the Bureau of Justice Assistance, an arm of the U.S. Department of Justice. The amount of Recovery Act funding funneled to various types of criminal justice programs is shown in Figure 9.1. Law enforcement agencies, as the figure shows, received the lion's share of the money. Most of them reported spending the funds they received on training (or retraining); the retention of personnel who would otherwise have been laid off; and equipment purchases, including items such as vehicles, weapons, Tasers™, protective vests, and communications devices.

DISCUSS Why is it important for today's police agencies to effectively justify budgetary outlays?

About a year later, in October 2010 the Government Accountability Office, the federal agency charged with assessing the benefits achieved by federal outlays, released a special report to Congress on the effective use of Recovery Act moneys by justice system agencies.[2] The report stated that performance measures that had been established by the U.S. Department of Justice to assess the effectiveness of expenditures made under the Recovery Act had been inadequate to the task. Those measures, said the GAO "lack key attributes of successful performance assessment systems . . . such as clarity, reliability, a linkage to strategic or programmatic goals, and objectivity and measurability of targets."[3]

While the GAO report may have seemed inconclusive to some, alert law enforcement administrators were quick to see the proverbial writing on the wall and realized that a new era in fiscal accountability had dawned with the release of that report. Not only would police agencies of the near future need to be cognizant of the legal environment surrounding enforcement activities, but they would also need to effectively justify budgetary outlays and demonstrate the exact nature of benefits to be received from planned expenditures.

Police departments, like other public agencies, have limited resources. They are almost wholly dependent on taxpayer funds for their continued existence, and budgets dictate their daily activities. Although they can always ask for more money, departments everywhere must make the most of available resources. Consequently, there can be only so many officers on the ground, and only limited funds are available to pay for overtime and to hire additional officers. Through

experience and research, police departments have also come to realize that traditional responses to crime, such as preventive patrol, have met with limited success. Fortunately, relatively inexpensive and widely available technological advances are aiding police departments today in their crime-fighting efforts, especially in the areas of information gathering and communications.

This chapter begins with an examination of the many advances in information and communications technology, including crime-mapping programs and Compstat. Next, it introduces the concept of intelligence-led policing. Not to be confused with evidence-based policing, which we have featured throughout this book, intelligence-led policing is about gathering information, analyzing it, and using the results to target specific crime problems. Finally, the chapter concludes with a look at the police response to terrorism. A focus on terrorism fits well in this chapter because *policing* the terrorist threat relies heavily on technology and intelligence-led policing.

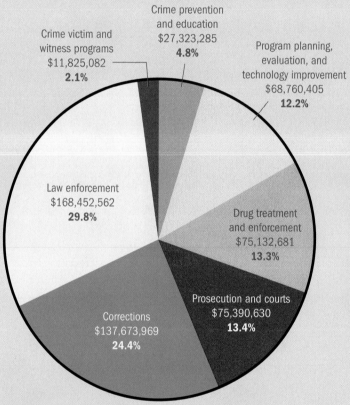

FIGURE 9.1 Recovery Act Moneys Awarded through the Bureau of Justice Assistance.

Source: U.S. Government Accountability Office, *Report to congressional requesters: Recovery Act – Department of Justice could better assess justice assistance grant program impact* (Washington, DC: GAO, October 2010), GAO-11-87, p. 19, www.gao.gov/new.items/d1187.pdf.

Advances in information and communications technology have worked wonders for law enforcement. From helping investigators reconstruct crime scenes to facilitating information sharing between agencies, they have transformed the way police do business. This section briefly examines some of the more interesting developments in this area.

LEARNING OUTCOMES 1 Discuss advances in information and communications technology as they apply to policing.

GLOSSARY

pin map An early crime-mapping technique that used colored pins to track criminal events on a map of the police department's jurisdictional area.

Crime Mapping Research Center (CMRC) A U.S. Justice Department agency that promotes research, training, and technical assistance for police agencies around the country and assists them in their crime-mapping efforts. Also called the *Mapping and Analysis for Public Safety (MAPS) Program.*

Crime Mapping

It used to be that patterns of criminal activity were identified on **pin maps**. Colored stick pins would literally be stuck in various places on a map of a city, county, district, precinct, or other area. Different colors corresponded to different types of crimes. This approach, while crude, permitted police to identify problem areas and patterns of criminal activity. The problem was that the maps were one-dimensional and could easily get crowded with pins, especially in the case of minor crimes that occurred with great frequency. The maps were also static, meaning that they could not easily be manipulated to serve different purposes, such

as tracking certain types of crime over time. Pin maps were large and could take up significant wall space. Enter crime-mapping software. (See Figure 9.2.)

Crime mapping has become so commonplace that the National Institute of Justice (an agency of the U.S. Justice Department) has created the **Crime Mapping Research Center (CMRC)**. The center promotes research, training, and technical assistance for police agencies around the country and assists them in their mapping efforts. CMRC is an enthusiastic supporter of **computerized crime mapping** for some simple reasons:

> Mapping crime can help law enforcement protect citizens more effectively in the areas they serve. Simple maps that display the locations where crimes or concentrations of crimes have occurred can be used to help direct patrols to places [where] they are most needed. Policy makers in police departments might use more complex maps to observe trends in criminal activity, and maps may prove invaluable in solving criminal cases. For example, detectives may use maps to better understand the hunting patterns of serial criminals and to hypothesize where these offenders might live.

Geographic Profiling

Geographic profiling makes use of crime-mapping technology. In particular, it maps connected criminal acts in an effort to determine the offender's residence location. It is used for a range of criminal acts, including murder, rape, robbery, and auto theft.

Geographic profiling can be made particularly effective when it is combined with databases used to track serial offenders. For

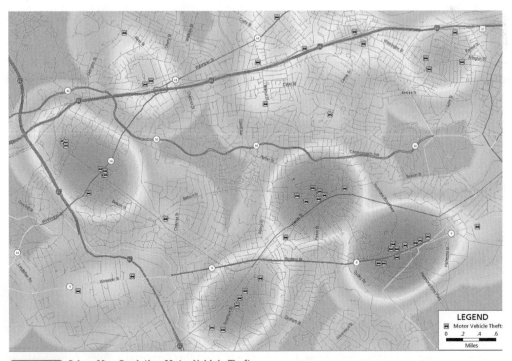

FIGURE 9.2 **Crime Map Depicting Motor Vehicle Thefts.**
Source: Produced by the Maptitude mapping software, © 2008 Caliper Corporation. Reprinted by permission.

Geographic profiling allows investigators to identify the likely whereabouts or residences of repeat or serial offenders.

example, the Washington State Attorney General's Office uses the **Homicide Investigation and Tracking (HITS) System**, which ties various databases together—including gang files, sex offender registries, parole records, and department of motor vehicle records—so that they can be searched simultaneously. According to University of Nevada at Reno criminologist Ken Peak,

> When an agency in the state has a major crime in its jurisdiction, the case is loaded into a central system, which scans every database and linking file for connections by comparing eyewitness descriptions of a suspect and vehicle. It builds a dataset containing profiles of the offender, the victims, and the incidents. The dataset then goes into a geographic information system, where the program selects and maps the names and addresses of those suspects whose method of operation fits the crime being investigated.[4]

Crime Intelligence Systems

Nowadays, nearly every patrol officer has a laptop computer in his or her car that is linked to various databases, such as vehicle registration records and criminal history information. Recently, though, the databases have become increasingly sophisticated. One of them, known as **CalGang** (in California) or GangNet (in other states) contains detailed information on known gang members that officers in the field can quickly access.

Compstat

During the early years of his tenure as police commissioner of New York City, William Bratton called for weekly meetings with representatives from each of the NYPD's eight bureaus. Deputy Commissioner Jack Maple, in conjunction with other high-ranking officials, placed pressure on the bureaus to generate crime statistics, which had not been kept up to date at the time. Precincts began to measure criminal activity more carefully; then the results were computerized and assembled into a document known as the *Compstat book.*[5] The crime figures reported in the Compstat book

Compstat is an acronym for "computer statistics" or, in some locations "compare statistics."

were eventually used to hold precinct commanders responsible for the crime rates in their areas.

Compstat is an acronym for "computer statistics" or, in some locations "compare statistics." The NYPD program has been widely imitated around the country,[6] and the programs have several different designations. Generally speaking, Compstat emphasizes four important elements:

1. Accurate and timely intelligence
2. Effective tactics
3. Rapid deployment
4. Relentless follow-up and assessment[7]

The logic behind the intelligence aspect is that "information describing how and where crimes are committed, as well as who criminals are, must be available to all levels of policing."[8] "Tactics are designed to respond directly to facts discovered during the intelligence gathering process."[9] Rapid deployment is important and often involves quick and effective coordination because "the most effective plans require that personnel from several units and enforcement functions work together as a team."[10] Relentless follow-up is necessary to ensure desired outcomes. Figure 9.3 lists the general elements of the Compstat model.

The last step, relentless accountability, is extremely important and is usually accomplished most effectively in intensive management meetings. According to Jack Maple, former deputy commissioner of the NYPD, "the first step to crime reduction itself—the gathering and analyzing of accurate, timely intelligence—has to be quickened by the heat of accountability."[11]

One important aspect of Compstat is crime mapping. Because crime data must be portrayed clearly and

geographic profiling Using crime-mapping technology to identify the likely whereabouts or residences of repeat or serial offenders.

Homicide Investigation and Tracking System (HITS) A geographic profiling system that ties various databases together (gang files, sex offender registries, parole records, and department of motor vehicle records) to facilitate simultaneous database searches.

CalGang A sophisticated software database of known gang members that field officers in California can access quickly. GangNet is a modified version of the software that is used nationwide.

Compstat A goal-oriented police management process that relies heavily on computer technology and accountability of top-level administrators.

---

computer-aided drafting (CAD) A technology, adapted to meet the needs of police officers and criminal investigators, that facilitates the drafting of crime scenes on a computer so that they can be viewed three-dimensionally.

(Think About It...

Compstat The effect of Compstat on crime has not received much research attention. Some researchers have attributed drops in crime to Compstat and similar managerial approaches, but to date, few researchers have applied rigorous scientific methods to the question of whether Compstat directly affects crime. Is it possible to know that Compstat, independent of all other possible explanations, reduces crime? Can Compstat alone reduce crime or are more means necessary? Explain.

Source: © Mikael Karlsson/Alamy

Innovative problem-solving tactics: Police responses are selected because they offer the best prospects of success, not because they are "what we have always done." Innovation and experimentation are encouraged and use of the best available knowledge about practices is expected.

Data-driven analysis of problems and assessment of department's problem-solving efforts: Data are made available to identify and analyze problems and to track and assess the department's response. Data are made accessible to all relevant personnel on a timely basis and in a readily usable format.

Mission clarification: Top management clarifies and exalts the core features of the department's mission. Management demonstrates commitment and states its goals. The organization and its leaders can be held accountable for specific goals—such as reducing crime by 10 percent in a year.

Organizational flexibility: The organization develops the capacity and habit of changing established routines as needed to mobilize resources when and where they are needed for strategic application.

Internal accountability: Operational commanders are held accountable for knowing their commands, being well acquainted with the problems in the command, and accomplishing measurable results in reducing those problems—or at least demonstrating a diligent effort to learn from that experience.

Geographic organization of operational command: Operational command is focused on the policing of territories, so central decision-making authority over police operations is delegated to commanders with territorial responsibility for districts. Functionally differentiated units and specialists—patrol, community-policing officers, detectives, narcotics, vice, juvenile, and traffic—are either placed under the command of the district commander, or arrangements are made to facilitate their responsiveness to the commander's needs.

FIGURE 9.3 **Core Elements of the Compstat Model.**
Source: J. J. Willis, S. D. Mastrofski, and D. Weisburd, *Compstat in Practice: An In-Depth Analysis of Three Cities* (Washington, DC: Police Foundation, 2004). Reprinted by permission of the Police Foundation.

firearms training system (FATS) A full-size, fully interactive training device, not unlike flight and driving simulators, that exposes police trainees to realistic shooting scenarios. The realism is enhanced by fully encasing the trainees in a particular surrounding rather than simply putting them in front of a television screen.

computerized crime mapping A computer-based system that combines a geographic information system with crime statistics generated by a police department, allowing crime data to be plotted on a map.

rapidly, computer technology is essential. According to one source, "A powerful software tool, MapInfo 94, became the NYPD's crime radar screen, with attention-grabbing colors and shapes. Red dots indicated drug complaints from the public, blue dots showed drug arrests, green triangles represented shooting incidents, and yellow dots indicated homicides."[12] Computerized images generated by MapInfo 94 brought together all the data in the Compstat books. Previously, crime statistics had not been kept or presented in any single source. As another

researcher observed, "These visual presentations are a highly effective complement to the Compstat report, since they permit precinct commanders and executive staff members to instantly identify and explore trends, patterns, and possible solutions for crime and quality-of-life problems."[13]

Crime statistics are the most popular measure of success for precinct commanders. However, Sam Houston State University criminologists Randall Garner and Larry Hoover question the appropriateness of crime statistics as the sole measure of success.[14] They cite quality-of-life issues and citizen complaints as barometers of police performance that agencies experimenting with Compstat may wish to consider. The appropriate measure of success, they suggest, "communicates what issues are valued most in the department."[15] They also raise concerns about the NYPD version of Compstat, which they regard as confrontational. While NYPD's program has established greater accountability, increased awareness, improved problem-solving endeavors, and increased managerial control, they caution that weekly meetings may be too shortsighted and aggressive an approach to reducing crime and may overemphasize outcomes rather than underlying causes of problems. Indeed, one researcher has observed that "Compstat's approach ignores decades of expert research that has shown that crime levels are determined by vast social forces beyond police control—poverty, racism, [and] demographics."[16]

Computer-Aided Drafting

Computer-aided drafting (CAD) is not a law enforcement technology per se, but it has been adapted to meet the needs of police officers and criminal investigators. Gone are the days of convincing jury members to convict based on tedious one-dimensional drawings and photographs. For instance, a three-dimensional crime scene image puts jurors at the crime scene almost as if they were actually there.

As this technology continues to develop, it is becoming more portable. For example, the Department of Energy has been working on a device that officers in the field can use to beam the information they gather (via pictures, laser range finders, Global Positioning System devices, etc.) to the crime lab for instant expert advice and accurate recording of the crime scene.[17]

CAD programs offer several advantages. First, they create images that are professional in their appearance, an improvement over traditional methods of drafting crime scene images by hand and relying on simple photographs. This is of great importance if the images are to be shared with jurors in a criminal trial. In this vein, the next CAD advantage is that the

Crime statistics are the most popular measure of success for precinct commanders.

software minimizes duplication of effort; there is no need to draft separate images for investigators and jurors. With a few keystrokes, a large image can be printed for sharing with a jury.

The software makes crime scene investigation much cheaper, too. Gone are the days when drafts people or engineers needed to take precise measurements of every detail of a crime scene. Delays in crime-scene reconstruction are now largely a thing of the past. Perhaps most important, it is easy to alter images as new information becomes available, thus eliminating the need to redraw the entire image.

Computer-Assisted Training

Computers also enhance the training of law enforcement officers. Veteran officers may have had the opportunity to participate in one of the old "shoot/don't shoot" training exercises in front of a television screen with a noninteractive video. Those days are largely over; computers have helped make such exercises much more realistic and dramatic.

One of the new technologies in this area, the **firearms training system (FATS)**, is about as realistic as shooting a simulated firearm can get. It is a full-size, fully interactive device, not

Computer-Aided Drafting	Permits drafting of crime scenes on a computer that can then be viewed three-dimensionally. CAD software has also been developed for animation purposes, enabling viewers to get a feel for the perpetrators' movements.
Computer-Assisted Training	Training now consists of simulators that fully encase trainees in a particular surrounding rather than simply putting them in front of a television screen. This makes the training more realistic, as threats can come from any direction on the job.
Computerized Crime Mapping	Combines geographic information systems with crime statistics generated by a police department so that the crimes can be plotted on a map, resulting in a clean image with details concerning the frequency with which certain crimes take place in given areas. Additionally, computerized crime maps can be overlaid with other information, such as demographic or law enforcement data (for example, unemployment levels or known gang territories).
Geographic Profiling	Using crime-mapping technology, geographic profiling allows investigators to identify the likely whereabouts or residences of repeat or serial offenders.
Crime Intelligence Systems	SRA International, a provider of crime intelligence software, created GangNet Solution, a browser-based investigative, analysis, and statistical resource for recording and tracking gang members and their activities. The database system enables information sharing on relationships between individuals involved in gangs, which gives law enforcement officials a tool to identify individuals, vehicles, tattoos, gang symbols, and locations, and to facilitate work on gang-related cases. Additional features, such as mapping and facial recognition, are continuously being added to the system[i].
Compstat	This is defined as a goal-oriented strategic management process that uses computer technology, operational strategy and managerial accountability to structure the manner in which a police department provides crime-control services.

FIGURE 9.4 The Impact of Technology on Policing.

unlike flight and driving simulators. Moreover, the technology is also relatively affordable and portable.

VirTra Systems, which markets FATS devices, uses a 300-degree immersive training platform that surrounds the trainee with a realistic judgmental use-of-force scenario in one of its products.[18]

Another company has gone so far as to develop a simulator that actually pelts the trainee with large-caliber nylon balls when he or she makes a mistake, further approximating reality. One such device, the Professional Range Instruction Simulator (PRISim), has been described as "training so real, you will not call it a simulator."[19] AIS Solutions, the company behind the device, says this:

> PRISim™ puts trainees into the middle of an interactive theatre to cause responses to potentially deadly mistakes, indecision, sudden fear, partial understanding, blindside surprise, eye-blink response and life or death choices. The PRISim™ system gives trainees the coaching they could never get in actual field operations and provides situational experiences far beyond the capability of conventional training. . . . The PRISim™ ShootBack cannon is a devastatingly effective tool to train effective use of cover. An instructor-aimed cannon is mounted above the centre of the screen to fire 17mm caliber nylon projectiles synchronized with the video scenario. The cannon fires accurate single, 3-round burst or full auto hostile fire.[20]

▶ Intelligence-Led Policing

In 2005, the U.S. Department of Justice embraced **intelligence-led policing (ILP)** as an important technique that American law enforcement agencies can employ in the battle against terrorism.[21] ILP can also be used to target other pressing problems, such as property crime, narcotics violations, and organized crime. Not every agency has the staff or resources needed to create a dedicated intelligence unit. Even without an intelligence unit, however, a law enforcement organization should have the ability to effectively utilize the information and intelligence products that are developed and disseminated by organizations at all levels of government. In other words, even though a police agency may not have its own resources for analyzing all the information it acquires, it should still be able to mount an effective response to credible threat information that it receives. The following sections take a closer look at the nature of intelligence, why it is important, the intelligence process, and the nature of intelligence-led policing, especially in comparison to some other approaches we discuss elsewhere in this book.

Intelligence

What is intelligence? It is tempting to liken it to information, but they are not the same. Rather, **intelligence** has been defined as the sum of information and analysis.[22] Another definition is "a formal process of taking information and turning it into knowledge while ensuring that the information is collected, stored, and disseminated appropriately."[23] Police expert David Carter's *Law Enforcement Intelligence: A Guide for State, Local, and Tribal Law Enforcement Agencies* defines criminal intelligence as "a

synergistic product intended to provide meaningful and trustworthy direction to law enforcement decision makers about complex criminality, criminal enterprises, criminal extremists, and terrorists."[24]

Intelligence is information that has been analyzed and integrated into a useful perspective. The information used in the development of effective intelligence is typically gathered from many sources as noted in Figure 9.5. Law enforcement intelligence, or **criminal intelligence**, is the result of a "process that evaluates information collected from diverse sources, integrates the relevant information into a cohesive package, and produces a conclusion or estimate about a criminal phenomenon by using the scientific approach to problem solving."[25] While criminal investigation is typically part of the intelligence-gathering process, the intelligence function of a police department is more exploratory and more broadly focused than a single criminal investigation.[26]

Key to these definitions is the idea that without analysis there is no intelligence. What, then, is analysis? It is not just information processing by trained crime analysts. Instead, "analysis requires thoughtful contemplation that results in conclusions and recommendations."[27] With this in mind, it is useful to distinguish between various types and levels of intelligence.

Tactical and Strategic Intelligence

Carter points out that there are two types of intelligence: tactical and strategic. **Tactical intelligence** "includes gaining or developing information related to threats of terrorism or crime and using this information to apprehend offenders, harden targets, and use strategies that will eliminate or mitigate the threat."[28] **Strategic intelligence**, in contrast, provides information to decision makers about the changing nature of threats for the purpose of "developing response strategies and reallocating resources"[29] to accomplish effective prevention.

GLOSSARY

intelligence-led policing (ILP) The collection and analysis of information to produce an intelligence end product designed to inform police decision making at both the tactical and strategic levels. Also called *intelligence-driven policing*.

intelligence Information that has been analyzed and integrated into a useful perspective.

criminal intelligence A synergistic product intended to provide meaningful and trustworthy direction to law enforcement decision makers about complex criminality, criminal enterprises, criminal extremists, and terrorists. Also, a process that evaluates information collected from diverse sources, integrates the relevant information into a cohesive package, and produces a conclusion or estimate about a criminal phenomenon by using the scientific approach to problem solving.

tactical intelligence A type of intelligence that includes gaining or developing information related to threats of terrorism or crime and using this information to apprehend offenders, harden targets, and use strategies that will eliminate or mitigate the threat.

strategic intelligence A type of intelligence that provides information to decision makers about the changing nature of threats, enabling them to develop response strategies and reallocate resources for effective threat prevention.

Decision Making
It is common for law enforcement agencies to gather information and to decide what to do with it. Having the most accurate and complete intelligence aids in decision making.

Strategic Targeting
Intelligence enables administrators to carefully target their efforts to achieve the best results with limited funds. Strategic targeting is about focusing on the individuals, groups, or locations where success is most likely.

Intelligence Gathering
- newspapers
- surveillance
- covert operations
- financial records
- electronic eavesdropping
- interviews
- interrogations

Crime Prevention
Every police agency hopes to prevent crime rather than just respond to it. Intelligence from previous crimes may arm decision makers with the information they need to prevent similar crimes from occurring. Analysts can compare the indicators from local neighborhoods to anticipate crime trends, and agencies can take preventive measures to intervene or mitigate the impact of those crimes.

Planning
Planning also depends on intelligence. Unfortunately, planning in many agencies is done without sufficient intelligence, such as the nature of specific crime problems facing an area.

FIGURE 9.5 Sources of Intelligence.

Intelligence is information that has been analyzed and integrated into a useful perspective.

National Criminal Intelligence Sharing Plan (NCISP) A formal intelligence sharing initiative that addresses the security and intelligence needs recognized after the tragic events of September 11, 2001. It describes a nationwide communications capability that will link together all levels of law enforcement personnel, including officers on the streets, intelligence analysts, unit commanders, and police executives for the purpose of sharing critical data.

fusion center An intelligence-gathering unit, often constituted as a collaborative effort that serves various agencies.

Law Enforcement Assistance and Partnership (LEAP) Strategy A plan introduced in the U.S. Congress that called for the establishment of a national center for intelligence-led policing.

Levels of Intelligence

There are four levels of intelligence. Level 1 intelligence is the highest. According to one study, "the law enforcement agency at [level 1] employs an intelligence manager, intelligence officers, and professional intelligence analysts."[30] The secretive Financial Crimes Enforcement Network (FINCEN) fits into this category. "Level 2 intelligence includes police agencies that produce tactical and strategic intelligence for internal consumption. . . . These agencies generally use intelligence to support investigations rather than to direct operations."[31] The typical agency at this level is a state police agency that may have intelligence units or officers on the payroll. Level 3

intelligence, the second most common form, includes local law enforcement agencies with anywhere from a few dozen to hundreds of sworn personnel. These agencies sometimes produce their own intelligence but often rely on other higher-level (state or federal) agencies that specialize in intelligence gathering. Level 3 agencies should not always rely on outside help, however. According to one study,

> While smaller agencies may not be able to devote a full-time position to the criminal intelligence function . . . [they] need to understand the proactive concept of criminal intelligence and recognize that most law enforcement agencies, regardless of size, are susceptible to organized criminal activity that may extend beyond jurisdictional boundaries. Their personnel should be trained to recognize and report indications of organized crime, gang activity, and criminal extremist and terrorist activity. The information should be shared with intelligence-trained personnel from neighboring agencies.[32]

Finally, level 4 intelligence characterizes the vast majority of law enforcement agencies in the United States. "If they assign someone to intelligence operations, that person generally has multiple responsibilities and is often a narcotics officer, gang officer, or counter-terrorism officer."[33]

Think About It...

Directed Patrol *Directed patrol* refers to patrol with direction—that is, patrol targeted at specific areas and problems. Directed patrol is heavily influenced by the gathering of intelligence. That is, with the right data, law enforcement officials can decide where to concentrate their efforts. Assuming police have a particular problem area in mind, is directed patrol the ideal approach? Should you worry about displacement of the problem into surrounding neighborhoods or cities? Why or why not?

Source: © Dnavarrojr/Dreamstime.com

Why Intelligence Is Important

Law enforcement agencies at all levels depend on intelligence and cannot function adequately without it.

The Intelligence Process

The Global Intelligence Working Group, consisting of approximately 30 intelligence professionals, met throughout 2003 to come up with a plan for intelligence sharing. The final product was called the **National Criminal Intelligence Sharing Plan (NCISP)**. It was approved and released by the U.S. attorney general in October 2003. Several recommendations for improved intelligence gathering were offered, and the group also organized the process into six steps (Figure 9.6). Note that the process is circular and that it starts with planning and direction. According to a recent report, *planning and direction* require

2003 The National Criminal Intelligence Sharing Plan (NCISP) was released by the U.S. attorney general in October 2003.

an agency to identify the outcomes it wants to achieve from its collection efforts. This identification directs the scope of the officers' and agents' investigations—for example, a straightforward inquiry to identify crime groups operating in a jurisdiction or a more complex inquiry to determine the likelihood that criminal extremists will attack a visiting dignitary.[34]

Next, *collection* refers to gathering and processing information. This can be accomplished through several strategies, including physical surveillance, electronic surveillance (for example, wiretapping), confidential informants, newspaper reports, and so on. Third, *processing* consists of sifting through all this information to organize and collate it. *Analysis* converts the information to intelligence. As one official put it, "Without the explicit performance of this function, the intelligence unit is nothing but a file unit."[35] Analysis includes crime analysis (for example, crime-pattern analysis with mapping software), but it also includes investigative analysis (bank record analysis) and strategic analysis (risk assessment). The next step is *dissemination*, which is the process of getting intelligence to the decision makers who need it. Finally, *reevaluation* is concerned with reanalysis of intelligence products to determine their accuracy and effectiveness. According to a report on the subject, "One way to reevaluate intelligence is to include a feedback form with each product that is disseminated."[36]

The Nature of Intelligence-Led Policing

We have spent significant time discussing intelligence in general, but what exactly is intelligence-led policing? The

Reevaluation
Planning and Direction
6
1
Collection
2
5
Dissemination
4
3
Analysis
Processing/ Collation

FIGURE 9.6 The Intelligence Process.
Source: Office of Justice Programs, *National criminal intelligence sharing plan* (Washington, DC: U.S. Department of Justice, 2003), p. 6.

term originated in the United Kingdom.[37] Specifically, the Kent Constabulary came up with the concept in response to a rise in property crime—a rise that occurred while police resources were being cut. Originally called the *Kent Policing Model*, this approach prioritized calls for service and referred nonemergency calls to other agencies, when appropriate. This freed up resources so that officers could focus on the property crimes that were on the rise. The result was a property crime drop of 24 percent over three years. According to one assessment of this effort,

> [I]ntelligence-led policing focuses on key criminal activities. Once crime problems are identified and quantified through intelligence assessments, key criminals can be targeted for investigation and prosecution. Because the groups and individuals targeted in Kent were those responsible for significant criminal activity, the ultimate reduction in crime was considerable.[38]

Since it has been imported into the United States, intelligence-led policing has remained largely the same, with some minor twists. For example, it has benefited from so-called **fusion centers**. These are essentially intelligence-gathering units—often collaborative efforts that serve various agencies. As David Lambert explains,

> A fusion center is a "collaborative effort of two or more agencies that provide resources, expertise, and information to the center with the goal of maximizing their ability to detect, prevent, investigate, and respond to criminal and terrorist activity." Fusion centers can identify potential threats through data analysis and enhance investigations through analytical support (e.g., flow charting and geographic analysis).[39]

Intelligence-Led versus Problem-Oriented Policing

Intelligence-led policing sounds similar to problem-oriented policing (see Chapter 8), but the two are somewhat different. Problem-oriented policing seeks to control crime through the study of problems. Common to problem-oriented policing, too, is the scanning, analysis, response, assessment (SARA) model.

Intelligence-led policing basically takes problem-oriented policing to the next level; it does the same for community-oriented policing. These strategies "have been used for crime analysis, which is statistical and incident-based, rather than strategic intelligence analysis, which looks at large-scope problems or models."[40] In other words, intelligence-based policing takes problem-oriented policing beyond the level of a single police agency.

Intelligence-led policing may also sound something like Compstat. As Table 9.1 shows, they are similar but not quite the same.

As recently as December 2006, U.S. Representative Bennie G. Thompson (D-MS) released a plan called the **Law Enforcement Assistance and Partnership (LEAP) Strategy**, in which he called for the establishment of a national center for intelligence-led policing. Initiatives proposed by others include providing funding for police chiefs to help defray the costs of intelligence gathering, improving border intelligence, providing funding for tribal participation, establishing a national counterterrorism center to include law enforcement officers in intelligence gathering, issuing security clearances to law enforcement executives who need them, and tracking the progress of intelligence-led policing efforts.[41] It will be most interesting to follow these developments over time.

TABLE 9.1 — Comparison of Compstat and Intelligence-Led Policing

Compstat	Commonalities	Intelligence-Led Policing
• Single jurisdiction	• Both have a goal of prevention	• Multiple jurisdictions
• Incident driven	• Both require	• Threat driven
• Street crime and burglary	– Organizational flexibility	• Criminal enterprises and terrorism
• Crime mapping	– Consistent information input	• Commodity flow; trafficking and transiting logistics
• Time sensitive (24-hour feedback and response)	– A significant analytic component	• Strategic
• Disrupt crime series (for example, burglary ring)	• Both are driven from the bottom up with respect to operational needs	• Disrupt enterprises
• Drives operations:		• Drives operations:
– Patrol		– JTIF
– Tactical unit		– Organized crime investigations
– Investigators		– Task forces
• Analysis of offender MOs		• Analysis of enterprise MOs

Source: Office of Community-Oriented Policing Services, *Intelligence-led policing: The integration of community policing and law enforcement intelligence, part 4* (Washington, DC: COPS Office, n.d.), p. 43, www.cops.usdoj.gov/pdf/e09042536_Chapter_04.pdf (accessed July 24, 2011).

A recent Bureau of Justice Assistance report offers some examples of how intelligence-led policing could be further utilized throughout the United States. Here are three of them:

- A county sheriff's office identifies narcotics control as its top priority and develops strategies accordingly. The office targets known offenders and groups, shuts down open-air drug markets and crack houses, and participates in school-based drug-awareness programs to help prevent drug use.
- A statewide agency identifies vehicle insurance fraud as a top area for enforcement. The agency targets those involved in staged accidents, identifies communities in which insurance fraud is prevalent, looks for similar methods of operation that may indicate ongoing fraudulent activity, and mounts a public education campaign.
- A police agency in a small city makes safe streets a priority. The agency focuses on directed enforcement in identified hot spots. It also targets career criminals whose apprehension will significantly reduce the number of crimes being committed. Preventive measures include enhanced patrols, improved street lighting, and crime-watch programs.

FIGURE 9.7 Examples of Intelligence Led Policing.
Source: From "Local and State Anti-Terrorism Analysis" by Marilyn B. Peterson, ILLINOIS LAW ENFORCEMENT EXECUTIVE FORUM 2(1): 77–84. Reprinted by permission.

▶ *Policing in an Age of Terrorism*

September 11, 2001, and the events in its wake have made clear the changed role of American police agencies in a new era of international terrorism. While the core mission of American police departments has not changed, law enforcement agencies at all levels now devote an increased amount of time and other resources to preparing for possible terrorist attacks and to gathering the intelligence necessary to thwart them.

Local police departments play an especially important role in responding to the challenges of terrorism. They must help prevent attacks and respond when attacks occur, offering critical evacuation, emergency medical, and security functions to help stabilize communities following an incident. A Police Executive Research Forum (PERF) survey of 250 police chiefs found that the chiefs strongly believe that their departments can make valuable contributions to terrorism prevention by using community policing networks to exchange information with citizens and to gather intelligence.[42]

The Council on Foreign Relations, headquartered in New York City and Washington, DC, agrees with PERF that American police departments can no longer assume that federal counterterrorism efforts alone will be sufficient to protect the communities they serve. Consequently, says the council, many police departments have responded by

- Strengthening liaisons with federal, state, and local agencies, including fire departments and other police departments
- Refining their training and emergency response plans to address terrorist threats, including attacks with weapons of mass destruction

Police chiefs strongly believe that their departments can make valuable contributions to terrorism prevention by using community policing networks.

- Increasing patrols and shoring up barriers around landmarks, places of worship, ports of entry, transit systems, nuclear power plants, and so on
- More heavily guarding public speeches, parades, and other public events
- Creating new counterterrorism divisions and reassigning officers to counterterrorism from other divisions, such as drug enforcement
- Employing new technologies such as X-ray-like devices to scan containers at ports of entry and sophisticated sensors to detect a chemical, biological, or radiological attack[43]

The extent of local departments' engagement in such preventive activities depends substantially on budgetary considerations and is strongly influenced by the assessed likelihood of attack. The New York City Police Department (NYPD), for example, which has firsthand experience in responding to terrorist attacks (23 of its officers were killed when the World Trade Center towers collapsed), has created a special bureau headed by a deputy police commissioner responsible for counterterrorism training, prevention, and investigation.[44] One thousand officers have been reassigned to antiterrorism duties, and the department is training its entire 39,000-member force in how to respond to biological, radiological, and chemical attacks.[45] The NYPD has assigned detectives to work abroad with law enforcement agencies in Canada, Israel, Southeast Asia, and the Middle East to track terrorists who might target

LEARNING OUTCOMES 3 Explain how terrorism has made an imprint on American policing.

GLOSSARY

Taking Command Initiative A project undertaken by the International Association of Chiefs of Police to assess the current state of homeland security efforts in the United States and to develop and implement the actions needed to protect American communities from the specter of both crime and terrorism.

Joint Terrorism Task Force (JTTF) An FBI-sponsored group composed of federal, state, and local law enforcement personnel who are brought together to focus on a specific threat.

boundaryless policing Any of various technology-based intelligence efforts designed to combat crime and terrorism.

IACP's Five Key Principles of an Effective Homeland Security Strategy

1. Homeland security proposals must be developed in a local context, acknowledging that local, not federal, authorities have the primary responsibility for preventing, responding to, and recovering from terrorist attacks.
2. Prevention, not just response and recovery, must be paramount in any national, state, or local security strategy. For too long, federal strategies have minimized the importance of prevention, focusing instead on response and recovery.
3. Because of their daily efforts to combat crime and violence in their communities, state and local law enforcement officers are uniquely situated to identify, investigate, and apprehend suspected terrorists.
4. Homeland security strategies must be coordinated nationally, not federally.
5. A truly successful national strategy must recognize, embrace, and value the vast diversity among state and local law enforcement and public-safety agencies. A one-size-fits-all approach will fail to secure our homeland.[i]

FIGURE 9.8 IACP's Five Key Principles of an Effective Homeland Security Strategy.
Source: From SACOP/IACP Committee Report, www.tacp.org, submitted by Gill Kendrick, March 28, 2006, p. 4. Reprinted by permission.

New York City,[46] and it now employs officers with a command of the Pashto, Farsi, and Urdu languages of the Middle East to monitor foreign television, radio, and Internet communications. The department has also invested heavily in new hazardous materials protective suits, gas masks, and portable radiation detectors.

In November 2004, in an effort to provide the law enforcement community and policy makers with guidance on critical issues related to antiterrorism planning and critical-incident response, the International Association of Chiefs of Police (IACP) announced its **Taking Command Initiative**. The IACP describes the initiative as "an aggressive project to assess the current state of homeland security efforts in the United States and to develop and implement the actions necessary to protect our communities from the specter of both crime and terrorism."[47] Initial deliberations under the initiative led IACP to conclude that "the current homeland security strategy is handicapped by a fundamental flaw: It was developed without sufficiently seeking or incorporating the advice, expertise, or consent of public safety organizations at the state, tribal or local level."[48]

As IACP recognizes that workable antiterrorism programs at the local level require the effective sharing of critical information between agencies. FBI-sponsored **Joint Terrorism Task Forces (JTTFs)** facilitate this by bringing together federal and local law enforcement personnel to focus on specific threats. The FBI currently has established or authorized JTTFs in each of its 56 field offices. In addition to the JTTFs, the FBI has created Regional Terrorism Task Forces (RTTFs) to share information with local enforcement agencies. Through the RTTFs, FBI special agents assigned to terrorism prevention and investigation meet twice a year with their federal, state, and local counterparts for common training, discussion of investigations, and intelligence sharing. The FBI says that "the design of this non-traditional terrorism task force provides the necessary mechanism and structure to direct counterterrorism resources toward localized terrorism problems within the United States."[49]

Some say that traditional distinctions between crime, terrorism, and war are fading and that direct military action and civil law enforcement are becoming integrated.

Six RTTFs are currently in operation: the Inland Northwest, South Central, Southeastern, Northeast Border, Deep South, and Southwest.

Given the changes that have taken place in American law enforcement since the terrorist attacks of September 11, 2001, some say that traditional distinctions between crime, terrorism, and war are fading and that, at least in some instances, direct military action and civil law enforcement are becoming integrated. The critical question for law enforcement administrators in the near future may be one of discerning the role that law enforcement is to play in the emerging global context.

Federal Agencies and Antiterrorism

The FBI's counterterrorism efforts became especially important following the September 11, 2001, attacks on American targets. Two months after the attacks, then-U.S. Attorney General John Ashcroft announced a major reorganization and mobilization of the FBI and other federal agencies, such as the Immigration and Naturalization Service. Speaking at a press conference in Washington, DC, Ashcroft said,

Our strategic plan mandates fundamental change in several of the most critical components of American justice and law enforcement, starting with the organization that is at the center of our counterterrorism effort, the Federal Bureau of Investigation. In its history, the FBI has been many things: the protector of our institutions when they were under assault from organized crime; the keeper of our security when it was threatened by international espionage; and the defender of our civil rights when they were denied to some Americans on the basis of their race, color or creed. Today the American people call upon the Federal Bureau of Investigation to put prevention of terrorism at the center of its law-enforcement and national-security efforts.[50]

Following the attorney general's lead, the FBI reshaped its priorities to focus on preventing future terrorist attacks. This effort is managed by the Counterterrorism Division at FBI headquarters and is emphasized at every field office, resident agency, and legal attaché (Legat) office. Headquarters administers a national threat warning system that allows the FBI to instantly distribute important terrorism-related bulletins to law enforcement agencies and public-safety departments throughout the country. "Flying Squads" provide specialized counterterrorism knowledge and experience, language capabilities, and analytic support as needed to FBI field offices and Legats. To combat terrorism, the FBI's Counterterrorism Division collects, analyzes, and shares information and critical intelligence with various federal agencies and departments—including the CIA, the National Security Agency, and the Department of Homeland Security—and with law enforcement agencies throughout the country.

An essential weapon in the FBI's battle against terrorism is the JTTF. A national JTTF, located at the FBI's Washington headquarters, includes representatives from the Departments of Defense and Energy, the Federal Emergency Management Agency, the CIA, U.S. Customs and Border Protection, the U.S. Secret Service, and U.S. Immigration and Customs Enforcement. In addition, through 66 local JTTFs, representatives from federal agencies, state and local law enforcement personnel, and first responders coordinate efforts to track down terrorists and to prevent acts of terrorism in the United States.

In testimony before Congress in 2005, FBI Director Robert S. Mueller III identified three areas of special concern relative to the bureau's ongoing antiterrorism efforts. First, said Mueller, "is the threat from covert operatives who may be inside the U.S. who have the intention to facilitate or conduct an attack."[51] The very nature of trained covert operatives is that they are difficult to detect. "I remain very concerned about what we are *not* seeing," Mueller said. Second, Mueller identified a concern "with the growing body of sensitive reporting that continues to show al-Qaeda's clear intention to obtain and ultimately use some form of chemical, biological, radiological, nuclear or high-energy explosives (CBRNE) material in its attacks against America." Finally, said Mueller, "[W]e remain concerned about the potential for al-Qaeda to . . . exploit radical American converts and other indigenous extremists."

Information Sharing and Antiterrorism

The need to effectively share criminal intelligence across jurisdictions and between law enforcement agencies nationwide became apparent with the tragic events of September 11, 2001. Consequently, governments at all levels are today working toward the creation of a fully integrated criminal justice information system.

According to a recent task force report, a fully integrated criminal justice information system is "a network of public safety, justice and homeland security computer systems which provides to each agency the information it needs, at the time it is needed, in the form that it is needed, regardless of the source and regardless of the physical location at which it is stored."[52] The information that is provided should be complete, accurate, and formatted in whatever way is most useful for the agency's tasks. In such a system, information would be made available at the practitioner's workstation, whether that workstation is a patrol car, desk, laptop, or judge's bench. Each agency shares information not only with other agencies in its own jurisdiction but with multiple justice agencies on the federal, state, and local levels. In such an idealized justice information system, accurate information is also available to nonjustice agencies with statutory authority and a legal obligation to check criminal histories before licensing, employment, weapons purchase, and so on.

Although a fully integrated nationwide criminal justice information system does not yet exist, efforts to create one began with the 2003 National Criminal Intelligence Sharing Plan (NCISP). The NCISP was developed under the auspices of the U.S. Department of Justice's Global Justice Information Sharing Initiative and was authored by its Global Intelligence Working Group.[53] Federal, local, state, and tribal law enforcement representatives all had a voice in the development of the plan. The NCISP provides specific steps that can be taken by law enforcement agencies to participate in the sharing of critical law enforcement and terrorism prevention information. Plan authors note that not every agency has the staff or resources needed to create a formal intelligence unit. Even without a dedicated intelligence unit, however, the plan says that every law enforcement organization must have the ability to effectively consume the intelligence available from a wide range of organizations at all levels of government.[54]

Efforts to share crime- and terrorism-related intelligence can result in what some have called **boundaryless policing**.[55] Examples of boundaryless policing can be found today in the Regional Information Sharing Systems Anti-Terrorism Information Exchange (RISS ATIX) Program and the State and Local Anti-Terrorism Training (SLATT) Program, both of which are supported through grants from the Bureau of Justice Assistance.[56] RISS, a nationwide communications and information-sharing network, serves more than 6,300 law enforcement member agencies from the 50 states, the District of Columbia, the U.S. territories, Canada, Australia, and England. A private, secure intranet (riss.net) connects six RISS centers and their participating law enforcement member agencies.[57] The RISS ATIX, a special aspect of the RISS Program that began operating in 2003, allows for the secure exchange of information between government and nongovernment officials who are responsible for planning and implementing terrorism-related prevention, response, mitigation, and recovery efforts.

The MATRIX project was an Internet-based proof-of-concept pilot program, jointly funded by the Departments of Justice and Homeland Security, to increase and enhance the exchange of sensitive information about terrorism and other criminal activity between enforcement agencies at the local, state, and federal levels.[58] Though it is no longer in operation, MATRIX used the Factual Analysis Criminal Threat Solution (FACTS) software application, which provides a technology-based investigative tool to facilitate free-form searches of available state and public records. FACTS analyzed and integrated disparate data from many different types of storage systems. The MATRIX system combined data from various sources to which agencies already had access into a single searchable database of 4 billion records. Available records included criminal histories, driver's license data, vehicle registration data, prison/corrections records, digitized photographs, and public data. Using FACTS, investigators were able to conduct searches using incomplete information, such as a portion of a vehicle license number. At the conclusion of the MATRIX pilot program, a number of participating states continued to use the FACTS application.

Finally, the federally funded SLATT Program provides specialized training for active state and local law enforcement personnel in combating terrorism and extremist criminal activity.[59] The SLATT Program has been central to antiterrorism research and training since the bombing of the Alfred P. Murrah Federal Building in Oklahoma City in 1995. SLATT focuses on the prevention of terrorism by training state and local law enforcement officers to understand, detect, deter, and investigate acts of terrorism in the United States by both international and domestic terrorists. Following the attacks of September 11, 2001, SLATT increased its training in the area of international terrorism.

A Dark Side to Compstat?

Former LAPD Chief William Bratton brought Compstat to Los Angeles after his years as commissioner of the New York City Police Department (NYPD). The strategy has been credited with reducing crime, but some critics have alleged that something other than good policing is at work. In 2007, the *LA Voice* published an article asking, "Is LAPD fudging our crime stats?"[60] The article alleged that *crime* was not actually down, but that *crime reporting* was. The *Voice* pointed to an anecdotal account of LAPD officers who had allegedly refrained from arresting a drunk driver, instead asking him not to drive until he sobered up. Why? So they wouldn't have to make an arrest and file an official report of the incident. These kinds of claims infuriated Detective Jeff Godown, the officer who, at the time, was in charge of the LAPD's Compstat unit. He said,

> I can assure you that no Captain, Commander, or Chief level staff officer is "cooking the books" to reduce crime in his area to make themselves look good. . . . I know of no LAPD command or staff officer who would "risk" their career by encouraging, or participating in, the "fudging" of crime statistics. . . . The anecdotal evidence of LAPD personnel attempting to artificially impact the accurate reporting of crime, as may be occurring in other jurisdictions, does not wash.[61]

The *LA Voice* article and the Detective's response to it represent a clash of perspectives and interests in the ongoing struggle to reduce crime. Throughout America, police departments are continually being pressured to reduce crime. They are also increasingly pressured to make decisions based on timely intelligence and careful analysis of crime trends. Crime statistics have been falling for over a decade, but it may be that crime numbers can only decline so far before hitting an impenetrable floor. As one critic said, "When you finally get a real handle on crime, you eventually hit a wall where you can't push it down any more. Compstat does not recognize that wall so the commanders have to get 'creative' to keep their numbers going down."[62]

These kinds of observations raise several questions:

1. What is Compstat, and is it an effective crime-reduction technique?

2. Compstat is just one example of the movement to make policing more effective. Is there a potential downside to this effort?

3. To what extent can information and intelligence be abused?

4. How have increased amounts of technology-generated information affected policing in America?

5. Has enhanced technology affected policing for better or for worse? How?

Source: Nicholas Moore/Shutterstock.com

LEARNING OUTCOMES 1

Discuss advances in information and communications technology as they apply to policing.

Advances in information and communications technology that have affected police agencies include computer-aided drafting, computer-assisted training, crime mapping, geographic profiling, and crime intelligence systems. Compstat, an innovative police management strategy, stresses intelligence gathering, rapid deployment of police resources, effective tactics, and follow-up.

1. How has information and communications technology improved law enforcement?

2. What is CompStat? How did it develop?

3. What is crime mapping? How can crime mapping be utilized to improve law enforcement outcomes?

4. What is "HITS," and how can it improve the outcome of efforts made by law enforcement agencies to prevent crime?

pin map An early crime-mapping technique that used colored pins to track criminal events on a map of the police department's jurisdictional area.

Crime Mapping Research Center (CMRC) A U.S. Justice Department agency that promotes research, training, and technical assistance for police agencies around the country and assists them in their crime-mapping efforts. Also called the *Mapping and Analysis for Public Safety (MAPS) Program.*

geographic profiling Using crime-mapping technology to identify the likely whereabouts or residences of repeat or serial offenders.

Homicide Investigation and Tracking System (HITS) A geographic profiling system that ties various databases together (gang files, sex offender registries, parole records, and department of motor vehicle records) to facilitate simultaneous database searches.

CalGang A sophisticated software database of known gang members that field officers in California can access quickly. GangNet is a modified version of the software that is used nationwide.

Compstat A goal-oriented police management process that relies heavily on computer technology and accountability of top-level administrators.

computer-aided drafting (CAD) A technology, adapted to meet the needs of police officers and criminal investigators, that facilitates the drafting of crime scenes on a computer so that they can be viewed three-dimensionally.

firearms training system (FATS) A full-size, fully interactive training device, not unlike flight and driving simulators, that exposes police trainees to realistic shooting scenarios. The realism is enhanced by fully encasing the trainees in a particular surrounding rather than simply putting them in front of a television screen.

computerized crime mapping A computer-based system that combines a geographic information system with crime statistics generated by a police department, allowing crime data to be plotted on a map.

LEARNING OUTCOMES 2

Define *intelligence-led policing* and provide examples of it.

Intelligence-led policing is a method of policing that focuses resources on key criminal activities. Once crime problems are identified and quantified through intelligence assessments, key criminals can be targeted for investigation and prosecution.

1. What is criminal intelligence? How does it differ from information?

2. What is intelligence-led policing? Provide some examples.

3. What is the difference between strategic intelligence and tactical intelligence? How can both forms of intelligence be used by law enforcement agencies?

4. What is National Criminal Intelligence Sharing Plan? What event provided the impetus for its creation?

intelligence-led policing (ILP) The collection and analysis of information to produce an intelligence end product designed to inform police decision making at both the tactical and strategic levels. Also called *intelligence-driven policing.*

intelligence Information that has been analyzed and integrated into a useful perspective.

criminal intelligence A synergistic product intended to provide meaningful and trustworthy direction to law enforcement decision makers about complex criminality, criminal enterprises, criminal extremists, and terrorists. Also, a process that evaluates information collected from diverse sources, integrates the relevant information into a cohesive package, and produces a conclusion or estimate about a criminal phenomenon by using the scientific approach to problem solving.

tactical intelligence A type of intelligence that includes gaining or developing information related to threats of terrorism or crime and using this information to apprehend offenders, harden targets, and use strategies that will eliminate or mitigate the threat.

strategic intelligence A type of intelligence that provides information to decision makers about the changing nature of threats, enabling them to develop response strategies and reallocate resources for effective threat prevention.

National Criminal Intelligence Sharing Plan (NCISP) A formal intelligence sharing initiative that addresses the security and intelligence needs recognized after the tragic events of September 11, 2001. It describes a nationwide communications capability that will link together all levels of law enforcement personnel, including officers on the streets, intelligence analysts, unit commanders, and police executives for the purpose of sharing critical data.

fusion center An intelligence-gathering unit, often constituted as a collaborative effort that serves various agencies.

Law Enforcement Assistance and Partnership (LEAP) Strategy A plan introduced in the U.S. Congress that called for the establishment of a national center for intelligence-led policing.

Explain how terrorism has made an imprint on American policing.

While the core mission of American police departments has not changed, law enforcement agencies at all levels now devote an increased amount of time and other resources to preparing for possible terrorist attacks and to gathering the intelligence necessary to thwart them.

1. In what ways has terrorism affected American policing?

2. What is boundaryless policing, and how can law enforcement agencies benefit from the concept?

3. What federal agency sponsors Joint Terrorism Task Forces? What do such task forces do?

4. What is the Taking Command Initiative? What organization sponsors it? What is the purpose of the initiative?

Taking Command Initiative A project undertaken by the International Association of Chiefs of Police to assess the current state of homeland security efforts in the United States and to develop and implement the actions needed to protect American communities from the specter of both crime and terrorism.

Joint Terrorism Task Force (JTTF) An FBI-sponsored group composed of federal, state, and local law enforcement personnel who are brought together to focus on a specific threat.

boundaryless policing Any of various technology-based intelligence efforts designed to combat crime and terrorism.

MyCJLab

Go to the Chapter 9 section in *MyCJLab* to test your understanding of this chapter, access customized study content, engage in interactive simulations, complete critical thinking and research assignments, and view related online videos.

Additional Links

Learn about the law enforcement intelligence function at **www.justicestudies.com/pubs/intelligencefunction.pdf**.

Two very readable articles about Compstat and its implementation can be found at **http://tinyurl.com/ynnv2r** and **www.justicestudies.com/pubs/june04leb.pdf**.

Crime mapping and the analysis of crime maps are topics for discussion at **www.justicestudies.com/pubs/forecasting.pdf** and **www.ojp.usdoj.gov/nij/maps**.

Crime activity by neighborhood across the United States can be seen at **www.crimemapping.com**.

A discussion of gunshot location systems for public safety can be seen at **http://tinyurl.com/6zaurqh**.

Special issues affecting the police, including drug use, juvenile gangs, and the elderly are available on the Web at **https://nsduhweb.rti.org**, **http://people.missouristate.edu/MichaelCarlie**, and **www.justicestudies.com/pubs/olderpops.pdf**.

Policing and the Law

"Effective police officers must be aware of how the law governs their everyday activities."

1 Discuss when Fourth Amendment provisions apply to activities undertaken by law enforcement officers, and describe existing rules governing the conduct of searches and seizures.

2 Discuss existing rules concerning interrogations undertaken by law enforcement officers and the in-court admissibility of obtained confessions, especially as established under the Fifth, Sixth, and Fourteenth Amendments.

Source: Frances A. Miller/Shutterstock.com

10

PLAYING BY THE RULES: A JOB REQUIREMENT

Not only do police officers enforce the law, but they are also held accountable under it. The principle that no one—not even those who make and enforce the law—is immune from the law's reach, is known as the rule of law. In societies where the rule of law operates, fairness and equal treatment before the law are accorded to everyone—no matter their social status or political position.

In a recent analysis of how the rule of law applies to law enforcement personnel, State University of New York at Albany professor David H. Bayley writes that "although the public is most concerned about dramatic infringements of the rule of law, such as brutality, planting false evidence, and lying in courts, most of the liberties taken by police are more mundane, routinized, and difficult to detect."[1] Bayley gives the example of an officer making an illegal vehicle stop on the pretext of offering assistance (that is, telling the driver that a taillight wasn't working). Bailey goes on to show that the costs to the police of violating rule of law principles are greater than any benefits that might accrue. In particular, he says "violating the rule of law

impairs crime control by alienating the public." In more general terms, Bayley stresses that, "when police act beyond the law, they lose their moral authority."

Effective police officers must be aware of how the law governs their everyday activities.[2] When they make arrests, search suspects, and interrogate them—and even when they make simple observations and draw certain actionable conclusions—various constitutional considerations come into play. Those constitutional issues, which are sometimes collectively referred to as *the law of search and seizure*, are the focus of this chapter. Here we will examine the rules governing searches and seizures, as well as those pertaining to confessions and interrogations. The rules we will be discussing stem largely from court interpretations of the Fourth and Fifth Amendments to the U.S. Constitution, and it would be a good idea to review both amendments before proceeding. While the language in these amendments may seem to be relatively straightforward, it has been scrutinized in scores of federal court cases.

> **DISCUSS** What is the rule of law? How does it apply to police officers?

▶ Search and Seizure

Of all the important legal issues in law enforcement today, the issue of how to properly conduct searches and seizures ranks as among the most important. Serving search warrants, arresting suspects, making traffic stops, stopping suspicious individuals on foot, inventorying impounded vehicles, and a host of other activities require an intimate knowledge of the Fourth Amendment. Fourth Amendment violations can result in lawsuits, complaints, difficulty convicting defendants, the release of criminals into the community, and even criminal charges against law enforcement officers.

When the Fourth Amendment Applies

The **Fourth Amendment** states the following:

> The right of the people to be secure in their persons, houses, papers, and effects, against unreasonable searches and seizures, shall not be violated, and no Warrants shall issue, but upon probable cause, supported by Oath or affirmation and particularly describing the place to be searched, and the persons or things to be seized.

The issue of how to properly conduct searches and seizures ranks as among the most important in law enforcement today.

The Fourth Amendment applies when a search or seizure is being contemplated (search warrants are discussed later in this chapter) or takes place. **Searches** are, as the term suggests, activities performed in order to find evidence to be used in a criminal prosecution. To define when a *Fourth Amendment search* takes place, however, two important elements must be considered: (1) whether the search is a product of **government action** and (2) whether the government action infringes upon the individual's **reasonable expectation of privacy**. We will return to this topic shortly.

The term **seizure** has a dual meaning in policing. First, property can be seized, and a search often results in the seizure of evidence. For example, if the police successfully serve a search warrant to look for illegal weapons at 345 Oak Street, any illegal weapons they find

LEARNING OUTCOMES 1 Discuss when Fourth Amendment provisions apply to activities undertaken by law enforcement officers, and describe existing rules governing the conduct of searches and seizures.

GLOSSARY

Fourth Amendment The amendment to the U.S. Constitution that governs search and seizure.

search An activity performed in order to find evidence to be used in a criminal prosecution.

government action In the context of search and seizure law, one of two elements that must be considered when defining a Fourth Amendment search. (The other element is a reasonable expectation of privacy.) Government actions consist of measures to effect a search undertaken by someone employed by or working on behalf of the government.

there will be seized. But people can also be seized. Seizures of people can occur almost anywhere and at any time. An arrest, for example, is considered a seizure within the meaning of the Fourth Amendment.

The next stage in the Fourth Amendment analysis requires that we focus on the **reasonableness** of the search or seizure. Once Fourth Amendment protections have been triggered, we must ask whether the officers acted in line with Fourth Amendment requirements. If a person has been arrested, for example, the question is whether the police had adequate reason to believe that the person arrested in fact committed the crime. When courts focus on the reasonableness of a search or seizure, they speak in terms of **justification**. If the police engage in searches or seizures without justification, they violate the Fourth Amendment.

The only justification mentioned in the Fourth Amendment is probable cause. Consequently, lay readers may be inclined to think that any search or seizure based on a lesser degree of certainty than probable cause would violate the Fourth Amendment. For a time this was the case, but in recent decades the U.S. Supreme Court has carved out exceptions to the Fourth Amendment's probable cause requirement. The Court has ruled that there are certain situations in which the police can seize people or look for evidence with a lesser degree of certainty than probable cause. These situations are described later in this chapter.

Defining Search and Seizure

Not every act of looking for evidence can be considered a search within the meaning of the Fourth Amendment, nor is every act of "grabbing" something or someone considered a seizure. For example, private citizens may look for evidence, but their actions are not bound by the Fourth Amendment because private citizens are not government actors. The Fourth Amendment protects citizens from *government* action. As such, one requirement in determining when a search occurs is to ascertain *who* is looking for evidence. And although the Fourth Amendment restricts government action, it is not the case that government actors always engage in searches when looking for evidence. There are many things the police can do to look for evidence—such as looking in open fields and public areas, examining items that have been discarded, observing people and things in public view, and so on—without being bound by the Fourth Amendment.

What Is a Search?

The Fourth Amendment's protection against unreasonable searches and seizures has been limited by the courts to behavior that is governmental in nature. When a private individual seizes evidence or otherwise conducts a search, Fourth Amendment protections are not triggered.[3]

For a Fourth Amendment search to occur, the government actor must also infringe on a person's reasonable expectation of privacy. What is a reasonable expectation of privacy? Prior to 1967, the definition of *search* was closely tied to property interests. Police action was only deemed a search if it physically infringed on an individual's property. Essentially, the activity had to amount to what would otherwise be considered common law trespass for it to be considered a search. Any police activity that was not trespassory in nature was not considered a search. This definition

became outdated in the landmark decision in *Katz* v. *United States* (1967).[4]

In *Katz*, federal agents placed a listening device outside a phone booth in which Katz was having a conversation. Katz made incriminating statements during the course of his conversation and the Federal Bureau of Investigation (FBI) sought to use the statements against him at trial. The lower court ruled that the FBI's activities did not amount to a search because there was no physical entry into the phone booth. The U.S. Supreme Court reversed the lower court's decision, holding that the Fourth Amendment "protects people, not places," so its reach "cannot turn upon the presence or absence of a physical intrusion into any given enclosure."[5] Instead, the Fourth Amendment definition of *search* turns on the concept of privacy. In the Court's words, "The Government's activities in electronically listening to and recording words violated the privacy upon which [Katz] justifiably relied while using the telephone booth and thus constituted a 'search and seizure' within the meaning of the Fourth Amendment."[6]

Despite the seemingly profound change in the *search and seizure* definition following *Katz*, several subsequent decisions have interpreted the *Katz* ruling rather narrowly. For example, the Supreme Court has since ruled that a Fourth Amendment search or seizure occurs only when there has been an infringement on an expectation of privacy that society (through the eyes of a court) is willing to accept as reasonable.[7] It further stated that "[w]hat a person knowingly exposes to the public, even in his own home or office, is not subject to Fourth Amendment protection."[8] Protection is only afforded for "what he seeks to preserve as private."[9]

reasonable expectation of privacy In the context of search and seizure law, one of two elements that must be considered when defining a Fourth Amendment search. (The other element is government action.) A reasonable expectation of privacy means that people who speak or act in private can reasonably expect that what they say or do will not be seen or heard by someone else.

seizure The confiscation of one's person (arrest) or property by a government agent.

reasonableness The elements of a situation that serve to justify a search or seizure.

justification The focus of a court's examination of the reasonableness of a search or seizure.

probable cause A set of facts and circumstances that would induce a reasonably intelligent and prudent person to believe that another particular person has committed a specific crime. Probable cause is the only justification for search and seizure mentioned in the Fourth Amendment.

reasonable suspicion A belief, based on a consideration of the facts at hand and on reasonable inferences drawn from those facts, that would induce an ordinarily prudent and cautious person under the same circumstances to conclude that criminal activity is taking place or that criminal activity has recently occurred. Reasonable suspicion is the standard for less intrusive stop-and-frisk searches; it is less than probable cause but more than a hunch.

administrative justification The standard for an administrative search based on the fact that government entities occasionally conduct searches in circumstances other than criminal investigations, such as a sobriety checkpoint set up for the purpose of apprehending drunk drivers. Sometimes called *special-needs* or *regulatory searches*, such searches attempt to achieve a balance between protecting individuals' privacy interests and protecting public safety.

Search

- Government actor must infringe on a person's reasonable expectation of privacy.
- Fourth Amendment protections only extend to government officials such as a police officer working in his or her official capacity.
- Private citizens are not government actors, unless they act at the behest of a governmental official (e.g., an officer asks a private citizen to conduct the search *for* him or her).

Seizure

- Meaningful interference with an individual's possessory interest in that property.
- A seizure of a person occurs when a police officer, by means of physical force or show of authority, intentionally restrains an individual's liberty in such a manner that a reasonable person would believe that he or she is not free to leave.

FIGURE 10.1 Search and Seizure.

What Is a Seizure?

The Supreme Court has concluded that the seizure of tangible property occurs "when there is some meaningful interference with an individual's possessory interest in that property."[10] A seizure of a person occurs when a police officer, by means of physical force or show of authority, intentionally restrains an individual's liberty in such a manner that a reasonable person would believe that he or she is not free to leave.[11] Another way to understand a Fourth Amendment seizure is by asking the question: Would a reasonable person believe that he or she is free to decline the officer's requests or otherwise terminate the encounter?[12] If the answer is no, a seizure has occurred.

There can be several types of seizures of a person, just as there can be many different types of searches. For example, a person can be arrested, perhaps the most significant form of seizure. But a stop-and-frisk situation also amounts to a seizure, as we will see later. A seizure can also occur without any physical contact; for example, an officer can block a person's path, which could amount to a seizure. Add to that the number of possible search scenarios, including searches with and without warrants, and things get even more complex.

Justification

To this point we have only addressed the threshold question of whether the Fourth Amendment applies, that is, has a search or a seizure occurred? If the answer is no, the matter would go no further, and justification would not matter because a search or seizure did not occur. However, if, in the case of a search, the government's action infringes upon a person's reasonable expectation of privacy, the next issue involves deciding whether the police acted within the limits of the Fourth Amendment.

The police must have justification, or cause, before they can conduct a search or a seizure. Justification must be in place *a priori*, that is, before a person or evidence is sought in an area protected by the Fourth Amendment. The police cannot conduct illegal searches to obtain evidence and then argue *after the fact* that what they did was appropriate.

Justification can be viewed as something of a sliding scale that hinges on the type of intrusion the police make. Generally,

The police must have justification, or cause, before they can conduct a search or a seizure.

the more intrusive the police action, the higher the level of justification required. Likewise, the lower the level of intrusion, the lower the justification the police need. Three primary levels of justification recognized by the courts are considered in this chapter: (1) **probable cause**—the standard for searches and seizures; (2) **reasonable suspicion**—the standard for stop-and-frisk activities; and (3) **administrative justification**—the standard for administrative searches.

Probable Cause

Probable cause has been defined by the U.S. Supreme Court as more than bare suspicion; it exists when "the facts and circumstances within [the officers'] knowledge and of which they [have] reasonably trustworthy information [are] sufficient to warrant a prudent man in believing that the [suspect] had committed or was committing an offense."[13] The Court had noted in an earlier case, "The substance of all the definitions of probable cause is a reasonable ground for belief of guilt."[14] A more practical definition of probable cause is that it consists of more than 50 percent certainty. Probable cause lies somewhere below absolute certainty and proof beyond a reasonable doubt (the latter is necessary to obtain a criminal conviction), but above a hunch or reasonable suspicion (the latter is required to conduct a stop and frisk). See Figure 10.2 for an overview of the components of probable cause.

Reasonable Suspicion

While the justification required to conduct a search or a seizure is probable cause, much police activity does not reach the level of intrusion that occurs when a search or seizure is carried out. For example, the police routinely confront people on the street to question them or pull over automobiles to enforce

Prior record
Flight from the scene
Suspicious conduct
Admission
Incriminating evidence
Unusual hour
Suspect resembling perpetrator
Evasive and untruthful responses to questions
Obvious attempt to hide something
Presence in a high-crime area or near the crime scene
Furtive gestures
Knowing too much

FIGURE 10.2 Components of Probable Cause.

Proof beyond a reasonable doubt = around 95 percent certainty
Probable cause = more than 50 percent certainty
Preponderance of the evidence = civil equivalent of probable cause
Reasonable suspicion = between 1 and 50 percent certainty
Administrative justification = balancing approach
Hunch = no justification or certainty at all

FIGURE 10.3 A Comparison of Levels of Proof.

Reasonable suspicion is something below probable cause but above a hunch.

traffic laws. If probable cause were required under such circumstances, there would be very little the police could do in terms of investigating suspicious activity.

Recognizing how essential these lesser intrusions are to the police mission, the Supreme Court established a different level of justification for such activities in *Terry* v. *Ohio* (1968).[15] The standard the Court created was "reasonable suspicion," something below probable cause but above a hunch.

The facts of the *Terry* case are interesting: An officer's attention was drawn to two men on a street corner who appeared to the officer to be "casing" a store for a robbery. The officer approached the men and asked them to identify themselves and then proceeded to pat the men down. Finding a gun on each man, he placed the men under arrest. They later sought to have the guns excluded as evidence from trial (the exclusionary rule is discussed in the next chapter), but the U.S. Supreme Court eventually held that the officer's actions were valid in the interests of "effective crime prevention and detection."[16] It also stated that because "street encounters between citizens and police officers are incredibly rich in diversity,"[17] a lower standard than probable cause is required.

As a level of justification lying below probable cause, reasonable suspicion is "considerably less than proof of wrongdoing by a preponderance of evidence"[18] but more than a mere hunch. Think of reasonable suspicion as more than 0 percent certainty (that is, more than a mere hunch) and less than 51 percent certainty (that is, less than probable cause).

Administrative Justification

A third level of justification has arisen by virtue of the fact that government entities occasionally conduct searches in circumstances other than criminal investigations. There are occasions where some sort of search is necessary, but that search is not conducted in an effort to detect evidence of a crime, such as a cache of illegal weapons. We have seen that searches and seizures aimed at obtaining evidence intended to be used in a criminal proceeding cannot occur without appropriate justification: probable cause for a search or seizure or reasonable suspicion

for a stop and frisk. The Supreme Court has created a different level of justification for noncriminal, or administrative, searches.

Administrative searches attempt to achieve a balance between protecting individuals' privacy interests and protecting public safety. Where public-safety concerns outweigh individual privacy interests, an administrative search may be permissible. One such search that has routinely been sanctioned by the courts is a sobriety checkpoint set up for the purpose of protecting the public by removing drunk drivers from roadways. Other examples of permissible administrative searches are discussed later in this chapter. For a summary of the various levels of proof, see Figure 10.3.

The Rules of Search and Seizure

Assuming that a case arises wherein the Fourth Amendment applies and officers have proper justification, what's next? The answer depends on whether the action in question is a search, a seizure, a stop, or an administrative search. It also depends on whether a warrant is required.

Arrest Warrant Requirements

The Fourth Amendment does not *require* an arrest warrant for all arrests, but the U.S. Supreme Court has adopted the view that arrest warrants are preferable. They can be obtained when the police know who they want to arrest, but the person is not immediately available (for example, he or she has escaped confinement). In contrast, if a police officer observes a person rob a bank, then it would obviously be impractical to require the officer to obtain an arrest warrant before arresting the suspect.

When are arrest warrants required? Essentially, the rule is this: An arrest made in a public place does not require an arrest warrant (but does require probable cause); an arrest made in a private place usually requires a warrant, unless special circumstances exist. In its landmark decision in *Payton* v. *New York* (1980),[19] the U.S. Supreme Court held that the Fourth Amendment prohibits warrantless, nonconsensual entries into private homes for the purpose of making an arrest. The Court has also required that

> ## Think About It...
>
> **Drug Courier Profiling** In *United States* v. *Montoya De Hernandez*, the U.S. Supreme Court ruled that "the detention of a traveler at the border, beyond the scope of a routine customs search and inspection, is justified at its inception if customs agents, considering all the facts surrounding the traveler and her trip, reasonably suspect that the traveler is smuggling contraband in her alimentary canal." Profiling is also used in airports and other ports of entry to detect suspected terrorists. What are the characteristics of suspected terrorists? How many otherwise law-abiding people are stopped and inconvenienced? Do the benefits of the practice outweigh the costs? Explain.

Source: United States Customs and Border Patrol

Search and Seizure **153**

arrests made in third-party homes require a warrant to search the property for the person to be arrested. To enter without a warrant could amount to a search without proper justification, in violation of the Fourth Amendment.[20]

Assuming that an arrest warrant is required, it must conform to certain requirements. First, a neutral and detached magistrate must authorize the warrant. Second, a showing of probable cause must be made. Finally, the warrant should be sufficiently particular so as to minimize the possibility of arresting the wrong person.

Neutral and Detached Magistrate. The U.S. Supreme Court has said,

> The point of the Fourth Amendment . . . is not that it denies law enforcement the support of the usual inferences reasonable men draw from evidence. Its protection consists in requiring that those inferences be drawn by a neutral and detached magistrate instead of being judged by the officer engaged in the often competitive enterprise of ferreting out crime.[21]

Most judges are considered neutral and detached. Even so, the Supreme Court has focused on this first critical warrant requirement in a number of cases. For example, the Court has declared that a state attorney general cannot issue a search warrant.[22] State attorneys generally are chief prosecutors and thus inclined to side with law enforcement officers. Similarly, in another case the Court decided that the president, acting through the attorney general of the United States, cannot authorize electronic surveillance without judicial approval.[23]

Probable Cause. The probable cause showing in an arrest warrant is not particularly complex. The Court has stated, "If there is sufficient evidence of a citizen's participation in a felony to persuade a judicial officer that his arrest is justified, it is constitutionally reasonable to require him to open his doors to the officers of the law."[24]

Particularity. There are two ways to satisfy the Fourth Amendment's particularity requirement with regard to arrest warrants, which are highlighted in Figure 10.4.

Search Warrant Requirements

Search warrants have the same three requirements as arrest warrants. The neutral and detached magistrate requirement remains the same, but there *are* differences in terms of probable cause and particularity, which have been highlighted in Figure 10.4.

Searches and Seizures without Warrants

Searches without warrants are far more common than those with warrants. Police can, for example, rely on the hot pursuit doctrine to chase a fleeing suspect into a private area and make an arrest without a warrant. Requiring officers to secure warrants in all such instances would be impractical. Similarly, it would endanger the public's safety if police were required to obtain a warrant in the face of a clear and sudden threat to public safety. Warrantless searches thus come in several varieties: (1) searches incident to arrest, (2) searches based on exigent circumstances, (3) automobile searches, (4) plain-view searches, and (5) consent searches.

	Neutral and Detached Magistrate	Probable Cause	Particularity
Arrest Warrant Requirements	A neutral and detached magistrate must authorize the arrest warrant.	The officer applying for the warrant must simply show probable cause that the person to be arrested committed the crime but not that the suspect will be found at a particular location.	If the suspect's name is known, then simply supplying the suspect's name is enough to meet the particularity requirement. There are some situations, however, where the suspect's name is *not* known. In such situations, a sufficiently specific description of the suspect supports issuance of a "John Doe" warrant. As long as other officers may locate the suspect with reasonable effort, the suspect's name is not required.
Search Warrant Requirements	Similar to the arrest warrant requirements, a neutral and detached magistrate must authorize the search warrant.	Unlike the arrest warrant requirements, the probable cause showing in a search warrant is twofold. First, the officer applying for the search warrant must show probable cause that the items to be seized are connected with criminal activity. Second, the officer must show probable cause that the items to be seized are in the location to be searched.	If a warrant does not "particularly" describe the place to be searched and the items to be seized, then it is not automatically deemed in violation of the Fourth Amendment. If there is a reasonable basis for the officers' mistaken belief, then the warrant will most likely be upheld.[i]

iNote: Some of the causes were triggering events, while others were predisposing factors.

FIGURE 10.4 Arrest and Search Warrant Requirements.

Searches Incident to Arrest. The first type of permissible warrantless search is known as a **search incident to arrest**. The U.S. Supreme Court has said that a warrantless search incident to arrest is permitted "to remove any weapons that the [arrestee] might seek to use in order to resist arrest or effect his escape" and to "seize any evidence on the arrestee's person in order to prevent its concealment or destruction."[25]

Probable cause to arrest must always precede a search incident to arrest.[26] This is to restrict officers from engaging in "fishing expeditions," searches based on less than probable cause that could potentially result in establishing the probable cause needed to make an arrest.

If probable cause to arrest is in place, the officer is not required to formally arrest the suspect before engaging in the search,[27] but the search should take place *soon* after the arrest if one is made. In other words, the search must be *contemporaneous* to the arrest. In *Preston* v. *United States* (1964),[28] the case that established this rule, Justice Hugo Black observed that the "justifications [for the search incident to arrest] are absent where a search is remote in time or place from the arrest."[29] In *Preston*, police officers arrested the occupants of a car and took them to jail. After this, the officers searched the car, which had been towed to an impound lot. In reversing the lower court's ruling, the Supreme Court noted that the possibilities of destruction of evidence or danger to the officers were no longer in place, as the suspects were no longer present to pose a threat.[30]

What is the scope of a search incident to arrest? In *Chimel* v. *California* (1969),[31] the Court held that "a warrantless search 'incident to a lawful arrest' may generally extend to the area that is considered to be in the 'possession' or under the 'control' of the person arrested."[32] It went on to create the so-called **arm-span rule**. In the Court's words, a search incident to arrest is limited to the area "within [the] immediate control" of the person arrested, that is, "the area from within which he might have obtained either a weapon or something that could have been used as evidence against him."[33]

In *Maryland* v. *Buie* (1990),[34] the Court further expanded the scope of the incident search in two ways. It held that the police may, as part of a search incident to arrest, look in areas immediately adjoining the place of arrest for other individuals who might attack the officers; no justification is required. The key is that such a search must occur immediately following an arrest. Next, the Court held that at any point up to the time the arrest is completed, the police may engage in a **protective sweep** (that is, "a cursory visual inspection of those places in which a person might be hiding"), but reasonable suspicion must exist for such a sweep to be justified. No justification is required *after* arrest, but reasonable suspicion is required to engage in a sweep up to the point of the arrest. If a suspect is arrested during a traffic stop, police may search him or her *and* the vehicle; however, they may only search the vehicle without a warrant if it is reasonable to assume the arrestee could access the vehicle or that the vehicle contains evidence of the offense for which the individual was arrested.[35]

Searches Based on Exigent Circumstances. Searches (and, by extension, arrests) based on **exigent circumstances** are permissible without warrants. Generally, three types of exigencies (emergencies) have been recognized: (1) hot pursuit, (2) the likelihood of a suspect's escaping or presenting a danger to others, and (3) evanescent evidence.

The Supreme Court established a **hot pursuit exception** to the Fourth Amendment's warrant requirement in *Warden* v. *Hayden* (1967).[36] In that case, the police were called by taxicab drivers who reported that their taxi company had been robbed. The police then located and followed the suspect to a house and were granted entry by the suspect's wife. When they entered, they found the suspect upstairs, pretending to be asleep. However, as they were searching the house for the suspect, the police found and seized clothing, a shotgun, and a pistol, which were used as evidence against the suspect at trial. The Court found that the warrantless entry was "reasonable" because the "exigencies of the situation made that course imperative."[37] Several reasons were offered for the decision. First, as Justice William Brennan stated, "The Fourth Amendment does not require police officers to delay in the course of an investigation if to do so would gravely endanger their lives or the lives of others."[38] Second, "[s]peed . . . was essential, and only a thorough search of the house for persons and weapons could have insured that Hayden was the only man present and that the police had control of all weapons which could be used against them or to effect an escape."[39]

> *Probable cause to arrest must always precede a search incident to arrest.*

search incident to arrest A warrantless search made at the time of or shortly following an arrest, which is conducted out of a concern for the safety of the arresting officer and others.

arm-span rule A doctrine established by the U.S. Supreme Court that limits a search incident to (that is, immediately following) arrest to the area "within [the] immediate control" of the person arrested—that is, the area from within which he might have obtained either a weapon or something that could have been used as evidence against him.

protective sweep A permissible cursory visual inspection of places in which a person might be hiding. A protective sweep may be conducted by police up to the point of an arrest but must be supported by reasonable suspicion.

exigent circumstances A situation that makes a warrantless search constitutionally permissible, such as hot pursuit, the likelihood of a suspect escaping or presenting a danger to others, and evanescent evidence.

hot pursuit exception One exception to the Fourth Amendment's warrant requirement, recognized by the U.S. Supreme Court in *Warden* v. *Hayden* (1967). The hot pursuit doctrine provides that police officers may enter the premises where they suspect a crime has been committed, or a perpetrator is hiding, without a warrant when delay would likely endanger their lives or the lives of others and possibly lead to the escape of the alleged perpetrator.

evanescent evidence Evidence that is likely to disappear quickly.

plain-view doctrine The rule that the police may seize evidence without a warrant if they have lawful access to the object and it is immediately apparent (that is, they have probable cause) that the object is subject to seizure.

stop and frisk The detaining of a person by a law enforcement officer for the purpose of investigation, accompanied by a superficial examination by the officer of the person's body surface or clothing to discover weapons, contraband, or other objects relating to criminal activity.

person inventory The search of an arrestee and his or her personal items, including containers found in his or her possession, as part of a routine inventory that is incident to the booking and jailing procedure. Often called *arrest inventory*.

vehicle inventory A warrantless inventory of a vehicle that is permissible on administrative or regulatory grounds. Vehicle inventories must follow a lawful impoundment, must be of a routine nature, must follow standard operating procedures, and must not be a pretext that attempts to conceal an investigatory search.

checkpoint A location at which a warrantless, suspicionless search is constitutionally permissible in furtherance of an overriding national or public-safety interest. National border entry points and sobriety checkpoints are examples.

Despite its sweeping language in the *Hayden* decision, the Supreme Court has imposed a number of restrictions on searches and seizures premised on hot pursuit. One court has observed that "[a] hot pursuit, by itself, creates no necessity for dispensing with a warrant."[40] Similarly, the Ninth Circuit has stated that police officers must reasonably believe (1) "that the suspect either knows or will learn at any moment that they are in immediate danger of apprehension"; (2) that "evidence is being currently removed or destroyed and it is impractical to avert the situation without immediately arresting the suspects or seizing the evidence"; or (3) that "a suspect is currently endangering the lives of themselves or others."[41]

Third, the police must begin hot pursuit from a lawful starting point. If officers are unlawfully on someone's private property, they will not succeed in claiming hot pursuit to justify any further warrantless action. However, in *United States* v. *Santana* (1976),[42] the Supreme Court upheld the warrantless arrest of a woman in her house when the police *observed* a crime on private property from a public vantage point. In that case, police officers observed Santana standing in the open doorway of her house with a brown paper bag, which they believed to contain narcotics. They pursued her into the house and arrested her. This decision suggests that the police can pursue from a public vantage point a suspect whom they observe on private property.

Fourth, the hot pursuit doctrine only applies to "serious" offenses. These include felonies and some serious misdemeanors.[43] This is perhaps the most important restriction on the hot pursuit doctrine—and, indeed, on exigent circumstance searches in general.

A fifth restriction on hot pursuits concerns the scope of the search. Generally, the scope of a search based on hot pursuit is broad. In *Hayden*, the Supreme Court stated, "The permissible scope of search must, at the least, be as broad as may reasonably be necessary to prevent the dangers that the suspect at large in the house may resist or escape."[44] However, the search must be "prior to or immediately contemporaneous with" the arrest of the suspect. Also, officers may only search where the suspect or weapons might reasonably be found.

Despite the fact that a vehicle search is permissible without a warrant, the search must still be based on probable cause.

Moving beyond hot pursuit, it is also permissible for police officers to dispense with the warrant requirement when it is likely that a suspect could escape or endanger others, even in the absence of hot pursuit.[45] Finally, **evanescent evidence** refers to evidence that is likely to disappear if the officers took the time to obtain a warrant.[46] Examples of evanescent evidence are alcohol in a person's bloodstream or drugs that are in the process of being destroyed, such as by flushing them down the toilet.[47]

Automobile Searches. The warrantless search of an automobile is permissible when (1) there is probable cause to believe that the vehicle contains evidence of a crime and (2) securing a warrant is impractical.[48] This rule resulted from a Prohibition-era case involving the vehicle stop of a suspect who was known to have previously engaged in the sale of bootleg whiskey. A warrantless search of the car revealed 68 bottles of illegal liquor. The Supreme Court upheld the warrantless search on the grounds that the evidence would have been lost if the officers had been required to secure a warrant. It pointed out that the inherent mobility of motor vehicles made it impractical to obtain a warrant, that people enjoy a lesser expectation of privacy in their vehicles, and that vehicles are subject to extensive government regulation, essentially making driving a privilege.

Several subsequent decisions have dealt with the definition of an automobile, the role of probable cause, whether warrants are required, and the scope of automobile searches. Concerning the first of these issues, any vehicle that serves a transportation function is considered to be an automobile. Four factors are used to determine whether a vehicle serves a transportation function: (1) whether it is mobile or stationary, (2) whether it is licensed, (3) whether it is connected to utilities, and (4) whether it has convenient access to the road. If, for example, a trailer is on blocks, unlicensed, connected to utilities, and in a trailer park, then it will almost certainly be treated as a residence for Fourth Amendment purposes.

Next, despite the fact that a vehicle search is permissible without a warrant, the search must still be based on probable cause. Even when probable cause to search exists, this does not automatically create probable cause to arrest; likewise, probable cause to arrest may not give rise to probable cause to search.

Given the circumstances surrounding most vehicle stops, it would seem foolish to require that the police obtain warrants before engaging in automobile searches. In *Husty* v. *United States* (1931),[49] a police officer, acting on a tip from an informant, found contraband in Husty's unattended car. Given that the car was unattended, one can argue that a warrant should have been secured, but the Court ruled that the officer "could not know when Husty would come to the car or how soon it would be removed."[50] Contrast *Husty* with *Coolidge* v. *New Hampshire* (1971).[51] In the *Coolidge* case, the Court ruled that the automobile exception did not apply to a warrantless search and seizure of two cars located on the defendant's property because the police had probable cause to act more than two weeks before the search.

Finally, what about the scope of an automobile search? In *United States* v. *Ross* (1982), the Supreme Court declared that as long as the police have justification to conduct a warrantless vehicle search, they may conduct a search "that is as thorough as a magistrate could authorize in a warrant."[52] The only limitation is "defined by the object of the search and the places in which there is probable cause to believe that it may be found."[53] Accordingly, if the contraband sought is small (for example, a syringe), the scope of the vehicle search exception is almost limitless.

Plain-View Searches. Plain-view searches can also be conducted without a warrant. In *Coolidge* v. *New Hampshire*,[54] the Supreme Court created the **plain-view doctrine** and held that seizure of evidence authorized when (1) the police are lawfully in the area where the evidence is located, (2) the item is "immediately apparent" as being subject to seizure, and (3) the discovery of the evidence is "inadvertent."[55] Police are lawfully in the area where the evidence is located when they have a warrant or are otherwise authorized to be there (for example, due to a hot pursuit exigency). "Immediately apparent" means that the police must have probable cause that the item of interest is subject to seizure.[56] The inadvertency

requirement was eliminated by the Court's subsequent ruling in *Horton* v. *California* (1990).[57]

Consent Searches. Consent searches are also permissible without a warrant—and even without probable cause. Consent cannot be "the result of duress or coercion, express or implied."[58] When does duress or coercion take place? There is no clear answer to this question. Instead, the Supreme Court has opted for a "totality of circumstances" test. This requires considering factors such as whether a show of force was made; whether the person's age, mental condition, or intellectual capacities inhibited understanding; whether the person was in custody; and whether consent was granted.

Importantly, consent to search may be valid even if the consenting party is unaware of the fact that he or she can refuse consent.[59] As the Court stated in *Ohio* v. *Robinette* (1996),[60] "[J]ust as it 'would be thoroughly impractical to impose on the normal consent search the detailed requirements of an effective warning,' so too would it be unrealistic to require police officers to always inform detainees that they are free to go before a consent to search may be deemed involuntary."[61] Nevertheless, the issue of one's awareness of the right to refuse consent is still factored into the totality of circumstances of analysis,[62] although ignorance of the right to refuse is not enough in and of itself to render consent involuntary.

Searches Incident to Arrest	Search made at the time of or shortly following an arrest, done out of a concern for the safety of the arresting officer and others.
Searches Based on Exigent Circumstances	Search based on (1) **Hot pursuit**—police have probable cause to believe that the person they are chasing has committed a crime and is on the premises entered. (2) Police have reason to believe that the suspect will escape or that further harm will occur if not immediately apprehended. (3) **Evanescent evidence**—evidence likely to disappear during time necessary to obtain a warrant.
Automobile Searches	Search admissible when (1) there is probable cause to believe that the vehicle contains evidence of a crime and (2) securing a warrant is impractical.
Plain-View Searches	Search authorized when (1) the police are lawfully in the area where the evidence is located, (2) the item is "immediately apparent" as being subject to seizure, and (3) the discovery of the evidence is "inadvertent."
Consent Searches	If a person gives consent to search, he or she effectively waives Fourth Amendment protection. *Consent must be voluntary and not the result of duress or coercion.

FIGURE 10.5 Searches and Seizures without Warrants.

To err on the side of constitutionality, many police departments have suspects complete consent-to-search forms. An example of one such form, from the Alabama Court of Criminal Appeals, is reprinted in Figure 10.6.

The scope of a consent search is limited to the terms of the consent. In other words, the person giving consent defines the limits of the search. This was the decision reached in *Florida* v. *Jimeno* (1991).[63] For example, if a person says "you may look around," that does not necessarily mean that the police can look *anywhere* for evidence of criminal activity.

Another issue concerning the scope of a consent search is whether the consent can be withdrawn once given. In *State* v. *Brochu* (1967),[64] the Maine Supreme Court held that a defendant's consent to search his house for evidence of his wife's murder did not extend to another search carried out the day after he was arrested as a suspect. Thus, although the man did not expressly request that the search end, the Maine court still decided that consent had been terminated.

Other Search and Seizure Issues

Earlier we talked about standards of justification, including reasonable suspicion. We pointed out that reasonable suspicion, which is a lesser standard of proof than probable cause, permits stop-and-frisk activities by police.[65] In this section, we look first at what constitutes a **stop and frisk**. Then we examine a few special-needs searches that must be based on administrative justification, which were also introduced earlier.

Stop and Frisk

In *Terry* v. *Ohio*,[66] the famous stop-and-frisk case mentioned earlier, the U.S. Supreme Court failed to provide a clear definition of a stop, but it did offer one in a later case, *United States* v. *Mendenhall* (1980):

> [A] person has been "seized" within the meaning of the Fourth Amendment only if, in view of all the circumstances surrounding the incident, a *reasonable person would have believed that he was not free to leave*. Examples of circumstances that might indicate a seizure, even where the person did not actually attempt

A frisk is a pat down of a person's outer clothing done out of a concern for the officer's safety.

to leave, would be the threatening presence of several officers, the display of a weapon by an officer, some physical touching of the person of the citizen, or the use of language or tone of voice indicating that compliance with the officer's request might be compelled.[67]

The Court's decision in this case stemmed from a confrontation between plainclothes Drug Enforcement Administration agents and a 22-year-old woman named Mendenhall in the Detroit airport. They had asked the woman for her ticket and identification. The name on the ticket did not match the name on the woman's identification, so the agents asked her to accompany them into a nearby private room. The Court did not actually decide whether Mendenhall had been "stopped," but it nevertheless articulated the "free to leave" test cited in the above quote.

The duration of a stop must also be given consideration. Sometimes a stop is drawn out until it evolves into an arrest, which would require probable cause rather than reasonable suspicion. At the other extreme, so-called nonstops, or consensual encounters, require no justification at all. See Figure 10.7 for a list of factors used to distinguish between a stop and a consensual encounter.

Frisks are often associated with stops. A frisk is a pat down of a person's outer clothing done out of a concern for the officer's safety. The officer is not permitted to reach into the person's pockets at the outset or to grope or manipulate the target area.[68] In one relevant case,[69] police officers observed an individual driving a vehicle with expired plates. The officers stopped the vehicle in order to issue the driver a traffic summons. When the officers asked the driver to step out of the car, they observed a large bulge in the pocket of his jacket. Fearing that the bulge might be a weapon, one of the officers frisked the driver. It turned out that the bulge was a .38-caliber revolver. The driver claimed at his trial that the gun was seized illegally, but the U.S. Supreme Court upheld

I, _____, having been informed of my constitutional right not to have a search made of the premises hereinafter mentioned without a search warrant and of my right to refuse consent to such a search, hereby authorize Officers _____ and _____ of the city of _____, state of Alabama, to conduct a complete search of
_____.

These officers are authorized by me to take from this location any property that they may desire. This written permission is being given by me to the above-mentioned officers voluntarily and without threats or promises of any kind.

Dated, signed, and witnessed

_____

FIGURE 10.6 **A Consent-to-Search Form.**
Used with permission of the Institute for Criminal Justice Education, Inc. (ICJE)

FIGURE 10.7 **Factors Used to Distinguish between a Stop and a Consensual Encounter.**

Source: J. L. Worrall, Criminal Procedure: From First Contact to Appeal, 2nd Edition, © 2007. Reprinted by permission of Pearson Education, Inc., Upper Saddle River, NJ.

the frisk. Even though a bulge in one's pocket is not necessarily indicative of a weapon, the Court felt that under these particular circumstances it was.

Special-Needs Searches

Special-needs searches (sometimes called *regulatory or administrative searches*) are those whose primary purpose is noncriminal. They are based on administrative justification, which was introduced earlier. Because such searches nonetheless intrude on people's privacy and can lead to the discovery of evidence, the Fourth Amendment is implicated. However, instead of focusing on probable cause or reasonable suspicion, the courts use a "balancing test" that weighs citizens' privacy interests with public-safety interests. When the latter outweighs the former, administrative searches are allowed—subject to certain limitations, such as department policy. There are many types of special-needs searches. We consider two that are most relevant in the policing context: inventories and checkpoints.

Inventories. There are two types of inventories: **person inventories** and **vehicle inventories**. The general rule is that the police may search an arrestee and his or her personal items, including containers found in his or her possession, as part of a routine inventory incident to the booking and jailing procedure. Neither a search warrant nor probable cause is required.[70] As for vehicle inventories,[71] the U.S. Supreme Court held that warrantless inventories are permissible on administrative or regulatory grounds; however, they must (1) follow a *lawful* impoundment, (2) be of a routine nature and follow standard operating procedures, and (3) not be a "pretext concealing an investigatory police motive."

Checkpoints. Many types of **checkpoints** have been authorized. First, brief border detentions are constitutionally permissible.[72] That is because it is in the interest of "national self-protection" to permit government officials to require "one entering the country to identify himself as entitled to come in, and his belongings as effects which may be lawfully brought in."[73] Second, the U.S. Supreme Court has upheld the establishment of roadblocks near the Mexican border designed to discover illegal aliens.[74] Third, warrantless, suspicionless sobriety checkpoints have also been authorized.[75]

The administrative search rationale is *not* acceptable for detecting evidence of criminal activity. This was the decision reached in *City of Indianapolis* v. *Edmond* (2000),[76] in which the Court examined whether a city's suspicionless checkpoints for detecting illegal drugs were constitutional. Here is how the Supreme Court described the checkpoints:

> The city of Indianapolis operated a checkpoint program under which the police, acting without individualized suspicion, stopped a predetermined number of vehicles at roadblocks in various locations on city roads for the primary purpose of the discovery and interdiction of illegal narcotics. Under the program, at least one officer would (1) approach each vehicle, (2) advise the driver that he or she was being stopped briefly at a drug checkpoint, (3) ask the driver to produce a driver's license and the vehicle's registration, (4) look for signs of impairment, and (5) conduct an open-view examination of the vehicle from the outside. In addition, a narcotics-detection dog would walk around the outside of each stopped vehicle.[77]

The Court held that stops like those conducted during Indianapolis's checkpoint operations require individualized suspicion. In addition, "because the checkpoint program's primary purpose [was] indistinguishable from the general interest in crime control,"[78] it was deemed to violate the Fourth Amendment.

In *Illinois* v. *Lidster* (2004),[79] the Supreme Court decided that officers at checkpoints are also authorized to ask questions related to crimes occurring at the same area earlier. In that case, police briefly detained motorists to ask them if they had any information about a hit-and-run accident between a vehicle and a bicycle that took place at the same location a week earlier. A driver entered the checkpoint, swerved, and nearly hit an officer. He was stopped and subjected to a field sobriety test. He was eventually convicted of drunk driving but challenged the constitutionality of the checkpoint. The Court rejected the challenge, thus permitting yet another type of checkpoint.

▶ Confessions and Interrogations

Just as the police need to be cognizant of Fourth Amendment requirements, they also need to be aware of the rules governing confessions and interrogations. It is possible to violate a suspect's rights by failing to adhere to legal requirements spelled out in the Constitution and interpreted by the courts. Accordingly, this section briefly reviews the leading constitutional rules governing confessions and interrogations.

Three Approaches to Confession Law

The primary focus in this section is on the **Fifth Amendment**, but for the sake of placing Fifth Amendment confession law into context, it is important to briefly consider the extent to which

If the person being questioned is not in custody, Miranda rights do not apply.

Miranda In simple terms, the *Miranda* decision sent a message to the police that they cannot question people who are in custody, most often under arrest, without first advising them that they don't have to talk. If they do, then any resulting confession cannot be used against such people during a criminal trial. Some believe that the *Miranda* decision should be abolished because it could cause convictions to be lost. They also claim that there are other constitutional protections that ensure suspects' rights are not violated. Is *Miranda* a loophole? Why or why not? Can you think of other supposed loopholes in the criminal justice process? Explain.

Source: © Marmaduke St. John/Alamy

confessions are protected by other constitutional provisions. Indeed, the very fact that three constitutional amendments place restrictions on how the government can obtain confessions suggests that our country places a high degree of value on the people's right to be free from certain forms of questioning.

Figure 10.8 illustrates the key learning points associated with the **due process voluntariness approach**, the Sixth Amendment approach, and the **Miranda rights** approach.

What is custody? The Court announced that *Miranda* applies when "a person has been taken into custody or otherwise

The Due Process Voluntariness Approach

A suspect's involuntary statement is not admissible in a criminal trial (or in any other criminal proceeding) to prove guilt. A confession is involuntary when, under the "totality of circumstances that preceded the confessions," the defendant is deprived of his or her "power of resistance." Courts take a case-by-case approach to determine voluntariness, focusing on two issues: (1) the police conduct in question and (2) the characteristics of the suspect.

Example: if the suspect is a minor and the police act with brutality, any subsequent confession will be deemed involuntary.

The Sixth Amendment Approach

Massiah v. *United States* (1964) led to the rule that the Sixth Amendment's guarantee to counsel in all "formal criminal proceedings" is violated when the government "deliberately elicits" incriminating responses from a person.

Two key elements:
(1) **deliberate elicitation:** an effort by a government actor to draw incriminating statements from a suspect who is not represented by counsel
(2) **formal criminal proceedings:** include the formal charge, preliminary hearing, indictment, information, and arraignment.

Example: If a police officer questions a person who has already been indicted and counsel is not present, the officer violates the person's Sixth Amendment rights.

The *Miranda* Approach

Miranda v. *Arizona* (1966) led to the rule that the prosecution may not use statements by the defendant stemming from custodial interrogation, unless it shows the use of procedural safeguards to secure privilege against self-incrimination.

*If the person being questioned is not in custody, *Miranda* rights do not apply. Simple police questioning—even full-blown interrogation—is not enough to trigger the protections afforded by the Fifth Amendment. The person subjected to such questioning *must* be in police custody.

Example: If police arrest and interrogate suspect without reading them their *Miranda* rights, anything suspect says cannot be used in court.

FIGURE 10.8 Three Approaches to Confession Law.

> You have the right to remain silent. Anything you say can and will be used against you in a court of law. You also have the right to an attorney. If you cannot afford an attorney, one will be provided to you at no cost. Do you understand these rights as they have been read to you?

deprived of his freedom of action in any significant way." An arrest is a clear-cut case of police custody, but what about a lesser intrusion such as an order not to leave the scene? Unfortunately, there is no easy answer to this question. Instead, courts focus on the circumstances surrounding each individual case. The Supreme Court has stated, however, that "the only relevant inquiry [in analyzing the custody issue] is how a reasonable man in the suspect's position would have understood his situation."[80]

The second major component of *Miranda* is interrogation. Custody by itself is not enough to require that *Miranda* warnings be given. For a person to be afforded Fifth Amendment protection—and particularly to be advised of his or her right to remain silent—then that person must be subjected to interrogation.

Miranda defined *interrogation* as "questioning initiated by law enforcement officers." Then, in *Rhode Island* v. *Innis* (1980), the Court noted that interrogation "must reflect a measure of compulsion above and beyond that inherent in custody itself."[81] Thus, any questions that tend to incriminate, that is, those that are directed toward an individual about his or her suspected involvement in a crime, are considered interrogation.

Unfortunately, many "questions" are not always readily identifiable as such. In *Innis*, the Supreme Court noted that in addition to "express questioning," the "functional equivalent" of a question is also possible. The **functional equivalent of a question**, according to the Court, includes "any words or actions on the part of the police (other than those normally attendant to arrest and custody) that the police should know are reasonably likely to elicit an incriminating response from the suspect."[82]

The *Miranda* decision was not without controversy. Shortly after the *Miranda* decision, Congress passed the Crime Control Act of 1968, which, among other things, attempted to overrule the *Miranda* decision. The statute, codified as **18 U.S.C. Section 3501**, states that in any federal prosecution a confession "shall be admissible in evidence if it is voluntarily given." Under the law, suspects need not be advised of their right to counsel, their right not to incriminate themselves, and so on.

For several years, Section 3501 remained dormant, but critics of *Miranda* continued to look for ways to bring it before the Court. That opportunity arose in 2000. The case involved Charles Dickerson, who had been indicted for bank robbery and related crimes. He moved to suppress a statement he made to agents from the Federal Bureau of Investigation on the grounds that he had not received his *Miranda* warnings. The district court granted Dickerson's motion to suppress but also noted that the confession was voluntary, despite the apparent *Miranda* violation. The Court of Appeals for the Fourth Circuit held (in a 2–1 decision) that "Congress, pursuant to its power to establish the rules of evidence and procedure in the federal courts, acted well within its authority in enacting Section 3501, [and] Section 3501, rather than *Miranda*, governs the admissibility of confession in federal court."[83] The case then went before the U.S. Supreme Court.[84] In a 7–2 opinion for the Court, Chief Justice Rehnquist wrote,

> We hold that *Miranda*, being a constitutional decision of this Court, may not be in effect overruled by an Act of Congress, and we decline to overrule *Miranda* ourselves. We therefore hold that *Miranda* and its progeny in this Court govern the admissibility of statements made during custodial interrogation in both state and federal courts.[85]

The Court further noted, "We do not think there is such justification for overruling *Miranda*. *Miranda* has become embedded in routine police practice to the point where the warnings have become part of our national culture."[86]

The Importance of *Miranda*

Subsequent Supreme Court cases have hinged on the substance and adequacy of the *Miranda* warnings and waivers. For example, if *Miranda* rights are not given "adequately," then the police risk having a confession thrown out of court.[87] Also, like many rights, *Miranda* rights can be waived, that is, suspects can elect *not* to remain silent.[88] To be safe, many police departments require that suspects complete a *Miranda* waiver before interrogation commences. Finally, suspects need not be advised of their *Miranda* rights when doing so could compromise public safety.[89]

Miranda continues to undergo refinement from one Supreme Court term to the next. Most recently, the Supreme

Court has decided that *Miranda* protections do not apply if a suspect is released from custody for at least 14 days and then re-questioned.[90] If the suspect is rearrested, however, *Miranda* warnings must be read. Also, the Court has held that the *Miranda* warnings do not require that police advise the suspect that he or she has the right to have an attorney present during questioning, only that the suspect has the right to talk with a lawyer.[91]

The Importance of Documenting a Confession

This section has been mainly concerned with the methods by which the police can extract incriminating information from criminal suspects. Assuming that the police are successful in terms of eliciting an incriminating response, it is not enough for the suspect to say, "I did it," or to offer some other form of a verbal confession. In fact, if the police hand the suspect a pencil and paper and say, "Write down your confession," this will not be enough, either. Instead, the police must follow specific procedures for documenting and reporting a confession.

14 *Miranda* protections do not apply if a suspect is released from custody for at least 14 days and then re-questioned.

The police should document every interrogation and even keep an interview log, which is a document containing information about the individuals involved in the interrogations and actions taken by both sides.[92] A list of topics to be recorded in an interview log can be found in Figure 10.9.

Also, the police should secure a signed statement from the accused. The statement should identify the suspect, the investigators, and the crime involved and should describe—in language that the suspect can understand—the details of the crime, what the suspect did, and how he or she did it. The statement should then be carefully reviewed with the suspect, even read aloud, so that its contents are clear. Finally, it should be signed by the suspect, the officer conducting the interrogation, and at least one witness, preferably another officer.

Interview Log
1. Identity of person interviewed
2. Identity of officers conducting interview
3. Location of interview
4. Date of interview
5. Time of arrest, if applicable
6. Location of arrest
7. Identity of officers making arrest
8. Time interview began
9. Time officers informed subject or suspect of his rights, and if more than one officer, name of officer advising subject or suspect
10. Time subject or suspect waived his rights
11. Time interview concluded
12. Time preparation of statement commenced
13. Identity of person preparing statement
14. Time statement completed
15. Time subject or suspect reviewed statement
16. Time subject or suspect signed written statement
17. A record of requests and complaints of subject and the action taken thereon, such as the time a subject requests permission to call an attorney, the time he made a call to his attorney, the time subject complained of illness, the time and action taken on this complaint, the time subject requested food, the time and action taken on this request, and the details as to how this request was handled

FIGURE 10.9 **Contents of a Typical Interview Log.**
Source: T. T. Burke, "Documenting and reporting a confession with a signed statement: A guide for law enforcement," *FBI Law Enforcement Bulletin* (February 2001): 21.

Privacy in the Waste Heat Leaving Someone's Home?

Agent William Elliott of the U.S. Department of the Interior suspected that Danny Kyllo was growing marijuana in his home, which was part of a triplex in Florence, Oregon—a town close to the ocean and west of Eugene.

At 3:20 AM one morning, Elliott and a colleague used an Agema Thermovision 210 thermal imager (an infrared heat detector about the size of a digital camera) to scan the triplex. The scan, conducted from the passenger seat of Elliott's vehicle, took only seconds, and the imager revealed unusual signs of high heat in part of Kyllo's home. The heat signature was consistent with the type of heat that would be emitted by an active marijuana-growing operation.

Elliott correctly concluded that Kyllo was using bright halide lights (a relatively common practice known to law enforcement officers at the time) to grow marijuana inside the house. He took the results of the scan, tips from informants, and copies of Kyllo's unusually high electric bills to a judge, who issued a warrant to search Kyllo's home. The search uncovered more than 100 marijuana plants under cultivation in the home.

Kyllo's attorney attempted to exclude the marijuana plants from evidence at his trial for marijuana manufacturing by arguing that the thermal imager scan was an unconstitutional search within the meaning of the Fourth Amendment. The attorney argued that Elliott shouldn't have been allowed to scan the house without first showing that he had probable cause to do so and obtaining a warrant permitting the scan. His attorney's motion to suppress the results of the scan was unsuccessful. Following conviction, Kyllo appealed to the Ninth Circuit Court of Appeals. After considering the fact that Kyllo had made no effort to conceal the heat escaping from his home, the court sided with the agents. Moreover, the court concluded that the scan did not "expose any intimate details of Kyllo's life," only "amorphous hot spots on the roof and exterior wall."

Kyllo continued appealing his conviction until he reached the U.S. Supreme Court. The Court issued its decision in 2001, reversing the findings of the lower courts. The justices held, "Where, as here, the Government uses a device that is not in general public use, to explore details of a private home that would previously have been unknowable without physical intrusion, the surveillance is a Fourth Amendment 'search,' and is presumptively unreasonable without a warrant."[93]

Court watchers find the *Kyllo* case to be especially interesting because it deals with the intersection of today's technology and our more than two-century-old Constitution. Significantly, in *Kyllo*, the Supreme Court did not limit its decision to thermal imagers. The justices talked about devices "not in general public use," a phrase that seems to cover many modern technologies, including those that are on the horizon.

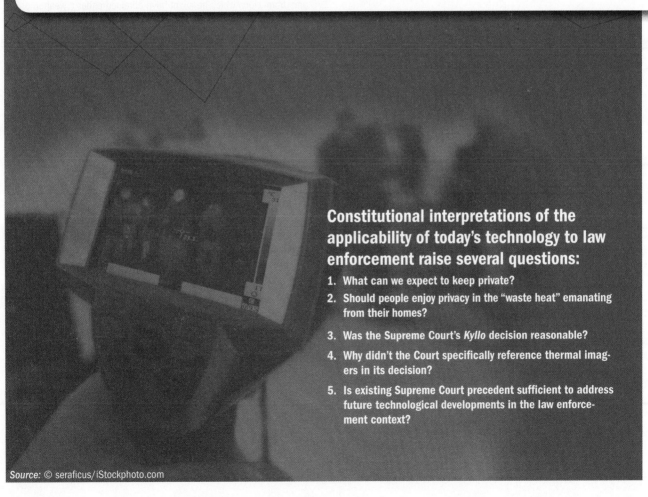

Constitutional interpretations of the applicability of today's technology to law enforcement raise several questions:

1. What can we expect to keep private?
2. Should people enjoy privacy in the "waste heat" emanating from their homes?
3. Was the Supreme Court's *Kyllo* decision reasonable?
4. Why didn't the Court specifically reference thermal imagers in its decision?
5. Is existing Supreme Court precedent sufficient to address future technological developments in the law enforcement context?

LEARNING OUTCOMES 1 Discuss when Fourth Amendment provisions apply to activities undertaken by law enforcement officers, and describe existing rules governing the conduct of searches and seizures.

A Fourth Amendment violation occurs when a government actor infringes on a person's reasonable expectation of privacy during a search or seizure. Seizures can be of people or property. Probable cause is more than 50 percent certainty; reasonable suspicion is between 1 and 50 percent certainty. Administrative justification balances society's interest in protecting public safety against individuals' privacy concerns. Search and arrest warrants must be issued by a neutral and detached magistrate and require a showing of probable cause and particularity. Searches that can be conducted without a warrant include searches incident to arrest, searches based on exigent circumstances, automobile searches, plain-view searches, and consent searches. Stop and frisk stems from the U.S. Supreme Court's decision in *Terry* v. *Ohio*, which permits police to briefly detain someone to determine whether criminal activity is afoot. Special-needs searches include inventories and checkpoints.

1. When does the Fourth Amendment apply to the activities of law enforcement officers?

2. What rules governing search and seizure are most relevant in the policing context?

3. What is the difference between a "frisk" and a "search" of a person?

4. Under what conditions is a warrantless vehicle inventory permitted?

5. What constitutes "reasonable suspicion"? How is the concept of reasonable suspicion relevant to police work?

Fourth Amendment The amendment to the U.S. Constitution that governs search and seizure.

search An activity performed in order to find evidence to be used in a criminal prosecution.

government action In the context of search and seizure law, one of two elements that must be considered when defining a Fourth Amendment search. (The other element is a reasonable expectation of privacy.) Government actions consist of measures to effect a search undertaken by someone employed by or working on behalf of the government.

reasonable expectation of privacy In the context of search and seizure law, one of two elements that must be considered when defining a Fourth Amendment search. (The other element is government action.) A reasonable expectation of privacy means that people who speak or act in private can reasonably expect that what they say or do will not be seen or heard by someone else.

seizure The confiscation of one's person (arrest) or property by a government agent.

reasonableness The elements of a situation that serve to justify a search or seizure.

justification The focus of a court's examination of the reasonableness of a search or seizure.

probable cause A set of facts and circumstances that would induce a reasonably intelligent and prudent person to believe that another particular person has committed a specific crime. Probable cause is the only justification for search and seizure mentioned in the Fourth Amendment.

reasonable suspicion A belief, based on a consideration of the facts at hand and on reasonable inferences drawn from those facts, that would induce an ordinarily prudent and cautious person under the same circumstances to conclude that criminal activity is taking place or that criminal activity has recently occurred. Reasonable suspicion is the standard for less intrusive stop-and-frisk searches; it is less than probable cause but more than a hunch.

administrative justification The standard for an administrative search based on the fact that government entities occasionally conduct searches in circumstances other than criminal investigations, such as a sobriety checkpoint set up for the purpose of apprehending drunk drivers. Sometimes called *special-needs* or *regulatory searches*, such searches attempt to achieve a balance between protecting individuals' privacy interests and protecting public safety.

search incident to arrest A warrantless search made at the time of or shortly following an arrest, which is conducted out of a concern for the safety of the arresting officer and others.

arm-span rule A doctrine established by the U.S. Supreme Court that limits a search immediately following an arrest to the area "within [the] immediate control" of the person arrested—that is, the area from within which he might have obtained either a weapon or something that could have been used as evidence against him.

protective sweep A permissible cursory visual inspection of places in which a person might be hiding. A protective sweep may be conducted by police up to the point of an arrest but must be supported by reasonable suspicion.

exigent circumstances A situation that makes a warrantless search constitutionally permissible, such as hot pursuit, the likelihood of a suspect escaping or presenting a danger to others, and evanescent evidence.

hot pursuit exception One exception to the Fourth Amendment's warrant requirement, recognized by the U.S. Supreme Court in *Warden* v. *Hayden* (1967). The hot pursuit doctrine provides that police officers may enter the premises where they suspect a crime has been committed, or a perpetrator is hiding, without a warrant when delay would likely endanger their lives or the lives of others and possibly lead to the escape of the alleged perpetrator.

evanescent evidence Evidence that is likely to disappear quickly.

plain-view doctrine The rule that the police may seize evidence without a warrant if they have lawful access to the object and it is immediately apparent (that is, they have probable cause) that the object is subject to seizure.

stop and frisk The detaining of a person by a law enforcement officer for the purpose of investigation, accompanied by a superficial examination by the officer of the person's body surface or clothing to discover weapons, contraband, or other objects relating to criminal activity.

person inventory The search of an arrestee and his or her personal items, including containers found in his or her possession, as part of a routine inventory that is incident to the booking and jailing procedure. Often called *arrest inventory*.

vehicle inventory A warrantless inventory of a vehicle that is permissible on administrative or regulatory grounds. Vehicle inventories must follow a lawful impoundment, must be of a routine nature, must follow standard operating procedures, and must not be a pretext that attempts to conceal an investigatory search.

checkpoint A location at which a warrantless, suspicionless search is constitutionally permissible in furtherance of an overriding national or public-safety interest. National border entry points and sobriety checkpoints are examples.

 LEARNING OUTCOMES 2

Discuss existing rules concerning interrogations undertaken by law enforcement officers and the in-court admissibility of obtained confessions, especially as established under the Fifth, Sixth, and Fourteenth Amendments.

The due process voluntariness approach to confessions and interrogations holds that all confessions must be voluntary. The Sixth Amendment applies to confessions and interrogations when officers deliberately elicit incriminating information from an accused person after the initiation of criminal proceedings. The *Miranda* approach to confessions and interrogations requires that an attorney be provided to an accused person who is in custody and is being interrogated. *Miranda* warnings must be read carefully; critical information should not be omitted. Miranda rights can be waived, and the warnings can be dispensed with—for a short time—if there is an imminent threat to public safety that would be worsened if the warnings were read.

1. What rules regarding confessions and interrogations should police officers be aware of?

2. Which U.S. Supreme Court decisions are most relevant in the area of confessions and interrogations?

3. What rights are established by the Fifth Amendment to the U.S. Constitution? How do they apply to police work?

4. What rights of criminal defendants were established by the U.S. Supreme Court in the 1966 case of *Miranda* v. *Arizona*? Why did the U.S. Congress seek to override the *Miranda* decision?

Fifth Amendment An amendment to the U.S. Constitution that establishes due process rights, including the right to remain silent in the face of criminal accusations.

due process voluntariness approach A means for determining the admissibility of a suspect's self-incriminating statement based on whether it was made voluntarily. Involuntariness is held to occur when, under the totality of circumstances that preceded the confessions, the defendant is deprived of his or her "power of resistance."

Miranda rights The set of rights that a person accused or suspected of having committed a specific offense has during interrogation and of which he or she must be informed prior to questioning, as stated by the U.S. Supreme Court in *Miranda* v. *Arizona* (1966) and related cases.

functional equivalent of a question Any words or actions on the part of the police (other than those normally attendant to arrest and custody) that the police should know are reasonably likely to elicit an incriminating response from the suspect.

18 U.S.C. Section 3501 The U.S. Code designation assigned to the Crime Control Act of 1968, which, among other things, attempted to invalidate the *Miranda* decision.

MyCJLab

Go to the Chapter 10 section in *MyCJLab* to test your understanding of this chapter, access customized study content, engage in interactive simulations, complete critical thinking and research assignments, and view related online videos.

Additional Links

Critical issues involving policing and the law are available at **www.justicestudies.com/pubs/knockandtalk.pdf** ("Knock and Talk" searches) and **www.justicestudies.com/pubs/gordonvmichigan.pdf** ("Knock and Announce" violations).

Special-needs searches are the topic discussed at **www.justicestudies.com/pubs/specialneeds.pdf**. Motor vehicle exceptions to search warrant requirements are reviewed at **www.justicestudies.com/pubs/motorvehicles.pdf**.

The full text of two U.S. Supreme Court cases of special importance to policing (*Kyllo* v. *United States* **www.law.cornell.edu/supct/html/99-8508.ZS.html** and *Katz* v. *United States* **www.law.cornell.edu/supct/html/historics/USSC_CR_0389_0347_ZS.html**) are viewable online.

Finally, a discussion about revoking consent to search can be seen at **www.justicestudies.com/pubs/revokingsearchconsent.pdf**.

Civil Liability and Accountability

"The police are held accountable for their actions by a number of means, including citizen oversight, the exclusionary rule, and civil litigation."

1 Identify the two main avenues available to aggrieved parties seeking to sue for police civil liability, and list some of the defenses against civil liability that law enforcement officers and their supervisors and departments might employ.

2 List and explain five external measures, other than litigation, for promoting police accountability.

3 Discuss procedures for promoting accountability from within police agencies.

Source: © Michael Matthews - Police Images / Alamy

POLICING UNDER A CONSENT DECREE

Following a series of scandals, administrators with the Los Angeles Police Department entered a consent decree through the federal courts in 2000, and undertook a number of efforts to improve policing in the city. The decree followed what some called "a decade of policing crises" that began with the widely televised beating of Rodney King in 1991 and culminated with the Rampart subdivision scandal of 1999. Today, according to authors of a 2009 report by the John F. Kennedy School of Government at Harvard University, "the Los Angeles Police Department is completing one of the most ambitious experiments in police reform ever attempted in an American city."[1] The report found that the department, under the leadership of a new chief, William Bratton, began to focus in 2002 on reducing crime, improving morale, and on "complying fully with the consent decree."

Since then, the report's authors note, public satisfaction with the police has risen substantially, with 83 percent of the city's residents saying that the LAPD is now doing a good or an excellent job. Moreover the use of force by officers has fallen annually since 2004. "Both the quantity and quality of enforcement activity have risen substantially," according to the report. "In sum," says the report, "the evidence here shows that with both strong police leadership and strong police oversight, cities can enjoy both respectful and effective policing." Access the full report at **http://justicestudies.com//policing/policinglosangeles.pdf**.

One of the core principles of the democratic system of government is public accountability. The American system of government is designed to ensure that public officials ultimately answer to the people whom they serve. Making elected officials accountable is relatively easy; they can be voted out of office. This is less true for workers in civil service positions; they answer to the public through a complex chain of relationships. The police have not always been held closely accountable to the public. Times have changed, however, and the mechanisms for ensuring public accountability of police activity are the focus of this chapter.

DISCUSS How can police officers be held accountable for their actions? Should they be?

While holding public officials accountable is certainly important, those officials enjoy many of the same legal protections that the rest of us do. Police officers who are sued, for example, can assert a number of defenses. Likewise, officers who are investigated by their departments for alleged misconduct enjoy a number of procedural protections. Bills of rights for police officers have emerged in an effort to preserve the due process rights of accused officers and to reduce the potential for wrongful firings, demotions, and transfers. This chapter examines efforts to balance the need for police accountability against the need to preserve due process protections for everyone, including the police.

One of the core principles of the democratic system of government is public accountability.

▶ Civil Liability

Whenever a person's constitutional or other federal civil rights are violated, a lawsuit can be filed. Even if a person merely *believes* that his or her rights have been violated, litigation is still an option. Litigation is also an option for tort violations, or civil wrongs that do not rise to the level of a constitutional rights violation. In either case, the worst that can happen for the plaintiff (the person bringing the lawsuit) is that the lawsuit will be dismissed and the plaintiff will be stuck with the attorney's bill.

What is the purpose of civil litigation? Aside from sometimes being the only remedy available to those who have been wronged, civil lawsuits are attractive because they sometimes result in monetary awards. Lawsuits in which people seek monetary compensation are called *damages suits*, and the money paid is called **damages**. In such suits, the plaintiff seeks payment for perceived or actual injuries. In addition to damages, plaintiffs can seek **injunctive relief**, which means that the plaintiff wants the court to bring the injurious or offensive action to a halt.

Section 1983 Liability

A portion of the U.S. Code, **42 U.S.C. Section 1983**, provides a remedy in federal court for the "deprivation of any rights . . . secured by the Constitution and laws" of the United States. Section 1983 states,

> Every person who, under color of any statute, ordinance, regulation, custom, or usage, of any State or Territory or the District of Columbia, subjects, or causes to be subjected, any citizen of the United States or other persons within the jurisdiction thereof to the deprivation of any rights, privileges, or immunities secured by the Constitution and laws, shall be liable to the party injured in an action at law, suit in equity, or other proper proceeding for redress.

LEARNING OUTCOMES 1 Identify the two main avenues available to aggrieved parties seeking to sue for police civil liability, and list some of the defenses against civil liability that law enforcement officers and their supervisors and departments might employ.

GLOSSARY

damages Monetary compensation awarded to the plaintiff in a successful civil lawsuit.

injunctive relief A court order to bring injurious or offensive action to a halt.

Someone acts under color of law when he or she acts in an official government capacity and with the appearance of legal power.

42 U.S.C. Section 1983 The federal statute that provides a remedy in federal court for the "deprivation of any rights . . . secured by the Constitution and laws" of the United States.

color of law The condition that exists when an individual acts in an official government capacity and with the appearance of legal power. Police officers, mayors, and a number of other government officials perform their duties under color of law.

constitutional rights violation Conduct that violates a specific constitutional provision.

culpability The state of deserving blame or being morally or legally responsible. Under the Section 1983 culpability requirement, plaintiffs generally must prove that the defendant officer *intended* for the violation to occur.

theory of liability Reasons offered as to why a particular person or other entity should be held answerable under law for some action.

Bivens* v. *Six Unknown Named Agents The 1971 U.S. Supreme Court ruling that held that federal law enforcement officers can be sued for Fourth Amendment violations. The decision has since been expanded to include liability for violations of constitutional rights embodied in other relevant amendments.

absolute immunity Protection from lawsuits enjoyed by federal officials when acting in their official capacities.

Color of Law

One of the requirements for a successful Section 1983 lawsuit is that the defendant, the person being sued, must have acted under color of law. The U.S. Supreme Court has said that someone acts under **color of law** when he or she acts in an official government capacity and with the appearance of legal power. This includes police officers, mayors, and a number of other government officials.[2] For example, a police officer who is on duty acts under color of law. Police officers also act under color of law when they (1) identify themselves as officers, (2) perform criminal investigations, (3) file official police documents, (4) make arrests, (5) invoke police powers inside or outside their jurisdiction, (6) settle personal vendettas with police power, or (7) display weapons or police equipment.[3] By contrast, someone acting in a private capacity (for example, an ordinary citizen) cannot be said to have acted under color of law.

Constitutional Violation

The second requirement for a successful Section 1983 lawsuit is that a federal or constitutional rights violation must have taken place. In the law enforcement context, the concern is almost exclusively over constitutional rights violations. In determining whether a **constitutional rights violation** has taken place, the plaintiff (the suing party) must establish that the conduct of the defendant (or defendants) violated a specific constitutional provision, such as the Fourth Amendment's prohibition against unreasonable searches and seizures (see Chapter 10), that is,

"in any given Section 1983 suit, the plaintiff must still prove a violation of the underlying constitutional right."[4]

Recently, the courts have begun to require that constitutional rights violations alleged under Section 1983 be committed with a certain level of **culpability**, that is, plaintiffs generally have to prove that the defendant officer *intended* for the violation to occur. The practical result of this is that Section 1983 is now reserved for the most serious of constitutional rights violations. The level of culpability required for a constitutional rights violation depends on the type of unconstitutional conduct alleged by the plaintiff.[5]

Theories of Liability

The term **theory of liability** refers essentially to reasons offered as to why a particular person or entity should be held answerable under civil law for some action. A typical Section 1983 lawsuit will target an individual officer, that officer's supervisor, the city or municipality for which the officer works, or some combination of these. Besides suing the officer who may have been responsible for a constitutional rights violation, it is often attractive for plaintiffs to go after the "bigger fish" because that is where the money is. Cities and counties tend to have deeper pockets than the average police officer and are therefore more attractive targets for civil litigation. To date, cities and counties have only been held liable for failing to train officers[6] and for adopting unconstitutional policies and customs.[7] For the latter, the plaintiff must prove that the city or county adopted and implemented a policy or custom that led to the injury. Isolated incidents are not sufficient to hold a city or county liable.

Suing Federal Officials

Before 1971, it was not clear whether federal officials could be sued under Section 1983. In the 1971 case of ***Bivens* v. *Six Unknown Named Agents***,[8] however, the U.S. Supreme Court held that federal law enforcement officers *can* be sued for Fourth Amendment violations. The decision has since been expanded to include liability for violations of constitutional rights embodied in other relevant amendments.[9]

Bivens claims are primarily limited to law enforcement officers, as many other federal officials enjoy absolute immunity. **Absolute immunity** means that the official cannot be sued under any circumstances. Federal officials who enjoy absolute immunity include judges[10] and prosecutors, among others.[11] By contrast, heads of federal agencies,[12] presidential aides,[13] and federal law enforcement officers *can* be sued. However, these and other federal officials enjoy qualified immunity, the same defense that applies to state officials in the Section 1983 context.

Defenses

The main defense to Section 1983 liability is **qualified immunity**. Qualified immunity is a judicially created defense. It emerged in response to two conflicting policy concerns: effective crime

In some cases, police have benefited from qualified immunity even when they violated clearly established constitutional rights.

control and the protection of people's civil liberties. On the one hand, Section 1983 lawsuits are intended to deter police misconduct. But on the other hand, the U.S. Supreme Court has recognized that it is not fair to hold officials liable for lapses in judgment and honest mistakes.[14]

Similar to the Fourth Amendment's test for reasonableness, the courts have applied an **objective reasonableness** standard in order to determine whether qualified immunity should bar a successful lawsuit. In other words, a defendant police officer is said to have acted in an objectively reasonable fashion if he or she did not violate clearly established rights of which a reasonable person would have known. In some Section 1983 cases, police have benefited from qualified immunity even when they violated clearly established constitutional rights, as long as the mistake was a reasonable one.[15]

State Tort Liability

State tort claims are an alternative for aggrieved people who do not choose to sue under Section 1983. Moreover, **state tort liability** is an important avenue of redress because negligent acts or misconduct by the police that result in minor injuries are usually not serious enough to make Section 1983 litigation a viable option. State tort claims tend to be reserved mostly for less serious claims. There are exceptions, however, such as tort lawsuits for wrongful death, an admittedly serious act.

Types of Torts

There are two types of state tort claims that matter in the law enforcement context. First, **intentional torts** consist of actions that are highly likely to cause injury or damage. For a plaintiff to successfully sue for an intentional tort, he or she must also show that the defendant officer knowingly engaged in the behavior. To be liable for an intentional tort, an officer need not intend to harm; it need only be shown that the officer intended to engage in the behavior that *led* to the harm. Common forms of intentional torts that are applicable to policing include wrongful death, assault and battery, false arrest, and false imprisonment.

A second and more far-reaching tort claim involves negligence. In a **negligence tort**, the mental state of the defendant officer is not at issue. Plaintiffs need only demonstrate the presence of four elements to succeed with a negligence claim: (1) a legal duty between the officer and the plaintiff, (2) a breach of that duty, (3) proximate (direct) causation between the officer's actions and the alleged harm, and (4) actual damage or injury.

Defenses

Police officers who are sued for tort violations benefit from the so-called **public-duty doctrine**. It states that police protection (like any other government function) is owed to the general public, not to individuals. This means that if a police officer is not present to thwart a criminal act, the officer cannot be held liable for failure to protect. The reason for this barrier to liability is clear: It would be unreasonable to hold law enforcement officials liable every

Section 1983 Liability

Provides a remedy in federal court for the deprivation of any rights secured by the Constitution and laws.

Two requirements for a successful lawsuit
1. The defendant (the person being sued) must have acted under color of law.
2. A federal or constitutional rights violation must have occurred.

Defense:
Qualified immunity: officer has lapse in judgment or makes an honest mistake.

State Tort Liability

Alternative for aggrieved people who do not choose to sue under Section 1983. State tort claims tend to be reserved mostly for less serious claims.

Two types of state tort claims that matter in the law enforcement context
1. **Intentional tort:** defendant officer knowingly engaged in behavior.
2. **Negligence tort:** the mental state of the defendant officer is not at issue.

Defenses:
Public-duty doctrine: police protection is owed to general public, not individuals.
Contributory negligence: if plaintiff was also negligent, officer is not liable.
Comparative negligence: looks at who is to blame and assigns liability accordingly.
Assumption of risk: plaintiff voluntarily engaged in dangerous activity, so officer is not liable.
Sudden Peril: officer required to make split-second decision.

FIGURE 11.1 Law Enforcement Liability.

Civil Litigation As part of one of the most visible branches of the executive arm of government, police officers occupy a precarious position with respect to civil liability (being sued for misconduct). This is complicated by the often confrontational nature of police work. Police officers must sometimes use force, which can upset people or injure them. Do the police get sued too much? Why or why not? Do they get sued more than people in other occupations? If so, why? What is your perspective on the issue of police civil litigation?

Source: Copyright © Bob Daemmrich/Photo Edit

---

intentional tort An action that is highly likely to cause injury or damage.

negligence tort A liability claim that must demonstrate that a legal duty existed between the officer and the plaintiff, that a breach of that duty occurred, that a proximate (direct) causation between the officer's actions and the alleged harm resulted, and that actual damage or injury occurred.

public-duty doctrine A doctrine stating that police protection (like any other government function) is owed to the general public, not to individuals. Police officers have used the public-duty doctrine as a liability defense.

contributory negligence A liability defense that holds that if an officer can show that the plaintiff or someone else was also negligent in an event, the officer should not be held liable. Contributory negligence can arise not only from the actions of a criminal suspect, but also from the actions of third parties.

comparative negligence A partial defense against state tort liability that examines who is to blame and assigns liability accordingly.

assumption of risk A defense against state tort liability that provides that if a plaintiff voluntarily engaged in a dangerous activity that led to his or her injury, then the police officer should not be held liable.

sudden peril A defense against state tort liability that is used for cases in which police officers were required to make split-second decisions.

---

time they do not intervene in criminal activity.

There are situations, however, in which police officers owe a legal duty to an individual and, as such, can be held liable for failing to perform that legal duty. For example, if a police officer stops a motorist, confirms that he is drunk, but lets him go, a special relationship has been created; the officer should arrest the drunk driver or, at a minimum, ensure that he does not drive until he is sober. The officer could therefore be held liable under state tort law for negligent failure to protect.

However, even in situations in which a special relationship exists between a police officer and a private citizen, the officer may be able to assert one of several defenses to liability. The first such defense is known as **contributory negligence**. This defense holds that if an officer can show that the plaintiff was also negligent in, say, causing an accident, the officer should not be held liable. Contributory negligence can arise not only from the actions of a criminal defendant, but also from those of third parties. If, during the course of a high-speed pursuit, a third motorist runs a red light and is struck by the officer, the officer may not be found liable because the motorist contributed to the crash by running a red light.

Unlike contributory negligence, the **comparative negligence** defense is not a total bar to state tort liability. Comparative negligence

looks at who is to blame and assigns liability accordingly. If it is found that the police officer is 20 percent liable and the plaintiff is 80 percent liable, damages would be awarded in accordance with these percentages. The comparative negligence defense permits courts to determine fault and the extent to which each party contributed to an incident or injury.

The **assumption of risk** defense against state tort liability provides that if a plaintiff voluntarily engaged in a dangerous activity that led to his or her injury, then the police officer should not be held liable. If a suspect is injured during the course of a high-speed pursuit and sues the officer, the court may decide that the suspect assumed the risk of injury by fleeing from the police.

Finally, police defendants in state tort claims enjoy a defense referred to as **sudden peril**. This is basically an "emergency" defense for situations in which officers were required to make split-second decisions. This defense only applies in situations in which the injury or death is *clearly* attributed to the heat of the moment. If the officer asserting such a defense contributed in any way to the creation of the emergency situation, courts (and juries) may be inclined to find in favor of the plaintiff.

▶ Other External Accountability Measures

Lawsuits serve as a powerful check on police misconduct. The problem, however, is that litigation is not always a viable or desirable alternative. Other measures have been put in place to pick up where litigation leaves off. This section looks at what we call *external accountability measures*, those stemming from outside law enforcement agencies. A later section looks at internal measures that police agencies employ to deal with complaints of misconduct and impropriety.

There is some debate over whether police accountability should be internal or external. Some feel that the police themselves are most capable of reviewing allegations against them. Others feel that a balance between internal and external review is necessary. For example, one researcher observed that "the departmental administrative structure has by far the greatest potential for efficient, effective action to prevent, to investigate, to adjudicate, or to punish police misconduct"[16] but that external review allows outside scrutiny of the process and thereby lends credibility to internal review. Others feel that external review of police agencies is critical, arguing that true control occurs only when civilians have the primary responsibility for investigating misconduct.

A more comprehensive view recognizes that the issue of control must be examined as a partnership between the police *and* the community. From this perspective, external accountability mechanisms are essential. We will look at several such mechanisms: citizen oversight, citizen complaints, agency accreditation, the exclusionary rule, and criminal prosecution for serious misconduct.

GLOSSARY

civilian review One of the stronger models of citizen oversight of a police agency in which a group of citizens investigates complaints against the police, adjudicates the complaints, and recommends punishment.

civilian input A model of civilian oversight of a police agency in which civilians receive and investigate complaints, but the next steps are taken by the police department.

civilian monitor A model of civilian oversight of a police agency that is similar to an ombudsman approach in which complaints are received by the police department and the process, from beginning to end, is monitored by civilians.

citizen complaint A document filed by someone who believes that he or she has been wronged by one or more police officers in a department.

accreditation Certification for having met all applicable requirements put in place by an accrediting body.

exclusionary rule A rule mandating that evidence obtained in violation of the U.S. Constitution cannot be admitted in a criminal trial. The exclusionary rule is an important mechanism for ensuring the accountability of police officials.

Citizen Oversight

Not too long ago, the vast majority of police departments used only an internal process to handle disciplinary actions.[17] A survey of police agencies conducted during the 1980s revealed that only about 15 percent of them allowed "outsiders" into the review process. Today, however, a host of police agencies have established external (citizen) complaint review procedures.[18] Figure 11.2 notes some of the reasons for citizen oversight.

There is little consistency in the way external review is structured,[19] but three distinct approaches have been identified:[20] **civilian review**, **civilian input**, and **civilian monitor**.

Civilian Review

The civilian review model is one of the stronger models of citizen oversight. It occurs when a group of citizens investigates complaints against the police, adjudicates the complaints, and recommends punishment. This approach has been taken in cities like Washington, DC; Philadelphia; Rochester; New York City; and Berkeley. The strongest argument against the civilian review model is that it vests responsibility and authority for police discipline in the hands of individuals who have no expertise in police work and who likely do not have the capacity for investigating and understanding the issues involved

in a disciplinary problem.[21] On the other hand, the civilian review model represents almost everything that critics of traditional internal review mechanisms desire.

Civilian Input

The civilian input model puts the reception and investigation of complaints in the hands of civilians, but the next steps are taken by the police department. In Kansas City, Missouri, the Office of Community Complaints (OCC) serves as the central clearing house for receiving complaints.[22] The OCC reviews all complaints and assigns them, as needed, to the police department's internal affairs unit for investigation. The internal affairs unit is staffed by sworn officers who investigate allegations of wrongdoing in the ranks. Once the investigation has been completed, the OCC reviews the results and makes recommendations to the chief. In Chicago, the Office of Professional Standards (OPS) is located in the police department but is staffed by nonsworn personnel. The OPS handles all citizen complaints involving excessive force, deadly force, and nondeadly force, while the department's internal affairs division is responsible for all other disciplinary issues.

Civilian Monitor

The civilian monitor model is similar to an ombudsman approach. With the civilian monitor model, complaints are received by the police department, and the process—from beginning to end—is monitored by the external unit. The key feature of this model is that the civilians *monitor* but do not *make* decisions. The monitoring consists of scrutinizing the internal process for inconsistencies or problems. For example, in San Jose, California, the Independent Police Auditor (IPA) receives and investigates complaints (as does the police department's internal affairs division). The IPA's mission consists of the following:

(a) Reviewing Police Department investigations of complaints against police officers to determine if the investigation was complete, thorough, objective and fair.

(b) Making recommendations with regard to Police Department policies and procedures based on the Independent Police Auditor's review of investigations of complaints against police officers.

(c) Conducting public outreach to educate the community on the role of the Independent Police Auditor and to assist the community with the process and procedures for investigation of complaints against police officers.[23]

Other Citizen Oversight Models

The three models we just mentioned are not the only methods of providing citizen oversight. One team of researchers identified *four* classes of citizen review.[24] They overlap to some extent with the three just described. The first involves independent citizen review bodies in which nonsworn investigators conduct investigations and make recommendations to the police executive. Citizen review bodies are found, for example, in New Orleans and Cincinnati.[25] The second approach involves initial investigations by sworn police officers, followed by a review of the officers' reports by an individual or board that

Today a host of police agencies have established external (citizen) complaint review procedures.

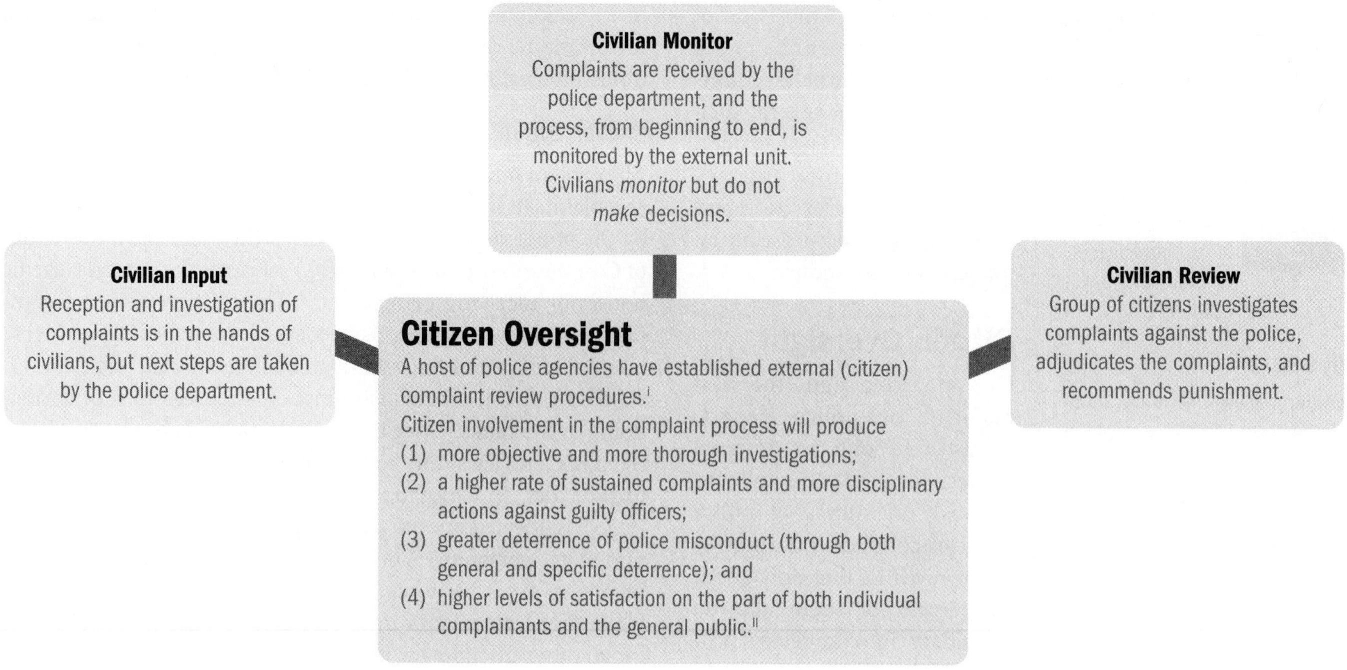

Civilian Monitor
Complaints are received by the police department, and the process, from beginning to end, is monitored by the external unit. Civilians *monitor* but do not *make* decisions.

Civilian Input
Reception and investigation of complaints is in the hands of civilians, but next steps are taken by the police department.

Civilian Review
Group of citizens investigates complaints against the police, adjudicates the complaints, and recommends punishment.

Citizen Oversight
A host of police agencies have established external (citizen) complaint review procedures.[i]
Citizen involvement in the complaint process will produce
(1) more objective and more thorough investigations;
(2) a higher rate of sustained complaints and more disciplinary actions against guilty officers;
(3) greater deterrence of police misconduct (through both general and specific deterrence); and
(4) higher levels of satisfaction on the part of both individual complainants and the general public.[ii]

[i]S. Walker and B. Wright, Citizen review of the police: A national survey of the 50 largest cities (Washington, DC: Police Executive Research Forum, 1995).

[ii]S. Walker and B. Wright, "Varieties of citizen review: The relationship of mission, structure, and procedures to police accountability," in Critical issues in policing: Contemporary readings, 3rd ed., ed. R. G. Dunham and G. P. Alpert (Prospect Heights, IL: Waveland, 1997).

FIGURE 11.2 Citizen Oversight and Police Accountability.

contains at least some nonsworn people. The individual or board then makes recommendations to the chief. Procedures of this type have been used in Kansas City (Missouri), Portland (Oregon), and Albuquerque.[26]

In the third approach, an internal affairs department investigates complaints and makes recommendations to the chief. Citizens who are not satisfied with the final disposition can appeal to a board containing at least some nonsworn individuals. The board reviews the case and may make different recommendations to the chief. In the fourth approach, auditors investigate citizen complaints. In both Seattle and San Jose, for example, an auditor reviews the department's complaint procedure and recommends changes as necessary. Also, the auditor often contacts complainants to assess their satisfaction with the complaint process.[27]

It is also important to distinguish between the independent review of citizen complaints and citizen oversight.[28] Independent review occurs when a civilian review body investigates complaints filed against law enforcement officers and then forwards its

fruit of the poisonous tree doctrine An expansion of the scope of the exclusionary rule that requires the exclusion of any secondary evidence (such as a confession) that derives from evidence originally obtained in violation of the U.S. Constitution.

18 U.S.C.A. Section 242 The most common federal statute used to hold police officers criminally liable.

public-duty defense A legal defense that shields a police officer from criminal liability in situations in which he or she is legally performing an assigned or implied public duty and engages in a necessary and reasonable action that, for ordinary citizens, would be considered a crime.

recommendations to the chief or sheriff. Citizen oversight, in contrast, stresses community outreach, review of complaint policies by a civilian group, audits of complaint investigation procedures, information dissemination, and the like.

Citizen oversight represents an important step in promoting accountability, but its effectiveness in reducing or eliminating misconduct is unclear. This is because most of the mechanisms only provide for disciplinary recommendations; that is, most oversight groups can only make advisory recommendations to the chief police.[29] As two noted researchers observed, "The powers of citizen review procedures are far more limited than those of judges in the criminal process."[30] Nevertheless, certain cities vest citizens with the ability to make disciplinary decisions. Examples include the San Francisco Office of Citizen Complaints, the Milwaukee Fire and Police Commission, the Chicago Police Board, and the Detroit Police Commission.[31]

Citizen Complaints

In general, citizen oversight is concerned with investigations of police misconduct, including investigations of citizen complaints. **Citizen complaints** are documents filed by people who feel they have been wronged by one or more police officers in a department. An example of a citizen's complaint form is provided in Figure 11.3.

Citizen complaints are sometimes seen by administrators as "a barometer of police performance."[32] Complaints can indicate how officers are behaving on the street, which is useful because police officers are not always directly supervised by their superiors. Agencies should not have to *rely* on complaints to

Abilene Police Department
Citizen Complaint/Commendations Form

File complaints or commendations about Police Department employees on this form. Return the completed form to the desk duty officer, 1st floor at the Police Department, 450 Pecan, or hand deliver to the City Manager's Office, 555 Walnut, Room 203, or by mail to P.O. Box 60 Abilene, Texas 79604.
Complaints will not be investigated until a Police Supervisor has contacted the Complaining Party.

Involved Officer/Employee(s) Information:

| Name: | |
| Name: | |

Person Making the Complaint/Commendation:

| Name: | | Phone: | |
| Address: | | Phone: | |

Information

Please provide as much information about the reason you were contacted by the officer/employee. Specific information about the date, time and location will help in locating computer-based information if you do not know the officer/employee's name.

| Date of Contact: | | Approximate Time: | | AM/PM |
| Location Contacted: | | | | |

Reason For The Complaint/Commendation: (attach additional pages if needed)

Witness Information:

Name:		Phone:	
Address:		Phone:	
Name:		Phone:	
Address:		Phone:	

Submitted by_____Date_____

FIGURE 11.3 **Citizen's Complaint Form.**
Source: Abilene (Texas) Police Department. Reprinted by permission.

understand how they are doing, but complaints can often send important messages that would not otherwise be clear.

Many police agencies have centralized areas where all citizen complaints about police misbehavior or ill-treatment of citizens must be reported. Complaints are confidentially received and permanently logged in chronological order of receipt. The complainant's information is also recorded, and an investigation is set into motion. Some agencies actively publicize their citizen complaint procedures. Visitors to the Los Angeles Police Department's website, for example, can find a link to a complaint form. Some agencies have even distributed citizen complaint forms to civic organizations and neighborhood groups.

Still others require any police employee who is approached by a citizen with a complaint to report the complaint to the internal investigation registration desk within a set period of time after receiving the information.

Agency Accreditation

Accreditation refers to certification for having met all applicable requirements put in place by an accrediting body. Accreditation is a big issue in the academic world. Universities have to satisfy their accrediting bodies' requirements, or they risk losing their accreditation, which is akin to losing credibility. Accreditation

Other External Accountability Measures **173**

Accreditation is a process intended to ensure that police agencies abide by the highest standards of conduct in the field.

has spilled over into law enforcement as well. It is a process intended to ensure that agencies remain accountable to the public and that they abide by the highest standards of conduct in the field.

The Commission on Accreditation for Law Enforcement Agencies (CALEA) was established in 1979 by the International Association of Chiefs of Police (IACP), the National Sheriffs' Association, the Police Executive Research Forum, and the National Organization of Black Law Enforcement Executives. Their goal was to evaluate and accredit police agencies that meet the commission's accreditation standards. CALEA has developed standards designed to do the following:

1. Increase the ability of law enforcement agencies to prevent and control crime

2. Increase agency effectiveness and efficiency in the delivery of law enforcement services

3. Increase cooperation and coordination with other law enforcement agencies and with other agencies of the criminal justice system

4. Increase citizen and employee confidence in the agency's goals, objectives, policies, and practices[33]

The standards set forth by CALEA address nine major law enforcement subjects: (1) role, responsibilities, and relationships with other agencies; (2) organization, management, and administration; (3) personnel structure; (4) personnel process; (5) operations; (6) operational support; (7) traffic operations; (8) detainee and court-related activities; and (9) auxiliary and technical services.[34] These subjects are then broken into 38 content areas consisting of (as of this writing) 439 standards.[35]

A police agency seeking accreditation must pass through five phases: application, self-assessment, on-site assessment, commission review and decision, and maintenance of compliance and reaccreditation. The accreditation process is a voluntary one, so only agencies interested in being accredited apply. Once eligibility has been confirmed, the agency and the commission both sign an agreement that identifies what is expected of each party. Then the agency completes an agency profile questionnaire. The responses to the questionnaire provide important information to the accreditation manager and facilitate interaction between the agency and the commission. Next, the agency conducts a self-assessment in which it determines whether it complies with standards set forth by the commission. Proof of compliance is required. The on-site assessment consists of a visit by commission officials during which the agency's compliance with commission standards is determined. The assessors' final report is then forwarded to the commission for review. If, during the review period, the commission is satisfied that the agency meets all relevant standards, accreditation is granted. Accredited agencies then submit annual reports to the commission attesting to their continued compliance with relevant standards.

Accreditation may also provide additional benefits besides accountability and the maintenance of high standards. One is a reduction in insurance premiums.[36] This is not unlike a reduction in auto insurance premiums for drivers who take a safe-driving course. A person who has taken the course is presumably at less risk for getting in an accident or filing a claim. The same goes for police agencies. Those who maintain the highest standards are presumably the least likely to be sued. Evidence also suggests that accredited law enforcement agencies may be more likely to receive grant funds.[37]

Despite the apparent benefits associated with national accreditation, there has been a great deal of debate and controversy over the accreditation process.[38] Some state law enforcement associations have vocally opposed national accreditation standards, arguing that state-level accreditation is preferable. This has resulted in an increase in state-level accreditation.[39] For example, the Washington Association of Sheriffs and Police Chiefs (WASPC) was directed by the state legislature to develop accreditation standards during the 1970s. The result was the WASPC Law Enforcement Accreditation Program.[40] Figure 11.2 depicts WASPC's outline of the benefits of state-level accreditation.

- Improved morale within the police agency
- Increased credibility with the agency's governing body
- Increased pride in the agency
- Systemized self-assessment
- Broadened perspectives
- Intensified administrative and operational effectiveness
- Confidence that recruitment, selection, and promotion processes are fair and equitable
- Strengthened understanding of agency policies and procedures by all police personnel
- Decreased susceptibility to litigation and costly civil court settlements
- Potential reduction in premiums for liability insurance
- Greater public confidence in the agency
- State and local acknowledgment of professional competence

FIGURE 11.4 **Benefits of Participating in the WASPC Accreditation Program.**
Source: Washington Association of Sheriffs and Police Chiefs, "Accreditation," www.waspc.org/index.php?c=accreditation (accessed January 14, 2011).

The Exclusionary Rule

Another important mechanism for ensuring the accountability of police agencies is the **exclusionary rule**, which mandates that evidence obtained in violation of the U.S. Constitution cannot be admitted in a criminal trial to prove guilt.[41] In the Supreme Court case of *Elkins* v. *United States*, Associate Justice Tom C. Clark provided eloquent reasoning for such a rule: "The criminal goes free, if he must, but it is the law that sets him free. Nothing can destroy a government more quickly than its failure to observe its own law, or worse, its disregard of the charter of its own existence."[42]

> *The exclusionary rule mandates that evidence obtained in violation of the U.S. Constitution cannot be admitted in a criminal trial to prove guilt.*

The so-called **fruit of the poisonous tree doctrine** has expanded the scope of the exclusionary rule to include evidence derived from materials that were unconstitutionally obtained. Suppose, for example, that a police officer illegally arrests someone. The fruit of the poisonous tree doctrine would not only require the exclusion of the evidence obtained in the search of the arrestee following that arrest but, potentially, any other evidence (such as a confession) obtained after that initial illegal act.[43] The question of what is considered "fruit," however, has become complicated over the years. This is partly due to the emergence of a number of exceptions to the fruit of the poisonous tree doctrine.

The intentions of the exclusionary rule are to promote accountability and to deter misconduct. Some would say, though, that the rule does not serve the same deterrent effect today that it perhaps once did. Its deterrent effect may have been diminished as the U.S. Supreme Court has become more conservative in its decisions. A variety of subsequently established exceptions to the rule helps to ensure that the criminal does not go free when reasonable mistakes are made. The deterrent effect is probably minimal, too, because the time elapsed between illegal police conduct and the decision to exclude evidence is usually rather lengthy.[44]

There is evidence, however, that many police organizations, fearful of losing criminal cases on technicalities, have instituted programs designed to teach trainees about constitutional guidelines. To that end, the exclusionary rule plays at least a minimal role in promoting accountability; when the police violate the Constitution, criminals go free. When criminals go free, the public demands answers. Thus law enforcement officials recognize the importance of operating within established constitutional and legal boundaries.

Criminal Prosecution

Various statutes at the state and federal levels provide criminal remedies for police misconduct. Some states make it a crime for police officers to trespass or to falsely arrest people. In fact, most criminal sanctions that apply to ordinary citizens also apply to police officers. Likewise, there are various statutes at the federal level that make it not only improper but criminal for police officers to engage in certain types of conduct.

Federal Prosecution

At the federal level, the most common statute for holding police officers criminally liable is **18 U.S.C.A. Section 242**. Section 242 is to criminal liability what Section 1983 (discussed earlier) is to civil liability. It can be used to prosecute either a state or a federal law enforcement officer. Section 242 states,

> Whoever, under color of any law, statute, ordinance, regulation, or custom, willfully subjects any inhabitant of any State, Territory, or District to the deprivation of any rights, privileges, or immunities secured or protected by the Constitution or laws of the United States, or to different punishments, pains, or penalties, on account of such inhabitant being an alien, or by reason of his color, or race, than are prescribed for the punishment of citizens, shall be fined not more than $1,000 or imprisoned not more than one year, or both; and if death results shall be subject to imprisonment for any term of years or for life.

To be held liable under Section 242, a law enforcement officer must act with specific intent to deprive a person of important constitutional or other federal rights.[45] A finding of criminal liability under Section 242 also requires that a constitutional right be clearly established.[46] These restrictions have resulted in relatively few Section 242 cases. In fact, criminal liability under Section 242 is reserved for the most egregious forms of police misconduct.

Despite its relatively infrequent application, there have been a few cases in which Section 242 was invoked. For example, in *Miller v. United States* (1968),[47] a police officer was held criminally liable for allowing his canine unit to bite a suspect. In *Williams v. United States* (1951),[48] a defendant had been beaten, threatened, and physically punished for several hours, and the police officer was held criminally liable.

> *To be held liable under Section 242, a law enforcement officer must act with specific intent to deprive a person of important constitutional or other federal rights.*

Section 242 has also been applied in cases involving assault and battery of criminal defendants.[49]

Additional federal statutes make it a criminal act to unlawfully search and seize individuals (18 U.S.C.A. Section 2236), although applications of this statute are rare. For example, 18 U.S.C.A. Section 2235 makes it a crime to maliciously procure a warrant, and Section 2234 makes it a criminal offense to exceed the authority of a warrant. Regardless of which criminal statute applies, an important distinction between the various criminal statutes and 42 U.S.C. Section 1983 is that officers who are held *criminally* liable receive criminal convictions and can even go to prison; Section 1983, by contrast, is civil, meaning that it is used independently of the criminal process. A successful Section 1983 lawsuit will never result in the imprisonment of the defendant.

State Prosecution

The same laws that apply to ordinary citizens also apply to police officers. For example, if a police officer knowingly and intentionally kills someone and is not legally justified in doing so (that is, it was not a justifiable killing that occurred in conjunction with the officer's official police duties), the officer can be held criminally liable for murder. Similarly, if a police officer trespasses on private property without appropriate justification, he or she can be held criminally liable. Criminal liability can extend to police officers for virtually any conceivable offense.

Three categories of offenses have been identified:[50] (1) violent and sex crimes, (2) drug crimes, and (3) other crimes. Examples of officers accused of violating state law include the so-called Miami River Cops, who were charged with murdering drug smugglers, and the police officer in Fort Myers, Florida, who was charged with sexual assault against a 19-year-old woman. Indeed, as of this writing, U.S. Border Patrol agents along the Arizona–Mexico border have become the targets of almost daily *criminal* complaints for a variety of actions.

Given the staggering amounts of money associated with the illegal drug trade, it is no wonder that some police officers cross the "thin blue line" and attempt to profit from illegal drugs. This appears to be the case with the infamous Rampart scandal in the Los Angeles Police Department. Officers in other cities have faced similar charges. In 1996, seven officers on the Chicago Police Department's Tactical Unit were charged with stealing and extorting drug money; seven officers in Atlanta were arrested in 1995 on drug charges; and a deputy in Tucson was arrested in 1999 for conspiracy to distribute drugs. The list, unfortunately, goes on.[51]

Police officers have also been held liable for such offenses as burglary, fabrication of evidence, perjury, and shoplifting. One report revealed that federal agents arrested three city police officers in Detroit who were planning a home invasion to steal $1 million in cash.[52]

This is not to suggest that police officers frequently engage in criminal activity—only that it does happen. No one is above the law, not even police officers. However, when officers break the law in order to protect the innocent or to prevent some greater harm, then they can claim a "law enforcement" or **public-duty defense**. Such a defense would, for example, be useful by an officer who finds the use of force necessary in effecting an arrest, but is later accused of assault by the person arrested. The public-duty defense is meant to shield police officers from criminal liability when they act reasonably in such situations.

▶ *Accountability from the Inside*

The preceding section may give the impression that there is something wrong with internal accountability mechanisms, the organizational steps that police departments take to address wrongdoing. Nothing could be further from the truth. Internal affairs divisions and codes of ethics are effective methods for promoting the accountability of those charged with serving the public.

Internal Affairs

Many police agencies have developed innovative and highly regarded internal complaint review units, most commonly known as **internal affairs (IA)** divisions. Internal investigation units receive complaints that are filed in various manners: verbally or in writing, openly or anonymously, by civilians or sworn police officers, in person or by telephone, or by other means. Complaints must be investigated regardless of the manner of filing or the type of incident involved.

The IA division in Oakland, California, for instance, is respected throughout the country.[53] According to one source, the "Internal Affairs Section of the Oakland Police Department works closely with the chief of police, who sets the tone for its rigorous investigations." Officers who have worked in IA "help to pass on [the unit's] knowledge about citizens' complaints and educate the everyday cop about how IA works. Ideally, these dynamics combine to make IA respected, understood, and feared by the cops it polices."[54]

LEARNING OUTCOMES 3 Discuss procedures for promoting accountability from within police agencies.

GLOSSARY

internal affairs (IA) An investigative agency within a police department that is tasked with investigating allegations of misconduct or criminality by members of the department.

police officers' bill of rights A police agency's formal statement of the rights of officers who are accused of misconduct.

code of ethics A statement of principles concerning the behavior of those who subscribe to the code.

Functions and Procedures

The effectiveness of internal investigations of police misconduct depends on the accurate receipt and recording of all relevant information of improper personnel or organizational behavior, regardless of its source. Administrative efforts to minimize the potential for manipulating complaints have led to the designation of specifically identified individuals or offices as the point for registering employee misconduct complaints.

Internal investigation units receive complaints that are filed in various manners: verbally or in writing, openly or anonymously, by civilians or sworn police officers, in person or by telephone, or by other means. Complaints must be investigated regardless of the manner of filing or the type of incident involved.

The following three types of complaints are critical to effective managerial control and must be fully investigated: (1) a citizen complaining about the police department or one of its employees, (2) a police employee complaining about another police employee, and (3) a police employee complaining about the police agency or its practices.[55]

Once they are recorded, complaints and reports must be managed in such a fashion as to ensure prompt, thorough, confidential investigations. Only the chief executive officer and police officials with a need to know are normally permitted access to information about the complainant, the complaint, or the investigation, at least during the initial investigative phase. Time limits for completing various aspects of the investigation and reporting to complainants are essential for the effective operation of internal affairs.

Another matter deserving careful consideration by the chief is the selection of staff investigators for internal affairs. Role conflicts are created when line police officers are assigned to investigate other line officers with whom they must work or when investigative officers are shifted back and forth between the internal affairs unit and operational units that are subject to investigations. In each of these instances, investigators may be tempted to be lenient with those officers accused of misconduct.

Although there is no universal agreement on this matter, internal investigations may be best served by police personnel who will never be reassigned to work under officers who have been the subject of their investigations. To prevent this situation from occurring, small police agencies sometimes use high-level staff commanders or investigators from other nearby police agencies or sheriff's departments. Larger organizations usually have the option of developing separate career paths for those who specialize in the investigation of other police officers. Such separate career routes have the advantage of permitting the use of rewards for vigorous, competent, and objective investigations.

Together, all of these concerns have led to sophisticated procedures for tracking and investigating complaints against the police through internal affairs. To illustrate one such process, Figure 11.3 shows how complaints are reviewed internally within the Claremont (California) Police Department. The Police Review Ad Hoc Committee referenced in the figure consists of no more than three commissioners drawn at random from the city's police commission.

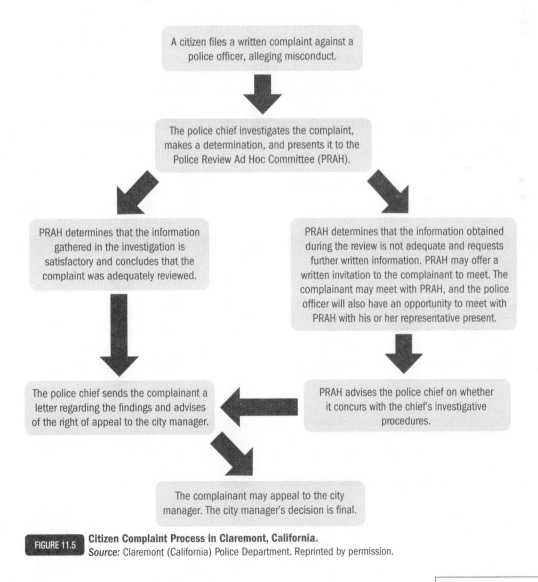

FIGURE 11.5 Citizen Complaint Process in Claremont, California.
Source: Claremont (California) Police Department. Reprinted by permission.

Officers' Rights during Investigations

A number of court cases have addressed the issue of police officers' rights during the course of internal investigations. For example, in *Garrity* v. *New Jersey* (1967),[56] the U.S. Supreme Court ruled that information gained from the interrogation of a police officer could not be used in a criminal trial because it was not voluntary. In that case, a state deputy attorney general was asking police officers about ticket fixing. The officers were read their rights and then told that if they failed to answer the questions, they would be dismissed. Subsequent criminal convictions based on the officers' admissions were deemed unconstitutional because the admissions were not voluntary. Similarly, in *Gardner* v. *Broderick* (1967),[57] the Supreme Court ruled that police officers could not be fired for invoking their constitutional rights against self-incrimination. In *Gardner*, a police officer refused to answer questions from a grand jury on the grounds that the answers might incriminate him. The department fired the officer, but the Court held that this termination was unconstitutional. A number of other pertinent decisions have been handed down over the years, but most are beyond the scope of this introductory text.

A Police Officers' Bill of Rights

To reduce the temptation for internal investigators to proceed against police employees in an insensitive fashion, some police agencies have formally adopted a statement of the rights of police officers who are accused of misconduct. Sometimes such conditions are contained in labor contracts; other times they are mandated by law. The typical **police officers' bill of rights** requires advanced notice to an officer who is being investigated, spells out procedures for resolving complaints that maintain due process protections, and limits the lengths to which an agency can go to secure information through interrogation and investigations.

Although the individual components of this list can be debated, fairness requires that officers deserve reasonable protection from inappropriate investigative practices. Procedures for ensuring that officers receive fair and appropriate treatment at the hands of specialized IA investigators and their supervisors should be observed in the investigative process.

Several states have adopted bills of rights for police officers,[58] beginning with Florida in 1974. Supporters of such legislation argue that "the bill of rights merely ensures [that] the officer under investigation knows the subject of the investigation and is afforded rights and protections against certain interrogation techniques subject to abuse."[59] Critics claim that

> *Some police agencies have formally adopted a statement of the rights of police officers who are accused of misconduct.*

"the basic premises of such legislation only confound an already complex area of public police without substantially improving police labor-management relations."[60]

Codes of Ethics

Another mechanism for promoting accountability from within the law enforcement agency is a **code of ethics**, a statement of principles concerning the behavior of those who subscribe to the code. According to Joycelyn Pollock,[61] a leading police ethicist, these codes consist of several standard elements: "legality (enforcing and upholding the law), service (protecting and serving the public), honesty and integrity (telling the truth, being honest in action), loyalty (to other police officers), and the Golden Rule (treating people with respect or the way one would like to be treated)."[62]

The development of a code of ethics for law enforcement can be traced back to early movements to professionalize policing. During the 1930s, the International Association of Chiefs of Police (IACP) created a committee to make recommendations designed to promote professionalism. The committee agreed that one of the criteria for accomplishing this goal was the creation of a code of ethics. It was not until 1957, however, that the Law Enforcement Code of Ethics was unanimously approved by delegates attending the sixty-fourth IACP conference in Honolulu. Then, in 1989, IACP voted to replace the 1957 code with a newer version that reflects concern over a wider range of issues.

Among the issues covered in the 1989 code of ethics are (1) the responsibilities of police officers, (2) the performance of police duties, (3) discretion, (4) use of force, (5) confidentiality, (6) integrity, (7) cooperation with other agencies, (8) personal and professional responsibilities, and (9) private life. For example, with respect to an officer's private life, the code states, "Police officers will behave in a manner that does not bring discredit to their agencies or themselves." With respect to use of force, the code states, "A police officer will never employ unnecessary force or violence and will use only such force in the discharge of duty as is reasonable in all circumstances."[63]

Can Reporters Accompany the Police When They Serve Arrest Warrants?

Some years ago, at around 6:45 in the morning, a group of deputy federal marshals and local sheriff's deputies invited a newspaper reporter and a news photographer to accompany them as they served an arrest warrant.

The team arrived at a private residence where they expected to find Dominic Wilson, a fugitive who had violated his probation following convictions for assault, robbery, and theft. The officers did not know, however, that the house they were about to enter belonged to Dominic's parents, Charles and Geraldine Wilson. The officers forcibly entered the home while the two were still in bed. Charles, dressed only in his underwear, ran into the living room to investigate the noises he heard. When he discovered five men in street clothes armed with guns, he demanded that they state their business.

The officers initially thought that Charles was Dominic, and they quickly subdued him. Meanwhile, Geraldine, dressed only in a nightgown, stepped out of the bedroom to find her husband handcuffed on the floor. The officers conducted a sweep of the residence, found no sign of Dominic Wilson, and quickly left.

The Wilsons were emotionally shaken by the experience, but what infuriated them was the presence of the reporter, who had been taking notes, and the photographer, who snapped several pictures. The news crew, *Washington Post* staffers, never wrote a story or published an account of what had occurred, but the Wilsons nevertheless sued the officers involved, alleging that the early-morning intrusion had violated their Fourth Amendment right to be free from unreasonable searches and seizures.

The officers who served the warrant made a mistake, but no one was physically harmed and they left the premises as soon as they realized that Dominic Wilson was not there. Would it be fair to hold the officers liable for their actions? If so, which of their actions were inappropriate?

This case eventually reached the U.S. Supreme Court, which declared that the officers violated the Fourth Amendment[64] by bringing members of the media with them into a private home. But the Court also decided that because the officers didn't know any better, they should not be required to pay damages.

This case raises several questions:

1. Did the officers go too far in bringing the reporters with them? After all, the *Washington Post* staffers did not *participate* in the service of the search warrant. They were simply observers, and other people (like neighbors) might also have observed what transpired.

2. Do lawsuits promote police accountability? Why or why not?

3. What mechanisms other than lawsuits can help ensure that the police are held accountable to the law?

4. Do we hold police officers and their departments to excessively high standards with respect to liability?

5. Is America too "litigious," that is, do people sue too often? If so, what might be done about it?

Identify the two main avenues available to aggrieved parties seeking to sue for police civil liability, and list some of the defenses against civil liability that law enforcement officers and their supervisors and departments might employ.

Police can be held liable for monetary and other damages under (1) 42 U.S.C. Section 1983, and (2) state tort law. For a Section 1983 lawsuit to succeed, the plaintiff must show that the defendant acted under color of law and violated an applicable constitutional provision. Defenses to Section 1983 liability include absolute and qualified immunity. Common state tort claims against police include intentional and negligent misconduct. There are several defenses to state tort liability, including the public-duty doctrine, contributory negligence, comparative negligence, assumption of risk, and sudden peril.

1. What are the two main avenues available to aggrieved parties seeking to sue for police civil liability?

2. What is a Section 1983 lawsuit? Who can be targeted by such suits?

3. What is meant by absolute immunity? Are law enforcement officers protected in the performance of their duties by the concept of absolute immunity? Why or why not?

4. What are some of the defenses against civil liability that law enforcement officers and their supervisors and departments might employ? How can civil liability promote accountability?

damages Monetary compensation awarded to the plaintiff in a successful civil lawsuit.

injunctive relief A court order to bring injurious or offensive action to a halt.

42 U.S.C. Section 1983 The federal statute that provides a remedy in federal court for the "deprivation of any rights . . . secured by the Constitution and laws" of the United States.

color of law The condition that exists when an individual acts in an official government capacity and with the appearance of legal power. Police officers, mayors, and a number of other government officials perform their duties under color of law.

constitutional rights violation Conduct that violates a specific constitutional provision.

culpability The state of deserving blame or being morally or legally responsible. Under the Section 1983 culpability requirement, plaintiffs generally must prove that the defendant officer *intended* for the violation to occur.

theory of liability Reasons offered as to why a particular person or other entity should be held answerable under law for some action.

Bivens* v. *Six Unknown Named Agents The 1971 U.S. Supreme Court ruling that held that federal law enforcement officers can be sued for Fourth Amendment violations. The decision has since been expanded to include liability for violations of constitutional rights embodied in other relevant amendments.

absolute immunity Protection from lawsuits enjoyed by federal officials when acting in their official capacities.

qualified immunity A liability defense that shields a police officer who has acted in an objectively reasonable fashion as long as he or she did not violate clearly established rights that a reasonable person would have known. Qualified immunity is an outgrowth of various U.S. Supreme Court decisions.

objective reasonableness A standard, used to determine whether qualified immunity applies, that looks at how a reasonable person would have acted under a given set of circumstances.

state tort liability An important avenue of redress for plaintiffs whose minor injuries, allegedly resulting from negligent acts or misconduct by the police, are not serious enough to make Section 1983 litigation a viable option.

intentional tort An action that is highly likely to cause injury or damage.

negligence tort A liability claim that must demonstrate that a legal duty existed between the officer and the plaintiff, that a breach of that duty occurred, that a proximate (direct) causation between the officer's actions and the alleged harm resulted, and that actual damage or injury occurred.

public-duty doctrine A doctrine stating that police protection (like any other government function) is owed to the general public, not to individuals. Police officers have used the public-duty doctrine as a liability defense.

contributory negligence A liability defense that holds that if an officer can show that the plaintiff or someone else was also negligent in an event, the officer should not be held liable. Contributory negligence can arise not only from the actions of a criminal suspect, but also from the actions of third parties.

comparative negligence A partial defense against state tort liability that examines who is to blame and assigns liability accordingly.

assumption of risk A defense against state tort liability that provides that if a plaintiff voluntarily engaged in a dangerous activity that led to his or her injury, then the police officer should not be held liable.

sudden peril A defense against state tort liability that is used for cases in which police officers were required to make split-second decisions.

LEARNING OUTCOMES 2

List and explain five external measures, other than litigation, for promoting police accountability.

External mechanisms for promoting police accountability in addition to civil liability include citizen oversight, citizen complaint procedures, agency accreditation, the exclusionary rule, and criminal prosecution. Citizen oversight refers to the oversight of police actions and the investigation of complaints by nonsworn personnel. Citizen complaints promote accountability, but the fate of a complaint depends on who files it. Police agencies, like universities, seek accreditation to demonstrate that they meet critical professional standards. The exclusionary rule requires that evidence obtained in violation of the U.S. Constitution be inadmissible in a criminal trial. The rule has been expanded with the fruit of the poisonous tree doctrine. There are several arguments for and against the exclusionary rule. Ultimately, however, it is rarely applied. Police officers, like ordinary citizens, can be held *criminally* liable for egregious misconduct.

1. What is meant by law enforcement agency accreditation? What is the accrediting agency? How does law enforcement accreditation promote police accountability?

2. What is the exclusionary rule? How does it promote police accountability?

3. What mechanisms are involved in civilian oversight of the police?

4. What is involved in the process of civilian review?

civilian review One of the stronger models of citizen oversight of a police agency in which a group of citizens investigates complaints against the police, adjudicates the complaints, and recommends punishment.

civilian input A model of civilian oversight of a police agency in which civilians receive and investigate complaints, but the next steps are taken by the police department.

civilian monitor A model of civilian oversight of a police agency that is similar to an ombudsman approach in which complaints are received by the police department and the process, from beginning to end, is monitored by civilians.

citizen complaint A document filed by someone who believes that he or she has been wronged by one or more police officers in a department.

accreditation Certification for having met all applicable requirements put in place by an accrediting body.

exclusionary rule A rule mandating that evidence obtained in violation of the U.S. Constitution cannot be admitted in a criminal trial. The exclusionary rule is an important mechanism for ensuring the accountability of police officials.

fruit of the poisonous tree doctrine An expansion of the scope of the exclusionary rule that requires the exclusion of any secondary evidence (such as a confession) that derives from evidence originally obtained in violation of the U.S. Constitution.

18 U.S.C.A. Section 242 The most common federal statute used to hold police officers criminally liable.

public-duty defense A legal defense that shields a police officer from criminal liability in situations in which he or she is legally performing an assigned or implied public duty and engages in a necessary and reasonable action that, for ordinary citizens, would be considered a crime.

LEARNING OUTCOMES 3

Discuss procedures for promoting accountability from within police agencies.

Accountability from inside police agencies is promoted via internal affairs divisions and professional codes of ethics. Internal affairs (IA) refers to either a division within a police agency or one or more officers who are tasked with investigating allegations of misconduct. The targets of IA investigations enjoy a number of protections today. Codes of ethics encourage officers to abide by various professional standards.

1. How do police agencies promote accountability from within?

2. What is the role of the internal affairs division in police departments?

3. Why would officers want to work in the internal affairs division?

4. Identify at least one law enforcement-related code of ethics. How seriously do police officers take codes of ethics?

internal affairs (IA) An investigative agency within a police department that is tasked with investigating allegations of misconduct or criminality by members of the department.

police officers' bill of rights A police agency's formal statement of the rights of officers who are accused of misconduct.

code of ethics A statement of principles concerning the behavior of those who subscribe to the code.

MyCJLab

Go to the Chapter 11 section in *MyCJLab* to test your understanding of this chapter, access customized study content, engage in interactive simulations, complete critical thinking and research assignments, and view related online videos.

Additional Links

Police civil liability is the subject of an article on failure to train at **www.justicestudies.com/pubs/ failuretotrain.pdf**.

Information on the doctrine of sovereign immunity can be found at **www.answers.com/topic/ sovereign-immunity**.

The exclusionary rule is the topic of discussion at **http://caselaw.lp.findlaw.com/data/constitution/ amendment04/06.html**.

Police gratuities are the focus of **www.justicestudies.com/pubs/gratuities01.pdf** and **www.justice-studies.com/pubs/gratuities02.pdf**.

The Commission on Accreditation for Law Enforcement Agencies website is available at **www.calea.org**.

Deviance, Ethics, and Professionalism

"With the enormous power afforded to law
enforcement officials comes the potential
for abuse of that power."

1 Discuss how various commissions established to examine
police misconduct in the United States have uncovered
deviance.

2 Identify several typologies of police deviance that scholars
have proposed.

3 Discuss explanations for police deviance, its incidence,
and methods of controlling it.

12

POLICING AND THE NEW PROFESSIONALISM

INTRO

In mid-2011, the John F. Kennedy School of Government, as part of its *New Perspectives in Policing* series, published an important paper on police professionalism entitled "Towards a New Professionalism in Policing." It was written by Christopher Stone and Jeremy Travis.[1] Travis is the president of New York's John Jay College of Criminal Justice; Stone is a highly-regarded professor at the Kennedy School.

Stone and Travis told readers that police organizations across the country are caught up today in a vigorous "traffic" in new ideas, including a strong striving for professionalism. "Their leaders," said the authors, "are committing themselves to stricter *accountability* for both their effectiveness and their conduct while they seek to increase their *legitimacy* in the eyes of those they police and to encourage continuous *innovation* in police practices." Because of the shared coherence of these ideals, Stone and Travis argued that a "New Professionalism" characterizes police work today. "The New Professionalism," they say, "can help police chiefs and commissioners keep their organizations focused on why they are doing what they do, what doing it better might look like, and how they can prioritize the many competing demands for their time and resources."

With the enormous power afforded to law enforcement officials comes the potential for abuse of that power. As in any job, when employees are given a large amount of autonomy coupled with a significant degree of control

DISCUSS What is the new professionalism in policing that this story describes? What are its central features?

over others, it is not surprising that some will step outside the bounds of acceptable conduct. Police training, supervision, professionalism, ethical standards, and legal constraints may deter some inappropriate behavior, but even the most effective controls do not work all the time or for all officers.

When talk of police improprieties comes up, the term **corruption** inevitably surfaces. Corruption can be defined as dishonest or fraudulent conduct by public officials in a position of power: "Police officers act corruptly when, in exercising or failing to exercise their authority, they act with the primary intention of furthering private or departmental/divisional advantage."[2]

Corruption, though, is but one example of improper conduct. Perhaps a better term to apply to the material discussed in this chapter is **deviance**. *Deviance* is a broad term that applies to any behavior that is at odds with socially expected or accepted behavior. *Police deviance* thus refers to police behavior that is not regarded as appropriate by those in a position to make such determinations. Usually, this means training authorities, supervisors, the authors of professional standards, and the like, but it also means members of the wider society. Viewed in this way, police deviance can take a number of forms. It can range from the most flagrant physical abuses to seemingly innocuous behaviors that probably wouldn't catch the eye of any but the most ardent police critics.

▶ *Discovering Deviance*

Varying degrees of deviance and corruption have characterized societies everywhere and are certainly not new. Criminal justice historian Samuel Walker describes police corruption during the eighteenth century:

> With few books and even less legal training available, many constables and justices of the peace simply did not know the law. Corruption was also a problem, as officials gave favored treatment to friends, relatives, and influential people. . . . [There were] also accounts of sheriffs and constables taking bribes to release prisoners or fix juries and assaulting citizens without any cause. In short, police corruption and brutality appeared at the very outset of American criminal justice history.[3]

Other historians have remarked that not only did early urban police protect the criminal element, but they practically encouraged crime:

> The police did not suppress vice; they licensed it. From New York . . . to San Francisco, and from Chicago . . . to New Orleans . . . they permitted gamblers, prostitutes, and saloon keepers to do business under certain well-understood conditions. These entrepreneurs were required to make regular payoffs [to the police].[4]

The Wickersham Commission

As patterns of misconduct were being revealed and policing entered the professional era, accounts of police deviance became even more common-place. This was partly due to the work of various crime commissions. The first of these to tackle the issue of improper police conduct was the 1929 Wickersham Commission (known officially as the *National Commission on Law Observance and Enforcement*). (See Figure 12.1.)

One of the Wickersham report's authors, Walter Pollak, went on to argue successfully for the defense in 1932 in *Powell v. Alabama*,[5] in which the U.S. Supreme Court held that a defendant facing the death penalty is entitled to an attorney at trial. *Powell* arose from the famous Scottsboro case, in which eight African-American

LEARNING OUTCOMES 1 Discuss how various commissions established to examine police misconduct in the United States have uncovered deviance.

GLOSSARY

corruption Dishonest or fraudulent conduct by public officials in a position of power.

deviance Any behavior that is at odds with socially expected or accepted behavior.

Wickersham Commission	1929: first commission to tackle the issue of improper police conduct. Its report, *Lawlessness in Law Enforcement*, provided a blistering critique of police corruption around the country. Its authors found that the "third degree," or "the inflicting of pain, physical or mental, to extract confessions or statements," was "extensively practiced across the country."[i]
Knapp Commission	1970: Report identified two types of corrupt police officers: **grass eaters** and **meat eaters**. Grass eaters are the police officers who accept small gifts and engage in minor deviance, mostly in response to peer pressure. Meat eaters are the officers who actively seek out opportunities to exploit their positions, in a proactive and planned fashion, and who may be involved in large-scale and far-reaching corrupt activities. The difficulty facing police reformers is that while meat-eating corruption is much more serious, grass-eating corruption is far more commonplace.

The first national commission to tackle the issue of improper police conduct was the 1929 Wickersham Commission.

[i]National Commission on Law Observance and Enforcement, *Report on lawlessness in law enforcement* (1931; repr., Montclair, NJ: Patterson Smith, 1968), p. 4.

FIGURE 12.1 **Police Deviance and Corruption.**

youths in Alabama were convicted of raping two white women and sentenced to die—without the assistance of counsel. This and some other successful cases that Pollak argued pointed to examples of questionable police conduct, shaky evidence, race discrimination, and other police misconduct.

The Knapp Commission

The formation of the **Knapp Commission** in 1970 marked another significant milestone in the investigation of police deviance. It was established in May of that year under the auspices of Mayor John V. Lindsay of New York in response to an article published by the *New York Times* that reported widespread corruption in the New York City Police Department (NYPD). Judge Whitman Knapp was appointed to chair the commission and investigate the extent to which the *New York Times* accurately portrayed the behaviors of the department.

The Knapp Commission's reference to grass- and meat-eating corruption (as noted in Figure 12.1) has since been expanded to include other types of police behaviors. Police expert Tom Barker, for example, expanded the commission's typology.[6] **White knights**, he argued, are the honest and upstanding officers who never step over the line between accepted and deviant conduct, no matter how great the pressure. **Straight shooters** are officers who, for the most part, are honest but will overlook some of the misconduct committed by their peers. Next are the **grass eaters** and **meat eaters** identified by the Knapp Commission. Finally, **rogues** are the most seriously deviant officers, according to Barker. In 2005, for example, a federal grand jury in Brooklyn indicted retired NYPD officers Stephen Caracappa and Louis Eppolito, saying that in the 1980s the two had routinely passed confidential law enforcement information to members of organized crime and had worked as hit men for the mob, killing rival gangsters.[7] Even meat eaters view rouges, who engage in serious criminal activity, as extraordinarily corrupt.

▶ Typologies Of Deviance

The Wickersham and Knapp crime commissions uncovered several varieties of police deviance. Since then, still other corrupt and deviant practices have come to light. This has prompted researchers to classify, or construct typologies of, police deviance. There are several such noteworthy efforts. We begin with one of the better-known typologies and then consider some others. The last part of this section looks at other forms of police deviance that do not fit neatly into any one category or set of categories.

The Dark Side of Policing

Victor Kappeler, Richard Sluder, and Geoffrey Alpert's popular book *Forces of Deviance: Understanding the Dark Side of Policing*[8] identifies four types of police deviance: police crime, occupational deviance, police corruption, and abuse of authority. Each is discussed in this section. The order in which they appear is not intended to suggest that one is any more serious than the other.

Police Crime

In Chapter 11, we discussed different mechanisms for preserving the accountability of law enforcement officials. One of those is the criminal law. Generally, when police officers break the criminal law, they do so during the course of their legitimate duties and thus cannot be prosecuted as the rest of us can. Indeed, there are a number of so-called affirmative

Knapp Commission A commission to investigate police corruption that was appointed by New York City Mayor John V. Lindsay in 1970 in response to a *New York Times* article that reported widespread corruption in the New York City Police Department.

white knight An honest and upstanding officer who never steps over the line between accepted and deviant conduct, no matter how great the pressure to do so.

straight shooter An honest police officer who will overlook some misconduct committed by peers.

grass eater A police officer who accepts small gifts and engages in minor acts of deviance but does not actively pursue opportunities for corruption.

meat eater A police officer who actively seeks out and plans opportunities to exploit his or her position for personal gain.

rogue A seriously deviant officer.

LEARNING OUTCOMES 2

Identify several typologies of police deviance that scholars have proposed.

defenses that police officers can assert that immunize them from charges of criminal activity when they engage in activities that would be considered criminal for the rest of us. These include entering private property without permission, using physical force to complete an arrest, and even shooting a person. This is what Kappeler and his colleagues meant by **police crime**. They defined police crime as an "officer's use of the official powers of his or her job to engage in criminal conduct*."[9] Researchers have uncovered several examples of police criminal behavior.[10]

Occupational Deviance

Occupational deviance refers either to behavior that does not conform to accepted standards of conduct or that is not part of normal patrol work and is committed under the guise of police authority. Almost anyone can engage in occupational deviance. Consider embezzlement, an offense that nearly anyone can commit during the course of legitimate employment. Embezzlement is basically theft without a trespassory element. The occupational deviance Kappeler and his colleagues refer to, however, is behavior that is facilitated by virtue of serving as a police officer, and it can include much more than just deviance for personal gain. Occupational deviance is perhaps the most intractable problem for police administrators because it's common, it's difficult to detect, and it does not always rise to the level of a criminal offense.

Police Corruption

Remember that our definition of deviance *includes* corruption. Knowing that, it should come as no surprise that Kappeler and his colleagues liken police corruption to deviance. They defined **police corruption** as the misuse of police authority for personal gain.

More often, the term *police corruption* connotes serious and even criminal conduct committed by law enforcement officers. Thus to minimize confusion, it is useful to put deviance in the *inappropriate*

The four types of police deviance are police crime, occupational deviance, police corruption, and abuse of authority.

but not necessarily flagrant category. Corruption is a bit more serious, but if corruption is for personal gain, then simply accepting a free cup of coffee fits the term. Can we logically argue that an officer who accepts a free cup of coffee is the same as one who routinely skims drugs or cash from big busts? Probably not.

Abuse of Authority

Abuse of authority is basically the catchall category for other inappropriate conduct that does not necessarily amount to crime, deviance, or corruption. Kappeler and his colleagues identify three elements of **abuse of authority**:

- Officers may physically abuse a citizen through the use of excessive force.

- Officers may psychologically abuse a citizen through the use of verbal assault, harassment, or ridicule.

- Officers may violate a citizen's constitutional, federal, or state rights*.[11]

Police Crime

Officer uses official police powers to engage in criminal conduct.
Examples: entering private property with no legitimate reason, unjustifiable homicide.

Occupational Deviance

Using one's position for personal gain.
Examples: committing theft from the evidence locker to helping a friend get a speeding ticket removed from his or her driving record

Police Corruption

Misusing police authority to receive material reward or gain. Material reward or gain must be some tangible object, either cash, service, or goods that have cash value.
Example: skimming drugs from big busts

Abuse of Authority

Abuse of authority is basically the catchall category for other inappropriate conduct that does not necessarily amount to crime, deviance, or corruption.
Examples: excessive force, psychological abuse of citizens

FIGURE 12.2 The Dark Side of Policing.

Physical abuse and brutality are arguably the most serious forms of police misconduct, but they can also overlap with some of the other behaviors we have already discussed. Police crime, for example, can contain physical elements. If a police officer wrongfully (and intentionally) kills someone, then what we have is police crime and abuse of authority all wrapped up in a single case. Given the serious nature of physical force, and particularly abuses of it, we return to this topic in Chapter 13.

Classifying Corruption

Some researchers have been content to use the term *corruption* to refer to all manner of police misconduct. For example, in his popular book *Conduct Unbecoming: The Social Construction of Police Deviance and Control*,[12] Maurice Punch identifies four categories of behavior that he considers to be corruption: **straightforward corruption**, **predatory corruption**, combative corruption, and the **perversion of justice**. The order in which they are presented in Figure 12.3 does not relate to their seriousness.

There have been many examples of police officers offering false testimony either to obtain a conviction or to satisfy vengeful motives. Officer Mark Fuhrman's perjured testimony during the famous O. J. Simpson trial is one example.[13] Then there are the findings of the **Mollen Commission**, which investigated allegations of police corruption in the NYPD during the 1990s. The commission drew this conclusion about the pervasiveness of police perjury:

> Officers reported a litany of manufactured tales. For example, when officers unlawfully stop and search a vehicle because they believe it contains drugs or guns, officers will falsely claim in police reports and under oath that the car ran a red light (or committed some other traffic violation) and that they subsequently saw contraband in the car in plain view. To conceal an unlawful search of an individual who officers believe is carrying drugs or a gun, they will falsely assert that they saw a bulge in the person's pocket or saw drugs and money changing hands. To justify unlawfully entering an apartment where officers believe narcotics or cash can be found, they pretend to have information from an unidentified civilian informant or claim they saw the drugs in plain view after responding to the premises on a radio run. To arrest people they suspect are guilty of dealing drugs, they falsely assert that the defendants had drugs in their possession when, in fact, the drugs were found elsewhere where the officers had no lawful right to be.[14]

If the commission's observations seem inaccurate or troubling, or even a little biased, then consider the findings from Myron Orfield's famous study of police perjury.[15] He interviewed prosecutors, judges, and defense attorneys and found that 52 percent believed that at least "half of the time" the prosecutor "knows or has reason to know" that police fabricate evidence at suppression hearings,

straightforward corruption Any form of police misconduct that provides direct financial benefit to police officers.

predatory corruption A form of police corruption that consists of more than just passive participation (for example, looking the other way while a fellow police officer commits a crime). In predatory corruption, officers actively promote and engage in criminal and other wrongful activities.

Straightforward Corruption

According to Punch, straightforward corruption is simply any form of misconduct that provides a direct financial benefit to the officer. An officer who is in cahoots with organized crime figures and receives money for "looking the other way," for example, is said to engage in straightforward corruption.

Predatory Corruption

Refers to the actions of police officers who actively promote and engage in criminal and other wrongful activities. For example, instead of "looking the other way" and ignoring organized crime, the police *are* the organized criminals. Predatory corruption is arguably more serious than straightforward corruption.

Combative Corruption

Combative corruption refers to making arrests, gaining convictions, and ensuring lengthy sentences at whatever the cost and may be among the most common forms of police misconduct. Here are several examples of combative corruption:

- Flaking: Planting evidence on a suspect
- Padding: Adding evidence to strengthen a case against a suspect
- Using verbals, or words, to describe and incriminate a suspect
- Intimidating a witness
- Scoring on an informant: Shaking down an informant for money, drugs, and other items
- Burning: Revealing an informant's identity
- Paying an informant with illegally obtained drugs

Perversion of Justice

Consists of serious actions by a police officer, such as lying under oath (perjury), intimidating a witness, and performing other activities that resemble combative corruption. The difference between the two lies in the officer's motivations. Where combative corruption was concerned with "doing justice" (in the police officer's view), the perversion of justice refers to acting vengefully, of using one's position as a police officer to exact revenge on others. There is, of course, some overlap between these categories. The common thread running throughout each is behavior that is at odds with accepted standards.

FIGURE 12.3 Four Categories of Police Corruption.

perversion of justice A kind of police corruption that consists of serious actions by a police officer, such as lying under oath (perjury), intimidating a witness, and performing other activities that resemble combative corruption.

Mollen Commission A commission appointed by New York City Mayor David N. Dinkins in 1992 to investigate allegations of police corruption in the New York City Police Department.

gratuity Something of value that is freely given to police officers simply because they are police officers. Examples include a cup of coffee, a lunch, or a "police price" discount on a meal or other service.

police sexual violence A sexually degrading, humiliating, violating, damaging, or threatening act committed by a police officer against a (usually female) citizen through the use of force or police authority.

use corruption Drug-related police corruption that consists of an officer's personal use of illicit drugs.

economic corruption Drug-related police corruption in which an officer seeks personal gain by stealing drugs, selling drugs, or extorting money from drug dealers.

police violence In the context of drug investigations, the use of improper physical force to extract a confession or to obtain evidence.

subjugation of defendants' rights In the context of drug investigations, an officer's lying or committing perjury or fabricating evidence in the name of securing a drug conviction.

noble-cause corruption Any corruption that occurs in connection with the goal of getting criminals off the streets and protecting the community.

where judges decide whether evidence should be excluded due to inappropriate police actions. More shocking still is the finding that more than nine of the ten prosecutors surveyed had knowledge of police perjury "at least some of the time." In fairness to police officers, Orfield's study also revealed that much of the perjured testimony given by police at suppression hearings was encouraged by prosecutors who would often say something like, "If this happens, we win. If this happens, we lose."[16]

Police Misconduct

Barker has argued that not only should deviance be couched in terms of corruption, but also that any focus on corruption should be limited to those activities for which there is a monetary reward for the officers.[17] In Figure 12.4 we briefly consider eight examples of this form of corruption.

Other Forms of Deviance

In addition to the deviance highlighted in Figure 12.4, there are other forms of deviance that either don't fit neatly into the categories we have already covered or overlap those categories. We wrap up our introduction to various forms of police deviance by exploring each of these problems: gratuities, police sexual misconduct, and temptations arising from the illicit drug trade.

Gratuities

Gratuities occur when officers accept something of value. Traditional examples of gratuities include a free cup of coffee, a free lunch, or a "police price" discount on a meal or other service. But gratuities can extend into other realms and include everything from free admission to sporting events to lavish gifts.

Shakedowns consist of corrupt officers demanding money, goods, or other valuables from people in exchange for some illegitimate service.

A person who simply gives a gift to a police officer may not expect anything in return, but there is always the possibility that it could *appear* otherwise. In other words, it just looks bad to accept free goods and services, whether the gift is an expression of someone's genuine thanks or is given with a more sinister motive in mind. The International Association of Chiefs of Police agrees; it considers gratuities to be unethical, but this does not stop officers from accepting them. In fact, the practice is actually quite common.

It is even a little risky to describe the acceptance of gratuities as a form of deviance. There are arguments for and against the practice. Stephen Coleman, a police ethics expert, has offered a series of arguments against the acceptance of gratuities:[18]

- The slippery slope to corruption: . . . It could be argued that although there seems to be a big difference between accepting a cup of coffee and accepting a six-figure bribe to look the other way while a murder is carried out, this is not really the case. For there is a logical slippery slope here, given that there is only a small difference between accepting a cup of coffee, and accepting a cup of coffee and a doughnut, and only a small difference between accepting a cup of coffee and a doughnut, and accepting a free meal. . .

- The democratic ethos of policing: Given that, in a democracy, public services should be equally available to all, allowing a fee-for-service system for policing would be "anti-democratic."

- The public perception: A public perception that police are corrupt, whether or not true, will have a deleterious effect on police performance. To avoid this problem, police need to avoid even the appearance of corruptibility.[19]

There are, of course, two sides to every story. Coleman goes on to call attention to some reasons why police *should* accept freebies. One is that they are the building blocks of positive relationships. Second, some people draw on police services more than others. Why shouldn't they be allowed to tip those who serve them? It happens elsewhere in the service sector, some would say, so why not in public service?

For the most part, police departments, training academies, and law enforcement associations discourage the practice of accepting gratuities, mainly due to the slippery slope argument: Given the stigma attached to the acceptance of gratuities, an officer who accepts them might *feel* corrupt, thus greasing the slippery slope toward more serious misconduct. As Coleman puts it, "If officers feel that they are already compromised, they might find it easier to make more significant compromises

Corruption of Authority

Occurs when an officer agrees to accept free meals, discounts, and rewards by virtue of his or her position as a police officer. This type of corruption is perhaps the most innocuous and does not require any significant degree of organization. An officer who receives a free cup of a coffee or a free lunch from a restaurant owner fits into this category.

It is likely that the restaurant owner is attempting to curry favor with the police and possibly benefit from some added attention and/or surveillance of the restaurant that other business owners in the area would not necessarily receive.

Kickbacks

Illegal payments for services performed. An example of this form of corruption hails from Illinois. In January 2001, the public safety director of Cicero, Illinois, Emil Schullo, was indicted in a kickback scheme. He was accused of contracting out town investigative work to a private investigative firm in exchange for kickbacks amounting to 10 percent of the contracted billings. To Schullo's chagrin, the investigator was working with federal law enforcement officials and tape-recorded their conversations. Surprisingly, Schullo was the *ninth* Cicero official to be indicted for corruption. In 2003, Schullo was sentenced to more than nine years in prison.

Opportunistic Theft

A theft that occurs when an opportunity presents itself. Examples include theft from arrestees, crime victims, crime scenes, and unprotected places. This type of theft can be quite lucrative.

Shakedowns

Shakedowns consist of corrupt officers demanding money, goods, or other valuables from people in exchange for lenient treatment, protection, or some other illegitimate service. Basically, shakedowns are extortion. Shakedowns are less common today than they were in the past, so we have to look back in time for examples. During the 1960s, for instance, Seattle police officers were paid $200 each month in exchange for protecting a gay bathhouse called the Atlas Club.

Protecting Illegal Activities

The protection of illegal activities is not unlike a shakedown in the sense that police receive money for their services. Here, though, instead of seeking payment for protection, they seek payment for turning a blind eye to criminal activity. It is safe to say that the police protection of criminal activity is very much the exception these days. It was perhaps most frequent during the Prohibition era, when corrupt officers would routinely protect establishments that continued to serve liquor. Many of these so-called speakeasies could not have operated without police protection.

Fixes

Fixes occur when police officers fix a speeding ticket or other infraction or charge—that is, remove it from someone's record. Examples of ticket fixing are commonplace. For example, during the late 1980s, an NYPD officer, Robert Hanes, was fired for a ticket-fixing scheme in Queens traffic court. As recently as 2006, a police chief and city councilperson in Edwardsville, Kansas, were charged in a driving under the influence (DUI) ticket-fixing scheme.

In response to these sorts of problems, a number of states have implemented so-called **no-fix laws**—with varying degrees of success. Massachusetts has had one such law in place since 1962. It requires officers to account for every ticket they issue, even the voided ones, in an effort to prevent favoritism and unequal treatment.

Crimes

Crimes are among the most serious forms of misconduct. Opportunistic theft is, of course, a type of crime, but Barker was referring mostly to serious criminal activity, including burglary, robbery, rape, and murder. These actions are very much the exception, as the vast majority of police officers are law-abiding and professional, but there are numerous accounts of egregious criminal activity nevertheless.

Internal Payoffs

Refer to the "sale" of anything within a police department, from work assignments and time off to evidence and promotion. The sale of work assignments is not particularly serious, at least not in comparison to criminal activity and other egregious forms of misconduct. In some departments, for example, officers can sell their scheduled shifts to colleagues who are happy to earn pay for the time worked, plus a little extra. This kind of practice may raise some ethical concerns, but it certainly is not criminal. At the other extreme, though, offering money in exchange for promotion or, worse, offering to sell evidence, including contraband, is a serious action that can lead to dismissal and even criminal charges.

FIGURE 12.4 Types of Police Misconduct Related to Money.

later, because they feel that they have nothing to lose."[20] See Table 12.1 for a summary of the arguments for and against accepting gratuities.

Police Sexual Misconduct

The position of authority a police officer enjoys provides ample opportunity for stepping over the line. Recently, researchers have called attention to another type of police misconduct: police sexual misconduct, or **police sexual violence**.[21] If we use the term *sexual misconduct*, we can identify two forms. First, there is consensual on-the-job sex. One study from the 1970s found that 32 percent of 43 officers surveyed in a southern police department reported having sex with women while on duty.[22]

Other researchers have chosen to focus on what they call *police sexual harassment*. This seems to fit somewhere between consensual encounters and violent or nonconsensual ones. One study presented this officer's observation:

> You bet I get [sex] once in a while by some broad who I arrest. Lots of times you can just hint that if you are taken care of, you could forget about what they did. One of the department stores here doesn't like to prosecute. . . . If it's a decent looking woman, sometimes I'll offer to take her home and make my pitch. Some of the snooty, high class broads turn on real quick if they think their friends and the old man doesn't have to find out about their shoplifting.[23]

Both of these studies were conducted some years ago, but it is a safe bet that neither of these forms of sexual misconduct has vanished from the law enforcement landscape. More disturbing still are nonconsensual, sometimes violent attacks by police officers. Not only are these inappropriate, they are also potentially criminal.

Pete Kraska and Victor Kappeler, who authored perhaps the most comprehensive study of police sexual violence, defined the problem as "those situations in which a female citizen experiences a sexually degrading, humiliating, violating, damaging, or threatening act committed by a police officer through the use of force or police authority."[24] They went on to develop a "continuum of sexual violence." It begins with "unobtrusive behavior," such as watching victims, viewing private photographs or videos, and otherwise invading a citizen's privacy. Next, "obtrusive behavior" consists of custodial strip searches, cavity searches, deception to gain sexual favors, and similar actions. Finally, "criminal behavior" is just that: harassment, involuntary sexual contact, sexual assault, and even rape. While most sexual victimization by police may be of women, the sexual abuse of power by policewomen has yet to be explored.

How common is police sexual violence? Kraska and Kappeler examined news sources from January 1991 to June 1993 and identified 124 cases.[25] Most of the cases were actual court cases, not just news accounts. Ninety-one of the cases were from the federal courts. Nine of these involved "unobtrusive" behaviors, 67 involved "obtrusive" behavior, and 15 were criminal.[26] The vast majority of the court cases involved allegations of improper strip searches, but there were a few violations of privacy, sexual assaults, and rapes, as well.

TABLE 12.1 | Arguments for and against Accepting Gratuities

Arguments in Support of Acceptance

Appreciation	It's natural and reasonable to show appreciation to those providing a public service. It's rude to refuse.
Not significant	Gratuities are not significant enough to buy or cultivate favors.
Officially offered	When offered officially by a company or corporation, no personal sense of obligation can develop.
Links with the community	It's part and parcel of fostering close links with the community, including businesspeople. In turn, it's a fundamental of "good policing."
Police culture	It's an entrenched part of police culture. Any attempt to end it will result in displeasure and cynicism.
Trust and discretion	Attempts to prohibit acceptance imply that officers cannot be trusted to exercise discretion and are incapable of making sensible moral judgments to guide their behavior.

Arguments against Acceptance

Sense of obligation	Even the smallest gift inevitably creates a sense of obligation if it becomes regularized.
"Slippery slope"	Gratuities lead to a "slippery slope" where the temptations become imperceptibly greater and refusal increasingly difficult.
Remove temptation	Not all officers can exercise proper judgment on what is reasonable to accept. It's more sensible for the organization to remove the temptation altogether.
Purchase preferential treatment	Businesses that offer gratuities are, in essence, seeking to purchase preferential treatment (for example, encourage greater police presence in the vicinity of their business).

Source: T. Newburn, *Understanding and preventing police corruption: Lessons from the literature* (London: Home Office, Policing and Reducing Crime Unit, 1999), p. 10. Reproduced under the terms of the Open Government License.

Drug War Temptations

Before the start of the "war on drugs" in the 1960s, police deviance was mostly connected with the protection of illegal gambling, prostitution, and other vice crimes. Officers were not faced with too many overt temptations to break the law. Since this country has sought to eradicate illicit drug use, however, those temptations have become quite pronounced.

Michigan State University police expert David Carter has identified two types of drug-related police corruption, both of which he says "have notably increased" in recent years.[27]

Type I drug corruption: This "occurs when an officer seeks to use his or her position simply for personal gain. This type of drug corruption includes the following: giving information to drug dealers about investigations, names of informants, planned raids, and so forth; accepting bribes from drug dealers in exchange for nonarrest, evidence tampering, or perjury; theft of drugs from the police property room for personal consumption; 'seizure' of drugs for personal use without arresting the person possessing the drugs; taking the profits of drug dealers' sales or their drugs for resale; extorting drug traffickers for money or property in exchange for nonarrest or nonseizure of drugs."[28]

Type II drug corruption: This "involves the officer's search for legitimate gains and may not even be universally perceived as being corrupt. 'Gain' may involve organizational benefit—perhaps a form of 'winning' or 'revenge.' Included are such actions as giving false statements to obtain arrest or search warrants against suspected or known drug dealers; perjury during hearings and trials of drug dealers; 'planting,' or creating evidence against known drug dealers; entrapment; and falsely spreading rumors that a dealer is a police informant in order to endanger that person."[29]

Victor Kappeler and his colleagues have come up with their own classification scheme for drug-related police corruption. It includes **use corruption**, **economic corruption**, **police violence**, and **subjugation of defendants' rights**. Use corruption refers to the personal use of illicit drugs. Two researchers found, for example, that 20 percent of the officers they surveyed reported using marijuana *on duty*.[30] Economic corruption is like Carter's Type I corruption cited above: Officers seek personal gain by stealing drugs, selling drugs, or extorting money from drug dealers. Police violence involves the use of improper physical force to extract confessions. Finally, the subjugation of defendants' rights refers to committing perjury or telling other lies or fabricating evidence in an attempt to secure drug convictions. The latter of these has also been called **noble-cause corruption**,[31] which has been defined as any corruption that occurs in connection with the goal of getting criminals off the streets and protecting the community.

The effort to eradicate illegal drugs has led to new forms of police corruption.

▶ Explanations, Incidence, and Controls

Criminological theory tells us why criminals offend. In much the same way, theories of police deviance explain what makes a law enforcement officer cross over to the dark side. There are far more theories of crime, however, than there are theories of police deviance. In addition to considering explanations of police deviance, it is also important to gauge the extent of the problem. The stories we have presented hardly capture the reality of police deviance. We described some of the more notorious cases, but what about the more mundane cases of police deviance—just how common are they? Finally, and perhaps most importantly, we need to consider what can be done to stop police deviance. It is not enough to wait around until something goes wrong. Administrators want to know what they can do to prevent police deviance before it becomes a problem.

LEARNING OUTCOMES 3 Discuss explanations for police deviance, its incidence, and methods of controlling it.

GLOSSARY

rotten apple theory A perspective that attributes police deviance primarily to a few individuals whose propensity toward corruption was not recognized during the recruitment and hiring phases.

first-page test A series of questions proposed by Joycelyn Pollock that police officers can ask themselves to reinforce professional ethical standards.

consent decree A legal settlement in which one entity agrees to take certain actions or rectify a particular problem without admitting to any illegality. Consent decrees are sometimes used in law enforcement following corruption scandals; a decree requires the police department to fix a particular problem and/or end a particular course of action.

Explaining Police Deviance

There are two main theories of police deviance. One explains deviance in terms of the isolated behavior of individual officers, while the other attributes deviance to the influence of environmental factors that could affect all police officers. These explanations roughly parallel classical and positivist theories of crime. Classical theories look at individual factors like personality; positivist theories look at environmental factors, including socialization and temptations in the environment.

The Rotten Apple Theory

The **rotten apple theory** attributes police deviance to a few individuals who should not have become police officers and whose propensity toward corruption was not recognized during the recruitment and hiring phases. The implication of this theoretical perspective is that police agencies must continue to refine and improve their hiring procedures. The hope is that adequate screening for candidates of the highest moral character will prevent deviance from taking root in the department.

Identifying "rotten apples"—that is, officer candidates with a propensity for deviance—is difficult. Skilled liars will not be screened out during hiring. Psychological exams can only do so much, usually identifying only the most unfit of applicants. In response to these problems, some researchers have studied citizen complaints against the police in an effort to determine which officers receive the most complaints—hoping to discern the most common characteristics of "problem" officers. The authors of one study found that 7 percent of the officers in one department were responsible for more than one-third of all the complaints. The officers were younger and had less experience, and the complaints against them were more likely to arise from their proactive (as opposed to reactive) contacts with citizens.[32] These findings suggest that it is important to monitor police-citizen encounters and to focus on less seasoned officers.

Environmental Factors

Positivist criminologists explain crime in terms of environmental factors like peer influence, family conditions, and neighborhood characteristics. Applying this line of thinking to police deviance, it may be that some officers become deviant as a result of either a corrupt political environment or the socialization process. If a city or its police department shows a pattern of

Rotten Apple Theory

Police deviance caused by a few individuals who should not have become police officers and whose propensity toward corruption was not recognized during the recruitment and hiring phases.

Environmental Factors

Some officers become deviant as a result of either a corrupt political environment or the socialization process.

FIGURE 12.5 Explaining Police Deviance.

problem behavior, then it is understandable that some officers will fall victim to it. Some of the examples discussed earlier revealed cultures of corruption within a department or city, making it pretty clear why police deviance spreads.

Cases of systemic corruption are rare, especially these days. This forces us to look at other environmental explanations of police deviance, namely those stemming from the socialization process. It is easier to conceive of a few officers working together and reinforcing one another's behavior through graft and corruption than it is to conceive of a whole police department doing the same. In Chapter 5's discussion of police subculture, we saw, for instance, that the code of silence pervades police work. The code certainly presents problems for

TABLE 12.2	Factors Affecting the Development of Police Deviance.
Constant Factors	
Discretion	The exercise of discretion is argued to have both legitimate and illegitimate bases.
Low managerial visibility	A police officer's actions are often low in visibility as far as line management is concerned.
Low public visibility	Much of what police officers do is not witnessed by members of the public.
Peer group secrecy	Police subculture is characterized by a high degree of internal solidarity and secrecy.
Managerial secrecy	Police managers have generally worked themselves up from the beat and share many of the values held by those they manage.
Status problems	Police officers are sometimes said to be poorly paid relative to their powers.
Association with lawbreakers, contact with temptation	Police officers inevitably come into contact with a wide variety of people who have an interest in police not doing what they have a duty to do. Such people may have access to considerable resources.
Variable Factors	
Community structure	Refers to the degree of "anomie," the political "ethos," and the extent of culture conflict
Organizational characteristics	Levels of bureaucracy, integrity of leadership, solidarity of work subcultures, moral career stages of police officers, and the perception of legitimate opportunities
Legal opportunities for corruption	Moral: so-called victimless crimes associated with the policing of vice Regulative: the exploitation of minor or trivial regulations, such as those associated with construction, traffic, and licensing
Corruption controls	How the guardians are themselves "guarded"
Social organization of corruption	Two basic forms: arrangements and events
Moral cynicism	Association with lawbreakers and contact with temptation are inevitable in police work, inclining officers toward moral cynicism

Source: T. Newburn, *Understanding and preventing police corruption: Lessons from the literature* (London: Home Office, Policing and Reducing Crime Unit, 1999), p. 17. Reproduced under the terms of the Open Government License.

administrators who are intent on rooting out corruption and deviance. This, in turn, allows problems to persist because they are difficult to bring to light.

Some researchers have attributed police deviance to a mixture of constant and variable factors unique to police work. Examples of these factors appear in Table 12.2. Some would also say that the explanations of corruption that we have covered are too simple and that corruption is a nasty and complex self-reinforcing cycle. This idea can be seen in Figure 12.6. Note that the flowchart is not limited specifically to policing, but addresses public service in general.

How Common Is Police Deviance?

Noted police researcher Lawrence Sherman offered this enlightening commentary on the incidence of police corruption in 1978: "Most police departments have members who commit corrupt acts from time to time. Only some police departments, however, become corrupt police departments."[33] In other words, corruption was—and still is—relatively rare. The vast majority of law enforcement officers are law-abiding, upstanding professionals. Even so, it is important to consider just how common police deviance is. We also need to look beyond the high-profile cases and consider the whole gamut of police deviance, most of which is not as serious as the stories from New York, Los Angeles, and Miami would have us believe.

Unfortunately, just as it is difficult to estimate the true extent of crime (the so-called dark figure of crime), it is also difficult to estimate the true prevalence of police deviance. Corrupt officers try to keep their activities private, just as criminals try

It is difficult to estimate the true prevalence of police deviance.

to hide theirs. As a result, researchers have had to get creative. One researcher surveyed officers in a police department that he called South City. They were asked to estimate how frequently they thought officers engaged in five behaviors: sleeping on duty, using excessive force, having sex on duty, committing perjury, and drinking on duty. Sleeping on duty, brutality, and sex on duty were, surprisingly, considered the most common (40, 39, and 32 percent, respectively). In other words, officers estimated that nearly four in ten officers slept on duty or used excessive force and that more than three in ten had sex on duty.

Cases of officers selling drugs, stealing evidence, and committing crimes are relatively rare in comparison to less extreme examples of police deviance. Sleeping on the job, sexual misconduct, harassment, and similar behaviors are perhaps easier to commit without getting caught. In addition, they may be viewed as relatively minor when compared to some of the more serious examples of deviance and corruption cited earlier in this chapter. The studies just cited probably cannot be generalized to all law enforcement officials or police departments, but they provide some needed insight into the extent of the problem.

Controlling Police Deviance

Perhaps the best control for police deviance is to screen out applicants who are unfit for the job by conducting background investigations, polygraph evaluations, and psychological evaluations. Obviously, though, this approach has failed on more than one occasion. A remaining option is to constantly remind officers of how they should act when presented with ethical dilemmas. This is accomplished through the promotion of professional standards and through police codes of ethics.

If we move away from policing and focus on corruption throughout the public sector, we find a large body of literature about prevention.[34] One scholar advocates treating corruption as a disease.[35] First, the disease has to be identified (Stage One). Once the disease has been identified, so-called Stage Two and Stage Three responses can be crafted (Table 12.3).

Professional Standards

As policing has matured over time, most of the rampant corruption we witnessed in the past has subsided. Continued reinforcement of professional standards, however, is critical. Joycelyn Pollock, one of the country's experts on police ethics, offers a number of suggestions in this regard.[36] She couches these in terms of some simple questions for officers to answer. The first is the

FIGURE 12.6 The Self-Reinforcing Cycle of Corruption.
Source: L. Cobb and M. Gonzalez, *Corruption as a system of interlocking vicious cycles: Lessons from the NationLab* (Louisville, CO: Aetheling Consultants, 2005). Reprinted by permission.

TABLE 12.3 | The "Medical" Response to Corruption.

	Stage Two: Fighting "Ordinary" Corruption	Stage Three: Fighting Systemic Corruption
Key metaphor	Controlling corruption	Subverting corruption
Medical analogy	Strengthen the body to prevent the disease from taking hold; examples: exercise, nutrition, lifestyle	Attack the disease itself; examples: antibiotics, chemotherapy, surgery
Use analysis to find out	Where healthy systems are vulnerable and how to strengthen them	Where organized corruption is itself vulnerable and how to weaken it
Some key analytical questions	How are agents selected? How is the principal–agent–client relationship structured? What are the incentives? How can discretion be clarified and circumscribed? How can accountability be enhanced? How can the moral costs of corruption be increased?	How are corrupt deals made and kept secret? How are corrupt goods and services delivered? How are members recruited and disciplined? What "footprints" are there from corrupt activities? How can risks and penalties be created or enhanced? How can corrupt activities be carried out with impunity, and where are they vulnerable?
Draw inspiration from	Best practices in business management; public health programs	Best practices in fighting organized crime: pathology and medicine
Key functions in the fight against corruption	Audit, systems design, incentive and personnel systems, control, citizen oversight	All of these, *plus* undercover agents, infiltrators, turncoats and key witnesses, "dirty tricks"
Key actors in the fight against corruption	People who run the system; the "principal" (metaphorically, the people; in practice, the people in charge)	People who can influence and, if necessary, subvert the corrupt system; citizens, professional associations, the press, business groups, some government agencies or levels of government

Source: R. Klitgaard, "Stages two and three in the fight against corruption," *Finance and development* (June 2000), 37 (2), http://www.imf.org. Copyright © the International Monetary Fund. Used with permission.

so-called **first-page test**. The question is, "How would you feel if your action appeared on the front page of the newspaper?" The second question is, "How will you feel about your action when looking back on it?" Finally, "Would you consider your action fair if you were each of the other parties involved?" Or, put differently, "Did you treat others the way you would want to be treated?"[37] Pollock goes on to note,

> These questions are sometimes overlooked when making day-to-day decisions. Thoughtful policing involves being sensitized to the ethical nature of decision-making and, if being egotistic at times, at least recognizing such actions for what they are.[38]

Pollock also points out that police officers, as professionals, need to distinguish between good police work and what it means to be a good person. The two do not always go hand in hand. "Good" police officers are those who make many arrests, catch criminals, and so on. But Pollock notes that "being a 'good' officer may be contradictory to being a 'good' person, and the good people who become officers may be distressed to find that being a good person is not 'good enough.'"[39] So police officers must be constantly aware that being a good person is part of being a good officer. It is not all about making good busts at all costs. Indeed, one of the hallmarks of a profession is abiding by certain standards of conduct, and that means following the rules and upholding the law.

Codes of Ethics

Those police departments that do not train their officers how to act when presented with ethical dilemmas can at least adopt appropriate codes of ethics. The professional associations that

Think About It...

Citizen Complaints Citizen complaints are one mechanism by which police deviance can be rectified. But do they work? While many agencies have taken great strides toward improving their complaint procedures (see previous chapter), a great deal of research suggests that it is much more difficult to have a complaint sustained—that is, resolved in favor of the person filing the complaint. In your view, what percentage of citizen complaints lack merit? Can we conclude that citizen complaints don't work simply because the "sustained" rate is low? Explain.

Source: © Mikael Karlsson/Alamy

Consent Decrees Consent decrees are intended to promote police department integrity, and researchers have concluded that federal intervention does encourage long-term police accountability. However, critics of consent decrees argue that federal district courts assert too much power over the defendant (police departments). Do you think consent decrees are a good thing? Are there any alternatives that would keep police departments accountable for their behavior?

Source: JustASC/Shutterstock.com

many officers are affiliated with (such as the Fraternal Order of Police) have them.

In fact, most professions have ethical codes of one form or another. Doctors, nurses, and attorneys have them. Even the authors of this textbook have to abide by ethical codes either established through their place of employment or promulgated by the professional associations with which they are affiliated (such as Academy of Criminal Justice Sciences).

Consent Decrees

During the 1990s, Congress gave the Civil Rights Division of the U.S. Justice Department authority to sue state and local governments in federal court in order to correct any "pattern or practice" of police misconduct. To avoid drawn-out courtroom battles, police departments that find themselves subjected to Justice Department misconduct investigations often enter into so-called consent decrees with the federal government. A **consent decree** is a voluntary agreement, approved by a federal court, between both parties that the police department in question will cease the improprieties of which it is suspected. The decree outlines specific policy and practice changes sought by the federal government.

A number of police departments have entered into consent decrees with the federal government in the wake of corruption scandals. Pittsburgh was the first to do so. It was required to make a number of changes. One was the implementation of a computerized early-warning system to track officers' compliance. Another was to more carefully document the use of force, traffic stops, and the like.

The decree also required reforms to the Bureau of Police citizen complaint procedure. Progress was monitored by a federal official who reported quarterly on Pittsburgh's progress.

Not only was Pittsburgh the first city to have its police department enter into a consent decree with the federal government, but it was also the first to have its progress subjected to research. The Vera Institute of Justice collected data from before and after the Pittsburgh consent decree was put in place.[40] The organization interviewed stakeholders in the community, conducted focus groups with officers, interviewed citizens, and analyzed official data. After analyzing the data, researchers concluded that "[t]here are strong signs a year after most of the decree has been lifted that federal intervention can encourage long-term improvements in police accountability."[41]

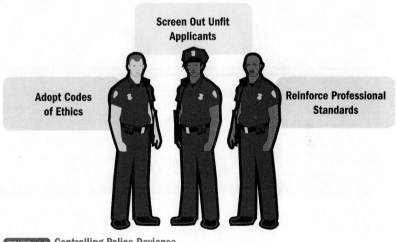

FIGURE 12.7 Controlling Police Deviance.

Media Bias

Police officers in California's Laguna Beach confronted a man and a woman who were apparently having a domestic dispute at a luxury oceanfront resort. Callers to the 911 emergency operators reported that the woman was running around the expensive hotel naked, waving a gun. When officers arrived at the couple's room, the pair passed the gun back and forth between them, and then the woman pointed it at the officers. At that point, the officers fired into the room, killing the couple.

Without knowing more about what actually happened, one might be inclined to criticize the police shooting of *both* the man and the woman. After all, only one of them could hold the gun at a time, and the officers might have taken better aim. Still, the officers who responded to the call were clearly in danger, and they may have thought that they had no choice but to shoot both people. What's interesting about this case, however, is the media's reaction to the shooting. It seemed as if reporters were *hoping* that the officers had acted improperly and that they *wanted* to inflame the public. The following day, for example, an MSNBC story based on details provided by the Associated Press recounted the incident in an article titled "Cops Kill Couple at Luxury Oceanfront Resort."[42] The story described the shootings as "the first homicides in Laguna Beach in nearly four years."

The language used by the media raises several questions that bear on the subject of police deviance:

1. Was the use of the phrase "cops kill" in the Associated Press headline unnecessarily inflammatory?

2. Was *homicide* a good choice of words, or should the reporter have made it clear that the police officers fired in self-defense?

3. Did the MSNBC story pass judgment on the officers too quickly?

4. Is there a preexisting bias in this country's media against the police?

5. What might explain the apparent desire by at least some members of the press to paint the police as deviant or even criminal?

6. Is police deviance a real problem in this country, or is it largely a creation of the media?

Source: Jerry Sharp/Shutterstock.com

Discuss how various commissions established to examine police misconduct in the United States have uncovered deviance.

The Wickersham (1929) and Knapp Commissions were credited with uncovering police deviance. The Wickersham Commission, in its report, *Lawlessness in Law Enforcement*, found that the "third degree," or "the inflicting of pain, physical or mental, to extract confessions or statements," was "extensively practiced across the country."

1. What did the Wickersham and Knapp Commissions investigate?

2. What did the commissions find? How did their findings differ, if at all?

3. What sources of information were especially important to members of both commissions?

4. What's the difference between a grass eater and a meat eater?

corruption Dishonest or fraudulent conduct by public officials in a position of power.

deviance Any behavior that is at odds with socially expected or accepted behavior.

Knapp Commission A commission to investigate police corruption that was appointed by New York City Mayor John V. Lindsay in 1970 in response to a *New York Times* article that reported widespread corruption in the New York City Police Department.

white knight An honest and upstanding officer who never steps over the line between accepted and deviant conduct, no matter how great the pressure to do so.

straight shooter An honest police officer who will overlook some misconduct committed by peers.

grass eater A police officer who accepts small gifts and engages in minor acts of deviance but does not actively pursue opportunities for corruption.

meat eater A police officer who actively seeks out and plans opportunities to exploit his or her position for personal gain.

rogue A seriously deviant officer.

Identify several typologies of police deviance that scholars have proposed.

Scholars have proposed several typologies of police deviance. Some focus on forms of corruption, while others focus on types of deviance. Gratuities (that is, gifts) are perhaps the most minor form of deviance. Some people don't regard them as deviance at all but rather as relationship builders. Police sexual misconduct includes everything from consensual sex on duty to rape. The ongoing "war on drugs" presents significant temptations to officers to step over the line.

1. Describe the typologies of police deviance discussed in this chapter, and give examples of each.

2. List and describe some infamous instances of police deviance.

3. When and where did the Mollen Commission function? What was its purpose? What did it find?

4. What is meant by the term *noble-cause corruption*? How does it apply to police work?

5. What is meant by the term *perversion of justice*? How does it apply to police corruption?

police crime An officer's use of the official powers of his or her job to engage in criminal conduct.

occupational deviance Behavior performed under the guise of police authority that either does not conform to accepted standards of conduct or is not part of normal patrol work.

police corruption The misuse of police authority for personal or organizational gain.

abuse of authority A catchall category for various forms of inappropriate police conduct that do not necessarily amount to crime, deviance, or corruption.

straightforward corruption Any form of police misconduct that provides direct financial benefit to police officers.

predatory corruption A form of police corruption that consists of more than just passive participation (for example, looking the other way while a fellow police officer commits a crime). In predatory corruption, officers actively promote and engage in criminal and other wrongful activities.

perversion of justice A kind of police corruption that consists of serious actions by a police officer, such as lying under oath (perjury), intimidating a witness, and performing other activities that resemble combative corruption.

Mollen Commission A commission appointed by New York City Mayor David N. Dinkins in 1992 to investigate allegations of police corruption in the New York City Police Department.

gratuity Something of value that is freely given to police officers simply because they are police officers. Examples include a cup of coffee, a lunch, or a "police price" discount on a meal or other service.

police sexual violence A sexually degrading, humiliating, violating, damaging, or threatening act committed by a police officer against a (usually female) citizen through the use of force or police authority.

use corruption Drug-related police corruption that consists of an officer's personal use of illicit drugs.

economic corruption Drug-related police corruption in which an officer seeks personal gain by stealing drugs, selling drugs, or extorting money from drug dealers.

police violence In the context of drug investigations, the use of improper physical force to extract a confession or to obtain evidence.

subjugation of defendants' rights In the context of drug investigations, an officer's lying or committing perjury or fabricating evidence in the name of securing a drug conviction.

noble-cause corruption Any corruption that occurs in connection with the goal of getting criminals off the streets and protecting the community.

Discuss explanations for police deviance, its incidence, and methods of controlling it.

Two theories of police deviance were offered in this chapter. The rotten apple theory argues that deviance is primarily the result of the corrupt activities of a few rogue officers. A second perspective, environmental theory, attributes deviance to peer pressure and other organizational factors. The true extent of police corruption remains elusive, rather like the dark figure of crime. Police deviance, however, can be controlled through rigorous hiring procedures, professional standards and training, and codes of ethics.

1. How common is police deviance?

2. How does the rotten apple theory explain police deviance?

3. How does environmental theory explain police deviance?

4. How can police deviance be controlled?

rotten apple theory A perspective that attributes police deviance primarily to a few individuals whose propensity toward corruption was not recognized during the recruitment and hiring phases.

first-page test A series of questions proposed by Joycelyn Pollock that police officers can ask themselves to reinforce professional ethical standards.

consent decree A legal settlement in which one entity agrees to take certain actions or rectify a particular problem without admitting to any illegality. Consent decrees are sometimes used in law enforcement following corruption scandals; a decree requires the police department to fix a particular problem and/or end a particular course of action.

MyCJLab

Go to the Chapter 12 section in *MyCJLab* to test your understanding of this chapter, access customized study content, engage in interactive simulations, complete critical thinking and research assignments, and view related online videos.

Additional Links

Measuring the professionalism of police officers is discussed at **http://tinyurl.com/2fgq6q**. The measurement of police integrity is reviewed at **www.justicestudies.com/pubs/policeintegrity.pdf**.

Papers about enhancing police integrity (**www.justicestudies.com/pubs/enhancing.pdf**) and principles for promoting police integrity (**www.justicestudies.com/pubs/promotingintegrity.pdf**) are available at the Justice Studies site.

Law enforcement ethics forms the subject matter of **www.justicestudies.com/pubs/leethics.pdf**, while developing and sustaining a culture of integrity within police organizations is discussed at **http://tinyurl.com/23lq7w**.

Studies of bad cops are available at **www.justicestudies.com/pubs/badcops.pdf** and **http://tinyurl.com/55jd5b**.

Education, training, and ethical dilemmas of relevance to policing can be reviewed at **www.justicestudies.com/pubs/education.pdf**.

The Use of Force

"Studies show that police use force
in fewer than 20 percent of adult
custodial arrests."

1 Identify the various levels of force, explain how they are controlled by policy, and describe their applications in police work.

2 Describe legal standards associated with the use of deadly force by law enforcement officers, explain the patterns of deadly force, and describe the problem of suicide by cop.

3 Describe legal standards governing nondeadly force, including less-lethal weapons.

4 List three types of excessive force.

13

In mid-2011, the Civil Rights Division of the U.S. Department of Justice released details of its investigation of the New Orleans Police Department (NOPD). The investigation was launched following a spate of what appeared to be inappropriate use-of-force incidents during and after Hurricane Katrina in 2005. It did not, however, focus on those incidents as many of them were under formal court review. Instead, the DOJ document looked at use-of-force incidents involving the department in 2009 and 2010. The investigation, "revealed a clear pattern of unconstitutional uses of force by NOPD officers." A study of officer-involved shootings found "many instances in which NOPD officers used deadly force contrary to NOPD policy or law." Investigators also discovered a pattern of unreasonable use of less-than-lethal force. Numerous incidents of the inappropriate use of force against individuals in handcuffs and against nonthreatening mentally ill persons were likewise identified and termed "not only unnecessary but deliberately retaliatory." In the words of DOJ investigators summarizing their findings, "Our investigation found reasonable cause to believe that NOPD has engaged in a pattern or practice of conduct that deprives individuals of rights, privileges, or immunities secured or protected by the Constitution or laws of the United States."[1] Read the entire document detailing the DOJ's investigation of the New Orleans Police Department online at http://justicestudies.com//policing/NOPDreport.pdf.

> **DISCUSS** What problems were identified within the NOPD? How might such problems be avoided in other departments?

Police **use of force** is defined as the use of physical restraint by a police officer when dealing with a member of the public.[2] Law enforcement officers are authorized to use the amount of force that is reasonable and necessary given the circumstances. Most officers are trained in the use of force and typically encounter numerous situations during their careers when the use of force is appropriate—for example, when making some arrests, restraining unruly combatants, or controlling a disruptive demonstration. Force may involve hitting; holding or restraining; pushing; choking; threatening with or using a baton, a flashlight, or chemical or pepper spray; restraining with a police dog; using a Taser* or a similar energy weapon; or threatening with or using a gun.

A more complex issue is the use of *excessive* force. The International Association of Chiefs of Police defines **excessive force** as "the application of an amount and/or frequency of force greater than that required to compel compliance from a willing or unwilling subject."[3] When excessive force is employed, the activities of the police often come under public scrutiny and receive attention from the media and legislators. A police officer's use of excessive force can also result in lawsuits by members of the public who feel that they have been treated unfairly. Whether the use of excessive force is aberrant behavior on the part of an individual officer or is the practice of an entire law enforcement agency, both the law and public opinion generally condemn it.

Kenneth Adams, an expert in the use of force by police, notes that there is an important difference between the terms *use of* *excessive force*, such as shoving or pushing when simply grabbing a suspect would be adequate, and the *excessive use of force*, which refers to the phenomenon of force being used unacceptably, often on a department-wide basis. The distinction "deals with relative comparisons among police agencies, and there are no established criteria for judgment."[4] The *use of excessive force* and the *excessive use of force* may also be distinguished from the *illegal use of force*, which refers to situations in which the use of force by police violates a law or statute.[5]

Excessive force can be symptomatic of **problem police officers**. Problem officers are those who exhibit problem behavior, as indicated by a large number of citizen complaints, frequent involvement in use-of-force incidents, and other evidence.[6] The **Christopher Commission**, which studied the structure and operation of the Los Angeles Police Department (LAPD) in the wake of the **Rodney King** beating, found a number of "repeat offenders" on the force.[7] According to the commission, approximately 1,800 LAPD officers were alleged to have used excessive force or improper tactics between 1986 and 1990. Of these officers, more than 1,400 had only one or two allegations against them. Another 183 officers had four or more allegations, 44 had six or more, 16 had eight or more, and 1 officer had sixteen such allegations. The commission also found that, generally speaking, the 44 officers with six complaints or more had received positive performance evaluations that failed to record "sustained" complaints or to discuss their significance.

▶ Use of Force

Use of force and *use of excessive force* are not one and the same. Most of this chapter is concerned with the legitimate use of force. We save the discussion of improper force for the end of the chapter. What, then, are the types of force? When can force be used? How often do officers use force? What distinguishes deadly force from nondeadly force? What are the rules governing an officer's use of force? We answer these and related questions in the next few sections.

Levels of Force

Whether police officers use force properly or improperly, seven levels of force have been identified and noted in Figure 13.1.

Our concern in this chapter is primarily with the last two types of force noted in Figure 13.1 (Impact Techniques and Deadly Force). These are the most likely to result in the injury or death of a suspect. Moreover, of all of the levels of

Deadly force. This is force that is capable of killing the suspect. An example is the use of a gun.[i]

Impact techniques. Impact techniques may involve physical contact or the use of chemical spray or stunning weapons.

Pain compliance. These tactics seek the suspect's compliance by causing pain. They should not cause lasting physical injury.

Firm grips. These are physical grips on the body directing a suspect when and where to move. They are not intended to cause pain.

Command voice. An officer's command voice is more vibrant than his or her speaking voice, and the officer's request takes the form of an order: "Sir, I asked you for your vehicle papers once. Now I'm *telling* you to give them to me *now*."

Verbalization. Officers are taught to speak persuasively. If verbalization doesn't work, officers move on to more forcible options.

Mere presence. It is believed that the simple presence of an officer, the embodiment of the authority of the state, will deter dangerous and criminal behavior.

[i] J. P. Crank, *Understanding police culture* (Cincinnati: Anderson, 1998), p. 78. See also J. H. Skolnick and J. J. Fyfe, *Above the law: Police and the excessive use of force* (New York: Free Press, 1993).

FIGURE 13.1 **Levels of Force.**

force, they attract the most attention. All too often, it seems, bystanders record what they perceive to be police brutality. Sometimes such recordings *do* reveal brutality. Other times, though, untrained bystanders may fail to understand that what an officer did to apprehend a resistant suspect followed the police agency's policy to the letter.

LEARNING OUTCOMES 1 Identify the various levels of force, explain how they are controlled by policy, and describe their applications in police work.

Use of Force Policy

Justifiable force is not applied arbitrarily. Police officers are trained to use only the necessary level of force to gain control over a situation or to subdue an unruly suspect. Sometimes

Police officers are trained to use only the minimum level of force necessary.

Suspect resistance

No resistance. Suspect was cooperative and followed all verbal instructions given by the officer.

Slight resistance. Suspect resisted the officer's actions, and the officer had to use strong directive language or minimal force (skills) to encourage suspect to cooperate and follow directions.

Moderate or high resistance. Suspect impeded officer's movement or resisted cuffing or placement in a car. This level of resistance required the officer to use arm/wrist locks, distraction techniques, or fighting skills to gain compliance and control.

Violent or explosive resistance. In this, the most extreme, level of resistance, the suspect struggled or fought violently and required the officer to (1) use fighting skills to disengage; (2) use a chemical agent, baton, or firearm; or (3) continue

fighting to gain control. In some cases in this resistance category, the officer may have decided that he or she needed to use weapons or other special tactics to gain control instead of engaging the suspect directly.

Officer force

No force. Officer used typical verbal commands.

Slight force. Officer had to use strong directive language or minimal physical force to encourage the suspect to cooperate and follow directions.

Forcibly subdued suspect with hands. Officer used an arm/wrist lock, take down, block, punch, or kick, or he or she struck or wrestled the suspect.

Forcibly subdued suspect using methods other than hands. Officer used chemical agent, baton, gun, or other special tactics or weapons.

FIGURE 13.2 **Force-Related Terminology.**
  Source: G.P. Alpert and R.G. Dunham, "The force factor: Measuring police use of force relative to suspect resistance," in *Use of force by police: Overview of national and local data* (Washington, DC: Bureau of Justice Statistics, 1999), p. 55. Full report available at http://bjs.ojp.usdoj.gov/index.cfm?ty=pbdetail&iid=809 (accessed April 30, 2011).

they are taught a **force continuum**, or use-of-force continuum. Other times their policy manuals contain elaborate descriptions of proper and improper force. Some agencies combine both approaches. Figure 13.2 contains some force-related terminology that will help you work through this section.

An example of a use-of-force continuum, this one from the Federal Law Enforcement Training Center (FLETC), appears in Figure 13.3. The left side looks at the suspect's action. The right side looks at the appropriate response the officer should use. So, for example, if the suspect is compliant, an officer should only use "cooperative controls." These include verbal commands. At the other end of the continuum, if the officer perceives that the suspect is assaultive and likely to inflict serious injury or death, deadly force is justified.

Another force continuum appears in Table 13.1. This one is from the Phoenix (Arizona) Police Department. Seven categories of suspect behavior are listed alongside seven categories of police response. No resistance should equate with no force. Passive resistance, such as laying down and obstructing a road or entrance to a facility, should be met with control and restraint, sometimes coupled with arrest and use of handcuffs. Finally, a suspect who wields a firearm could very likely be shot—and justifiably so. More often than not, law enforcement agencies adopt use-of-force policies that are far more detailed and restrictive than the force continuums just presented.

Additionally, the agency's policy manual explains in detail what type of force can be used and when. A list of suspect actions is provided, along with proper responses deputies can use.

In a study reported in 2001, police experts Geoffrey Alpert and Roger Dunham found that the **force factor**—the level of force used by the police relative to the suspect's

FIGURE 13.3 **Use-of-Force Continuum.**
  Source: Federal Law Enforcement Training Center, Department of Homeland Security.

TABLE 13.1 | Phoenix Police Department Force Continuum

Police	Suspects
0. No force	0. No resistance
1. Police presence	1. Psychological intimidation
2. Verbal commands	2. Verbal noncompliance
3. Control and restraint (handcuffs)	3. Passive resistance
4. Chemical agents	4. Defensive resistance
5. Tactics and weapons[a]	5. Active aggression
6. Firearms/deadly force	6. Firearms/deadly force

[a]Includes all physical tactics and weapons except chemical agents and firearms.

Source: J. Garner and others, Understanding the use of force by and against the police (Washington, DC: National Institute of Justice, 1996), p. 5.

level of resistance—is a key element to consider in attempting to reduce injuries to both the police and suspects.[8] The force factor is calculated by measuring both the suspect's level of resistance and the officer's level of force on an equivalent scale and by then subtracting the level of resistance from the level of police force used. Results from the study indicate that, on average, the level of force that officers use is closely related to the type of training that their departments emphasize.

force continuum The spectrum of force available to a police officer, from the absence of physical force to the use of a deadly weapon.

force factor The level of force used by a police officer relative to the suspect's level of resistance.

Applications of Force

The National Institute of Justice estimates that nearly 45 million people nationwide have face-to-face contact with the police over a typical 12-month period and that approximately 700,000 of them are subjected to the use of force or the threat of force.[9] When handcuffing is included in the definition of force, the number of people subjected to force increases to 1.2 million, or slightly more than 2.5 percent of those having contact with the police. Other studies show that police use weaponless tactics in approximately 80 percent of use-of-force incidents and that half of all use-of-force incidents involve merely grabbing or holding the suspect.[10]

Studies show that police use force in fewer than 20 percent of adult custodial arrests. Even in instances where force is used, the police primarily use weaponless tactics. For example, a study of more than 7,000 police arrests in Phoenix revealed that no weapon was displayed, much less used, in about 95 percent of the arrests.[11] In addition, female officers are less likely to use physical force and firearms and are more likely to use

20% Studies show that police use force in fewer than 20 percent of adult custodial arrests.

chemical weapons (mostly pepper spray) than are their male counterparts.

Who is most likely to experience police force? Perhaps not surprisingly, males, African-Americans, and younger people are most likely to experience force:

Blacks (4.4%) and Hispanics (2.3%) were more likely than whites (1.2%) to experience use of force during contact with police in 2005. Blacks accounted for 1 out of 10 contacts with police but 1 out of 4 contacts where force was used. Persons age 16 to 29 (2.8%) who had contact with police were more likely than those over age 29 (1.0%) to have had force used against them. Persons age 16 to 29 made up a smaller percentage of persons who had a police contact (34.5%) compared to the percentage of persons experiencing force during a contact (60.3%). The median age of those experiencing force was 26.[12]

The nature of the contact is also associated with whether force is used. People whose contact was initiated by the police were much more likely to see force used. Indeed, about 80 percent of the contacts involving use of force were initiated by the police. This, too, is not surprising because police-initiated contacts are those where officers generally witness a criminal act or a person they suspect of having committed a crime. Sometimes these suspects flee, and force is required to stop them.

▶ Deadly Force

Generally speaking, **deadly force** is force that is likely to cause death or significant bodily harm. *Black's Law Dictionary* adopts a more general definition, namely "force that may result in the death of the person against whom the force is applied."[13] According to a report released by the Bureau of Justice Statistics in 2001, the number of justifiable homicides by police averages nearly 400 per year.[14]

The use of deadly force by law enforcement officers, especially when it is *not* considered justifiable, is one area of potential civil liability that has received considerable attention in recent years. Historically, the "fleeing-felon rule" applied to most U.S. jurisdictions. It held that officers could use deadly force to prevent the escape of a suspected felon, even when that person represented no immediate threat to the officer or to the public. This, as we will see, has changed.

Legal Standards

The 1985 U.S. Supreme Court case of **Tennessee v. Garner**[15] specified the conditions under which deadly force can be used to apprehend a suspected felon. Edward Garner, a 15-year-old suspected burglar, was shot to death by Memphis police after he refused their order to halt and attempted to climb over a chain-link fence. In an action initiated by Garner's father, who claimed that his son's constitutional rights had been violated, the Court held that the use of deadly force by the police to prevent the escape of a fleeing felon could

LEARNING OUTCOMES 2

Describe legal standards associated with the use of deadly force by law enforcement officers, explain the patterns of deadly force, and describe the problem of suicide by cop.

GLOSSARY

deadly force Force that is likely to cause death or significant bodily harm.

Tennessee v. Garner The 1985 U.S. Supreme Court case that specified the conditions under which deadly force could be used to apprehend suspected felons.

suicide by cop An incident in which an individual who is determined to die engages in behavior meant to provoke responding officers to resort to deadly force.

be justified only where the suspect could reasonably be thought to represent a significant threat of serious injury or death to the public or to the officer and where deadly force is necessary to effect the arrest. In reaching its decision, the Court declared that "[t]he use of deadly force to prevent the escape of *all* felony suspects, whatever the circumstances, is constitutionally unreasonable."

More specifically, the Court ruled that deadly force may be used when two criteria are present: (1) It is necessary to prevent the suspect's escape, and (2) the officer has probable cause to believe that the suspect poses a serious threat of death or serious physical injury to others. Given the nature of the *Garner* case, one would think the Court would have handed down a unanimous decision, but three justices dissented, noting that the statute struck down by the majority "assist[s] the police in apprehending suspected perpetrators of serious crimes and provide[s] notice that a lawful police order to stop and submit to arrest may not be ignored with impunity."[16] In any case, to further grasp the reach of *Garner*, it is important to consider the notion of what kind of offender poses a "serious threat." Courts will generally consider present and/or past dangerousness.

Present Dangerousness

According to Victor Kappeler of Eastern Kentucky University, "[A] dangerous suspect is, generally, an armed suspect who can inflict serious physical harm."[17] Fingernail clippers, for

Deadly force is force that is likely to cause death or significant bodily harm.

example, cannot be considered a deadly weapon.

In one illustrative case, one of the federal district courts concluded that the police used deadly force inappropriately in killing a woman (Hegarty) when

Hegarty repeatedly asked the officers to leave, but she neither threatened them nor did she fire any shots while the officers were present. In fact, the officers decided to enter Hegarty's home forcibly only after it appeared that she had put down her rifle. Hegarty did not threaten injury to herself at any time, nor were there other individuals in danger.[18]

Past Dangerousness

A suspect can also pose a serious threat based on his or her past conduct or based on the nature of the crime in question. Less serious offenses, in general, do not enhance the police authority to use deadly force.

It should be emphasized that only a handful of courts have permitted deadly force based solely on past dangerousness, and the U.S. Supreme Court has never sanctioned such action. In fact, a federal circuit court of appeals has held that the use of deadly force to apprehend a suspect charged with a serious crime is unconstitutional.[19] For example, if a suspect committed robbery but was then confronted by the police and, following their orders, raised his hands, he could not then be shot.

Finally, if police are going to defend deadly force based on past dangerousness, then the serious offense that the suspect is alleged to have committed must have been committed in the recent past. In other words, officers should avoid deadly force if too much time has elapsed between the crime and the use of deadly force. For example, if a police officer used deadly force based solely on the fact that a suspect committed homicide several months ago, the officer's actions would probably be considered unconstitutional. This is especially true if the officer could have used other methods besides the use of deadly force to apprehend the suspect.

Federal Policy

In 1995, following investigations into the actions of federal agents at the deadly siege of the Branch Davidian compound at Waco, Texas, and the tragic deaths associated with a 1992 FBI assault on antigovernment separatists in Ruby Ridge, Idaho, the federal government announced that it was adopting an "imminent danger" standard for the use of deadly force by federal agents. The imminent danger standard restricts the use of deadly force to situations in which the

The federal imminent danger standard restricts the use of deadly force to situations in which the lives of agents or others are in danger.

Think About It...

Tennessee v. Garner *Tennessee* v. *Garner* was important because it set the standard for police deadly force; no longer could an officer shoot an unarmed fleeing felon. Many law enforcement agencies were forced to revise their deadly force policies, but other agencies already had restrictive deadly force policies in place prior to *Garner*, suggesting that the decision may have only had a modest effect. Do you think the *Garner* decision made a difference in how often officers shoot their weapons? Why or why not? Read the *Garner* decision and summarize the court's logic for its rule. Three justices dissented. Read the case and summarize their perspective.

Source: 1qaz7ty / Shutterstock.com

lives of agents or others are in danger. When the new standard was announced, federal agencies were criticized for not adopting it sooner. The federal policy, as adopted by the FBI, is highlighted in Figure 13.4.

Patterns of Deadly Force

Studies of killings by the police have often focused on claims of discrimination—that is, that African-American and minority suspects are more likely to be shot than Caucasians. But research has not provided solid support for such claims. While individuals shot by police are more likely to be minorities, an early study by criminologist James Fyfe found that police officers will generally respond with deadly force when mortally threatened and that minorities are considerably more likely to use weapons in assaults on officers than are whites.[20] Complicating the picture further, Fyfe's study showed that minority officers are involved in the shootings of suspects more often than other officers, a finding that may be due to the assignment of minority officers to poor inner-city areas. However, a later study by Fyfe, which analyzed police shootings in Memphis, Tennessee, found that African-American property offenders were twice as likely as Caucasians to be shot by police.[21]

Although relatively few police officers ever fire their weapons at suspects during the course of their careers, those who do may become embroiled in social, legal, and personal

---

Federal Policy The federal deadly force policy, as adopted by the FBI, contains the following elements:[i]

Defense of life. Agents may use deadly force only when necessary—that is, only when they have probable cause to believe that the subject poses an imminent danger of death or serious physical injury to the agent or to others.

Fleeing subject. Deadly force may be used to prevent the escape of a fleeing subject if there is probable cause to believe that the subject has committed a felony involving the infliction or threatened infliction of serious physical injury or death and that the subject's escape would pose an imminent danger of death or serious physical injury to the agents or to others.

Verbal warnings. If feasible, and if doing so would not increase the danger to the agent or to others, a verbal warning to submit to the authority of the agent should be given prior to the use of deadly force.

Warning shots. Agents may not fire warning shots.

Vehicles. Agents may not fire weapons solely to disable moving vehicles. Weapons may be fired at the driver or other occupant of a moving motor vehicle only when the agent has probable cause to believe that the subject poses an imminent danger of death or serious physical injury to the agent or to others and when the use of deadly force does not create a danger to the public that outweighs the likely benefits of its use.

[i] J. C. Hall, "FBI training on the new federal deadly force policy," *FBI Law Enforcement Bulletin* (April 1996): 25–32.

FIGURE 13.4 Deadly Force.

complications. It is estimated that in an average year, 600 suspects are killed by police officers in America, 1,200 are shot and wounded, and 1,800 are shot at and missed.[22] The personal side of police shootings is well summarized in the title of an article that appeared in *Police Magazine*. The article, "I've Killed That Man Ten Thousand Times," demonstrates how police officers who have to use their weapons may be haunted by years of depression and despair.[23] According to author Anne Cohen, all departments did to help officers who had shot someone was to "give him enough bullets to reload his gun." The stress and trauma that police officers suffer from having shot someone are now being realized, and many departments have developed mechanisms for dealing with them.[24]

Suicide by Cop

Police officers have particular difficulty dealing with instances of **suicide by cop**, in which individuals who are determined to die engage in behavior that causes responding officers to resort to deadly force. On March 10, 2005, for example, John T. Garczynski, Jr., a father of two preteen boys, died in a hail of 26 police bullets fired by officers who had surrounded his vehicle in a Boca Raton, Florida, condominium parking lot.[25] Garczynski, a Florida Power and Light Company employee, appeared to have been despondent over financial problems and the breakup of his marriage. The night before his death, Garczynski met his wife at a bowling alley and handed her a packet containing a suicide note, a typed obituary, and a eulogy to be read at his funeral. After he left, Garczynski's wife called police, and officers used the help of a cell phone company to locate Garczynski. As deputies surrounded Garczynski's 2003 Ford Explorer, he attempted to start the vehicle. One of the officers yelled "Freeze," and then "Let me see your hands." It was at that point, deputies said, that Garczynski pointed a gun at them and they fired.

Rebecca Stincelli, author of the book *Suicide by Cop: Victims from Both Sides of the Badge*,[26] says that an incident like the one involving Garczynski can be devastating for police officers. "In the past, people have used rope, a gun, gas, jumped off a building. A police officer is just another method," says Stincelli. "They say it's nothing personal. [But] they are wrong. It's very personal" for the officers involved.[27] The FBI notes that "suicide-by-cop incidents are painful and damaging experiences for the surviving families, the communities, and all law enforcement professionals."[28]

A study of fatal shootings by Los Angeles police officers found that an astonishingly large number—more than 10 percent—could be classified as suicide by cop.[29] Recently, researchers have identified three main categories of suicide by cop: direct confrontations, in which suicidal subjects instigate attacks on police officers for the purpose of dying; disturbed interventions, in which potentially suicidal subjects take advantage of

600

In an average year, 600 suspects are killed by police officers in America, 1,200 are shot and wounded, and 1,800 are shot at and missed.

police intervention in their suicide attempt in order to die; and criminal interventions, in which criminal suspects prefer death to capture and arrest.[30]

Several steps for managing suicide-by-cop scenarios have been suggested:

- Contain the area, while remaining aware that too close a containment may allow the precipitator [the suicidal person] to provoke a deadly confrontation.
- If time and circumstances allow, make a clear demand for compliance—a demand that will usually be ignored.
- Ask the person what he or she wants (specifically, ask if they are trying to die).
- If family, friends, or acquaintances of the subject are present, ask if they are aware of the subject's mental health history, chemical dependency, or any criminal record.
- Remain a good listener, while avoiding making promises or committing to anything.
- Use a less-lethal weapon only as a diversionary tactic before making a planned attempt to apprehend but never as a stand-alone tactic, as the use of such devices without an immediate attempt to apprehend may in fact escalate the situation.[31]

It may seem silly to ask the apparently suicidal individual about his or her intentions, but failure to do so can result in needless death:

> While the individual shot by police may have committed a suicidal act, he may not have been suicidal. In fact, the offender's physical survival probably did not enter his thought processes at the moment he made his fateful decision. Instead, this person was momentarily indifferent to the consequences of his threatening behavior. Rather than suicide by cop, he committed "death by indifference."[32]

▶ *Nondeadly Force*

We defined *deadly force* as force that is likely to cause death or significant bodily harm. **Nondeadly force** is basically the opposite: force that is *unlikely* to cause death or significant bodily harm. We cannot safely say that nondeadly force will always prevent injury or preserve loss of life because sometimes—rarely—people die as a result of injuries suffered from nondeadly force. This is more true of so-called less-lethal weapons, which we will introduce shortly, than physical force, although people sometimes die or suffer long-term injury from physical force, too.

Legal Standards

In the 1989 case of **Graham v. Connor**,[33] the U.S. Supreme Court declared that claims of excessive nondeadly force must be judged under the Fourth Amendment's reasonableness clause:

> [A]ll claims that law enforcement officers have used excessive force—deadly or not—in the course of an arrest, investigatory stop, or other "seizure" of a free citizen should be analyzed under the Fourth Amendment and its "reasonableness" standard.[34]

The Court also said that whether deadly force has been used appropriately should be judged from the perspective of a reasonable officer on the scene and not with the benefit of 20/20 hindsight. The justices wrote, "The calculus of reasonableness must embody allowance for the fact that police officers are often forced to make split-second judgments—in circumstances that are tense, uncertain, and rapidly evolving—about the amount of force that is necessary in a particular situation."[35]

In helping to decide what a reasonable police officer would do, courts need to consider three factors: the severity of the crime, whether the suspect poses a threat, and whether the suspect is resisting or attempting to flee the scene. Generally, if the crime in question is a serious one and the suspect is dangerous or resists arrest, the suspect will have difficulty prevailing with a claim of excessive force.

LEARNING OUTCOMES 3 Describe legal standards governing nondeadly force, including less-lethal weapons.

GLOSSARY

nondeadly force Force that is unlikely to cause death or significant bodily harm.

Graham v. Connor The 1989 U.S. Supreme Court case in which the Court declared that claims of excessive nondeadly force must be judged under the Fourth Amendment's reasonableness clause.

less-lethal weapon A weapon that is designed to disable, capture, or immobilize, rather than kill.

Less-Lethal Weapons

Less-lethal weapons offer what may be a problem-specific solution to potential incidents of suicide by cop, as well as a generic solution to at least some charges of use of excessive force. Less-lethal weapons are designed to disable, capture, or immobilize, rather than kill.

Efforts to provide law enforcement officers with less-lethal weapons like stun guns, Tasers, rubber bullets, beanbag projectiles, and pepper spray began in 1987.[36] More exotic types of less-lethal weapons are available today. They include snare nets fired from shotguns, disabling sticky foam that can be sprayed from a distance, microwave beams that heat the tissue of people exposed to them until they desist or lose consciousness, and high-tech guns that fire bolts of electromagnetic energy at a target, causing painful sensory overload and violent muscle spasms. The National Institute of Justice says, "The goal

Less-lethal weapons are not always safe and may sometimes cause death.

is to give line officers effective and safe alternatives to lethal force."[37]

As their name implies, however, less-lethal weapons are not always safe. On October 21, 2004, for example, 21-year-old Emerson College student Victoria Snelgrove died hours after being hit in the eye with a plastic pepper-spray-filled projectile. Police officers had fired the projectile at a rowdy crowd celebrating after the Red Sox won the American League Championship. Witnesses said that officers fired into the crowd after a reveler near Fenway Park threw a bottle at a mounted Boston police officer.[38] The following sections look at three families of less-lethal weapons. There are others besides those we discuss here, but these are some of the most widely used.

Conducted Energy Devices

The most popular **conducted energy device (CED)** is the familiar Taser. One of the most common Taser models is the so-called X26 ECD. The Taser International website explains how it works:

> The TASER X26 Electronic Control Device (ECD) uses a replaceable cartridge containing compressed nitrogen to deploy two small probes that are attached to the TASER X26 ECD by insulated conductive wires with a maximum length of 35 feet (10.6 meters). The TASER X26 ECD transmits electrical pulses through the wires and into the body affecting the sensory and motor functions of the peripheral nervous system. The energy can penetrate up to two cumulative inches of clothing, or one inch per probe.[39]

Some Tasers have two modes: "probe" and "touch stun." In the "probe" mode, a cartridge projects and attaches to a suspect's clothing or penetrates the skin with barbs. Between the barbs and the pistol-like Taser unit are two small wires. An electrical charge is then sent down the wires, disabling the suspect. The "touch stun" mode requires the officer to touch the suspect with the unit (similar to a stun gun); wires are not used. For obvious reasons, the "probe" mode is safer for the officer.

There are some concerns over the use and safety of conducted energy devices. A recent Police Executive Research Forum study called attention to the need for national guidelines governing their use, particularly the use of Tasers, and the organization offered more than 50 recommendations for proper and safe operation of the devices.[40] Their recommendations included the following:

1. CEDs should only be used against suspects who are actively resisting or exhibiting active aggression or to prevent individuals from harming themselves or others. CEDs should not be used against passive suspects.

2. No more than one officer at a time should activate a CED against a person.

3. When activating a CED, law enforcement officers should use it for one standard cycle (five seconds) and stop to evaluate the situation. If subsequent cycles are necessary, agency policy should restrict the number and duration of those cycles to the minimum activations necessary to place the subject in custody.

4. Training protocols should emphasize that multiple activations and continuous cycling of a CED appear to increase

The Severity of the Crime

Whether the Suspect Is Resisting or Attempting to Flee the Scene

Whether the Suspect Poses a Threat

FIGURE 13.5 Legal Standards for the Use of Nonlethal Weapons.

the risk of death or serious injury and should be avoided where practical.

5. Officers should be trained to recognize the limitations of CED activation and should be prepared to transition to other force options as needed.[41]

The need for such guidelines is critical because despite their supposedly nonlethal nature, conducted energy devices *have* been implicated in some deaths. Medical examiners have attributed some Taser-related deaths (and other deaths in police custody) to a condition known as **excited delirium**, an overdose of adrenaline that can occur in heated confrontations with the police.

Impact Munitions

Earlier in this chapter, we mentioned a force continuum. There is also a **weapons continuum**. Traditional less-lethal technologies require that officers be in close proximity to suspects. Whether employing a baton, a can of pepper spray, or a Taser in "touch stun" mode to get the job done, an officer has to be a few feet from the suspect. Lethal weapons, especially guns, by contrast, do not require close proximity. These devices can be put on a continuum that moves the threat of injury to the officer from low to high. Guns generally present a low risk to officers, whereas batons present a fairly high risk. In response to this problem, less-lethal technologies have been developed that can be used from a distance. Such devices are most commonly called **impact munitions**. For example, the 12-gauge launching cap produced by Combined Tactical Systems (CTS) can fire a large rubber projectile from a distance of 75 to 100 meters. Beanbags can also be fired from these types of devices.

Law enforcement officers need to be careful to use impact munitions from proper distances. When employed from too great a distance, less-lethal weapons can be ineffective. On the other hand, when fired from less than 30 or so feet, these devices can cause serious injury, including broken bones. Death can even occur if the devices are not used as intended. A National Institute of Justice study of 373 incidents involving impact munitions found that eight individuals died as a result of injuries sustained from the weapons.[42] Most of the deaths were caused by broken ribs that pierced the heart or lungs. At least one suspect died as a result of being hit in the neck with a beanbag round. Additional findings from this study appear in Figure 13.6.

Pepper Spray (Oleoresin Capsicum)

Pepper spray, or oleoresin capsicum (OC), is a so-called lachrymatory (inflammatory) agent that causes irritation to the eyes and skin. There are two forms of tear gas: chlorobenzylidenemalononitrile (CS) gas and chloroacetophenone (CN) gas.

These gases are irritants and are used more often than pepper spray to control unruly crowds, rather than to gain compliance from an individual.

The active ingredient in pepper spray is capsaicin, a derivative of the fruit from plants in the *Capsicum* genus, which includes certain peppers, notably the cayenne pepper—hence the term *pepper spray*. The spray is usually packaged in small pressurized canisters that are carried on the person and can be dispensed quickly to subdue a suspect or for self-defense. The spray is most effective when sprayed in the eyes. Pepper spray, unlike some of the other less-lethal technologies, can be acquired legally by non–law enforcement personnel, but not in all states. Most states that permit its sale have laws that penalize improper use of the spray.

Pepper spray is aptly called a less-lethal weapon because some people *have* died as a result of its use.[43] A study of pepper spray's effectiveness was conducted by researchers at the University of North Carolina.[44] They examined injuries to officers and suspects and complaints of excessive force before and after police departments adopted the use of pepper spray. The researchers found an overall decline in officer injuries, but the decline apparently preceded the introduction of pepper spray, and the effect varied across police departments. The researchers found fewer suspect injuries due to the introduction of pepper spray. Finally, complaints of excessive force declined markedly after pepper spray came into use.

Another study looked at in-custody deaths following the use of pepper spray. Researchers at the University of Texas Southwestern Medical Center identified 63 such cases and concluded, for the most part, that pepper spray was not the culprit.[45] The researchers went on to conclude that pepper spray did not cause *or* contribute to death in 61 of the 63 identified cases. The two remaining deaths were of

conducted energy device (CED) A device that uses electrical shock to incapacitate a suspect. Examples are the Taser® and the Sticky Shocker®. Also called *electromuscular disruption technology*.

excited delirium A condition in which a suspect experiences an overdose of adrenaline during a heated confrontation with the police.

weapons continuum The array of nonlethal and lethal weaponry available to police officers, the selection of which depends on the situation.

impact munitions Munitions designed to stun or otherwise temporarily incapacitate a suspect or a dangerous individual so that law enforcement officers can subdue and arrest that person with less risk of injury or death to themselves and to others.

pepper spray A so-called lachrymatory (inflammatory) agent that causes irritation to the eyes and skin. Also called *oleoresin capsicum (OC)*.

Think About It…

Conducted Energy Devices Conducted energy devices (CEDs) have become very popular with law enforcement organizations across the country. CEDs can be safely used in the vast majority of circumstances, but they have still come under scrutiny as a result of some high-profile incidents, such as the June 2009 "tasing" of 72-year-old woman during a traffic stop in Texas. A handful of CED-related deaths, too, have prompted a focus on the devices. What are your thoughts concerning CED effectiveness? Do the benefits outweigh the costs? Why or why not? What would you do to minimize the potential for problems associated CED usage in law enforcement?

Source: © Howard Sayer b/a Alamy

The Targets

The study found that 181, or nearly half, of the reported 373 incidents involved emotionally disturbed individuals who were armed and showed signs of suicidal intent. The reported incidents also included the following:

- Nonsuicidal but armed individuals in open areas who had refused police orders to drop their weapons (70 incidents)
- Individuals barricaded inside buildings or vehicles (48 incidents)
- Hostage takers (9 incidents)

The data showed the characteristics of those who were shot by law enforcement officers firing impact munitions:

- Most individuals were in their 30s, though ages ranged from 14 to 83.
- Nearly all were men (291 of 315 cases in which gender was recorded).
- Nearly two-thirds were white (200 out of 301 cases in which information on race or ethnic group was included), followed Hispanics (49) and African-Americans (40).

Armed and Dangerous

Subjects were armed in almost 90 percent of the 306 cases for which weapons data were available. (In the few instances in which suspects possessed multiple weapons, the researchers counted only the most dangerous one.)

- Cutting instruments (knives, swords, axes, machetes)—50 percent of the 306 cases
- Firearms (handguns, shotguns, rifles)—29 percent
- Blunt instruments (bats, clubs, sticks)—6 percent
- Other objects (rocks, bottles, Molotov cocktails)—4 percent
- No weapon—11 percent

Number of Shots Fired

Law enforcement officers fired 1 to 141 shots at individual targets. Often, multiple shots were needed to subdue an individual because a single hit by an impact munition was not always immediately effective. In the overwhelming number of cases, however, the number of shots fired was few.

Ten or fewer rounds were fired in 98 percent of the 316 cases for which information was available, five or fewer in 93 percent, and one shot in 38 percent of the cases.

Respondents in 313 of the cases reported on the number of shots that struck their intended target, with the number of hits ranging from 1 to 13. In one case, the individual being fired at surrendered after the shots missed. Others surrendered when follow-up shots missed but the initial shots hit their target.

Type of Munition Used

The type of impact munition used was identified in 962 of the 969 reported discharges of devices. Of the 21 different types of munitions used, beanbags shot from 12-gauge shotguns were the most common, accounting for 65 percent of all the projectiles fired. Plastic baton rounds were the second most common, used in 28 percent of the cases.

Where Struck

Most often, targets were struck in the abdomen (34 percent) or the chest (19 percent), followed by the legs (15 percent), arms (14 percent), and back (11 percent). Only 2 percent of the impacts were on the head, and only 1 percent each in the groin and neck, the more vulnerable parts of a person's body. Of the 969 reported discharges of impact munitions, 782 resulted in injuries. Of those, more than 80 percent were bruises and abrasions, both relatively minor injuries that may not require medical treatment. Bruises accounted for 51 percent of the injuries, and abrasions added another 31 percent. More serious lacerations accounted for 5.5 percent of the injuries; broken bones accounted for 3.5 percent. Of the 782 injuries, there were 14 instances (1.8 percent) in which the impact munition penetrated the target's skin and caused a more serious injury.

Impacts to the head produced a greater proportion of nonfatal serious injuries than other areas struck. Of the 19 head impacts reported, 14 resulted in a laceration, bone fracture, or penetration wound.

FIGURE 13.6 **Findings from a Study of Incidents Involving Impact Munitions.**
Source: National Institute of Justice, *Impact munitions use: Types, targets, effects* (Washington, DC: National Institute of Justice, 2004), pp. 4–5.

asthmatics whose conditions were exacerbated by pepper spray.

Researchers at the University of California, San Diego, measured the effects of both pepper spray and a placebo spray on police recruits who were then placed in either a sitting position or in the "hogtie" (feet and hands bound behind the back) position.[46] The study found that pepper spray alone does not cause respiratory problems in either position. It should be noted, however, that the study participants were healthy police recruits and that they were allowed to wear goggles to minimize the harmful effects of the pepper spray. Even so, it is safe to say that pepper spray is likely the safest less-lethal weapon, especially when compared to some of the other weapons we have discussed in this chapter.

▶ Excessive Force and Abuse of Authority

Recall that excessive force is not the same as use of force. Excessive force is *inappropriate* force. To clarify even further, consider the distinction between ends and means. In our democratic system of government, we are very concerned with process. Applied to policing, *process* refers to the means or procedures police use to perform their jobs. We are nervous about the prospect of giving police unlimited authority. On the other hand, we don't like to ignore the ends either—in other words, crime control. We want police to control crime *and* preserve our liberty. But when the ends become more of a concern than the means, inappropriate or excessive force is a likely result.

Excessive force is not the only form of inappropriate police conduct. It is also possible to abuse one's authority. We saw some examples of this in the preceding chapter. We also

Excessive force is inappropriate force.

looked at the consequences of violating people's legal rights in Chapters 11 and 12. It is important here, however, to point out that in addition to excessive force, abuse of authority is also inappropriate. Abuse of authority, which was defined in the last chapter, can be thought of as something of an umbrella under which excessive force falls. An officer can abuse his or her authority without resorting to physical force. In either case, the end result is a person who is improperly and unjustly made to suffer in one way or another.

Types of Excessive Force

Excessive force and abuse of authority take at least three distinct forms. Neither is quite the same as, say, accepting a gratuity or receiving a kickback (see Chapter 12). Each leads to a measure of discomfort, if not pain or even death, on the part of a criminal suspect—or even an innocent person. Physical brutality, verbal and psychological abuse, and other so-called rights violations are discussed in this section. Think of these as appearing on a continuum that moves from most to least serious.

Physical Brutality

Perhaps the most notorious example of police brutality in recent years is the infamous 1991 Rodney King incident, which was mentioned at the beginning of this chapter. King was stopped for speeding and for fleeing from police. He did not cooperate once he was stopped, and officers applied force to subdue him, but a bystander's video recording of the incident revealed something else. King was hit and kicked more than 50 times, as 27 officers from various agencies stood by. What's more, the beating continued even after King appeared to be under control. King received 11 fractures to his skull, a broken ankle, and several other serious injuries. So serious was the incident that an independent commission, the Christopher Commission (named for Warren Christopher, former deputy attorney general and deputy secretary of state for the United States), was appointed to investigate it—along with other alleged problems in the Los Angeles Police Department. Three officers who were criminally charged in the incident were acquitted in 1992, inciting one of the largest riots in Los Angeles history.

In 2008, LAPD officers were once again criticized by the press for their handling of another incident, an immigration rally. Two officers were reassigned after the incident, but this has not stopped people from trying to connect the dots—from Rodney King to the Rampart Division scandal to the crackdown at the 2000 Democratic National Convention, which took place at Los Angeles's Staples Center. Critics argue that the LAPD is plagued by a warrior culture that, like an ocean liner, is difficult to turn around.

Conducted Energy Devices

Example: TASER. The typical CED shocks a person with 50,000 volts, causing involuntary contractions of the skeletal muscles and leading to instant immobilization. Although the device has been used inappropriately in a few noteworthy cases, the CED is arguably one of the most effective tools in the law enforcement arsenal.

Impact Munitions

Examples: foam rubber bullets, wooden dowels, beanbags, and other projectiles that are usually fired from 12-gauge shotguns or 37/40-millimeter gas grenade launchers. Impact munitions are designed to stun or otherwise temporarily incapacitate a suspect or dangerous individual so that law enforcement officers can subdue and arrest that person with less danger of injury or death to themselves and others.[i]

Pepper Spray

Pepper spray or oleoresin capsicum (OC), is a so-called lachrymatory (inflammatory) agent that causes irritation to the eyes and skin. Pepper spray, like tear gas, causes the eyes to close tightly and tear up, and it may even cause temporary blindness. It also causes the mucous membranes of the nose, throat, and sinuses to burn and swell, making breathing difficult. OC spray is very effective when used to subdue a resistant suspect. Note that pepper spray is not the same as tear gas.

[i]National Institute of Justice, *Impact munitions use: Types, targets, effects* (Washington, DC: National Institute of Justice, 2004).

FIGURE 13.7 Less-Lethal Weapons

Verbal and Psychological Abuse

The old idiom "sticks and stones may break my bones, but words will never hurt me" couldn't be further from the truth. We know from some high-profile school shootings that words definitely hurt. Any child of a dysfunctional family, even one where physical abuse was never a problem, knows that communication problems and insults can take their toll. There is no reason why police officers should be excused when they engage in verbal abuse. When the things they say and do exclusive of the application of physical force go beyond standards of acceptability, they can be considered abusive. Such actions include everything from insulting suspects to denying them basic necessities during the course of an aggressive interrogation.

LEARNING OUTCOMES 4 — List three types of excessive force.

GLOSSARY

third degree A formerly common coercive interrogation technique that combined psychological pressures with physical force.

legal abuse Any violation of a person's constitutionally, federally, or state-protected rights.

There is a fine line between psychological pressure and abuse. Consider police interrogation. Assume that a detective lies to a suspect by saying that an accomplice has implicated him. Is this abuse or just good detective work? On the one hand, it is not a verbal assault, ridicule, harassment, or even a threat of harm. It is, however, something that could instill fear. What if, to take it one step further, the detective *indirectly* threatened the suspect, perhaps by claiming that a jury would surely find him guilty? This type of deception is increasingly common, especially in the wake of the U.S. Supreme Court's famous *Miranda* decision (see Chapter 10). *Miranda* has, for better or for worse, made it more difficult for police to secure confessions. As such, they have had to resort to creative means of doing so, including deception. Richard Leo, a researcher who has documented this trend, summarized one exchange between a detective and a suspect that illustrates the point:

> Detective: If you take this to a jury trial, they're going to hit you hard. They're going to slam you real hard. He's trying to lie to us, he must think we're stupid. Ladies and gentlemen of the jury, we have the evidence that shows he broke the window. He says "no, I didn't do it." Now do you want to be lenient with this guy?
>
> The suspect interjects: No, I'm not going to go for this one.
>
> Detective: Fine, we'll take it to a jury trial, but they're going to say he's guilty, he's guilty. You had a chance to tell the truth. They'll say: he had a chance. The

sergeants talked to him and gave him an opportunity to explain how it happened, to give his side of the story, and what did he do? He lied. That's what he's going to say. He's going to say you lied. You had a chance to tell the truth but you lied. That's exactly what he's going to say.[47]

We are not suggesting that this exchange amounts to abuse, but at what point does deception go too far? This is not an easy question to answer. Gone are the days where psychological pressures were combined with physical force in a mix commonly called the **third degree**, but words alone can go pretty far toward directly harming an individual.

Other Rights Violations

If an officer physically and unnecessarily abuses a suspect during an arrest, there is a clear rights violation that might enable the suspect to claim a violation of the Fourth Amendment right to be free from unreasonable seizures. Likewise, a detective who coerces a suspect into confessing or who violates the suspect's *Miranda* rights also commits a rights violation. Specifically, the detective violates the suspect's Fifth Amendment right to be free from compelled self-incrimination. There are other rights, however, that can also be violated without physical abuse and in the absence of verbal or psychological abuse. David Carter calls this **legal abuse**:

> This form of abuse occurs with greater frequency than the other categories. Legal abuse is defined as any violation of a person's constitutional, federally protected, or state-protected rights. Although the individual may not suffer any apparent psychological damage in the strictest sense, an abuse of authority has nonetheless occurred. In all cases of physical abuse and in many cases of verbal abuse, there will also be a legal question. However, legal abuse can—and does—occur frequently without the other forms.[48]

What if, for example, a police officer pushes a suspect up against a brick wall before conducting a pat-down search, and the suspect bumps his head, causing it to bleed? The injury is by no means serious, and we would probably be remiss to call it brutality. A bystander may not even take notice. But what if the force is unnecessary? If it is not abuse and it is not psychological pressure, what can the suspect do? If the seizure in this case is not justified, what remedies are available? There are not too many (see Chapter 11), but this doesn't make the incident any more acceptable than a full-on physical assault.

Physical Brutality
Excessive physical assaults that likely result in injury or even possible death.

Verbal and Psychological Abuse
Words and actions that go beyond standards of acceptability, from insulting suspects to denying them basic necessities during the course of an aggressive interrogation.

Legal Abuse
Any violation of a person's constitutional, federally protected, or state-protected rights.

FIGURE 13.8 Examples of Excessive Force.

A Post-9/11 Surge in Police Brutality?

Police brutality cases have been on the rise since the terrorist attacks of September 11, 2001, and federal prosecutors are targeting an increasing number of abusive officers. Brooklyn, New York, tops the list, with 11 criminal prosecutions of police officers during the first 10 months of fiscal year 2007.[49] Several other cities, including Milwaukee; Jackson, Mississippi; New Orleans; Chicago; and Cleveland, have seen a similar upsurge in uncalled for police violence. On the whole, U.S. Justice Department statistics show a 25 percent increase in the incidence of police brutality between 2001 and 2007. The vast majority of police abuse cases are never prosecuted, so the real numbers could be even higher.

One explanation that has been offered for this trend is the growing difficulty that police departments face in finding qualified police officer applicants, partially because of the war in the Middle East. Throughout the country, many agencies have been forced to revise their recruitment policies or lower their standards to fill vacancies. Age, height, and weight requirements have been relaxed; test standards have been revised; hiring bonuses are being offered; and some agencies have become more tolerant of recruits' past drug use.[50] Since many police officers and applicants are steadily being drawn into military service, agencies have had to ramp up their hiring efforts.

This raises some interesting questions:

1. Does a nationwide increase of 25 percent in police brutality cases over a six-year period seem significant?

2. If police brutality has risen substantially since the terrorist attacks of September 11, can those events somehow be blamed?

3. To what extent have relaxed recruitment standards affected police brutality?

4. If it is necessary to relax police hiring standards to meet the realities of police recruiting today, then at what point do we draw the line?

Source: Lilac Mountain/Shutterstock.com

LEARNING OUTCOMES 1

Identify the various levels of force, explain how they are controlled by policy, and describe their applications in police work.

Levels of force range from an officer's mere presence all the way up to deadly force. Use-of-force policies usually refer to a force continuum that describes the appropriate levels of force to use in response to the level of resistance or force used by the suspect.

1. What are the kinds of police use of force that this chapter discusses?

2. Which is the type of force most commonly used by police officers?

3. What is meant by the term *force continuum*? Provide examples of levels of force that might be identified by a force continuum.

4. What is meant by the term *force factor*? How does it relate to a suspect's level of resistance?

use of force The use of physical restraint by a police officer when dealing with a member of the public.

excessive force The application of an amount and/or frequency of force greater than that required to compel compliance from a willing or unwilling subject.

problem police officer An officer who exhibits problem behavior, as indicated by a large number of citizen complaints, frequent involvement in use-of-force incidents, and other evidence.

Christopher Commission The commission that studied the structure and operation of the Los Angeles Police Department in the wake of the Rodney King beating incident.

Rodney King A suspect whose videotaped beating by members of the Los Angeles Police Department led to civil unrest across the nation.

force continuum The spectrum of force available to a police officer, from the absence of physical force to the use of a deadly weapon.

force factor The level of force used by a police officer relative to the suspect's level of resistance.

LEARNING OUTCOMES 2

Describe legal standards associated with the use of deadly force by law enforcement officers, explain the patterns of deadly force, and describe the problem of suicide by cop.

Deadly force is force that is likely to cause death or significant bodily harm. Strict legal standards govern the use of deadly force. In general, it is unconstitutional for an officer to shoot an unarmed fleeing felon. Such shootings are only permissible if the officer has probable cause to believe that the suspect poses a serious risk of danger to others. Roughly 3,600 suspects are shot at by police officers each year. Of these, about 600 die from injuries they receive. Suicide by cop refers to situations in which individuals who are determined to end their lives engage in behavior that causes responding officers to resort to deadly force.

1. What is the meaning of deadly force within the law enforcement context?

2. What legal standards govern the use of deadly force by police officers?

3. What is meant by *suicide by cop*? How can suicide-by-cop situations be avoided?

4. What is the significance of the U.S. Supreme Court case of *Tennessee* v. *Garner* for law enforcement officers? What standards did it set?

deadly force Force that is likely to cause death or significant bodily harm.

Tennessee v. Garner The 1985 U.S. Supreme Court case that specified the conditions under which deadly force could be used to apprehend suspected felons.

suicide by cop An incident in which an individual who is determined to die engages in behavior meant to provoke responding officers to resort to deadly force.

LEARNING OUTCOMES 3

Describe legal standards governing nondeadly force, including less-lethal weapons.

Nondeadly force is the opposite of deadly force; it is force that is unlikely to cause death or significant bodily harm. Claims of excessive force are judged under the Fourth Amendment's reasonableness clause. Nondeadly force would be excessive if a "reasonable person" would feel it was unreasonable to employ such force in a given situation. Less-lethal weapons, including conducted energy devices, impact munitions, and pepper spray, have been developed as alternatives to (but not replacements for) deadly force.

1. What legal standards govern the use of nondeadly force by police officers?

2. What kinds of less-lethal technologies are available to law enforcement agencies today?

3. How might today's less-lethal weapons be effectively employed in place of deadly force?

4. What is the significance of the 1989 U.S. Supreme Court case of *Graham* v. *Connor* for considerations involving the use of nondeadly force by police officers?

nondeadly force Force that is unlikely to cause death or significant bodily harm.

Graham* v. *Connor The 1989 U.S. Supreme Court case in which the Court declared that claims of excessive nondeadly force must be judged under the Fourth Amendment's reasonableness clause.

less-lethal weapon A weapon that is designed to disable, capture, or immobilize, rather than kill.

conducted energy device (CED) A device that uses electrical shock to incapacitate a suspect. Examples are the Taser® and the Sticky Shocker®. Also called *electromuscular disruption technology*.

excited delirium A condition in which a suspect experiences an overdose of adrenaline during a heated confrontation with the police.

weapons continuum The array of nonlethal and lethal weaponry available to police officers, the selection of which depends on the situation.

impact munitions Munitions designed to stun or otherwise temporarily incapacitate a suspect or a dangerous individual so that law enforcement officers can subdue and arrest that person with less risk of injury or death to themselves and to others.

pepper spray A so-called lachrymatory (inflammatory) agent that causes irritation to the eyes and skin. Also called *oleoresin capsicum (OC)*.

LEARNING OUTCOMES 4

List three types of excessive force.

Excessive force falls into three general categories: (1) physical abuse, (2) verbal and psychological abuse, and (3) other rights violations. The latter includes constitutional rights violations that result from police actions besides abuse. An example would be a shove or a push.

1. Identify three types of excessive force, and provide examples of each.

2. What is meant by the term *the third degree*?

3. Do you believe that excessive force is a serious problem in policing today? Explain.

4. What can police administrators do to ensure that officers under their command refrain from using excessive force?

third degree A formerly common coercive interrogation technique that combined psychological pressures with physical force.

legal abuse Any violation of a person's constitutionally, federally, or state-protected rights.

MyCJLab

Go to the Chapter 13 section in *MyCJLab* to test your understanding of this chapter, access customized study content, engage in interactive simulations, complete critical thinking and research assignments, and view related online videos.

Additional Links

Citizen complaints about police use of force forms the subject matter of **www.justicestudies.com/pubs/citizencomplaints.pdf**.

An analysis of police use-of-force data can be read at **www.justicestudies.com/pubs/analysis.pdf**.

Excessive use of force is covered at **www.justicestudies.com/pubs/excessiveforce.pdf**.

Police attitudes toward abuse of authority are revealed at **www.justicestudies.com/pubs/policeattitudes.pdf**.

Papers on the early detection of problem officers (**www.justicestudies.com/pubs/problemofficers.pdf**) and methods for curbing police brutality (**www.justicestudies.com/pubs/curbing.pdf**) are available online.

Understanding the use of force by and against the police is discussed at **www.justicestudies.com/pubs/understandingforce.pdf**.

Glossary

18 U.S.C. Section 3501 The U.S. Code designation assigned to the Crime Control Act of 1968, which, among other things, attempted to invalidate the *Miranda* decision.

18 U.S.C.A. Section 242 The most common federal statute used to hold police officers criminally liable.

42 U.S.C. Section 1983 The federal statute that provides a remedy in federal court for the "deprivation of any rights . . . secured by the Constitution and laws" of the United States.

absolute immunity Protection from lawsuits enjoyed by federal officials when acting in their official capacities.

abuse of authority A catchall category for various forms of inappropriate police conduct that do not necessarily amount to crime, deviance, or corruption.

accepted lie A lie that is necessary in furthering the police mission.

accreditation Certification for having met all applicable requirements put in place by an accrediting body.

administrative justification The standard for an administrative search based on the fact that government entities occasionally conduct searches in circumstances other than criminal investigations, such as a sobriety checkpoint set up for the purpose of apprehending drunk drivers. Sometimes called *special-needs* or *regulatory searches*, such searches attempt to achieve a balance between protecting individuals' privacy interests and protecting public safety.

affirmative action The practice of taking proactive steps to boost the presence of historically marginalized groups (typically minorities and women) in the ranks of an organization by giving preference to members of those groups.

affront According to John Van Maanen, the first of three steps police officers use in identifying an "asshole." It occurs when an officer's authority is questioned.

Americans with Disabilities Act (ADA) U.S. legislation passed in 1990 that forbids discrimination against the disabled.

anthropometry A technique developed by Alphonse Bertillon in 1882 for identifying people based on their body measurements. Also called *Bertillon measurements*.

arm-span rule A doctrine established by the U.S. Supreme Court that limits a search immediately following an arrest to the area "within [the] immediate control" of the person arrested—that is, the area from within which he might have obtained either a weapon or something that could have been used as evidence against him.

assumption of risk A defense against state tort liability that provides that if a plaintiff voluntarily engaged in a dangerous activity that led to his or her injury, then the police officer should not be held liable.

August Vollmer (1876–1955) An early and especially effective advocate of police reform whose collaboration with the University of California established the study of criminal justice as an academic discipline.

Bivens v. Six Unknown Named Agents The 1971 U.S. Supreme Court ruling that held that federal law enforcement officers can be sued for Fourth Amendment violations. The decision has since been expanded to include liability for violations of constitutional rights embodied in other relevant amendments.

bobby The popular British name given to a member of Sir Robert Peel's Metropolitan Police Force.

booking The process of fingerprinting, processing, and photographing a suspect, after which he or she is typically placed in a holding cell. The suspect may also be required to submit to testing (such as for alcohol) or be required to participate in a lineup.

boundaryless policing Any of various technology-based intelligence efforts designed to combat crime and terrorism.

Bow Street Runners An early English police unit formed under the leadership of Henry Fielding, magistrate of the Bow Street region of London. Also referred to as *thief takers*.

broken windows model A model of policing based on the notion that physical decay in a community (for example, litter and abandoned buildings) can breed disorder and lead to crime by signaling that laws are not being enforced. Such decay is thought to push law-abiding citizens to withdraw from the streets, which signals that lawbreakers can operate freely. The model suggests that by encouraging the repair of run-down buildings and by controlling disorderly behavior in public spaces, police agencies can create an environment in which serious crime cannot easily flourish.

Bureau of Alcohol, Tobacco, Firearms and Explosives (ATF) A tax-collection, enforcement, and regulatory arm of the U.S. Department of Justice.

bureaucracy The administrative structure of a large or complex organization, typically employing task-specialized bureaus or departments.

burnout The progressive loss of idealism, energy, purpose, and concern that results from the conditions of work.

CalGang A sophisticated software database of known gang members that field officers in California can access quickly. GangNet is a modified version of the software that is used nationwide.

centralized policing model The less prevalent model of state police organization, in which the tasks of major criminal investigations are combined with the patrol of state highways.

chain of command The supervisory channel within a law enforcement organization.

checkpoint A location at which a warrantless, suspicionless search is constitutionally permissible in furtherance of an overriding national or public-safety interest. National border entry points and sobriety checkpoints are examples.

Christopher Commission The commission that studied the structure and operation of the Los Angeles Police Department in the wake of the Rodney King beating incident.

citizen complaint A document filed by someone who believes that he or she has been wronged by one or more police officers in a department.

citizen patrol A preventive patrol program staffed by citizen volunteers.

citizen police academy A training experience that offers citizens an opportunity to learn about the policing profession and even to experience some of the same situations that uniformed officers experience.

civil disobedience Law-breaking used as a political tactic to prove a point or to protest against something.

civil law The branch of modern law that governs relationships between parties.

civil service A system in which employees are hired, retained, advanced, disciplined, and discharged on the basis of merit (that is, their abilities and qualifications).

civil service commission A federal, state, or local agency charged with ensuring that employees in civil service positions receive specific protections.

civilian input A model of civilian oversight of a police agency in which civilians receive and investigate complaints, but the next steps are taken by the police department.

civilian monitor A model of civilian oversight of a police agency that is similar to an ombudsman approach in which complaints are received by the police department and the process, from beginning to end, is monitored by civilians.

civilian review One of the stronger models of citizen oversight of a police agency in which a group of citizens investigates complaints against the police, adjudicates the complaints, and recommends punishment.

civilianization "A law enforcement agency's hiring of non-sworn personnel to replace or augment its corps of sworn officers" in an effort to reduce costs and improve service.

clarification According to John Van Maanen, the second of three steps police officers use in identifying an "asshole." It occurs when the officer attempts to ascertain what kind of person he or she is dealing with.

code of ethics A statement of principles concerning the behavior of those who subscribe to the code.

college system A police academy training model intended to enhance the professional aspects of police training curricula by exposing trainees to problem solving, sensitivity to marginalized groups, and other valuable topics in addition to required technical knowledge.

color of law The condition that exists when an individual acts in an official government capacity and with the appearance of legal power. Police officers, mayors, and a number of other government officials perform their duties under color of law.

community era By most accounts, the contemporary era of U.S. law enforcement, which stresses service and an almost customer-friendly approach to police work.

community justice A relatively new and innovative set of ideas about how the goals of the criminal justice system can be achieved. It favors original, nontraditional approaches to crime control that draw heavily on input and cooperation from the community.

community policing A collaborative effort between the police and the community that identifies problems of crime and disorder and involves all elements of the community in the search for solutions to these problems.

comparative negligence A partial defense against state tort liability that examines who is to blame and assigns liability accordingly.

Compstat A goal-oriented police management process that relies heavily on computer technology and accountability of top-level administrators.

computer-aided drafting (CAD) A technology, adapted to meet the needs of police officers and criminal investigators, that facilitates the drafting of crime scenes on a computer so that they can be viewed three-dimensionally.

computerized crime mapping A computer-based system that combines a geographic information system with crime statistics generated by a police department, allowing crime data to be plotted on a map.

conducted energy device (CED) A device that uses electrical shock to incapacitate a suspect. Examples are the Taser® and the Sticky Shocker® Also called *electromuscular disruption technology*.

consent decree A legal settlement in which one entity agrees to take certain actions or rectify a particular problem without admitting to any illegality. Consent decrees are sometimes used in law enforcement following corruption scandals; a decree requires the police department to fix a particular problem and/or end a particular course of action.

constitutional rights violation Conduct that violates a specific constitutional provision.

contingency theory A management theory that recognizes that there are often different types of tasks within a single organization, including repetitive tasks that call for standardization and control and nonrepetitive tasks that call for flexibility and participatory management.

contributory negligence A liability defense that holds that if an officer can show that the plaintiff or someone else was also negligent in an event, the officer should not be held liable. Contributory negligence can arise not only from the actions of a criminal suspect, but also from the actions of third parties.

corruption Dishonest or fraudulent conduct by public officials in a position of power.

council-manager form The most common form of city government in cities of more than 12,000 people. It consists of an elected city council (usually between five and twelve people) responsible for all policy decisions for the city. Mayors under this form of municipal government generally perform ceremonial duties and serve as the voice, and often the leader, of the city council.

Crime Mapping Research Center (CMRC) A U.S. Justice Department agency that promotes research, training, and technical assistance for police agencies around the country and assists them in their crime-mapping efforts. Also called the *Mapping and Analysis for Public Safety (MAPS) Program*.

crime peak A time of day when a particular crime increases in frequency.

criminal intelligence A synergistic product intended to provide meaningful and trustworthy direction to law enforcement decision makers about complex criminality, criminal enterprises, criminal extremists, and terrorists. Also, a process that evaluates information collected from diverse sources, integrates the relevant information into a cohesive package, and produces a conclusion or estimate about a criminal phenomenon by using the scientific approach to problem solving.

criminalistics The use of technology in the service of criminal investigation; the application of scientific techniques to the detection and evaluation of criminal evidence.

critical incident An emergency situation that evokes immediate police response and that takes priority over all other police work.

culpability The state of deserving blame or being morally or legally responsible. Under the Section 1983 culpability requirement, plaintiffs generally must prove that the defendant officer *intended* for the violation to occur.

culture A set of shared values, norms, and behaviors that form a way of life.

Customs and Border Protection (CBP) The U.S. law enforcement agency, established after the terrorist attacks on September 11, 2001, that combined the entire U.S. Border Patrol with portions of the U.S. Customs Service, U.S. Immigration, and the Animal and Plant Health Inspection Service. CBP was given the mission of controlling and protecting America's borders and ports of entry, including international airports and international shipping ports.

dactylography An early name for fingerprinting.

damages Monetary compensation awarded to the plaintiff in a successful civil lawsuit.

deadly force Force that is likely to cause death or significant bodily harm.

decentralized policing model A model of policing in which central governments exercise relatively few police powers and in which the majority of police services are provided by separate local and regional agencies.

democracy A form of government that vests supreme authority in the people, usually through their freely elected representatives.

deterrence theory A perspective that holds that crime will be less likely to occur when the potential for getting caught outweighs any likely benefits from breaking the law.

deviance Any behavior that is at odds with socially expected or accepted behavior.

deviant lie A lie that expressly violates the rules and legal requirements.

directed patrol A form of patrol that involves concentrating the police presence in areas where certain crimes are a significant problem.

distress A harmful form of stress that can threaten an individual's functioning or overload his or her capacity to cope with environmental stimuli.

dominion John Crank's substitute for the term *territoriality*, which refers to an officer's sense of personal ownership over the area for which he or she is responsible.

double marginality A situation in which black officers treat black suspects harshly to gain the respect of their white counterparts and to avoid giving the impression that they are biased toward members of their own race.

dramaturgical discipline Achieving a balance between merely reporting facts and putting a "spin" on those facts to create a desired impression.

dramaturgy In the law enforcement context, the act of putting on a display of high-mindedness.

Drug Enforcement Administration (DEA) The U.S. law enforcement agency tasked with enforcing controlled-substance laws and regulations.

dual federalism An interpretation of the U.S. Constitution that suggests a system in which the only powers vested in the federal government are those explicitly listed in the document, with the remaining powers being left to the states.

due process of law A right guaranteed by the Fifth, Sixth, and Fourteenth Amendments and generally understood, in legal contexts, to mean the due course of legal proceedings according to the rules and forms established for the protection of individual rights. In criminal proceedings, due process of law is generally understood to include the following basic elements: a law creating and defining the offense, an impartial tribunal having jurisdictional authority over the case, accusation in proper form, notice and opportunity to defend, trial according to established procedure, and discharge from all restraints or obligations unless convicted.

due process voluntariness approach A means for determining the admissibility of a suspect's self-incriminating statement based on whether it was made voluntarily. Involuntariness is held to occur when, under the totality of circumstances that preceded the confessions, the defendant is deprived of his or her "power of resistance."

economic corruption Drug-related police corruption in which an officer seeks personal gain by stealing drugs, selling drugs, or extorting money from drug dealers.

equal employment opportunity Fair employment practices mandated by Title VII of the Civil Rights Act of 1964.

Equal Employment Opportunity Commission (EEOC) The federal agency that is empowered by Title VII of the Civil Rights Act of 1964 to "intervene on behalf of affected individuals," to "file suit against businesses or governmental entities in cases of discrimination," to intervene in cases of alleged sexual harassment, and to investigate cases of employer retaliation.

eustress A positive form of stress that does not threaten or harm the individual but is pleasurable, challenging, or exciting.

evanescent evidence Evidence that is likely to disappear quickly.

excessive force The application of an amount and/or frequency of force greater than that required to compel compliance from a willing or unwilling subject.

excited delirium A condition in which a suspect experiences an overdose of adrenaline during a heated confrontation with the police.

exclusionary rule A rule mandating that evidence obtained in violation of the U.S. Constitution cannot be admitted in a criminal trial. The exclusionary rule is an important mechanism for ensuring the accountability of police officials.

exigent circumstances A situation that makes a warrantless search constitutionally permissible, such as hot pursuit, the likelihood of a suspect's escaping or presenting a danger to others, and evanescent evidence.

Federal Bureau of Investigation (FBI) The investigative arm of the U.S. Department of Justice.

federalism A political doctrine holding that power is divided (often constitutionally) between a central governing body (the federal government, for example) and various constituent units (the states).

field training officer (FTO) A veteran police officer tasked with providing on-the-job training and performance critique during a rookie police officer's initial assignment following graduation from the academy.

Fifth Amendment An amendment to the U.S. Constitution that establishes due process rights, including the right to remain silent in the face of criminal accusations.

firearms training system (FATS) A full-size, fully interactive training device, not unlike flight and driving simulators, that exposes police trainees to realistic shooting scenarios. The realism is enhanced by fully encasing the trainees in a particular surrounding rather than simply putting them in front of a television screen.

first-page test A series of questions proposed by Joycelyn Pollock that police officers can ask themselves to reinforce professional ethical standards.

focused patrol A form of patrol that focuses police efforts on certain problems, locations, or times.

foot patrol The oldest method of police patrol, which entails officers walking through neighborhoods. Foot patrol tends to enhance rapport between citizens and officers, but it clearly limits an officer's ability to give chase if the need arises.

force continuum The spectrum of force available to a police officer, from the absence of physical force to the use of a deadly weapon.

force factor The level of force used by a police officer relative to the suspect's level of resistance.

forensic evidence Physical evidence whose usefulness in a court of law may not be immediately apparent to an untrained observer but can be demonstrated through the application of accepted scientific techniques.

Fourth Amendment The amendment to the U.S. Constitution that governs search and seizure.

frankpledge system The ultimate outgrowth of the night watch system of social control, dating to the twelfth century, in which ten households were grouped into a tithing, and each adult male member of the tithing was held responsible for the conduct of the others.

Frederick W. Taylor (1856–1915) A classical organizational theorist who posited that worker productivity could be increased through careful attention to how work was allocated and who performed what functions.

fruit of the poisonous tree doctrine An expansion of the scope of the exclusionary rule that requires the exclusion of any secondary evidence (such as a confession) that derives from evidence originally obtained in violation of the U.S. Constitution.

functional equivalent of a question Any words or actions on the part of the police (other than those normally attendant to arrest and custody) that the police should know are reasonably likely to elicit an incriminating response from the suspect.

fusion center An intelligence-gathering unit, often constituted as a collaborative effort that serves various agencies.

geographic profiling Using crime-mapping technology to identify the likely whereabouts or residences of repeat or serial offenders.

government action In the context of search and seizure law, one of two elements that must be considered when defining a Fourth Amendment search. (The other element is a reasonable expectation of privacy.) Government actions consist of measures to effect a search undertaken by someone employed by or working on behalf of the government.

Graham v. Connor The 1989 U.S. Supreme Court case in which the Court declared that claims of excessive nondeadly force must be judged under the Fourth Amendment's reasonableness clause.

grass eater A police officer who accepts small gifts and engages in minor acts of deviance but does not actively pursue opportunities for corruption.

gratuity Something of value that is freely given to police officers simply because they are police officers. Examples include a cup of coffee, a lunch, or a "police price" discount on a meal or other service.

Henry Fielding (1707–1754) An English magistrate who founded what some have called London's first police force, the Bow Street Runners.

Homeland Security Act of 2002 U.S. legislation enacted after the terrorist attacks of September 11, 2001, that created the cabinet-level Department of Homeland Security.

Homicide Investigation and Tracking System (HITS) A geographic profiling system that ties various databases together (gang files, sex offender registries, parole records, and department of motor vehicle records) to facilitate simultaneous database searches.

hostile work environment A form of sexual harassment involving situations in which unwelcome sexual contact and comments have the effect of "unreasonably interfering with an individual's work performance or creating an intimidating environment."

hot pursuit exception One exception to the Fourth Amendment's warrant requirement, recognized by the U.S. Supreme Court in *Warden* v. *Hayden* (1967). The hot pursuit doctrine provides that police officers may enter the premises where they suspect a crime has been committed, or a perpetrator is hiding, without a warrant when delay would likely endanger their lives or the lives of others and possibly lead to the escape of the alleged perpetrator.

hot spot A concentrated area of significant criminal activity, such as a street corner known for its prostitution traffic.

hot time A period during the day when crime is particularly problematic, such as after dark on a Friday night.

Illinois Crime Survey A series of influential reports, published in 1929, on homicide, juvenile justice, and justice operations in Chicago that criticized the corrupt political influence on the justice system.

Immigration and Customs Enforcement (ICE) The largest investigative component of the federal Department of Homeland Security. ICE focuses specifically on illegal immigration.

impact munitions Munitions designed to stun or otherwise temporarily incapacitate a suspect or a dangerous individual so that law enforcement officers can subdue and arrest that person with less risk of injury or death to themselves and to others.

impression management A media relations concept that involves controlling the presentation of information to achieve a desired public perception.

injunctive relief A court order to bring injurious or offensive action to a halt.

institution An organizational structure through which values and norms are transmitted over time and from one location to another within a society.

institutional value A sense of agreement within a particular culture about how to accomplish a valued objective.

intelligence-led policing (ILP) The collection and analysis of information to produce an intelligence end product designed to inform police decision making at both the tactical and strategic levels. Also called *intelligence-driven policing*.

intelligence Information that has been analyzed and integrated into a useful perspective.

intentional tort An action that is highly likely to cause injury or damage.

internal affairs (IA) An investigative agency within a police department that is tasked with investigating allegations of misconduct or criminality by members of the department.

International Association of Chiefs of Police (IACP) Founded in 1893, the best-known association for law enforcement professionals.

International Police Association (IPA) Founded in 1950, the largest police professional association in the world.

International Union of Police Associations (IUPA) An international police association, founded in 1954 and chartered by the AFL-CIO, that represents all rank-and-file officers and functions more as a lobbying group than as a professional association.

Joint Terrorism Task Force (JTTF) An FBI-sponsored group composed of federal, state, and local law enforcement personnel who are brought together to focus on a specific threat.

justification The focus of a court's examination of the reasonableness of a search or seizure.

Knapp Commission A commission to investigate police corruption that was appointed by New York City Mayor John V. Lindsay in 1970 in response to a *New York Times* article that reported widespread corruption in the New York City Police Department.

Law Enforcement Assistance and Partnership (LEAP) Strategy A plan introduced in the U.S. Congress that called for the establishment of a national center for intelligence-led policing.

legal abuse Any violation of a person's constitutionally, federally, or state-protected rights.

less-lethal weapon A weapon that is designed to disable, capture, or immobilize, rather than kill.

local agency One of the three levels of law enforcement activity in the United States—the other two being state and federal—that encompasses organizations like municipal police departments, sheriff's departments, and other lesser-known agencies (including campus police, transit police, and specialized agencies at public schools, airports, state capitols, medical facilities, state parks, certain prosecutor's offices, and others). Together, the personnel in these local agencies far outnumber all state and federal law enforcement officials combined.

Max Weber (1864–1920) A classical organizational theorist, widely acknowledged as the father of bureaucracy, who identified five principles that he suggested are characteristic of an effective bureaucratic organization.

mayor-council form A form of municipal government that can be categorized in two ways. The strong-mayor variation gives the mayor almost limitless authority over city operations, including the hiring and dismissal of key officials. In the weak-mayor variation, which is more common in small towns, the mayor serves largely at the behest of the city council.

meat eater A police officer who actively seeks out and plans opportunities to exploit his or her position for personal gain.

Metropolitan Police Act The legislation adopted by the British Parliament in 1829 that established the world's first large-scale organized police force in London.

Miranda **rights** The set of rights that a person accused or suspected of having committed a specific offense has during interrogation and of which he or she must be informed prior to questioning, as stated by the U.S. Supreme Court in *Miranda* v. *Arizona* (1966) and related cases.

Mollen Commission A commission appointed by New York City Mayor David N. Dinkins in 1992 to investigate allegations of police corruption in the New York City Police Department.

money laundering The process by which criminals or criminal organizations seek to disguise the illicit nature of their proceeds by introducing them into the stream of legitimate commerce and finance.

municipal police department One of the types of local law enforcement agencies in the United States. Specifically, the law enforcement agency that serves a municipality.

National Black Police Association The parent association, founded in 1972, for local and regional associations of African-American police professionals.

National Criminal Intelligence Sharing Plan (NCISP) A formal intelligence sharing initiative that addresses the security and intelligence needs recognized after the tragic events of September 11, 2001. It describes a nationwide communications capability that will link together all levels of law enforcement personnel, including officers on the streets, intelligence analysts, unit commanders, and police executives for the purpose of sharing critical data.

negligence tort A liability claim that must demonstrate that a legal duty existed between the officer and the plaintiff, that a breach of that duty occurred, that a proximate (direct) causation between the officer's actions and the alleged harm resulted, and that actual damage or injury occurred.

noble-cause corruption Any corruption that occurs in connection with the goal of getting criminals off the streets and protecting the community.

nondeadly force Force that is unlikely to cause death or significant bodily harm.

nonsworn personnel Support staff members of a law enforcement agency who are not empowered to make arrests.

norm A rule or expectation for behavior that characterizes a particular social group.

objective reasonableness A standard, used to determine whether qualified immunity applies, that looks at how a reasonable person would have acted under a given set of circumstances.

occupational deviance Behavior performed under the guise of police authority that either does not conform to accepted standards of conduct or is not part of normal patrol work.

Office of Community Oriented Policing Services (COPS Office) An agency within the U.S. Department of Justice tasked with administering and supervising federal funds allocated to improve community policing capabilities.

organization A group in which individuals work together to accomplish specified tasks or goals.

Orlando Winfield "O. W." Wilson (1900–1972) A progressive era reformer, professor of police administration, and protégé of August Vollmer whose writings and teachings continue to influence contemporary U.S. law enforcement.

paradox of policing A phenomenon in which a police officer's fear of being injured or killed is stronger than is justified by actual rates of injury or death within the profession.

parish Under the frankpledge system, a group of ten tithings. Also referred to as a *hundred*.

participatory management A form of leadership that allows subordinates to participate in decision making and planning, especially with regard to the manner in which their own units are operated.

particularistic perspective The view that individual officers differ from one another in various ways, including values, role orientation, and preferred styles of policing.

patronage system A system of hiring in which decisions are based more on an individual's political support for an officeholder than on his or her abilities and qualifications. Patronage was common in police agencies during the political era.

pepper spray A so-called lachrymatory (inflammatory) agent that causes irritation to the eyes and skin. Also called *oleoresin capsicum (OC)*.

person inventory The search of an arrestee and his or her personal items, including containers found in his or her possession, as part of a routine inventory that is incident to the booking and jailing procedure. Often called *arrest inventory*.

perversion of justice A kind of police corruption that consists of serious actions by a police officer, such as lying under oath (perjury), intimidating a witness, and performing other activities that resemble combative corruption.

pin map An early crime-mapping technique that used colored pins to track criminal events on a map of the police department's jurisdictional area.

plain-view doctrine The rule that the police may seize evidence without a warrant if they have lawful access to the object and it is immediately apparent (that is, they have probable cause) that the object is subject to seizure.

plebe system A police academy model that closely parallels a military-style boot camp and that aims to produce well-groomed and disciplined officers.

police commission An agency maintained in some large cities that acts like a corporate board of directors, setting policy and overseeing the police department's operations.

police corruption The misuse of police authority for personal or organizational gain.

police crime An officer's use of the official powers of his or her job to engage in criminal conduct.

police officers' bill of rights A police agency's formal statement of the rights of officers who are accused of misconduct.

police sexual violence A sexually degrading, humiliating, violating, damaging, or threatening act committed by a police officer against a (usually female) citizen through the use of force or police authority.

police subculture The shared values and norms and the established patterns of behavior that tend to characterize policing; also called *police culture*.

police training officer (PTO) program A police training method that focuses on developing an officer's learning capacity, leadership, and problem-solving skills.

police violence In the context of drug investigations, the use of improper physical force to extract a confession or to obtain evidence.

political era The period of American policing during the late nineteenth and early twentieth centuries during which police forces served more to regulate crime pursuant to the wishes of corrupt politicians (who used patronage to give police jobs to handpicked loyalists) than to control crime in the interests of the public good.

post-traumatic stress disorder (PTSD) A condition that sets in following a traumatic event with which the sufferer cannot cope. It has been described as an event outside the usual human experience—one that is experienced in a markedly distressing way, with intense fear, terror, bewilderment, and a sense of helplessness.

predatory corruption A form of police corruption that consists of more than just passive participation (for example, looking the other way while a fellow police officer commits a crime). In predatory corruption, officers actively promote and engage in criminal and other wrongful activities.

pretext stop A traffic stop based on more than one motive. For example, an officer stops a vehicle for a legitimate reason but is also suspicious about the driver.

preventive patrol The practice of canvassing neighborhoods in an effort to discourage people from committing crime.

private policing The acquisition and use of security products and services, as well as the application of specialized knowledge in areas like crime control, investigation, and risk management, by nonsworn personnel.

private security The industry that provides for-profit security products and services, which include three broad categories: the provision of guards, equipment, and investigative or consulting services.

probable cause A set of facts and circumstances that would induce a reasonably intelligent and prudent person to believe that another particular person has committed a specific crime. Probable cause is the only justification for search and seizure mentioned in the Fourth Amendment.

problem police officer An officer who exhibits problem behavior, as indicated by a large number of citizen complaints, frequent involvement in use-of-force incidents, and other evidence.

problem-oriented policing (POP) A method of policing that is geared toward identifying and solving problems within a community that are particularly troublesome and then crafting creative solutions to them. Also called *problem-solving policing*.

protective sweep A permissible cursory visual inspection of places in which a person might be hiding. A protective sweep may be conducted by police up to the point of an arrest but must be supported by reasonable suspicion.

public information officer A police department's spokesperson. The media must go through the public information officer to gather information about the department.

public-duty defense A legal defense that shields a police officer from criminal liability in situations in which he or she is legally performing an assigned or implied public duty and engages in a necessary and reasonable action that, for ordinary citizens, would be considered a crime.

public-duty doctrine A doctrine stating that police protection (like any other government function) is owed to the general public, not to individuals. Police officers have used the public-duty doctrine as a liability defense.

qualified immunity A liability defense that shields a police officer who has acted in an objectively reasonable fashion as long as he or she did not violate clearly established rights that a reasonable person would have known. Qualified immunity is an outgrowth of various U.S. Supreme Court decisions.

quality circle A group of qualified employees from all ranks who work together, often around one table, to solve organizational problems.

quality-of-life offense A minor law violation that demoralizes residents and businesspeople by creating disorder. Sometimes called *petty crime*.

quasi-military An organizational structure that follows the military model to some extent, but with subtle differences.

quid pro quo **harassment** A form of sexual harassment that generally involves a demand for sexual favors in exchange for some perk or benefit, such as a promotion or a favorable job assignment.

racial profiling The use of discretionary authority by law enforcement officers in encounters with minority motorists, typically within the context of a traffic stop, that results in the disparate treatment of minorities.

racial quota A requirement for hiring and promoting a specified number of minorities.

reasonable expectation of privacy In the context of search and seizure law, one of two elements that must be considered when defining a Fourth Amendment search. (The other element is government action.) A reasonable expectation of privacy means that people who speak or act in private can reasonably expect that what they say or do will not be seen or heard by someone else.

reasonable suspicion A belief, based on a consideration of the facts at hand and on reasonable inferences drawn from those facts, that would induce an ordinarily prudent and cautious person under the same circumstances to conclude that criminal activity is taking place or that criminal activity has recently occurred. Reasonable suspicion is the standard for less intrusive stop-and-frisk searches; it is less than probable cause but more than a hunch.

reasonableness The elements of a situation that serve to justify a search or seizure.

reform era The period of American policing during the early to mid-twentieth century, during which efforts were made to professionalize police forces and to eliminate the influence of corrupt politicians.

remedy According to John Van Maanen, the last of three steps police officers use in identifying an "asshole." It consists of the officer's response to an affront.

response time The time it takes for police officers to respond to a call for service.

reverse discrimination Discrimination against nonminorities that occurs when the hiring and promotion of minorities are based more on race than on any other criterion.

Rodney King A suspect whose videotaped beating by members of the Los Angeles Police Department led to civil unrest across the nation.

rogue A seriously deviant officer.

rotten apple theory A perspective that attributes police deviance primarily to a few individuals whose propensity toward corruption was not recognized during the recruitment and hiring phases.

saturation patrol A form of patrol that involves concentrating the police presence in a certain area in an effort to catch criminals and to deter would-be offenders.

search incident to arrest A warrantless search made at the time of or shortly following an arrest, which is conducted out of a concern for the safety of the arresting officer and others.

search An activity performed in order to find evidence to be used in a criminal prosecution.

seizure The confiscation of one's person (arrest) or property by a government agent.

sexual harassment Unwelcome sexual advances, requests for sexual favors, and other verbal or physical conduct of a sexual nature.

sheriff's department One of the types of local law enforcement agencies in the United States. Specifically, the law enforcement agency that serves a county or parish.

sheriff The modern-day term for the Old English *shire-reeve*. In the United States today, the senior law enforcement official in a county.

shire-reeve The Old English term for *sheriff*. Literally, "the keeper of the shire."

shire Under the frankpledge system, a collection of several parishes.

Sir Robert Peel (1788–1850) A former British home secretary whose criticisms of the state of policing in London led to the pas-sage of the Metropolitan Police Act and the establishment of the world's first large-scale organized police force in that city in 1829.

sixth sense A healthy sense of suspicion; the experience-based ability to intuit when something is amiss.

slave patrol A crude form of private policing, often carried out by citizen volunteers. Slave patrols were created in the eighteenth century to apprehend runaway slaves and to ensure that slaves did not rise up against their owners.

solidarity The tendency among police officers to stick together and associate with one another.

span of control The number of subordinates supervised by one person.

split-second syndrome A condition confronting police officers that involves three central features of policing—the urgency of police–citizen encounters, the involuntariness of such encounters, and a public setting—all of which combine to place officers in the position of having to make quick on-the-spot decisions.

state tort liability An important avenue of redress for plaintiffs whose minor injuries, allegedly resulting from negligent acts or misconduct by the police, are not serious enough to make Section 1983 litigation a viable option.

stop and frisk The detaining of a person by a law enforcement officer for the purpose of investigation, accompanied by a superficial examination by the officer of the person's body surface or clothing to discover weapons, contraband, or other objects relating to criminal activity.

straight shooter An honest police officer who will overlook some misconduct committed by peers.

straightforward corruption Any form of police misconduct that provides direct financial benefit to police officers.

strategic intelligence A type of intelligence that provides information to decision makers about the changing nature of threats, enabling them to develop response strategies and reallocate resources for effective threat prevention.

street environment One of two settings identified by John Crank (the other is the traffic stop) in which police officers perform daily tasks that involve interaction with ordinary citizens and with other criminal justice professionals.

stress Anything that places a positive or negative adjustive demand on an organism.

subculture Cultural patterns that distinguish some segment of a society's population.

subjugation of defendants' rights In the context of drug investigations, an officer's lying or committing perjury or fabricating evidence in the name of securing a drug conviction.

sudden peril A defense against state tort liability that is used for cases in which police officers were required to make split-second decisions.

suicide by cop An incident in which an individual who is determined to die engages in behavior meant to provoke responding officers to resort to deadly force.

sworn personnel Members of a law enforcement agency who are empowered to make arrests.

systems perspective A view of organizational style, rooted in biology, that posits that organizations are living organisms that strive for a state of equilibrium, or balance, and that affect or are affected by their environment.

tactical intelligence A type of intelligence that includes gaining or developing information related to threats of terrorism or crime and using this information to apprehend offenders, harden targets, and use strategies that will eliminate or mitigate the threat.

Taking Command Initiative A project undertaken by the International Association of Chiefs of Police to assess the current state of homeland security efforts in the United States and to develop and implement the actions needed to protect American communities from the specter of both crime and terrorism.

Tammany Hall The corrupt Democratic Party political "machine" that operated in New York City in the late nineteenth and early twentieth centuries and that used patronage to control city operations.

technical training model A police academy training model that emphasizes the technical aspects of police work and provides little or no training in such nontechnical areas as stress management, interaction with difficult people, problem solving, and sensitivity to marginalized groups.

Tennessee* v. *Garner The 1985 U.S. Supreme Court case that specified the conditions under which deadly force could be used to apprehend suspected felons.

territorial imperative The sense of obligation, even protectiveness, that develops in officers who routinely patrol the same area.

Texas Rangers A militia originally formed by Stephen F. Austin in 1823 to protect the territory of Texas against Native American raids, criminals, and intruders. Today, the Rangers serve as part of the Texas Department of Public Safety.

theory of liability Reasons offered as to why a particular person or other entity should be held answerable under law for some action.

thief taker An alternative name for Henry Fielding's Bow Street Runners.

third degree A formerly common coercive interrogation technique that combined psychological pressures with physical force.

third-party policing A recently coined term that describes police efforts to persuade or coerce nonoffending persons to take actions that are outside the scope of their routine activities, and that are designed to indirectly minimize disorder caused by other persons or to reduce the possibility that crime may occur.

tithing Under the frankpledge system, a group of ten households.

tolerated lie A lie that is used to defend a questionable discretionary decision.

trace evidence Minute, nearly invisible evidence of a crime that would escape all but the most skilled investigators.

U.S. Marshals Service (USMS) The oldest American law enforcement agency. Its mission includes judicial security and fugitive investigation and apprehension.

universalistic perspective The view that all police officers are similar and that they exhibit some of the same characteristics and behavior patterns.

use corruption Drug-related police corruption that consists of an officer's personal use of illicit drugs.

use of force The use of physical restraint by a police officer when dealing with a member of the public.

value A standard of goodness, desirability, behavior, beauty, or interaction that serves as a guideline for living within a particular culture.

vehicle inventory A warrantless inventory of a vehicle that is permissible on administrative or regulatory grounds. Vehicle inventories must follow a lawful impoundment, must be of a routine nature, must follow standard operating procedures, and must not be a pretext that attempts to conceal an investigatory search.

Violent Crime Control and Law Enforcement Act of 1994 The U.S. legislation that established the Office of Community Oriented Policing Services (the COPS Office) in the U.S. Justice Department.

watchman An early officer on foot patrol who, during the hours of darkness, watched for fires and criminal activities. Upon detecting such events, the watchman's role was to sound the "hue and cry" to evoke a defensive response from the citizenry. This style of policing dates back to the early to mid-eighteenth century in England.

weapons continuum The array of nonlethal and lethal weaponry available to police officers, the selection of which depends on the situation.

white knight An honest and upstanding officer who never steps over the line between accepted and deviant conduct, no matter how great the pressure to do so.

Wickersham Commission A commission appointed by President Herbert Hoover in 1929 to investigate the operations and problems of the criminal justice system. Formally known as the National Commission on Law Observance and Enforcement.

William M. "Boss" Tweed (1823–1878) A corrupt American politician who became notorious as the powerful leader of New York City's Tammany Hall.

References

Chapter 1, Origins and Evolution of American Policing

1 David Weisburd and Peter Neyroud, "Police Science: Toward a New Paradigm," Harvard University, John F. Kenedy School of Government, 2011.

2 Ibid.

3 F. Schmalleger, *Criminal justice today: An introductory text for the twenty-first century,* 9th ed. (Upper Saddle River, NJ: Prentice Hall, 2007), p. 162.

4 B. L. Berg, *Law enforcement: An introduction to police in society* (Boston: Allyn and Bacon, 1992), pp. 15–16.

5 W. Kunkel, *An introduction to Roman legal and constitutional history,* 2nd ed. (Oxford: Clarendon Press, 1973).

6 W. J. Bopp and D. D. Schultz, *A short history of American law enforcement* (Springfield, IL: Charles C. Thomas, 1972), pp. 9–10.

7 There are three "historical" Statutes of Westminster, dated 1275, 1285, and 1290 (known as "First," "Second," and "Third"), relating to the government of the Kingdom of England. There is also a 1931 Statute of Westminster, relating to the British Empire and its dominions.

8 W. L. M. Lee, *A history of police in England* (repr., Montclair, NJ: Patterson Smith, 1971).

9 D. H. Bayley, *Patterns of policing: A comparative international analysis* (New Brunswick, NJ: Rutgers University Press, 1985), p. 29.

10 J. J. Tobias, "Police and public in the United Kingdom," *Journal of Contemporary History* (January–April 1972): 201–19.

11 G. Armitage, *The history of the Bow Street Runners, 1729–1829* (London: Wishart, n.d.), p. 123.

12 A. C. Germann, F. D. Day, and R. R. Gallati, *Introduction to law enforcement and criminal justice* (Springfield, IL: Charles C. Thomas, 1978).

13 S. Spitzer and A. T. Scull, "Social control in historical perspective: From private to public responses to crime," in *Correction and punishment,* ed. D. F. Greenberg, pp. 265–86 (Beverly Hills, CA: Sage, 1977).

14 Bayley, *Patterns of policing,* pp. 31–32.

15 Germann, Day, and Gallati, *Introduction to law enforcement and criminal justice.*

16 J. L. Lyman, "The Metropolitan Police Act of 1829: An analysis of certain events influencing the passage and character of the Metropolitan Police Act in England," *Journal of Criminal Law, Criminology, and Police Science,* vol. 55, no. 1 (March 1964): 141.

17 Roy Ingleton, "The early days of policing in Kent" (Part 6), The Kent Police Museum, www.kent-police-museum. co.uk/core_pages/pasttimes_early_days_pt6.shtml (accessed July 4, 2008).

18 L. Radzinowicz, *A history of English criminal law and its administration since 1750* (New York: Macmillan, 1957), p. 177.

19 E. L. Ayers, *Vengeance and justice: Crime and punishment in the nineteenth century American South* (New York: Oxford University Press, 1984), p. 181.

20 B. Chapin, *Criminal justice in colonial America, 1606–1660* (Athens: University of Georgia Press, 1983), p. 146.

21 F. Browning and J. Gerassi, *The American way of crime* (New York: G. P. Putnam's Sons, 1980).

22 L. H. Randolph, *Biographical sketches of distinguished officers of the army and navy* (New York: Henry E. Huntington, 1905), pp. 82–88.

23 R. B. Fosdick, *American police systems* (New York: The Century Co., 1920), p. 62.

24 G. L. Lankevich, *American metropolis: A history of New York City* (New York: New York University Press, 1998), pp. 84–85.

25 Fosdick, *American police systems,* p. 82.

26 Others date the NYPD's official beginning as January 1, 1898—the day that the five boroughs of Manhattan, the Bronx, Brooklyn, Queens, and Staten Island, joined together under a charter as the City of Greater New York. What should be clear, however, is that what was essentially a citywide police force operated in the area prior to the 1898 charter.

27 Some of the information in this paragraph comes from Bernard Whalen, "The birth of the NYPD," www.nycop. com/Aug_00/The_ Birth_of_the_NYPD/body_the_birth_ of_the_ nypd.html (accessed July 5, 2008). The department was further expanded in 1995, when the city's housing and transit police were merged into the NYPD.

28 B. Vila and C. Morris, eds., *The role of police in American society: A documentary history* (Westport, CT: Greenwood Press, 1999), p. 25.

29 W. Miller, *Cops and bobbies* (Chicago: University of Chicago Press, 1977), p. 2.

30 Vila and Morris, eds., *The role of police in American society.*

31 Ibid.

32 R. Brown, *Strain of violence* (New York: Oxford University Press, 1975).

33 S. Walker, *Popular justice* (New York: Oxford University Press, 1998), p. 15.

34 B. Smith, *Police systems in the United States* (New York: Harper and Brothers, 1949).

35 Walker, *Popular justice*, p. 55.

36 Illinois Association for Criminal Justice, *Illinois crime survey* (1929; repr. Montclair, NJ: Patterson Smith, 1968), p. 359.

37 G. L. Kelling and M. H. Moore, "The evolving strategy of policing," in *Perspectives on policing*, vol. 4 (Washington, DC: National Institute of Justice, 1988).

38 Walker, *Popular justice*, p. 57.

39 J. C. Schneider, *Detroit and the problem of order, 1830–1880* (Lincoln: University of Nebraska Press, 1980), pp. 26–27, 121.

40 Walker, *Popular justice*, p. 59.

41 A. von Hoffman, "An officer of the neighborhood: A Boston patrolman on the beat in 1895," *Journal of Social History*, vol. 26, no. 2 (Winter 1992), pp. 309–30.

42 E. H. Monkkonen, *Police in urban America, 1860–1920* (Cambridge: Cambridge University Press, 1981), pp. 87, 89.

43 Walker, *Popular justice*, p. 62.

44 "Thomas F. Byrnes," in *Wikipedia, The free encyclopedia*, revised May 18, 2008, http://en.wikipedia.org/w/index.php?title=Thomas_F._Byrnes&oldid=213279082 (accessed June 19, 2008).

45 C. H. Parkhurst, *Our fight with Tammany* (1895; repr., New York: Arno Press, 1970), p. 5.

46 H. P. Jeffers, *Commissioner Roosevelt: The story of Theodore Roosevelt and the New York City Police, 1895-97* (New York: Wiley, 1994).

47 Walker, *Popular justice*, p. 65.

48 A. Vollmer, "Predelinquency," in *Proceedings, 1919*, ed. International Association of Chiefs of Police, pp. 77–80 (New York: Arno Press, 1971).

49 Walker, *Popular justice*, p. 131.

50 Illinois Association for Criminal Justice, *Illinois crime survey* (1929; repr., Montclair, NJ: Patterson Smith, 1968), p. 359.

51 For more on Vollmer's legacy, see J. Liss and S. Schlossman, "The contours of crime prevention in August Vollmer's Berkeley," in *Research in law, deviance, and social control*, vol. 6 (Greenwich, CT: JAI Press, 1984); A. Vollmer and A. Schneider, "The school for police as planned at Berkeley," *Journal of Criminal Law and Criminology* 7 (1917): 877–98; and G. E. Carte and E. H. Carte, *Police reform in the United States: The era of August Vollmer* (Berkeley: University of California Press, 1975).

52 Walker, *Popular justice*, p. 172.

53 O. W. Wilson and R. C. McLaren, *Police administration*, 4th ed. (New York: McGraw-Hill, 1977).

54 O. W. Wilson, *The distribution of police patrol forces* (Chicago: Public Administration Service, 1941).

55 Walker, *Popular justice*, p. 173.

56 J. E. Angell, "Toward an alternative to the classic police organizational arrangements: A democratic model," *Criminology* 9 (1971): 185–206.

57 See the Minuteman Project website, www.minutemanproject.com.

Chapter 2, Policing in American Context

1 "Large cuts in staff for Camden, Newark police could threaten anti-crime progress," NJ.com, December 05, 2010, www.nj.com/news/index.ssf/2010/12/large_cuts_in_staff_for_camden.html (accessed February 7, 2011).

2 George Berkin, "Camden police layoffs and economics," NJ.com, January 21, 2011, http://blog.nj.com/njv_george_berkin/2011/01/camden_police_layoffs_and_econ.html (accessed June 28, 2011).

3 G. T. Marx, "Police and democracy," http://web.mit.edu/gtmarx/www/dempol.html (accessed December 2, 2010).

4 Robert F. Kennedy quotations from MemorableQuotations.com, www.memorablequotations.com/rfk.htm (accessed December 2, 2010).

5 See, e.g., S. K. Ivkovich, "Shades of blue: A cross-national study of public support for the police," paper presented at the annual meeting of the American Society of Criminology, Toronto, June 20, 2008; S. G. Brandl, J. Frank, J. Wooldredge, and R. C. Watkins, "On the measurement of public support for the police: A research note," *Policing: An International Journal of Police Strategies & Management*, vol. 20, no. 3 (1997): 473–80; and E. Erez, "Self-defined desert and citizen's assessment of the police," *Journal of Criminal Law and Criminology* 75 (1984): 1276–99.

6 J. L. Worrall, "Public perceptions of police efficacy and image: The fuzziness of support for the police," *American Journal of Criminal Justice* 24 (1999): 47–66.

7 D. Bayley, *Forces of order: Police behavior in Japan and the United States* (Berkeley: University of California Press, 1976); and S. M. Lipset and W. Schneider, *The confidence gap: Business, labor, and government in the public mind* (New York: Free Press, 1983).

8 S. Albrect and M. Green, "Attitudes toward the police and the larger attitude complex: Implications for police-community relations," *Criminology* 15 (1977): 67–87; T. Jefferson and M. A. Walker, "Ethnic minorities in the criminal justice system," *Criminal Law Review* 28 (1993): 83–95; and R. B. Parks, "Linking objective and subjective measures of performance," *Public Administration Review* 44 (1984): 118–27.

9 Associated Press, "Town to police: 'You're fired,'" October 23, 2006, www.cbsnews.com/stories/2006/10/23/national/main2114983.shtml (accessed December 2, 2010).

10 City of San Diego, "Strong mayor form of governance," www.sandiego.gov/mayortransition/index.shtml (accessed December 2, 2010).

11 James Sterngold, "Police chief rebuffed in Los Angeles," *New York Times*, April 18, 2002, http://query.nytimes.com/gst/fullpage.html?res=9B04E3DE173FF93BA25757C0A9649C8B63 (accessed December 2, 2010).

12 GovernmentExecutive.com, "Park police chief fired," July 9, 2004, www.govexec.com/dailyfed/0704/070904a1.htm (accessed December 2, 2010).

13 J. L. Worrall, "Constitutional issues in reality-based police television programs: Media ride-alongs," *American Journal of Criminal Justice* 25 (2000): 41–64. Also see P. G. Kooistra, J. S. Mahoney, and S. D. Westervelt, "The world of crime according to 'COPS,'" in *Entertaining crime: Television reality programs*, ed. M. Fishman and G. Cavender, pp. 141–58 (New York: Aldine De Gruyter, 1998); and M. B. Oliver, "Portrayals of crime, race, and aggression in 'reality-based' police shows: A content analysis," *Journal of Broadcasting and Electronic Media* 38 (1994): 179–92.

14 J. M. Carlson, "Crime show viewing by preadults: The impact on attitudes toward civil liberties," *Communication Research* 10 (1983): 529–52; J. M. Carlson, *Prime time law enforcement: Crime show viewing and attitudes toward the criminal justice system* (New York: Praeger, 1985); R. M. Entman, "Modern racism and the images of blacks in local television news," *Critical Studies in Mass Communication* 7 (1990): 332–45; R. M. Entman, "Blacks in the news: Television, modern racism and cultural change," *Journalism Quarterly* 60 (1992): 341–61; G. Gerbner and L. Gross, "Living with television: The violence profile," *Journal of Communication* 26 (1976): 173–99; and R. P. Hawkins and S. Pingree, "Uniform messages and habitual viewing: Unnecessary assumptions in social reality effects," *Human Communication Research* 7 (1981): 291–301.

15 R. Costello and F. Biafora, "Just the facts ma'am: The supreme court says 'no' to media ride-alongs," *Journal of Criminal Justice and Popular Culture* 7 (1999): 15–25, quote on p. 15.

16 J. L. Worrall, "Constitutional issues in reality-based police television programs: Media ride-alongs," *American Journal of Criminal Justice* 25 (2000): 41–64, quote on pp. 42–43.

17 J. S. Lovell, *Media power and information control*, p. 179.

18 Ibid.

19 Ibid.

20 Ibid.

21 Ibid.

22 Ibid., pp. 188–89.

23 International Association of Chiefs of Police, CONSTITUTION (Alexandria, VA: International Association of Chiefs of Police, 2006). Reprinted by permission.

24 The National Black Police Association website, www.blackpolice.org (accessed December 2, 2010).

25 International Union of Police Associations Mission Statement, http://www.iupa.org. Reprinted by permission.

26 International Police Association, www.ipa-usa.org/index.php (accessed December 2, 2010).

27 From "What is the IPA?" http://ipa-ica.org. Reprinted by permission of the International Police Association.

28 E. Glazer, "Thinking strategically: How federal prosecutors can reduce violent crime," *Fordham Urban Law Journal* 26 (1999): 573–606.

29 From "The use of force / When SFPD officers resort to violence," by Susan Sward, Bill Wallace and Elizabeth Fernandez, SAN FRANCISCO CHRONICLE, February 5, 2006, p. A1. Reprinted by permission.

30 From "The use of force / When SFPD officers resort to violence," by Susan Sward, Bill Wallace and Elizabeth Fernandez, SAN FRANCISCO CHRONICLE, February 5, 2006, p. A1. Reprinted by permission.

31 From "The use of force / When SFPD officers resort to violence," by Susan Sward, Bill Wallace and Elizabeth Fernandez, SAN FRANCISCO CHRONICLE, February 5, 2006, p. A1. Reprinted by permission.

Chapter 3, Law Enforcement Agencies and Their Organization

1 This story is taken from FBI "Mafia takedown," January 20, 2011, from which much of the wording comes. Web available at www.fbi.gov/news/stories/2011/january/mafia_012011 (accessed February 8, 2011).

2 E. R. Maguire and others, "Counting cops: Estimating the number of police departments and police officers in the USA," Policing: An International Journal of Police Strategies and Management 21 (1998): 109.

3 Ibid.

4 We divided 311 million (there are approximately this many people in the United States as of this writing) by 680,000.

5 U.S. Customs and Border Protection, "This is CBP," www.cbp.gov/xp/cgov/about/mission/cbp.xml (accessed December 5, 2010).

6 U.S. Customs and Border Protection, "Snapshot: A summary of CBP facts and figures," www.cbp.gov/linkhandler/cgov/about/accomplish/snapshot.ctt/snapshot.pdf (accessed December 5, 2010).

7 U.S. Immigration and Customs Enforcement, "ICE overview," www.ice.gov/about/overview/ (accessed December 5, 2010).

8 16Stat. 162.

9 Federal Bureau of Investigation, "Today's FBI," www.fbi.gov/stats-services/publications/facts-and-figures-2010-2011/facts-and-figures-2010-2011-pdf (accessed December 5, 2010).

10 Ibid.

11 More historical details can be found at U.S. Marshals Service, "Historical Perspective," www.usmarshals.gov/history/index.html (accessed December 5, 2010).

12 These and other facts draw from U.S. Marshals Service, *Fact sheet* (Washington, DC: U.S. Department of Justice, U.S. Marshals Service, Pub. No. 21-A, January 13, 2006).

13 U.S. Drug Enforcement Administration, "DEA mission statement," www.dea.gov/agency/mission.htm (accessed December 5, 2010).

14 New York City Police Department website, www.nyc.gov/html/nypd/html/faq/faq_police.shtml#1 (accessed December 5, 2010).

15 B. A. Reaves and M. J. Hickman, *Census of state and local law enforcement agencies, 2004* (Washington, DC: Bureau of Justice Statistics, 2007). These are most recent figures available as of this writing (December 5, 2010).

16 Ibid.

17 Reaves and Hickman, *Census of state and local law enforcement agencies, 2004*.

18 This is not the case in every state.

19 Ohio Revised Code, Section 3313.616 (2006).

20 S. P. Robbins, *Organization theory: Structure, design, and applications* (Englewood Cliffs, NJ: Prentice Hall, 1990).

21 H. G. Rainey, *Understanding the managing of public organizations* (San Francisco: Jossey-Bass, 1991).

22 A. Germann, F. Day, and R. Gallati, *Introduction to law enforcement and criminal justice* (Springfield, IL: Charles C. Thomas, 1978).

23 M. Weber, "Bureaucracy," in *Organizations*, vol. 1, ed. J. Litterer, pp. 29–31 (New York: Wiley, 1969).

24 T. Burns and G. Stalker, *The management of innovation* (London: Tavistock, 1961).

25 J. Kuykendall and R. Roberg, *Police administration* (Los Angeles: Roxbury, 1997).

26 L. Bertalanffy, "General systems theory: A new approach to the unity of science," *Human Biology* 23 (1951): 302–61.

27 Ibid.

28 E. E. Joh, "The paradox of private policing," *Journal of Criminal Law and Criminology* 95 (2004): 67.

29 See, e.g., M. K. Nalla and C. G. Heraux, "Assessing the goals and functions of private police," *Journal of Criminal Justice* 31 (2003): 237–47.

30 Joh, "The paradox of private policing," pp. 491–31.

31 R. Behar, "Thugs in uniform," *Time* (March 9, 1992): 44.

32 W. C. Cunningham and J. J. Strauchs, "Security industry trends: 1993 and beyond," *Security Management* 36 (1992): 27–30, 32, 34–36.

33 P. S. Bailin and D. K. Cole, *Industry study 1244: Private security services* (Cleveland: Freedonia Group, 2000).

34 Cunningham and Strauchs, "Security industry trends," pp. 27–30, 32, 34–36.

35 D. A. Sklansky, "The private police," *UCLA Law Review* 46 (1999): 1165–1287, quote on p. 1166.

36 Joh, "The paradox of private policing," p. 67.

37 Ibid.

38 Ibid., p. 62.

39 C. D. Shearing and P. Stenning, "Modern private security: Its growth and implications," in *Crime and justice: A review of research*, ed. M. Tonry, pp. 193–246 (Chicago: University of Chicago Press, 1981). See also C. D. Shearing and P. C. Stenning, *Private policing* (Newbury Park, CA: Sage, 1987).

40 Joh, "The paradox of private policing," p. 62.

41 Shearing and P. Stenning, "Modern private security: Its growth and implications."

42 Joh, "The paradox of private policing," p. 62.

43 Ibid., p. 63.

44 See, e.g., D. Shichor and M. J. Gilbert, eds., *Privatization in criminal justice: Past, present, and future* (Dayton, OH: Lexis-Nexis, 2001).

45 Sklansky, "The private police," p. 1166.

46 Ibid., pp. 1230–31.

47 *Griffin* v. *Maryland*, 378 U.S. 130 (1964).

48 See, e.g., *Wade* v. *Byles*, 83 F.3d 902 (7th Cir. 1996); *Gallagher* v. *Neil Young Freedom Concert*, 49 F.3d 1442 (10th Cir. 1995); *United States* v. *Francoeur*, 547 F.2d 891 (5th Cir. 1977); *People* v. *Taylor*, 271 Cal. Rptr. 785 (Ct. App. 1990); *United States* v. *Lima*, 424 A.2d 113 (D.C. 1980) (en banc); *People* v. *Toliver*, 377 N.E.2d 207 (Ill. App. Ct. 1978); *People* v. *Holloway*, 267 N.W.2d 454 (Mich. Ct. App. 1978); and *State* v. *Buswell*, 460 N.W.2d 614 (Minn. 1990).

49 See, e.g., *United States* v. *Antonelli*, 434 F.2d 335 (2d Cir. 1970); and *City of Grand Rapids* v. *Impens*, 327 N.W.2d 278 (Mich. 1982).

50 See, e.g., *United States* v. *Cruz*, 783 F.2d 1470, 1473 (9th Cir. 1986); *State* v. *Garcia*, 528 So. 2d 76 (Fla. Dist. Ct. App. 1988); *Perez* v. *State*, 517 So. 2d 106 (Fla. Dist. Ct. App. 1987); *People* v. *Gorski*, 494 N.E.2d 246 (Ill. App. Ct. 1986); *State* v. *Farmer*, 510 P.2d 180 (Kan. 1973); and *Commonwealth* v. *Lindenmuth*, 554 A.2d 62 (Pa. Super. Ct. 1989).

51 Joh, "The paradox of private policing," p. 64.

52 See, e.g., J. Hall, "Legal and social aspects of arrest without a warrant," *Harvard Law Review* 49 (1935): 566.

53 J. T. Gilliland, "Ireland refuses to extradite alleged pedophile to Arizona," July 29, 2005, Cybercast News Service, www.cnsnews.com/news/article/22523 (accessed December 5, 2010).

54 Ibid.

55 Joh, "The paradox of private policing," p. 67.

Chapter 4, Becoming a Cop

1 K. J. Peak, *Policing America: Methods, issues, challenges*, 5th ed. (Upper Saddle River, NJ: Prentice Hall, 2006), p. 69.

2 Quoted in V. A. Leonard and H. W. More, *Police organization and management*, 3rd ed. (Mineola, NY: Foundation Press, 1971), p. 128.

3 J. Nislow, "Is anyone out there?" *Law Enforcement News*, October 31, 1999, p. 1.

4 N. Z. Dizon, "Searching for police," June 3, 2000, Associated Press news service.

5 M. Lifsher, "State strains to recruit new police," *Wall Street Journal*, November 10, 1999, p. CA1.

6 Peak, *Policing America*, p. 72.

7 For a thorough review of studies in this area, see J. G. Varela et al., "Personality testing in law enforcement employment settings: A meta-analytic review," *Criminal Justice and Behavior* 31 (2004): 649–75. See also S. Daniels and E. King, "Predictive validity of MMPI-2 content scales for small-town police officer performance," *Journal of Police and Criminal Psychology* 17 (2002): 54–62; and W. U. Weiss and others, "Personality assessment inventory as a selection device for law enforcement personnel," *Journal of Police and Criminal Psychology* 19 (2004): 23–29.

8 K. Peak, D. Farenholtz, and G. Coxey, "Physical abilities testing for police officers: A flexible, job-related approach," *Police Chief* (January 1992): 51–56.

9 See, for example, Truth or Lie Polygraph Lie Detector Examination Agency, "How can you beat the polygraph?" http://www.truthorlie.com/beatpoly.html (accessed December 6, 2010).

10 Peak, *Policing America*, p. 78.

11 Ibid.

12 See, e.g., New York State Division of Criminal Justice Services, "Pre-employment police basic course," http://criminaljustice.state.ny.us/ops/training/bcpo/bcpo04.htm (accessed December 6, 2010).

13 See, e.g., D. Bradford and J. E. Pynes, "Police academy training: Why hasn't it kept up with practice?" *Police Quarterly* 2 (1999): 283–301; N. Marion, "Police academy training: Are we teaching recruits what they need to know?" *Policing: An International Journal of Police Strategies and Management* 21 (1998): 54–79; and R. F. Brand and K. Peak, "Assessing police training curriculums: 'Consumer reports,'" *Justice Professional* 9 (winter 1995): 45–58.

14 J. J. Broderick, *Police in a time of change*, 2nd ed. (Prospect Heights, IL: Waveland, 1987), p. 215.

15 Ibid.

16 Ibid.

17 Bradford and Pynes, "Police academy training."

18 Peak, *Policing America*, p. 81.

19 M. S. McCampbell, *Field training for police agencies: The state of the art* (Washington, DC: U.S. Department of Justice, National Institute of Justice, 1986).

20 K. J. Peak, S. Pitts, and R. W. Glensor, "From 'FTO' to 'PTO': A contemporary approach to post-academy recruit training," paper presented at the annual meeting of the Western and Pacific Association of Criminal Justice Educators, Reno, NV, 2006. Reprinted by permission of Ken Peak.

21 R. G. Dunham and G. P. Alpert, *Critical issues in policing: Contemporary readings* (Prospect Heights, IL: Waveland Press, 1989), pp. 111–15.

22 Peak, Pitts, and Glensor, "From 'FTO' to 'PTO,'" p. 6.

23 See, e.g., J. Dewey, *How we think: A restatement of the relation of reflective thinking on the educative process* (Boston: D. C. Heath, 1933).

24 M. Knowles, *Andragogy in action: Applying modern principles of adult learning* (San Francisco: Jossey-Bass, 1981).

25 H. Barrows and R. M. Tamblyn, *Problem-based learning: An approach to medical education* (New York: Springer, 1980).

26 B. S. Bloom, *Taxonomy of educational objectives, handbook I: The cognitive domain* (New York: David McKay, 1956).

27 Peak, Pitts, and Glensor, "From 'FTO' to 'PTO,'" pp. 8–9.

28 The organization's website is www.pspbl.com (accessed December 6, 2010).

29 Equal Employment Opportunity Commission, www.eeoc.gov (accessed November 9, 2008).

30 Equal Employment Opportunity Commission, "Retaliation," www.eeoc.gov/laws/types/retaliation.cfm (accessed December 6, 2010).

31 J. Frank and others, "Reassessing the impact of citizens' attitudes toward the police: A research note," *Justice Quarterly* 13 (1996): 231–34.

32 J. L. Sichel and others, *Women on patrol: A pilot study of police performance in New York City* (New York: Vera Institute of Justice, 1978).

33 R. Weitzer, "White, black, or blue cops? Race and citizen assessments of police officers," *Journal of Criminal Justice* 28 (2000): 313–24.

34 S. Walker, *Employment of black and Hispanic police officers, 1983–1988: A follow-up study* (Omaha: Center for Applied Urban Research, University of Nebraska at Omaha, 1989).

35 C. S. Johnson, *Into the mainstream: A survey of best practices in race relations in the South* (Chapel Hill: University of North Carolina Press, 1947).

36 J. L. Kuykendall and D. E. Burns, "The black police officer: An historical perspective," *Journal of Contemporary Criminal Justice* 4 (1980): 5.

37 E. Rudwick, *The unequal badge: Negro policemen in the South—Report of the Southern Regional Council* (Atlanta: Southern Regional Council, 1962).

[38] P. S. Sullivan, "Minority officers: Current issues," in *Critical issues in policing: Contemporary readings*, ed. R. G. Dunham and G. P. Alpert, pp. 331–45 (Prospect Heights, IL: Waveland, 1989). Adapted with permission from the International Association of Police Chiefs.

[39] H. F. Gosnell, *Negro politicians: The rise of negro politics in Chicago* (Chicago: University of Chicago Press, 1935).

[40] S. Leinen, *Black police, white society* (New York: New York University Press, 1984).

[41] M. J. Hickman and others, "Does race influence the police disciplinary process?" *Justice Research and Policy* 3 (2001): 97–113.

[42] President's Commission on Law Enforcement and Administration of Justice, *Task force report: The police* (Washington, DC: U.S. Government Printing Office, 1967), p. 162.

[43] L. W. Landrum, "The case of Negro police," *New South* 11 (1947): 5–6; and G. Myrdal, *An American dilemma: The Negro problem and modern democracy* (New York: Harper and Brothers, 1944).

[44] W. M. Kephart, *Racial factors and urban law enforcement* (Philadelphia: University of Pennsylvania Press, 1957).

[45] N. Alex, *New York cops talk back* (New York: Wiley, 1976).

[46] N. Alex, *Black in blue* (Englewood Cliffs, NJ: Prentice Hall, 1969).

[47] D. Parsons and P. Jesilow, *In the same voice: Women and men in law enforcement* (Santa Ana, CA: Seven Locks Press, 2001).

[48] Ibid.

[49] S. Walker, *A critical history of police reform* (Lexington, MA: Lexington Books, 1977), p. 85.

[50] C. Owings, *Women police* (New York: F. H. Hitchcock, 1925).

[51] G. E. Berkeley, *The democratic policeman* (Boston: Beacon, 1969).

[52] C. Milton, *Women in policing* (Washington, DC: Police Foundation, 1972).

[53] C. Sulton and R. A. Townsey, *Progress report on women in policing* (Washington, DC: Police Foundation, 1981).

[54] Police Foundation, *Community policing: A binding thread through the fabric of our society* (Washington, DC: Police Foundation, 1990).

[55] P. Bloch and D. Anderson, *Policewomen on patrol: Final report* (Washington, DC: Police Foundation, 1974); L. J. Sherman, "Evaluation of policewomen on patrol in a suburban police department," *Journal of Police Science and Administration* 3 (1975): 434–38; and J. L. Sichel and others, *Women on patrol: Pilot study of police performance in New York City* (New York: Vera Institute of Justice, 1978).

[56] S. Grennan, "Findings on the role of officer gender in violent encounters with citizens," *Journal of Police Science and Administration* 15 (1988): 78–85.

[57] Ibid. See also M. Morash and J. R. Greene, "Evaluating women on patrol: A critique of contemporary wisdom," *Evaluation Review* 10 (1986): 231–55.

[58] Parsons and Jesilow, *In the same voice.*

[59] B.A. Reaves, *Local police departments, 2007* (Washington, DC: Bureau of Justice Statistics, 2010), p. 14.

[60] D. A. Snyder, *The Americans with Disabilities Act* (Portland, OR: Labor Relations Information Systems, 1991).

[61] *Tanberg* v. *Weld County Sheriff*, 787 F.Supp. 970 (D. Colo. 1992).

[62] *Bombrays* v. *Toledo*, 849 F.Supp. (N.D. Ohio 1933).

[63] *Champ* v. *Baltimore County*, 884 F.Supp. 991 (1995).

[64] J. Jacobs and J. Cohen, "The impact of racial integration on the police," *Journal of Police Science and Administration* 6 (1978): 168–83.

[65] R. N. Haarr, "Patterns of interaction in a police patrol bureau: Race and gender barriers to integration," *Justice Quarterly* 14 (1997): 53–85.

[66] *Detroit Police Officers Association* v. *Young*, 446 F.Supp. 979 (1978).

[67] *United States* v. *Paradise*, 107 U.S. 1053 (1987).

[68] For more information, see Adversity.net, "Case 49: Dayton, Ohio police dept. loses reverse discrimination suit," www. adversity.net/Dayton_OH_PD/default.htm (accessed December 6, 2010).

[69] For more information, see Adversity.net, "Milwaukee police reverse discrimination," www.adversity.net/milwaukee_police/alexander_v_jones.htm (accessed December 6, 2010).

[70] C. McHenry, "Stress in the police service: Preventing the long-term effects of trauma," *Occupational Health Review* (July–August 1995), p. 18.

[71] *Hall* v. *GHS Construction Co.*, 842 F.2d 101 (8th Cir. 1988).

[72] See, e.g., J. Grencik, "Toward an understanding of stress," in *Job stress and the police officer: Identifying stress reduction techniques*, ed. W. Kroes and J. Hurrell (Washington, DC: U.S. Department of Health, Education, and Welfare, 1975), pp. 163–81.

[73] See, e.g., J. Blackmore, "Are police allowed to have problems of their own?" *Police Magazine* 1 (1978): 47–55; and L. Territo and H. Vetter, *Stress and police personnel* (Boston: Allyn and Bacon, 1981).

[74] J. Selye, *Stress without distress* (Philadelphia: Lippincott, 1981).

[75] Ibid.

[76] R. L. Veniga and J. Spradley, *How to cope with job burnout* (Englewood Cliffs, NJ: Prentice Hall, 1981), p. 6.

[77] M. Silbert, "Job stress and burnout of new police officers," *Police Chief* 49 (1982): 46–48.

[78] R. M. Solomon, "Post-shooting trauma," *Police Chief* 55 (1988): 40, 42, 44.

79 S. Carson, "Post-shooting stress reduction," *Police Chief* (October 1982): 66–68.

80 Ibid.

81 Solomon, "Post-shooting trauma."

82 C. McHenry, "Stress in the police service: Preventing the long-term effects of trauma," *Occupational Health Review* (July–August 1995): 17–20, quote on p.18.

83 Ibid.

84 Cited in B. Vila and D. J. Kenney, "Tired cops: The prevalence and potential consequences of police fatigue," *NIJ Journal* 248 (2002): 16–21, quote on p. 20.

85 B. Vila, *Tired cops: The importance of managing police fatigue* (Washington, DC: Police Executive Research Forum, 2000).

86 Vila and Kenney, "Tired cops," p. 18.

87 Ibid., p. 17.

88 Ibid.

89 Ibid., p. 18.

90 Ibid., p. 17.

91 Ibid., p. 18.

92 Ibid., p. 18.

93 Ibid., p. 19.

94 *Barnes* v. *Costle*, 561 F.2d 983 (D.C. Cir. 1977).

95 *Meritor Savings Bank* v. *Vinson*, 474 U.S. 1047 (1986).

96 *Hall* v. *GHS Construction Co.*, 842 F.2d 101 (8th Cir. 1988).

97 *Sorlucco* v. *New York City Police Department*, 971 F.2d 864 (2nd Cir. 1992).

98 S. C. Collins, "Sexual harassment and police discipline: Who's policing the police?" *Policing: An International Journal of Police Strategies and Management* 27 (2004): 512–38.

99 T. Mahoney, "Sexual harassment in California law enforcement: A survey of women police officers," *Journal of California Law Enforcement* 30 (1996): 82–87.

100 National Center for Women and Policing, *Equity denied: The status of women in policing, 1997* (Los Angeles: Feminist Majority Foundation, 1998), p. 5.

101 For more information, see the Wonderlic website, www.wonderlic.com (accessed December 7, 2010).

102 *Jordan* v. *New London*, 1999 U.S. Dist. LEXIS 14289 (1999).

103 Ibid., pp. 6–7.

104 Equal Employment Opportunity Commission, http://eeoc.gov (accessed November 9, 2008).

105 C. McHenry, "Stress in the police service: Preventing the long-term effects of trauma," *Occupational Health Review* (July–August 1995), p. 18.

106 *Hall* v. *GHS Construction Co.*, 842 F.2d 101 (8th Cir. 1988).

Chapter 5, Police Subculture

1 J. P. Crank, *Understanding police culture* (Cincinnati: Anderson, 1998). His book was an invaluable resource |in the organization of this chapter. We cite it in several places.

2 Ibid., p. 14.

3 Ibid., p. 15.

4 See, for example, D. Guyot, "Bending granite: Attempts to change the rank structure of American police departments," *Journal of Police Science and Administration* 7 (1979): 253–84.

5 Crank, *Understanding police culture*, p. 15.

6 J. Rubinstein, *City police* (New York: Farrar, Strauss, and Giroux, 1973), pp. 32–43.

7 Note that *platoon* and *squad* are terms commonly used in the military.

8 M. R. Pogrebin and E. D. Poole, "Humor in the briefing room," *Journal of Contemporary Ethnography* 17 (1988): 183–210, quote on pp. 188–89.

9 T. Rubinstein, *City police*, p. 32.

10 J. Crank, *Understanding police culture*, p. 30. See also J. Van Maanen, "Observations on the making of policemen," *Human Organization* 32 (1973): 407–18.

11 M. Felson, *Crime and everyday life* (Thousand Oaks, CA: Pine Forge Press, 1994).

12 J. Crank, *Understanding police culture*, p. 30. See also A. Niederhoffer, *Behind the shield* (Garden City, NY: Doubleday, 1967).

13 Crank, *Understanding police culture*, p. 32.

14 Ibid., p. 32. See also Pogrebin and Poole, "Humor in the briefing room."

15 D. N. Allen and M. G. Maxfield, "Judging police performance: Views and behavior of patrol officers," in *Police at work: Policy issues and analysis*, ed. R. R. Bennett, pp. 65–86 (Beverly Hills, CA: Sage, 1983).

16 See *Houston Chronicle*, "The TASER Effect," www.chron.com/disp/story.mpl/metropolitan/4464516.html (accessed December 23, 2010).

17 E. Bittner, *The functions of police in modern society* (Washington, DC: National Institute of Mental Health, 1970).

18 Crank, *Understanding police culture*, p. 40.

19 Ibid., p. 44.

20 Van Maanen, "Observations on the making of policemen," p. 226.

21 Rubinstein, *City police*, p. 318.

22 Crank, *Understanding police culture*, p. 69.

23 Crank, *Understanding police culture*, p. 82.

24 J. H. Skolnick and D. H. Bayley, *The new blue line: Police innovation in six American cities* (New York: Free Press, 1986), pp. 141–42.

25 Crank, *Understanding police culture*, p. 86.

26 W. A. Geller and M. S. Scott, "Deadly force: What we know," in *Thinking about police*, 2nd ed., ed. C. Klockars and S. Mastrofski, pp. 446–76 (New York: McGraw-Hill, 1991), p. 449.

27 P. Ragonese, *The soul of a cop* (New York: St. Martin's Paperbacks, 1991), pp. 200–202.

28 V. E. Kappeler, R. D. Sluder, and G. P. Alpert, *Forces of deviance: The dark side of policing* (Prospect Heights, IL: Waveland, 1994), p. 100.

29 F. Cullen and others, "Paradox in policing: A note on perceptions of danger," *Journal of Police Science and Administration* 11 (1983): 457–62.

30 Federal Bureau of Investigation, *Law enforcement officers killed and assaulted, 2009,* www2.fbi.gov/ucr/killed/2009/officersassaulted.html (accessed December 23, 2010).

31 E. Bittner, *Aspects of police work* (Boston: Northeastern University Press, 1990).

32 P. K. Manning, *Police work: The social organization of policing.* (Cambridge: The MIT Press, 1977); J. Van Maanen, "Working the street: A developmental view of police behavior," in *The potential for reform in criminal justice*, vol. 3, ed. H. Jacob, pp. 83–129 (Beverly Hills, CA: Sage, 1974).

33 Rubinstein, *City police*, p. 224.

34 J. J. Fyfe, "The split-second syndrome and other determinants of police violence," in *Critical issues in policing*, 4th ed., ed. R. G. Dunham and G. P. Alpert, pp. 583–98 (Prospect Heights, IL: Waveland, 2001).

35 Ibid.

36 Crank, *Understanding police culture*, p. 151. See also G. W. Sykes, "Street justice: A moral defense of order maintenance policing," *Justice Quarterly* 3 (1986): 497–512.

37 J. Van Maanen, "The asshole," in *Policing: A view from the street*, ed. P. K. Manning and J. Van Maanen, pp. 221–38 (Santa Monica, CA: Goodyear, 1978).

38 Crank, *Understanding police culture*, p. 160.

39 C. Fletcher, *Pure cop* (New York: Pocket Books, 1991), p. 278.

40 Crank, *Understanding police culture*, p. 164.

41 Ibid., pp. 172–73.

42 Ibid., p. 180.

43 A. Bouza, *The police mystique: An insider's look at cops, crime, and the criminal justice system* (New York: Plenum Press, 1990), p. 74.

44 P. Bonifacio, *The psychological effects of police work: A psychodynamic approach* (New York: Plenum Press, 1991), p. 39.

45 *The report of the City of New York Commission to Investigate Allegations of Police Corruption and the Anti-Corruption Procedures of the Police Department* (The Mollen Commission, 1994), pp. 51–52.

46 Reprinted by permission of Waveland Press, Inc. from Victor E. Kappeler, et al., "Breeding Deviant Conformity, *Forces of deviance: The dark side of policing.* (Long Grove, IL: Waveland Press, Inc., 1998). All rights reserved.

47 C. Bahn, "Police socialization in the eighties: Strains in the forging of an occupational identity," *Journal of Police Science and Administration* 12 (1984): 390–94, quote on p. 392.

48 T. Barker, R. N. Friery, and D. L. Carter, "After L.A., would your local police lie?" in *Police Deviance*, 3rd ed., ed. T. Barker and D. Carter, pp. 155–68 (Cincinnati: Anderson, 1994).

49 R. Gearty, "Blue wall whistleblower gets day in court after demotion," *Daily News*, June 13, 2004, p. 27.

50 K. Makin, "Police chief denies 'blue wall of silence' in corruption probe," *National News*, January 21, 2004, p. A6.

Chapter 6, Police Discretion and Behavior

1 *Castle Rock* v. *Gonzales*, 545 U.S. 748 (2005).

2 Karen J. Kruger, "Mandatory arrest statutes: Are they really mandatory?" *Police Chief*, vol. 76, no. 12 (December, 2009); www.policechiefmagazine.org/magazine/index.cfm?fuseaction=display&article_id=1961&issue_id=122009 (accessed April 10, 2011).

3 *Gonzalez*, 545 U.S. at 760.

4 J. Q. Wilson and G. L. Kelling, "Broken windows: The police and neighborhood safety," *Atlantic Monthly* (March 1982): 28–29.

5 D. H. Bayley and E. Bittner, "Learning the skills of policing," in *Critical issues in policing: Contemporary readings*, ed. R. G. Dunham and G. P. Alpert, pp. 87–110 (Prospect Heights, IL: Waveland, 1989).

6 K. C. Davis, *Police discretion* (St. Paul: West, 1975), p. 73.

7 J. Zhao, Q. Thurman, and N. He, "Sources of job satisfaction among police officers: A test of demographic and work environment models," *Justice Quarterly* 16 (1999): 153–73.

8 K. Peak, *Policing America: Methods, issues, challenges*, 5th ed. (Upper Saddle River, NJ: Prentice Hall, 2006).

9 D. Black, *The manners and customs of the police* (New York: Academic Press, 1980).

10 S. E. Martin, *Breaking and entering: Policewomen on patrol* (Berkeley: University of California Press, 1980).

[11] R. Worden, "Situational and attitudinal explanations of police behavior: A theoretical reappraisal and empirical assessment," *Law and Society Review* 23 (1989): 687.

[12] Ibid.

[13] S. O. White, "A perspective on police professionalization," *Law and Society Review* 7 (1982): 61.

[14] Worden, "Situational and attitudinal explanations of police behavior," p. 687.

[15] White, "A perspective on police professionalization," p. 61.

[16] Worden, "Situational and attitudinal explanations of police behavior," p. 688.

[17] See, e.g., Brown, *Working the street*, p. 162

[18] *Atwater* v. *City of Lago Vista* 121 S.Ct. 1536 (2001).

[19] Worden, "Situational and attitudinal explanations of police behavior," p. 689.

[20] J. A. Gardiner, *Traffic and the police: Variations in law enforcement policy* (Cambridge, MA: Harvard University Press, 1969).

[21] See, e.g., Brown, *Working the street*.

[22] Worden, "Situational and attitudinal explanations of police behavior," p. 690.

[23] M. Rokeach, M. Miller, and J. Snyder, "The value gap between police and policed," *Journal of Social Issues* 27 (1971): 155–71.

[24] M. Caldero and A. P. Larose, "Value consistency within the police: The lack of a gap," *Policing: An International Journal of Police Strategies and Management* 24 (2003): 162–80, quote on p. 162.

[25] See also J. Crank and M. Caldero, *Police ethics: The corruption of noble cause* (Cincinnati: Anderson, 1999), for an examination of this issue.

[26] G. Alpert and W. Smith, "Developing police policy: An evaluation of the control principle," in L. Gaines and G. Cordner (eds.), *Policing Perspectives: An Anthology*, pp. 353–62 (Los Angeles, CA: Roxbury, 1998). See also J. Auten, "Preparing written guidelines," *FBI Law Enforcement Bulletin* 57 (1988): 1–7.

[27] G. Cordner, "Written rules and regulations: Are they necessary?" *FBI Law Enforcement Bulletin*, July (1989): 17–21. See also, T. Adams, *Police Field Operations* (Englewood Cliffs, NJ: Prentice-Hall, 1990).

[28] R. Roberg, K. Novak, and G. Cordner, *Police and society*, 4th ed. (New York: Oxford, 2008), p. 285.

[29] S. D. Mastrofski, "Policing the beat: The impact of organizational scale on patrol officer behavior in urban residential neighborhoods," *Journal of Criminal Justice* 9 (1981): 343–58.

[30] S. D. Mastrofski, R. Ritti, and D. Hoffmaster, "Organizational determinants of police discretion: The case of drinking-driving," *Journal of Criminal Justice* 15 (1987): 387–402.

[31] Brown, *Working the street*, p. 58; P. V. Murphy and T. Pate, *Commissioner* (New York: Simon and Schuster, 1977), p. 39.

[32] Murphy and Pate, *Commissioner*.

[33] L. W. Brooks, "Police discretionary behavior: A study of style," in *Critical issues in policing: Contemporary readings*, 4th ed., ed. R. G. Dunham and G. P. Alpert (Prospect Heights, IL: Waveland, 1989), p. 123.

[34] E. M. Davis, *Staff one: A perspective on effective police management* (Englewood Cliffs, NJ: Prentice Hall, 1978), p. 135.

[35] S. Walker, *The police in America*, 2nd ed. (New York: McGraw-Hill, 1991); and P. F. Nardulli and J. M. Stonecash, *Politics, professionalism, and urban services: The police* (Cambridge, MA: Oelgeschlager, Gunn, and Hain, 1981).

[36] Nardulli and Stonecash, *Politics, professionalism, and urban services*, pp. 86–88.

[37] Roberg, Novak, and Cordner, *Police and society*, p. 286.

[38] D. A. Smith, "The neighborhood context of police behavior," in *Crime and justice: An annual review of research*, vol. 8, ed. A. J. Reiss and M. Tonry (Chicago: University of Chicago Press, 1986).

[39] E. C. Riksheim and S. M. Chermak, "Causes of police behavior revisited," *Journal of Criminal Justice* 21 (1993): 353–82; D. A. Smith, "The organizational aspects of legal control," *Criminology* 22 (1984): 19–38; Smith, "The neighborhood context of police behavior"; and D. A. Smith and J. R. Klien, "Police agency characteristics and arrest decisions," in *Evaluating performance of criminal justice agencies*, ed. G. D. Whitaker and C. D. Phillips (Beverly Hills, CA: Sage, 1984).

[40] D. A. Klinger, "Negotiating order in patrol work: An ecological theory of police response to deviance," *Criminology* 35 (1997): 277–306.

[41] L. W. Brooks, A. Piquero, and J. Cronin, "Workload rates and police officer attitudes: An examination of 'busy' and 'slow' precincts," *Journal of Criminal Justice* 22 (1994): 277–86.

[42] L. W. Sherman, "Causes of police behavior: The current state of quantitative research," in *The ambivalent force*, 3rd ed., ed. A. S. Blumberg and E. Niederhoffer (New York: Holt, Rinehart, and Wilson, 1985), p. 187.

[43] J. Van Maanen, "The Asshole," in *Policing: A view from the streets*, ed. P. K. Manning and J. Van Maanen, pp. 221–38 (Santa Monica, CA: Goodyear, 1978).

[44] See, e.g., D. Black and A. Reiss, "Police control of juveniles," *American Sociological Review* 35 (1970): 63–77; R. Ericson, *Reproducing order: A study of police patrol work* (Toronto: University of Toronto Press, 1982); D. A. Smith, "The neighborhood context of police behavior," in *Crime and justice: An annual review of research*, vol. 8, ed. A. J. Reiss and M. Tonry (Chicago: University of Chicago Press, 1986); and C. A. Visher, "Gender, police arrest decisions, and notions of chivalry," *Criminology* 21 (1983): 5–28.

45 K. M. Lersch and J. R. Feagin, "Violent police-citizen encounters: An analysis of major newspaper accounts," *Critical Sociology* 22 (1996): 29–49.

46 D. Klinger, "Demeanor or crime: Why 'hostile' citizens are more likely to be arrested," *Criminology* 32 (1994): 475–93.

47 See, e.g., R. J. Lundman, "Demeanor or crime? The midwest city police-citizen encounter," *Criminology* 32 (1994): 631–56; and R. E. Worden and R. L. Shepard, "Demeanor, crime, and police behavior: A reexamination of the police services study data," *Criminology* 34 (1996): 83–105.

48 V. E. Kappeler, R. D. Sluder, and G. P. Alpert, *Forces of deviance: Understanding the dark side of policing* (Prospect Heights, IL: Waveland, 1994); W. Chambliss, "Policing the ghetto underclass: The politics of law and law enforcement," in *Public policy: Crime and criminal justice*, ed. B. Handcock and P. Sharp, pp. 146–65 (Upper Saddle River, NJ: Prentice Hall, 1997); and M. Maurer, *Young black men and the criminal justice system: A growing national problem* (Washington, DC: Sentencing Project, 1993).

49 Roberg, Novak, and Cordner, *Police and society*, p. 288.

50 G. P. Alpert, J. M. Macdonald, and R. G. Dunham, "Police suspicion and discretionary decision making during citizen stops," *Criminology* 43 (2005): 407–34.

51 For some examples, see D. A. Harris, "The stories, the statistics, and the law: Why 'driving while black' matters," *Minnesota Law Review* 84 (1999): 265–326; and E. Spitzer, *The New York City Police Department's 'stop and frisk' practices: A report to the people of the state of New York from the office of the attorney general* (Albany: New York Attorney General's Office, 1999).

52 C. A. Visher, "Gender, police arrest decisions, and notions of chivalry," *Criminology* 21 (1983): 5–28.

53 P. B. Kraska and V. E. Kappeler, "To serve and pursue: Exploring police sexual violence against women," *Justice Quarterly* 12 (1995): 85–112.

54 Kappeler, Sluder, and Alpert, *Forces of deviance*.

55 See, e.g., D. Black, *The behavior of law* (New York: Academic Press, 1976).

56 K. J. Novak and others, "Revisiting the decision to arrest: Comparing beat and community officers," *Crime and Delinquency* 48 (2002): 70–98.

57 Y. G. Hurst and J. Frank, "How kids view cops: The nature of juvenile attitudes toward the police," *Journal of Criminal Justice* 28 (2000): 189–202.

58 See, e.g., S. D. Mastrofski, R. E. Worden, and J. B. Snipes, "Law enforcement in a time of community policing," *Criminology* 33 (1995): 539–63; and G. Cordner, "Community policing: Elements and effects," *Police Forum* 5 (1995): 1–8.

59 Black and Reiss, "Police control of juveniles"; D. Black, "The social organization of arrest," *Stanford Law Review* 23 (1971): 1087–1111; and R. J. Friedrich, "The impact of organizational, individual, and situational factors on police behavior," Ph.D. dissertation (Department of Political Science, University of Michigan, 1977).

60 Black and Reiss, "Police control of juveniles"; Black, "The social organization of arrest"; L. W. Brooks, "Determinants of police officer orientations and their impact on police discretionary behavior," Ph.D. dissertation (Institute of Criminal Justice and Criminology, University of Maryland, 1986); Friedrich, "The impact of organizational, individual, and situational factors on police behavior"; D. A. Smith, "Police response to interpersonal violence: Defining the parameters of legal control," *Social Forces* 65 (1987): 767–82; D. A. Smith and C. Visher, "Street level justice: Situational determinants of police arrest decisions," *Social Problems* 29 (1981): 167–78; C. A. Visher, "Gender, police arrest decisions, and notions of chivalry," *Criminology* 21 (1983): 5–28; and Worden, "Situational and attitudinal explanations of police behavior."

61 See, e.g., Black, *The manners and customs of the police.*

62 Roberg, Novak, and Cordner, *Police and society*, p. 291.

63 See, e.g., Brooks, "Police discretionary behavior," p. 126; and Sherman, "Causes of police behavior," pp. 189–92.

64 See, e.g., S. E. Martin, "Female officers on the move?" in *Critical issues in policing: Contemporary readings*, ed. R. G. Dunham and G. P. Alpert, pp. 312–30 (Prospect Heights, IL: Waveland, 1989); and S. A. Grennan, "Findings on the role of officer gender in violent encounters with citizens," *Journal of Police Science and Administration* 15 (1988): 78–85.

65 W. F. Walsh, "Police officer arrest rates," *Justice Quarterly* 3 (1986): 271–90.

66 Mastrofski and others, "Law enforcement in a time of community policing."

67 "Was it 'excited delirium' or police brutality?" CBS News, *60 Minutes*, December 10, 2003, www.cbsnews.com/stories/2003/12/09/60II/main587569.shtml (accessed January 4, 2011).

Chapter 7, Core Police Functions

1 George Gascon and Todd Fogleson, "Making Policing More Affordable," Harvard University's John F. Kennedy School of Management, December, 2010.

2 C. D. Hale, *Police patrol: Operations and management* (Englewood Cliffs, NJ: Prentice Hall, 1994).

3 V. Kappeler and others, *The mythology of crime and criminal justice* (Prospect Heights, IL: Waveland Press, 1996).

4 See, e.g., http://pdf.plano.gov/planning/neigh_serv/ServicesandProgramsBrochure.pdf (accessed January 5, 2011).

5 See S. P. Lab, *Crime prevention at a crossroads* (Cincinnati: Anderson, 1997).

6 R. H. Langworthy and L. P. Travis III, *Policing in America: A balance of forces*, 2nd ed. (Upper Saddle River, NJ: Prentice Hall, 1999), p. 194.

7 L. Mazerolle and others, "Managing citizen calls to the police: An assessment of nonemergency call systems," *Criminology*, Vol. 2, No. 1 (2002), pp. 97–124.

8 Ibid.

9 Terence Dunworth, "Criminal justice and the IT revolution," in *Criminal justice 2000 (*Washington, DC: National Institute of Justice, 2000), pp. 371–426. Available at www.ncjrs.gov/criminal_justice2000/vol_3/03h.pdf (accessed January 5, 2011).

10 J. Fuller, "Rethinking foot patrol," *Police and Security News* (May–June 2004): 63–66, quote on p. 63.

11 K. D. Vonk, "Bike patrol successes," *Law and Order* (April 2003): 82–86, quote on p. 85.

12 J. Bellah, "Low-speed ahead," *Law Enforcement Technology* (October 2001): 76–82, quote on p. 78.

13 J. C. Fine, "Police on horseback: A new concept for an old idea," *FBI Law Enforcement Bulletin* (July 2001): 6–7, quote on p. 6.

14 S. Slahor, "MEU: Mounted units for crowd control," *Law and Order* (October 2001): 234–37, quote on p. 237.

15 B.A. Reaves, *Local police departments, 2007 (*Washington, DC: Bureau of Justice Statistics, 2010), p. 34.

16 *City crime rankings*, 2010–2011 (Washington, DC: CQ Press, 2011). Available at http://os.cqpress.com/citycrime/2010/citycrime2010-2011.htm (accessed January 5, 2011).

17 S. Walker, *Sense and nonsense about crime and drugs: A policy guide*, 5th ed. (Belmont, CA: Wadsworth, 2001), p. 81.

18 Ibid.

19 Much of this material is adapted from Walker, *Sense and nonsense about crime and drugs*.

20 Ibid., p. 86.

21 W. K. Rashbaum, "Response time to police calls is 29% faster," *New York Times*, September 26, 2002, p. B1.

22 Details for this story come from K. Streeter, "Girl, 2, rescued from washer," *Los Angeles Times*, May 26, 2003, http://articles.latimes.com/2003/may/26/local/me-laundry26 (accessed January 5, 2011).

23 See M. S. Scott, *Problem-oriented policing: Reflections on the first 20 years* (Washington, DC: Office of Community Oriented Policing Services, 2000), p. 87, from which much of this material is adapted.

24 G. Carrick, "Traffic safety in the new millennium," *Law and Order* (April 2003): 44–50.

25 *Whren* v. *United States*, 517 U.S. 806 (1996).

26 *Maryland* v. *Wilson*, 519 U.S. 408, 410 (1997); and *Pennsylvania* v. *Mimms*, 434 U.S. 106, 111 (1977).

27 *Ohio* v. *Robinette*, 519 U.S. 33 (1996).

28 *Horton* v. *California*, 496 U.S. 128, 133–37 (1990).

29 *Michigan* v. *Long*, 463 U.S. 1032, 1035 (1983).

30 *New York* v. *Belton*, 453 U.S. 454, 460 (1981).

31 C. Batton and C. Kadleck, "Theoretical and methodological issues in racial profiling research," *Police Quarterly* (March 2004): 30–64.

32 See, for example, "Driving while Black: Study shows minorities more likely to question why police stopped them, how they were treated," *Ohio State Research*, February 10, 2003. Available at http://researchnews.osu.edu/archive/dwbstudy.htm (accessed January 5, 2011).

33 *Whren* v. *United States* (1996).

34 R. S. Engel and J. M. Calnon, "Examining the influence of drivers' characteristics during stops with the police: Results from a national survey," *Justice Quarterly* (March 2004): 49–90, quote on p. 49.

35 J. Rojek, R. Rosenfeld, and S. Decker, "The influence of driver's race on traffic stops in Missouri," *Police Quarterly* (March 2004): 126–47, quote on p. 143.

36 J. Nislow, "Are Americans ready to buy into racial profiling?" *Law Enforcement News*, October 15, 2001, p. 11.

37 Ibid.

38 O. Cox, "2003 traffic safety data," *Police Chief* (July 2004): 15.

39 Ibid.

40 H. E. Cauvin, "D.C. ordered to pay in police chase: Woman maimed in crash is awarded almost $1 million," *Washington Post*, December 14, 2006, p. B1.

41 G. P. Alpert, *Police pursuit: Policies and training* (Washington, DC: National Institute of Justice, 1997), p. 1.

42 G. P. Alpert and others, *Police pursuits: What we know* (Washington, DC: Police Executive Research Forum, 2000).

43 Alpert, *Police pursuits*, p. 4.

44 Ibid.

45 Ibid., p. 3.

46 Ibid.

47 National Institute of Justice, "New Technologies Demonstrated for Law Enforcement" (Washington, DC: National Institute of Justice, 1995). Available at www.justnet.org/TechBeat%20Files/tbt-0995.pdf (accessed January 5, 2011).

48 Adapted from Bronx County (New York) District Attorney's Office, "Quality of life offenses," December 24, 2002, http://bronxda.nyc.gov/fcrime/qol.htm (accessed January 5, 2011).

49 Other violations may be involved, as well. On December 29, 2000, for example, Judge John S. Martin, Jr., of the Federal District Court in Manhattan, ruled that homeless people in New York City could be arrested for sleeping in cardboard boxes in public. Judge Martin held that a city sanitation department regulation barring people from abandoning cars or boxes on city streets could be applied to the homeless who were sleeping in boxes.

50 For example, Norman Siegel, executive director of the New York Civil Liberties Union, as reported in "Quality of life offenses targeted," *Western Queens Gazette*, November 22, 2000, www.qgazette.com/News/2000/1122/Editorial_pages/e01.html (accessed January 5, 2011).

51 The broken windows thesis was first suggested by G. L. Kelling and J. Q. Wilson in "Broken windows: The police and neighborhood safety," *Atlantic Monthly* (March 1982).

52 For a critique of the broken windows thesis, see B. E. Harcourt, *Illusion of order: The false promise of broken windows policing* (Cambridge: Harvard University Press, 2001).

53 P. Schuler, "Law professor Harcourt challenges popular policing method, gun violence interventions," *Chicago Chronicle*, March 20, 2003.

54 G. L. Kelling, C. M. Coles, and J. Q. Wilson, *Fixing broken windows: Restoring order and reducing crime in our communities* (repr., New York: Touchstone, 1998).

55 C. R. Swanson, L. Territo, and R. W. Taylor, *Police administration: Structures, processes, and behavior*, 4th ed. (Upper Saddle River, NJ: Prentice Hall, 1998), p. 1.

56 Ibid.

57 K. M. Hess and H. M. Wrobleski, *Police operations: Theory and practice*, 4th ed. (Belmont, CA: Wadsworth, 2006), pp. 188–89.

58 C. A. Rohr, "Training for managing crowds and responding to civil disobediences," *Police Chief* (October 2001): 10–11, especially p. 10.

59 F. Butterfield, "Student's death returns crowd control to the fore," *New York Times*, November 1, 2004.

60 P. W. Greenwood and J. Petersilia, *The criminal investigation process*, vol. 1, *Summary and policy implications* (Santa Monica, CA: RAND, 1975).

61 J. Thorwald, *The century of the detective* (New York: Harcourt, Brace, and World, 1965), pp. 9–10.

62 Ibid., p. 62.

63 A. L. Califana and J. S. Levkov, *Criminalistics for the law enforcement officer* (New York: McGraw-Hill, 1978), p. 20.

64 J. Thorwald, *The marks of Cain* (London: Thames and Hudson, 1965), pp. 78–79.

65 Ibid., pp. 87–88.

66 Ibid., p. 164.

67 C. R. Swanson, N. C. Chamelin, and L. Territo, *Criminal investigation*, 4th ed. (New York: Random House, 1988), p. 19.

68 A. S. Osborn, *Questioned documents: A study of questioned documents with an outline of methods by which the facts may be discovered and shown* (Rochester, NY: The Lawyers' Co-operative Publishing Co., 1910).

69 P. R. DeForest, R. E. Gaensslen, and H. C. Lee, *Forensic science: An introduction to criminalistics* (New York: McGraw-Hill, 1983), p. 19.

70 K. J. Peak, *Policing America: Methods, issues, challenges*, 5th ed. (Upper Saddle River, NJ: Prentice Hall, 2006).

Chapter 8, Community Policing and Community Involvement

1 Steve Neavling and Gina Damron, "Detroit police offered renovated homes for as little as $1,000," *Detroit Free Press*, February 8, 2011, www.ongo.com/v/365982/-1/D3810DBAF56A7D71/detroit-police-offered-renovated-homes-for-as-little-as-1000 (accessed July 28, 2011).

2 Several portions of this chapter borrow from Chapter 5 of J. L. Worrall, *Crime control in America: An assessment of the evidence* (Boston: Allyn and Bacon, 2006).

3 V. G. Strecher, *Planning community policing* (Prospect Heights, IL: Waveland, 1997).

4 H. Goldstein, *Problem oriented policing* (New York: McGraw-Hill, 1990); and H. Goldstein, "Improving policing: A problem-oriented approach," *Crime and Delinquency* 25 (1979): 236–58.

5 M.D. Reisig, "Community and problem-oriented policing," *Crime and Justice: A Review of Research* 39(2010): 2–53, p. 2.

6 J. E. Angell, "Toward an alternative to the classic police organizational arrangements: A democratic model," *Criminology* 9 (1971): 185–206.

7 G. L. Kelling, "Police and communities: The quiet revolution," in *Criminal justice in America: Theory, practice, and policy*, ed. B. W. Hancock and P. M. Sharp, pp. 134–44 (Upper Saddle River, NJ: Prentice Hall, 1996).

8 Ibid., p. 138.

9 Ibid.

10 Ibid.

11 R. Trojanowicz and others, *Community policing: A contemporary perspective*, 2nd ed. (Cincinnati: Anderson, 1988).

12 Ibid., p. 53.

13 D. Hayeslip and G. Cordner, "The effects of community-oriented patrol on police officer attitudes," *American Journal of Police-Special Issue on Foot Patrol and Community Policing* 4 (1987): 95–119.

14 P. K. Manning, "Community policing as a drama of control," in *Community policing: Rhetoric or reality?* ed. J. R. Greene and S. D. Mastrofski, pp. 27–45 (New York: Praeger, 1988).

15 D. Garland, "The limits of the sovereign state: Strategies of crime control in contemporary society," *British Journal of Criminology* 36 (1996): 445–71.

16 J. Zhao, *Why police organizations change* (Washington, DC: Police Executive Research Forum, 1996).

17 See, for instance, W. G. Skogan and S. M. Hartnett, *Community policing: Chicago style* (New York: Oxford University Press, 1997).

18 Police Executive Research Forum, *Themes and variations in community policing* (Washington, DC: Police Executive Research Forum, 1996).

19 G. W. Cordner, "Community policing: Elements an effects," in *Critical issues in policing: Contemporary readings,* 3rd ed., ed. R. G. Dunham and G. P. Alpert (Prospect Heights, IL: Waveland, 1997), p. 452.

20 J. A. Roth, J. Roehl, and C. C. Johnson, "Trends in the adoption of community policing," in *Community policing: Can it work?* ed. W. G. Skogan, pp. 3–29 (Belmont, CA: Wadsworth, 2003).

21 Ibid., p. 24.

22 See also J. Zhao, Q. Thurman, and N. Lovrich, "Community oriented policing across the U.S.: Facilitators and impediments to implementation," *American Journal of Police* 14 (1995): 11–28; and J. Zhao, N. Lovrich, and Q. Thurman, "The status of community policing in American cities," *Policing: An International Journal of Police Strategies and Management* 22 (1999): 152–70.

23 J. R. Greene, "Community policing and organization change," in *Community policing: Can it work?* ed. W. G. Skogan (Belmont, CA: Wadsworth, 2003), p. 49.

24 Ibid.

25 See, for example, D. Guyot, "Bending granite: Attempts to change the rank structure of American police departments," *Journal of Police Science and Administration* 7 (1979): 253–384.

26 E. R. Maguire, "Structural change in large municipal police organizations during the community-policing era," *Justice Quarterly* 14 (1997): 547–76. See also J. A. Roth, ed., *National evaluation of the COPS program: Title 1 of the 1994 Crime Act* (Washington, DC: National Institute of Justice, 2000).

27 W. G. Skogan, ed., *Community policing: Can it work?* (Belmont, CA: Wadsworth, 2003), p. xxviii.

28 D. P. Rosenbaum and D. L. Wilkinson, "Can police adapt? Tracking the effects of organizational reform over six years," in *Community policing: Can it work?* ed. W. G. Skogan, pp. 79–108 (Belmont, CA: Wadsworth, 2003). See also D. P. Rosenbaum, S. Yeh, and D. L. Wilkinson, "Estimating the effects of community policing reform on police officers," *Crime and Delinquency* 40 (1994): 331–53.

29 W. Terrill and S. D. Mastrofski, "Working the street: Does community policing matter?" in *Community policing: Can it work?* ed. W. G. Skogan, pp. 109–35 (Belmont, CA: Wadsworth, 2003). See also W. Terrill and S. D. Mastrofski, "Situational and officer based determinants of police coercion," *Justice Quarterly* 19 (2002): 101–34.

30 R. L. Wood, M. Davis, and A. Rouse, "Diving into quicksand: Program implementation and police subcultures," in *Community policing: Can it work?* ed. W. G. Skogan, pp. 136–61 (Belmont, CA: Wadsworth, 2003).

31 J. Zhao, N. P. Lovrich, and Q. Thurman, "The status of community policing in American cities: Facilitators and impediments revisited," *Policing* 22:1 (1999): 74.

32 Michael D. Reisig and Roger B. Parks, "Experience, quality of life, and neighborhood context: A hierarchical analysis of satisfaction with police," *Justice Quarterly* 17:3 (2000): 607.

33 Mark E. Correia, "The conceptual ambiguity of community in community policing: Filtering the muddy waters," *Policing* 23:2 (2000): 218–33.

34 Adapted from D. R. Fessler, *Facilitating community change: A basic guide* (San Diego: San Diego State University, 1976), p. 7.

35 D. W. Flynn, *Defining the "community" in community policing* (Washington, DC: Police Executive Research Forum, 1998).

36 R. C. Trojanowicz and M. H. Moore, *The meaning of community in community policing* (East Lansing: Michigan State University's National Neighborhood Foot Patrol Center, 1988).

37 R. M. Bohm, K. M. Reynolds, and S. T. Holms, "Perceptions of neighborhood problems and their solutions: Implications for community policing," *Policing* 23:4 (2000): 439.

38 Ibid., p. 442.

39 M. K. Sparrow, "Implementing community policing," *Perspectives on policing,* no. 9 (Washington, DC: National Institute of Justice, 1988).

40 "L.A. police chief: Treat people like customers," *USA Today,* March 29, 1993, p. 13A.

41 R. Wasserman and M. H. Moore, "Values in policing," *Perspectives in policing,* no. 8 (Washington, DC: National Institute of Justice, 1988), p. 7.

42 "New York City mayor sparks debate on community policing," *Criminal Justice Newsletter,* January 18, 1994, p. 1.

43 C. Wexler, "Foreword," in *Solving crime and disorder problems: Current issues, police strategies, and organizational tactics,* ed. M. Reuland, C. S. Brito, and L. Carroll (Washington, DC: Police Executive Research Forum, 2001), p. vii.

44 B. Bucqueroux and D. Diamond, "Community policing is our best bet against terror," *Subject to Debate* (January 2002): 1, 6, especially p. 6.

45 Ibid.

46 U.S. Department of Justice, *Citizen patrol projects: National evaluation program phase 1 summary report* (Washington, DC: U.S. Department of Justice, 1976).

47 J. Hilson, "Fort Worth's citizens on patrol program," *TELEMASP Bulletin* 1 (1994): full issue.

48 See, e.g., V. W. Bumphus, L. K. Gaines, and C. R. Blakely, "Citizen police academies: Observing goals, objectives, and recent trends," *American Journal of Criminal Justice* 24 (1999): 67–79.

49 See, e.g., G. A. Aryani and others, "Citizen police academy: Success through community partnership," *FBI Law Enforcement Bulletin* 69 (2000): 16–21.

50 M. J. Palmiotto and N. P. Unninthan, "Impact of citizen police academies on participants: An exploratory study," *Journal of Criminal Justice* 30 (2002): 101–6.

51 J. A. Schafer and E. M. Bonello, "Citizen police academy: Measuring outcomes," *Police Quarterly* 4 (2001): 434–48; and E. G. Cohn, "Citizen police academy: A recipe for improving police-community relations," *Journal of Criminal Justice* 24 (1996): 265–71.

52 W. T. Jordan, "Citizen police academies: Community policing or community politics," *American Journal of Police* 25 (2000): 93–118.

53 Ibid.

54 B. Forst, "The privatization and civilianization of policing," in *Boundary changes in criminal justice organizations*, ed. C. M. Friel (Washington, DC: National Institute of Justice, 2000), p. 23.

55 Ibid., p. 25.

56 Ibid.

57 Ibid., p. 403.

58 Ibid.

59 Ibid., p. 408.

60 Ibid.

61 San Diego Municipal Code, chapter 5, article 2, division 52.5301.

62 Washington, DC, Metropolitan Police, "Neighborhood Crime Data," press release, July 20, 1999, http://newsroom.dc.gov/show.aspx/agency/mpdc/section/2/release/240/year/1999/month/7 (accessed January 6, 2011).

Chapter 9, Policing in the Modern Era

1 Pub. L. 111-5.

2 U.S. Government Accountability Office, *Report to congressional requesters: Recovery Act – Department of Justice could better assess justice assistance grant program impact* (Washington, DC: GAO, October 2010), GAO-11-87, www.gao.gov/new.items/d1187.pdf.

3 U.S. Government Accountability Office, *Highlights of GAO-11-87, A report to congressional requesters* (Washington, DC: GAO, October 2010), p. 1, www.gao.gov/highlights/d1187high.pdf.

4 K. J. Peak, *Policing in America: Methods, issues, challenges,* 5th ed. (Upper Saddle River, NJ: Prentice Hall, 2006), pp. 430–31.

5 E. Silverman, *NYPD battles crime: Innovative strategies in policing* (Boston: Northeastern University Press, 1999).

6 D. Weisburd and others, *Compstat and organizational change: Findings from a national survey* (Washington, DC: Police Foundation, 2001). For a review of Compstat-like strategies in six cities, see also M. H. Moore and A. A. Braga, "Measuring and improving police performance: The lessons of Compstat and its progeny," *Policing: An International Journal of Police Strategies and Management* 26 (2003): 439–53.

7 E. Brady, "Compstat: Mapping, accountability, equal less crime," *USA Today*, December 1, 1997, p. 18A.

8 K. Harries, *Mapping crime: Principle and practice* (Washington, DC: National Institute of Justice, 1999), p. 79.

9 Ibid.

10 Ibid.

11 J. Maple, *The crime fighter* (New York: Doubleday, 1999), p. 93.

12 Silverman, *NYPD battles crime*, p. 104.

13 Harries, *Mapping crime*, p. 80.

14 R. Garner and L. Hoover, "The Compstat craze: Emphasizing accountability in policing," paper presented at the annual meeting of the Academy of Criminal Justice Sciences in New Orleans, 2000.

15 Ibid., p. 11.

16 D. Pederson, "Bullets in the big easy," *Newsweek* (December 23, 1996), p. 29.

17 J. Raymond, "Forget the pipe, Sherlock: Gear for tomorrow's detectives," *Newsweek* (June 22, 1998): 12.

18 VirTra Systems, *VirTra 300 LE*, http://virtrasystems.com/law-enforcement-training (accessed July 28, 2011).

19 Advanced Interactive Solutions, "PRISim," www.ais-solutions.co.uk/prisim.php (accessed January 10, 2011).

20 Ibid.

21 The concept of intelligence-led policing appears to have been first fully articulated in A. Smith, ed., *Intelligence-led policing* (Richmond: International Association of Law Enforcement Intelligence Analysts, 1997).

22 M. Peterson, *Intelligence-led policing: The new intelligence architecture* (Washington, DC: Bureau of Justice Assistance, 2005), p. 3.

23 Ibid., p. 11.

24 I. D. L. Carter, *Law enforcement intelligence: A guide for state, local, and tribal law enforcement agencies* (Washington, DC: U.S. Department of Justice, 2004), p. 7.

25 Ibid.

26 Much of the information and some of the wording in this section is taken from Carter, *Law enforcement intelligence*.

27 Peterson, *Intelligence-led policing*, p. 3.

28 Carter, *Law enforcement intelligence*, p. 8.

29 Ibid.

30 Peterson, *Intelligence-led policing*, p. 12.

31 Ibid.

32 R. Wright, "Management of the intelligence unit," in *Intelligence 2000: Revising the basic elements,* ed. M. B. Peterson, R. Wright, and B. Morehouse, p. 69 (Lawrenceville, NJ: International Association of Law Enforcement Intelligence Analysts and Law Enforcement Intelligence Units, 2001).

33 Peterson, *Intelligence-led policing*, p. 13.

34 Ibid., p. 6.

35 Ibid., p. 7.

36 Ibid.

37 This section draws from Peterson, *Intelligence-led policing*, p. 9.

38 Ibid.

39 D. Lambert, "Intelligence-Led Policing in a Fusion Center," *FBI Law Enforcement Bulletin* December (2010), www.fbi.gov/stats-services/publications/law-enforcement-bulletin/Dec2010/intelligence_feature (accessed January 14, 2011).

40 Ibid., p. 11.

41 International Association of Chiefs of Police, *IACP Capitol Report* 5:19 (December 14, 2006).

42 Police Executive Research Forum, *Local law enforcement's role in preventing and responding to terrorism* (Washington, DC: Police Executive Research Forum, October 2, 2001). See also www.cops.usdoj.gov/files/RIC/Publications/e02021441.pdf (accessed January 10, 2011).

43 Council on Foreign Relations, "Terrorism questions and answers: Police departments," www.cfr.org/publication/10214/police_departments.html?breadcrumb=default (accessed January 10, 2011).

44 Ibid.

45 M. Weissenstein, "NYPD shifts focus to terrorism, long considered the turf of federal agents," Associated Press, March 21, 2003.

46 Ibid.

47 International Association of Chiefs of Police, *From hometown security to homeland security: IACP's principles for a locally designed and nationally coordinated homeland security strategy* (Alexandria, VA: International Association of Chiefs of Police, 2005).

48 Ibid.

49 R. J. Jordan, Federal Bureau of Investigation, Congressional statement on information sharing before the U.S. Senate Committee on the Judiciary, Subcommittee on Administrative Oversight and the Courts, Washington, DC, April 17, 2002, www2.fbi.gov/congress/congress01/mcchesney111301.htm (accessed January 10, 2011).

50 U.S. Department of Justice, "Attorney General Ashcroft and Deputy Attorney General Thompson announce reorganization and mobilization of the nation's justice and law enforcement resources," press release, November 8, 2001.

51 R. S. Mueller III, Federal Bureau of Investigation, Testimony before the Senate Committee on Intelligence, February 16, 2005.

52 Governor's Commission on Criminal Justice Innovation, *Final report* (Boston: Governor's Commission on Criminal Justice Innovation, 2004), p. 57, from which much of the wording in the rest of this paragraph is taken.

53 The plan was an outgrowth of the IACP Criminal Intelligence Sharing Summit held in Alexandria, Virginia, in March 2002. Results of the summit are documented in International Association of Chiefs of Police, *Recommendations from the IACP intelligence summit, criminal intelligence sharing* (Washington, DC: COPS Office, 2002).

54 Office of Justice Programs, *The national criminal intelligence sharing plan* (Washington, DC: U.S. Department of Justice, 2003).

55 The term comes from Bud Levin, as quoted in Gene Stephens, "Policing the future: Law enforcement's new challenges," *The Futurist* (March–April 2005): 55.

56 Much of the information in this section comes from Bureau of Justice Assistance, *Promoting partnerships for public safety, annual report FY 2002* (Washington, DC: December 2003), www.ncjrs.gov/pdffiles1/bja/200252.pdf (accessed January 10, 2011).

57 Visit RISS at www.riss.net/centers.aspx (accessed January 10, 2011).

58 MATRIX Data Mining System is Unplugged, www.privacyinternational.org/article.shtml?cmd%5B347%5D=x-347-205261 (accessed January 10, 2011).

59 State and Local Anti-Terrorism Training Program, www.slatt.org/default.aspx (accessed January 10, 2011).

60 "Is LAPD fudging our crime stats?" LAVoice.org, http://lavoice.org/index.php?name=News&file=article&sid=2525 (accessed January 10, 2011).

61 J. Godown, "Compstat and crime reduction," January 25, 2007, http://lapdblog.typepad.com/lapd_blog/2007/01/compstat_and_cr.html (accessed January 10, 2011).

62 R. Zink, "The trouble with Compstat," *PBA Magazine*, www.nycpba.org/publications/mag-04-summer/compstat.html (accessed January 10, 2011).

Chapter 10, Policing and the Law

1 David H. Bayley, "Law Enforcement and the Rule of Law: Is There a Tradeoff?" *Criminology and Public Policy*, Vol. 2, No. 1 (November 2002): 133–154; published online March 7, 2006 at http://onlinelibrary.wiley.com/doi/10.1111/j.1745-9133.2002.tb00113.x/pdf (accessed April 11, 2011).

2 Portions of this chapter were borrowed from J. L. Worrall, *Criminal procedure: From first contact to appeal*, 3rd ed. (Boston, MA: Prentice Hall, 2010).

3 Of course, other questions then arise, including whether the private citizen had the right to be in the place where the evidence was thought to be, how he or she gained access to that place, and so on. While the private seizure of evidence might not lead to its inadmissibility at court, it might provide grounds for a civil suit against the citizen or even for his or her arrest (in case of burglary or theft).

4 *Katz* v. *United States*, 389 U.S. 347 (1967).

5 Ibid., p. 353.

6 Ibid.

7 *California* v. *Greenwood*, 486 U.S. 35 (1988).

8 *Katz* v. *United States*, p. 351.

9 Ibid.

10 *United States* v. *Jacobsen*, 466 U.S. 109 (1984).

11 *Terry* v. *Ohio*, 392 U.S. 1 (1968); and *United States* v. *Mendenhall*, 446 U.S. 544 (1980).

12 *Florida* v. *Bostick*, 501 U.S. 429 (1991).

13 *Beck* v. *Ohio*, 379 U.S. 89 (1964), p. 91.

14 *Brinegar* v. *United States*, 338 U.S. 160 (1949), p. 175.

15 *Terry* v. *Ohio*, 392 U.S. 1 (1968).

16 Ibid., p. 22.

17 Ibid., p. 13.

18 *United States* v. *Sokolow*, 490 U.S. 1 (1989), p. 7.

19 *Payton* v. *New York*, 445 U.S. 573 (1980).

20 *Steagald* v. *United States*, 451 U.S. 204 (1981).

21 *Johnson* v. *United States*, 333 U.S. 10 (1948), pp. 13–14.

22 *Coolidge* v. *New Hampshire*, 403 U.S. 443 (1971).

23 *United States* v. *United States District Court*, 407 U.S. 297 (1972).

24 *Payton* v. *New York*, 445 U.S. 573 (1980), pp. 602–3.

25 *Chimel* v. *California*, 395 U.S. 752 (1969), p. 763.

26 *Sibron* v. *New York*, 392 U.S. 40 (1968).

27 See *Rawlings* v. *Kentucky*, 448 U.S. 98 (1980).

28 *Preston* v. *United States*, 376 U.S. 364 (1964).

29 Ibid., p. 367.

30 See also *Chambers* v. *Maroney*, 399 U.S. 42 (1970).

31 *Chimel* v. *California*, 395 U.S. 752 (1969).

32 Ibid., p. 759.

33 Ibid., p. 768.

34 *Maryland* v. *Buie*, 494 U.S. 325 (1990).

35 *Arizona* v. *Gant*, 556 U.S. 332 (2009).

36 *Warden* v. *Hayden*, 387 U.S. 294 (1967).

37 Ibid., p. 298.

38 Ibid., pp. 298–99.

39 Ibid., p. 299.

40 *State* v. *Wren*, 115 Idaho 618 (1989), p. 625.

41 *United States* v. *George*, 883 F.2d 1407 (9th Cir. 1989).

42 *United States* v. *Santana*, 427 U.S. 38 (1976).

43 See, e.g., *Welsh* v. *Wisconsin*, 466 U.S. 740 (1984).

44 *Warden* v. *Hayden*, 387 U.S. 294 (1967), p. 299.

45 *Minnesota* v. *Olson*, 495 U.S. 91 (1990).

46 *Breithaupt* v. *Abram*, 352 U.S. 432 (1957).

47 See, e.g., *Kentucky* v. *King*, No. 09-1272 (2011).

48 *Carroll* v. *United States*, 267 U.S. 132 (1925).

49 *Husty* v. *United States*, 282 U.S. 694 (1931).

50 Ibid., p. 701.

51 *Coolidge* v. *New Hampshire*, 403 U.S. 443 (1971).

52 *United States* v. *Ross*, 456 U.S. 798 (1982), p. 800.

53 Ibid., p. 824.

54 *Coolidge* v. *New Hampshire*, 403 U.S. 443 (1971).

55 Ibid.

56 *Arizona* v. *Hicks*, 480 U.S. 321 (1987).

57 *Horton* v. *California*, 496 U.S. 128 (1990).

58 *Schneckloth* v. *Bustamonte*, 412 U.S. 218 (1973).

59 Ibid.

60 *Ohio* v. *Robinette*, 519 U.S. 33 (1996).

61 Ibid., pp. 39–40.

62 *United States* v. *Mendenhall*, 446 U.S. 544 (1980).

63 *Florida* v. *Jimeno*, 500 U.S. 248 (1991).

64 *State* v. *Brochu*, 237 A.2d 418 (Me. 1967).

65 *Terry* v. *Ohio*, 392 U.S. 1 (1968).

66 Ibid.

67 *United States* v. *Mendenhall*, 446 U.S. 544 (1980), p. 554, emphasis added.

68 *Sibron* v. *New York*, 392 U.S. 40 (1968).

69 *Pennsylvania* v. *Mimms*, 434 U.S. 106 (1977).

70 *Illinois* v. *Lafayette*, 462 U.S. 640 (1983).

71 *South Dakota* v. *Opperman*, 428 U.S. 364 (1976).

72 *Carroll* v. *United States*, 267 U.S. 132 (1925).

73 Ibid., p. 154. See also *United States* v. *Montoya de Hernandez*, 473 U.S. 531 (1985), p. 538.

74 *United States* v. *Martinez-Fuerte*, 428 U.S. 543 (1976).

75 *Michigan Dept. of State Police* v. *Sitz*, 496 U.S. 444 (1990).

76 *City of Indianapolis* v. *Edmond*, 531 U.S. 32 (2000).

77 Ibid., p. 32.

78 Ibid., p. 44.

79 *Illinois* v. *Lidster*, 540 U.S. 419 (2004).

80 *Berkemer* v. *McCarty*, 468 U.S. 420 (1984), p. 442.

81 *Rhode Island* v. *Innis*, 446 U.S. 291 (1980), p. 300.

82 Ibid., p. 302, n. 8.

83 *United States* v. *Dickerson*, 166 F.3d 667 (4th Cir. 1999), p. 671.

84 *Dickerson* v. *United States*, 530 U.S. 428 (2000).

85 Ibid., p. 431.

86 Ibid., p. 443.

87 See, e.g., *California* v. *Prysock*, 453 U.S. 355 (1981), p. 359; *Duckworth* v. *Eagan*, 492 U.S. 192 (1989), p. 198.

88 See, e.g., *Miranda* v. *Arizona*, 384 U.S. 436 (1966), p. 475; *Colorado* v. *Connelly*, 479 U.S. 157 (1986); *Fare* v. *Michael C.*, 442 U.S. 707 (1979), p. 725; *North Carolina* v. *Butler*, 441 U.S. 369 (1979).

89 *New York* v. *Quarles*, 467 U.S. 649 (1984).

90 *Maryland* v. *Shatzer*, 559 U.S. ___ (2010).

91 *Florida* v. *Powell*, 559 U.S. ___ (2010).

92 T. T. Burke, "Documenting and reporting a confession with a signed statement: A guide for law enforcement," *FBI Law Enforcement Bulletin* (February 2001): 17.

93 *Kyllo* v. *United States*, 533 U.S. 27 (2001).

Chapter 11, Civil Liability and Accountability

1 Christopher Stone, Todd Fogelsong, and Christine M. Cole, "Policing Los Angeles Under a Consent Decree: The Dynamics of Change at the LAPD," The John F. Kennedy School of Government, May 2009.

2 *Lugar* v. *Edmondson Oil Co.*, 457 U.S. 922 (1982), p. 937.

3 Vaughn and Coomes, "Police civil liability under Section 1983," p. 409.

4 *Daniels* v. *Williams*, 474 U.S. 327 (1986), p. 330.

5 J. L. Worrall, "Culpability standards in Section 1983 litigation against criminal justice officials: When and why mental state matters," *Crime and Delinquency* 47 (2001): 28–59.

6 See, e.g., *City of Canton* v. *Harris*, 489 U.S. 378 (1989).

7 See, e.g., *Monell* v. *Department of Social Services*, 436 U.S. 658 (1978).

8 *Bivens* v. *Six Unknown Named Agents*, 403 U.S. 388 (1971).

9 See, e.g., *Davis* v. *Passman*, 442 U.S. 228 (1979); *Sonntag* v. *Dooley*, 650 F.2d 904 (7th Cir. 1981); and *Carlson* v. *Green*, 446 U.S. 14 (1980).

10 *Bradley* v. *Fisher*, 80 U.S. 335 (1871).

11 *Yaselli* v. *Goff*, 275 U.S. 503 (1927).

12 *Butz* v. *Economou*, 438 U.S. 478 (1978).

13 *Harlow* v. *Fitzgerald*, 457 U.S. 800 (1982).

14 See, e.g., *Harlow* v. *Fitzgerald*, 457 U.S. 800 (1982); and *Wood* v. *Strickland*, 420 U.S. 308 (1975).

15 See, e.g., *Anderson* v. *Creighton*, 483 U.S. 635 (1987); and *Malley* v. *Briggs*, 475 U.S. 335 (1988).

16 W. A. Kerstetter, "Who disciplines the police? Who should?" in *Police leadership in America*, ed. W. Geller, pp. 178, 188 (Chicago: American Bar Association, 1985).

17 P. West, "Investigation of complaints against the police: Summary report of a national survey," *American Journal of Police* 7 (1988): 101–22.

18 S. Walker and B. Wright, *Citizen review of the police: A national survey of the 50 largest cities* (Washington, DC: Police Executive Research Forum, 1995).

19 A. J. Goldsmith, *Complaints against the police: The trend toward external review* (Oxford: Clarendon Press, 1991).

20 Kerstetter, "Who disciplines the police?"

21 A. E. Wagner and S. H. Decker, "Evaluating citizen complaints against the police," in *Critical issues in policing: Contemporary readings*, 3rd ed., ed. R. G. Dunham and G. P. Alpert, pp. 302–18 (Prospect Heights, IL: Waveland, 1997); and Americans for Effective Law Enforcement, *Police civilian review boards*, AELE Defense Manual, Brief #82-3 (San Francisco: Americans for Effective Law Enforcement, 1982).

22 For more details, see the Kansas City (Missouri) Police Department home page, www.kcpd.org/ (accessed January 14, 2011).

23 City of San Jose, Office of the Independent Auditor, "Charter," www.sanjoseca.gov/ipa/Charter.html (accessed January 14, 2011).

24 S. Walker and V. W. Bumphus, *Civilian review of the police: A national survey of the 50 largest cities* (Omaha: University of Nebraska at Omaha, 1991).

25 S. Walker, *Citizen review resource manual* (Washington, DC: Police Executive Research Forum, 1995).

26 Ibid.

27 Ibid.

28 S. Walker, *Police accountability: The role of citizen oversight* (Belmont, CA: Wadsworth, 2001).

29 D. W. Perez, *Common sense about police review* (Philadelphia: Temple University Press, 1994).

30 S. Walker and B. Wright, "Varieties of citizen review: The relationship of mission, structure, and procedures to police accountability," in *Critical issues in policing: Contemporary readings*, 3rd ed., ed. R. G. Dunham and G. P. Alpert, p. 333 (Prospect Heights, IL: Waveland, 1997).

31 Ibid.

32 A. E. Wagner and S. H. Decker, "Evaluating citizen complaints against the police," in *Critical issues in policing: Contemporary readings*, 3rd ed., ed. R. G. Dunham and G. P. Alpert, p. 310 (Prospect Heights, IL: Waveland, 1997).

33 Commission on Accreditation for Law Enforcement Agencies, *Standards for law enforcement agencies*, 4th ed. (Fairfax, VA: Commission on Accreditation for Law Enforcement, 1999), p. xiii.

34 Commission on Accreditation for Law Enforcement Agencies, *Standards for law enforcement agencies*, 5th ed. (Fairfax, VA: Commission on Accreditation for Law Enforcement Agencies, 2006), www.calea.org (accessed January 14, 2011). © 2006. Reprinted with permission.

35 Ibid.

36 J. A. Conser and G. D. Russell, *Law enforcement in the United States* (Gaithersburg, MD: Aspen, 2000).

37 S. J. Hill, "The significance of police credentialing," *Police* 23 (March 1999): 40–42.

38 W. E. Eastman, "National accreditation: A costly, unneeded make-work scheme," in Police management today, ed. J. Fyfe, pp. 49–54 (Washington, DC: International City Managers Association, 1985); and J. Pearson, "National accreditation: A valuable management tool," in *Police management today*, ed. J. Fyfe, pp. 45–48 (Washington, DC: International City Managers Association, 1985).

39 J. W. Bizzack and V. Delacruz, "Demystifying police accreditation," *Law Enforcement News*, April 30, 1994, pp. 8, 11.

40 Washington Association of Sheriffs and Police Chiefs, *Accreditation program* (Olympia: Washington Association of Sheriffs and Police Chiefs, 1998).

41 *Weeks* v. *United States*, 232 U.S. 383 (1914); and *Mapp* v. *Ohio*, 367 U.S. 643 (1961).

42 *Elkins* v. *United States*, 364 U.S. 206 (1960).

43 *Silverthorne Lumber Co.* v. *United States*, 251 U.S. 385 (1920).

44 M. Wilkey, "Why suppress evidence?" *Judicature* 62 (1978): 214.

45 *Screws* v. *United States*, 325 U.S. 91 (1945).

46 *United States* v. *Lanier*, 520 U.S. 259 (1997).

47 *Miller* v. *United States*, 404 F.2d 611 (5th Cir. 1968).

48 *Williams* v. *United States*, 341 U.S. 97 (1951).

49 *Lynch* v. *United States*, 189 F.2d 476 (5th Cir. 1951).

50 M. L. Birzer, "Crimes committed by police officers," in *Police misconduct*, ed. M. J. Palmiotto, pp. 168–81 (Upper Saddle River, NJ: Prentice Hall, 2001).

51 Ibid.

52 M. W. Lyman, *The police: An introduction* (Upper Saddle River, NJ: Prentice Hall, 1999).

53 J. Douglas and J. Johnson, *Official deviance* (New York: Lippincott, 1977); and D. Guyot, *Policing as though people matter* (Philadelphia: Temple University Press, 1991).

54 D. W. Perez and W. K. Muir, "Administrative review of alleged police brutality," in *And justice for all: Understanding and controlling police abuse of force*, ed. W. A. Geller and H. Toch, pp. 207–8 (Washington, DC: Police Executive Research Forum, 1995).

55 J. Angell, "The adequacy of the internal processing of citizen complaints by police departments," master's thesis (Michigan State University, 1966).

56 *Garrity* v. *New Jersey*, 385 U.S. 483 (1967).

57 *Gardner* v. *Broderick*, 392 U.S. 273 (1967).

58 M. Chiuchiolo, "The law enforcement officer's bill of rights: Panacea or problem?" *Police Chief* 68 (1981): 70–72.

59 H. Johnson, "A police officer's bill of rights: A needed protection for cops?" in *Controversial issues in policing*, ed. J. D. Sewell, p. 42 (Boston: Allyn and Bacon, 1999).

60 M. Scott, "A police officer's bill of rights: A needed protection for cops?" in *Controversial issues in policing*, ed. J. D. Sewell, pp. 36–41 (Boston: Allyn and Bacon, 1999).

61 J. M. Pollock, "Ethics in law enforcement," in *Critical issues in policing: Contemporary readings*, 4th ed., ed. R. G. Dunham and G. P. Alpert, p. 366 (Prospect Heights, IL: Waveland, 2001).

62 J. Pollock and R. Becker, "Ethical dilemmas in police work," in *Justice, crime, and ethics*, ed. M. Braswell, B. McCarthy, and B. McCarthy, pp. 83–103 (Cincinnati, OH: Anderson, 1996).

63 L. K. Gaines, V. E. Kappeler, and J. B. Vaughn, *Policing in America*, 3rd ed., pp. 344–45 (Cincinnati: Anderson, 1999).

64 *Wilson* v. *Layne*, 526 U.S. 603 (1999).

Chapter 12, Deviance, Ethics, and Professionalism

1 Christopher Stone and Jeremy Travis, "Toward a new professionalism in policing," The John F. Kennedy School of Government at Harvard University, 2011.

2 J. Kleinig, *The ethics of policing* (Cambridge: Cambridge University Press, 1996), p. 166.

3 S. Walker, *Popular justice: A history of American criminal justice*, 2nd ed. (New York: Oxford University Press, 1998), pp. 26–27.

4 R. M. Fogelson, *Big-city police* (Cambridge, MA: Harvard University Press, 1977), p. 32.

5 *Powell* v. *Alabama*, 287 U.S. 45 (1932).

6 T. Barker, *Police ethics: Crisis in law enforcement* (Springfield, IL: Charles Thomas, 1996).

7 Associated Press, "Ex-cops accused of doubling as mob hitmen," www.msnbc.msn.com/id/7434863/ns/us_news-crime_and_courts/ (accessed January 17, 2011) and http://tinyurl.com/55jd5b.

8 Reprinted by permission of Waveland Press, Inc. from Victor E. Kappeler, et al., "Breeding Deviant Conformity, FORCES IN DEVIANCE: UNDERSTANDING THE DARK SIDE OF POLICING. (Long Grove, IL: Waveland Press, Inc., 1998). All rights reserved.

9 Reprinted by permission of Waveland Press, Inc. from Victor E. Kappeler, et al., "Breeding Deviant Conformity, FORCES IN DEVIANCE: UNDERSTANDING THE DARK SIDE OF POLICING. (Long Grove, IL: Waveland Press, Inc., 1998). All rights reserved.

10 For a fairly thorough account, see M. L. Birzer, "Crimes committed by police officers," in *Police misconduct: A reader for the 21st century*, ed. M. J. Palmiotto, pp. 168–81 (Upper Saddle River, NJ: Prentice Hall, 2001).

11 Reprinted by permission of Waveland Press, Inc. from Victor E. Kappeler, et al., "Breeding Deviant Conformity, FORCES IN DEVIANCE: UNDERSTANDING THE DARK SIDE OF POLICING. (Long Grove, IL: Waveland Press, Inc., 1998). All rights reserved.

12 Punch, *Conduct unbecoming*.

13 "Mark Fuhrman's 10/2/96 plea agreement to felony perjury at O.J. Simpson's criminal trial," The 'Lectric Law Library, www.lectlaw.com/files/case63.htm (accessed January 17, 2011).

14 Cited in C. Slobogin, "Testifying: Police perjury and what to do about it," *University of Colorado Law Review* 67 (1996): 1037–60, quote on pp. 1042–43.

15 M. W. Orfield, Jr., "Deterrence, perjury, and the heater factor: An exclusionary rule in the Chicago criminal courts," *University of Colorado Law Review* 107 (1992): 75.

16 Ibid.

17 Barker, *Police ethics*.

18 S. Coleman, "When police should say 'no!' to gratuities," *Police Ethics* (winter–spring 2004): 33–44.

19 Ibid, pp. 34–37.

20 Ibid., p. 39.

21 See P. B. Kraska and V. E. Kappeler, "To serve and pursue: Exploring police sexual violence against women," *Justice Quarterly* 12 (1995): 85–109.

22 T. Barker, "An empirical study of police deviance other than corruption," *Journal of Police Science and Administration* 3 (1978): 264–72.

23 A. D. Sapp, "Sexual Misconduct by Police Officers," in T. Barker and D. Carter (eds.), *Police deviance*, pp. 83–95 (Cincinnati: Anderson, 1986), p. 88.

24 See Kraska and Kappeler, "To serve and pursue."

25 Ibid.

26 Ibid.

27 D. L. Carter, "Drug use and drug-related corruption of police officers," in *Policing perspectives: An anthology*, ed. L. K. Gaines and G. W. Cordner, pp. 311–23 (Los Angeles, CA: Roxbury, 1999).

28 K. J. Peak, *Policing America: Methods, issues, challenges*, 5th ed. (Upper Saddle River, NJ: Prentice Hall, 2006), p. 307.

29 Ibid.

30 P. B. Kraska and V. E. Kappeler, "Police on-duty drug use: A theoretical and descriptive explanation," *American Journal of Police* 7 (1988): 1–28.

31 J. Crank and M. Caldero, *Police ethics: The corruption of noble cause* (Cincinnati: Anderson, 1999).

32 K. Lersch and T. Mieczkowski, "Who are the problem-prone officers? An analysis of citizen complaints," *American Journal of Police* 15 (1996): 23–44.

33 L. W. Sherman, *Controlling police corruption: The effects of reform policies* (Washington, DC: U.S. Department of Justice, 1978), p. 32.

34 See, for example, R. Klitgaard, "Subverting corruption," *Finance and development* (June 2000), http://www.imf.org/external/pubs/ft/fandd/2000/06/klitgaar.htm (accessed January 17, 2011).

35 Ibid.

36 J. M. Pollock, "Ethics and law enforcement," in *Critical issues in policing: Contemporary readings*, 4th ed., ed. R. G. Dunham and G. P. Alpert, pp. 356–73 (Prospect Heights, IL: Waveland, 2001).

37 Ibid., p. 369.

38 Ibid.

39 Ibid., p. 370.

40 R.C. Davis, N.J. Henderson, and C.W. Ortiz, *Can federal intervention bring lasting improvement in local policing? The Pittsburgh consent decree* (New York: Vera Institute of Justice, 2005).

41 Ibid., p. 4.

42 Associated Press, "Cops kill couple at luxury oceanfront resort," April 23, 2007, www.msnbc.msn.com/id/18270556 (accessed January 17, 2011).

Chapter 13, The Use of Force

1 United States Department of Justice, Civil Rights Division, *Investigation of the New Orleans Police Department* (Washington, DC: USDOJ, March 16, 2011).

2 Some of the material in this section is adapted or derived from National Institute of Justice, *Use of force by police: Overview of national and local data* (Washington, DC: National Institute of Justice, 1999).

3 International Association of Chiefs of Police, *Police use of force in America, 2001* (Alexandria, VA: International Association of Chiefs of Police, 2001), p. 1.

4 K. Adams, "Measuring the prevalence of police use of force," in *Police violence: Understanding and controlling police abuse of force*, eds. William A. Geller and Hans Toch, pp. 52–93 (New Hartford: Yale University Press, 2005).

5 *Police use of force in America, 2001*, op. cit.

6 S. Walker, G. P. Alpert, and D. J. Kenney, *Responding to the problem police officer: A national study of early warning systems* (Washington, DC: National Institute of Justice, 2000).

7 Some of the wording in this paragraph is adapted from Human Rights Watch, "The Christopher Commission report," www.hrw.org/reports98/police/uspo73.htm (accessed January 17, 2011).

8 G. P. Alpert and R. G. Dunham, *The force factor: Measuring police use of force relative to suspect resistance—A final report* (Washington, DC: National Institute of Justice, 2001).

9 M. R. Durose, E. L. Smith, and P. A. Langan, *Contacts between police and the public* (Washington, DC: Bureau of Justice Statistics, 2007).

10 J. H. Garner and C. D. Maxwell, "Measuring the amount of force used by and against the police in six jurisdictions," in *Use of force by police: Overview of national and local data*, p. 41 (Washington, DC: Bureau of Justice Statistics, 1999). Full report available at www.ncjrs.gov/pdffiles1/nij/176330-2.pdf (accessed January 17, 2011).

11 Ibid., p. 30.

12 Durose, Smith, and Langan, *Contacts between police and the public*, p. 8.

13 *Black's law dictionary*, 6th ed. (St. Paul, MN: West Publishing Co., 1990), p. 398.

14 J.M. Brown, *Policing and Homicide, 1976–98: Justifiable Homicide by Police, Police Officers Murdered by Felons* (Washington, DC: Bureau of Justice Statistics, 2001).

15 *Tennessee v. Garner*, 471 U.S. 1 (1985).

16 Ibid., p. 28.

17 V. E. Kappeler, *Critical issues in police civil liability*, 3rd ed. (Prospect Heights, IL: Waveland, 2001), p. 72.

18 *Hegarty v. Somerset County*, 848 F.Supp. 257 (1994), p. 257.

19 *Hemphill v. Schott*, 141 F.3d 412 (1998).

20 J. Fyfe, *Shots fired: An examination of New York City Police firearms discharges* (Ann Arbor, MI: University Microfilms, 1978).

21 J. Fyfe, "Blind justice? Police shootings in Memphis," paper presented at the annual meeting of the Academy of Criminal Justice Sciences, Philadelphia, March 1981.

22 See W. Geller, *Deadly force study guide*, Crime File Series (Washington, DC: National Institute of Justice, no date).

23 A. Cohen, "I've killed that man ten thousand times," *Police Magazine* (July 1980).

24 For more information, see Joe Auten, "When police shoot," *North Carolina Criminal Justice Today*, 4:4 (Summer 1986): 9–14.

25 Details for this story come from S. Slater, "Suicidal man killed by police fusillade," *Palm Beach Post*, March 11, 2005, p. 1A.

26 R. Stincelli, *Suicide by cop: Victims from both sides of the badge* (Folsom, CA: Interviews and Interrogations Institute, 2004).

27 Slater, "Suicidal man killed by police fusillade."

28 A. J. Pinizzotto, E. F. Davis, and C. E. Miller III, "Suicide by cop: Defining a devastating dilemma," *FBI Law Enforcement Bulletin* 74:2 (February 2005): 15.

29 "Ten percent of police shootings found to be 'suicide by cop,'" *Criminal Justice Newsletter*, September 1, 1998, pp. 1–2.

30 R. J. Homant and D. B. Kennedy, "Suicide by police: A proposed typology of law enforcement officer–assisted suicide," *Policing: An International Journal of Police Strategies and Management*, 23:3 (2000): 339–55.

31 A. L. Honig, "Police-assisted suicide: Identification, intervention, and investigation," *Police Chief*, October (2001): 89–93, quote on p. 93.

32 G. T. Williams, "Death by indifference," *Law and Order* (December 2003): 66–69, quote on p. 67.

33 *Graham v. Connor*, 490 U.S. 386, 396–397 (1989).

34 Ibid, p. 490.

35 Ibid.

36 D. W. Hayeslip and A. Preszler, *NIJ initiative on less-than-lethal weapons*, NIJ Research in Brief (Washington, DC: National Institute of Justice, 1993).

37 Ibid.

38 T. Farragher and D. Abel, "Postgame police projectile kills an Emerson student," *Boston Globe*, October 22, 2004, www.boston.com/news/local/massachusetts/articles/2004/10/22/postgame_police_projectile_kills_an_emerson_student/ (accessed January 17, 2011).

39 TASER International, "TASER X26 ECD," www.taser.com/products/law/Pages/TASERX26.aspx (accessed January 17, 2011). Courtesy of TASER International, Inc., Scottsdale, AZ, USA.

40 J. M. Cronin and J. A. Ederheimer, *Conducted energy devices: Development of standards for consistency and guidance* (Washington, DC: Police Executive Research Forum, 2006), www.ojp.usdoj.gov/BJA/pdf/CED_Standards.pdf (accessed January 17, 2011).

41 Ibid., p. 23.

42 National Institute of Justice, *Impact munitions use*, p. 3.

43 For some research in this area, see R. J. Kaminski, S. M. Edwards, and J. W. Johnson, "Assessing the incapacitative effects of pepper spray during resistive encounters with police," *Policing: An International Journal of Police Strategies and Management* 22 (1999): 7–29; and

R. J. Kaminski, S. M. Edwards, and J. W. Johnson, "The deterrent effects of oleoresin capsicum on assaults against police: Testing the velcro-effect hypothesis," *Police Quarterly* 1 (1998): 1–20.

44 National Institute of Justice, *The effectiveness and safety of pepper spray: Research for practice* (Washington, DC: National Institute of Justice, 2003), www.ncjrs.gov/pdffiles1/nij/195739.pdf (accessed January 17, 2011).

45 Ibid., p. 10.

46 Ibid., p. 11.

47 R. A. Leo, "*Miranda's* revenge: Police interrogation as a confidence game," *Law and Society Review* 30 (1996): 259–88, quote on p. 278.

48 Cited in R. Roberg, K. Novak, and G. Cordner, *Police and society*, 3rd ed. (Los Angeles: Roxbury, 2005), p. 333. See also Carter, "Theoretical dimensions in the abuse of authority by police officers," p. 273.

49 K. Johnson, "Police brutality cases on rise since 9/11," *USA Today*, January 18, 2007, www.usatoday.com/news/nation/2007-12-17-Copmisconduct_N.htm (accessed January 17, 2011).

50 See, e.g., B. Taylor and others, *Cop crunch: Identifying strategies for dealing with the recruiting and hiring crisis in law enforcement* (Washington, DC: Police Executive Research Forum, 2006); A. Sharp, "Departmental divergences on marijuana use and new recruits," *Law and Order* 51 (2003): 80–84; S. F. Domash, "Who wants this job?" *Police* 26 (2002): 34–39; L. K. Decker and R. G. Huckabee, "Raising the age and education requirements for police officers: Will too many women and minority candidates be excluded?" *Policing: An International Journal of Police Strategies and Management* 25 (2002): 789–802.

Name Index

Subject Index